THE EDUCATION OF A WOMAN

The Life of Gloria Steinem

CAROLYN G. HEILBRUN

THE DIAL PRESS

Published by
The Dial Press
Bantam Doubleday Dell Publishing Group, Inc.
1540 Broadway
New York, New York 10036

Library of Congress Cataloging in Publication Data
Heilbrun, Carolyn G., 1926–
The education of a woman : a life of Gloria Steinem / Carolyn G. Heilbrun.
p.   cm.
ISBN 0-385-31371-3 (hardcover)
1. Steinem, Gloria.   2. Feminists—United States—Biography.   I. Title.
HQ1413.S675H44   1995
305.42′0973—dc20   95-19683
                                                                         CIP

Manufactured in the United States of America
Published simultaneously in Canada

October 1995

10   9   8   7   6   5   4   3   2   1

BVG

THE EDUCATION
OF A WOMAN

To Penelope Heilbrun Duus
Born October 12, 1994

and

In memory of her great-grandmother
Estelle Roemer Gold
Born November 29, 1895

CONTENTS

ACKNOWLEDGMENTS

A BIOGRAPHER, trying to mold some version of truth from the scattered evidence of a life, incurs countless debts. I am grateful to have had the opportunity to talk with the many who contributed to my writing of this book; I am eager to acknowledge, even with a sense of inadequacy, my profound appreciation of all those whose cooperation with me made this biography possible.

Gloria Steinem, whom I met for the first time only two weeks before beginning work on this book, answered questions over many hours, gave me access to all her papers, urged those I wished to interview to talk to me, and was patience personified with all my endless requests and queries. She had no right of approval over the contents of the manuscript. Her cooperation was the more gracious in that, during the course of our many meetings, she frequently differed from me and my interpretations.

Susanne Steinem Patch, Gloria Steinem's sister, apart from granting me valuable interviews, answered more questions than I dare to remember, particularly but not exclusively about events preceding Gloria Steinem's birth. Her graciousness throughout has been elegant.

To all those who with great generosity and patience allowed me to interview them, sometimes more than once and for extended periods, my debt is profound.

Kathleen Banks Nutter, a noble research assistant, worked for months in the Sophia Smith Collection of Smith College on the numerous and totally unorganized papers of Gloria Steinem, who had kept her memorabilia in no particular order in cardboard boxes, not yet cataloged in any way. Kathleen, an experienced archivist and a historian, rendered these papers useful to me; I am beholden.

Mary Thom, who is writing a history of *Ms.* magazine, has been wonderfully generous in her guidance, on which I have depended sometimes shamefully. Joanne Edgar deserves special thanks for answering endless picky questions day and night, and for much kind advice. Pat Carbine offered me valuable documents, and, often on a moment's notice, the benefit of her recollections.

Steinem's support staff has tolerated my endless questions and requests with astonishing patience and good humor. I heartily thank Diana James and Amy Richards.

Special thanks are due to Frank Musial, for information on the Youth Festivals; to Seymore Rothman of *The Toledo Blade* for important information and clippings; to Susan Nerheim, who chased down my sudden research requests, many of them odd and all needed yesterday, with marvelous efficiency; to Professor Patsy Yaeger of the University of Michigan, who drove me to Toledo, Ohio, and Clark Lake, Michigan, and helped in the exploration of places where Steinem and her family had lived; to Ron Grele, director of Columbia's Oral History Project; to Carol Polsgrove, who has published (W. W. Norton) a book on *Esquire* magazine under the editorship of Harold Hayes, and who told me about letters at Wake Forest and Michigan universities concerning Steinem.

Many thanks also to the following:

Bella Abzug, Robert Benton, Andy Bernstein, Sallie Bingham, Mary Kay Blakely, Ivy Bontini, Ruth Bower, Susan Braudy, Donna Brunstad, Jacqueline Ceballos, Phyllis Chesler, Blair Chotzinoff, Jane McKenzie Davidson, Slavenka Drakulić, Nora Ephron, Brenda Feigen, Clay Felker, Jo Freeman, Marilyn French, Betty Friedan, Vivian Gornick, Tom Guinzberg, Betty Forsling Harris, Aileen Hernandez, Koryne Horbal, Ann Hornaday, Dorothy Pitman Hughes, Devaki Jain, Mim Kelber, Flo Kennedy, Jayne Keyes, Kristine Kiehl, Juanita Kreps, Kitty LePerriere, John Leonard, Robert Levine, Suzanne Braun Levine, Sally Lunt, Harriet Lyon, Philip Mandell, Wilma Mankiller, Jim Marshall, Juliet Mitchell, Robin Morgan, Carla Morganstern, Marion Moses, Barbara Nessim, Jane O'Reilly, Joan Palevsky, Mary Peacock, Letty Cottin Pogrebin, Stan Pottinger, Denise Rathben, Carmine Robinson, Phyllis Rosser, Herb Sargent, Arthur Schlesinger, Jr., Barbara Seaman, Donna Shalala, Alix Kates Shulman, Patsy Goodwin Sladdin, Margaret Sloan, Liz Smith, Ann Snitow, Tom Stoddard, Ellen Sweet, Franklin Thomas, Marlo Thomas, Sheila Tobias, Mary Jean Tully, Edie Van Horn, Alice Walker, Rebecca Walker, Nancy Wechsler, Judith Wenning, Judith Wheeler, Ellen Willis, Ming-Ji Zhank, and Mortimer Zuckerman.

At The Dial Press, I was lucky to have Vincent Virga as my photo editor, Suzanne Telsey as my careful legal reader, and Jolanta Benal as an ever-vigilant copy editor. In addition Tracy Devine provided fine editorial support and Kathleen Jayes offered innumerable kindnesses.

I am deeply grateful to my editor, Susan Kamil, who, with

intelligence and imagination, advanced my endeavors. From her combination of warmth, enthusiasm, a strict objectivity laced with kindness, and respect for my own sometimes eccentric assertions, I learned what good editing can be.

Susan Heath, troubleshooter par excellence, has been my prop and stay, without whom I would probably have long since jumped off the Brooklyn Bridge, the manuscript clutched to my breast. There is no phrase that has not received her meticulous attentions, even when I could no longer bear to focus my eyes on it; her patience is as astonishing as are her skills. I am profoundly grateful for her hours of work with me, for the high quality of that work, above all for her conversation and her friendship.

My agent, Ellen Levine, has long been my single steady support in a giddy publishing world, and I thank her now for the blessings of that long association.

The weekly exchanges with Nancy K. Miller, throughout the writing of this book, illuminated dark corners, led me to many insights, and was a much needed support during this sometimes awesome task. Tom F. Driver read through the manuscript at an early stage and offered, as always, valuable amendments and observations.

My husband, Jim Heilbrun, found less of his life pirated by this book than is the usual case with my writings. Nonetheless, he served heroically at many points, and, most important, put up with me when, driven to biographical distraction, I was far from easy to put up with. My children graced my life, as they have long done, with their presence and their astonishing range of information.

Since this is the biography of a controversial figure living in parlous times rife with disagreement and anger, it is the more urgent that I lay claim to all errors.

A NOTE ON DOCUMENTATION

THERE ARE NO source notes in this book. Quotations from printed works are followed by page numbers; the books from which the quotations are taken are listed alphabetically by author in the section headed "Bibliography." I have not quoted directly from each of the books listed there, but have found them all useful.

Within the text, the writer of a quoted letter is identified, as is the letter's date when it is known. Quotations from newspapers and journals are identified within the text. All other quotations not otherwise identified, including quotations from Steinem, are from interviews conducted by the author from 1990 to 1994.

INTRODUCTION

CHILDHOOD CAN MAKE a destiny, and most of us believe that it does. But it is also possible, if childhood trauma has not imprisoned us in a cycle of unconscious repetition, that the early years, or memories of them, serve mainly to reveal a pattern only discernible when the life is considered as a whole. In adulthood we can, if we look, find in childhood the seeds of the life we have lived. Whether that life was made inevitable by the childhood, or whether we remember only that part of childhood that explains what we have become, may be less important to the biographer than to the therapist or the suffering individual requiring therapy.

Autobiography is not the story of a life; it is the recreation or the discovery of one. In writing of experience, we discover what it was, and in the writing create the pattern we seem to have lived. Often, of course, autobiography is merely a collection of well-rehearsed anecdotes; but, intelligently written, it is the revelation, to the reader and the writer, of the writer's conception of the life he or she has lived. Simply put, autobiography is a reckoning.

Biography is another matter. A two-person dialogue, biography is the imposition of the biographer's perception upon the life of the subject. There is no truth; there are, indeed, remarkably few facts. Biographers differ in their objectivity, but those who consider themselves most objective are probably those who fail to see their own biases and assumptions. I, as the biographer of a feminist, begin from the desire to write the life of a woman who became, simultaneously, the epitome of female beauty and the quintessence of female revolution. I see as valiant her questioning of the powerful on behalf of the dispossessed; others might see it as deleterious. That is why there need to be many biographies of a complex subject—at least one every generation—if an individual life is to hold meaning for readers born in a different time and place from the subject, if a life is to be usefully interpreted for an ever-changing audience.

Gloria Steinem's life offers testimony to the power of contradictory behavior. Equipped with the attributes necessary for success on a conventionally established path, she turned another way, early on becoming a creature of contrasts, a complex woman.

Until recently, it has been difficult to accept complexity in a woman; some find it impossible: the conventions circumscribing female behavior have been both narrower and stricter than those relating to men. Yet to understand Steinem's apparent anomalies is to reckon profoundly with the possibilities of female destiny. The seeming incongruities of her life, even in the early days when they were not of her own making, offer clues to the creation of a feminist. There are the obvious contradictions of the expected: a feminist in a miniskirt; a woman frequently offered marriage who did not marry; a successful journalist who eschewed opportunities to write stories hurtful to women; a woman of courage who avoided direct personal conflict, but who confronted all the shibboleths of a patriarchal culture.

These contradictions are superficial. Far more challenging to consider is the disjunction between the deprived child and the accomplished, generous adult; between her father's obesity and her own eternal slimness; between her high intelligence and her irreverence toward academic intellectuals and the male theorists like Freud and Marx they so relentlessly honor; between the autonomy of a woman owning her own life and that same woman's relish of the uninterrupted companionship of desirable men; between her blatant attractiveness and her habit of underplaying it, if not denying it outright.

In only one aspect of Steinem's life was ambiguity in fact absent. Rare is the woman of accomplishment who has not revealed at some point, in childhood or later, her awareness of the great advantage in being born male. Other American women writers of Steinem's generation have been explicit. Anne Sexton said that she wished for a destiny that had nothing to do with gender; Sylvia Plath wrote in her journal: "I am at odds, I dislike being a girl, because as such I must come to realize that I cannot be a man. . . . I am part man. . . . Being born a woman is my awful tragedy." Steinem, on the other hand, had no ambivalence on the question of gender and, unusual among achieving women, never for a moment wished to be other than female.

Perhaps Steinem is one of the women Robert Bly had in mind when he wrote *Iron John,* his otherwise less than compelling book about men. In attempting not to confront feminists head-on, he noted, perhaps with a touch of envy: "Women in the 1970s needed to develop what is known in the Indian tradition as Kali energy— the ability really to say what they want, to dance with skulls around their neck, to cut relationships when they need to." [27]

Steinem was glad to be a woman, and lived that role with no longing glances either toward the clearer, more open male destiny, or toward its opposite: devotion to men as a sex. She happily searched within her own gender for a destiny unconstrained and unprescribed—for herself, and for other women less unambiguously at home in their bodies. Katie Roiphe and Naomi Wolf, writing as the younger generation of feminists in the early 1990s, found those of Steinem's generation to be antiman and antisex. Steinem's life indicates that this is youth ignorant of its predecessors, whose history is just beginning to be written.

Steinem's love affairs have been called minimarriages, and in a sense they were that. But if marriage, mini or maxi, may be defined as an association in which the other partner must always be taken into account, must always be considered in all major decisions, hers were not marriages at all. They were passionate associations between lovers who were not partners in any legal sense, sharing neither ownership of property nor dependents nor finances. Steinem was committed only as long as she and her lover chose; most often, it was she who ended the love relationship, prepared to welcome friendship, which for the most part was readily and enduringly offered.

In many ways unique, Steinem's journey toward feminism is markedly distinguishable from the lives of other feminists of her time. Betty Friedan's *The Feminine Mystique,* published in 1963, was rightly viewed as a revolutionary text, inciting women weary of their suburban, dependent life to something more rewarding. But Steinem had never lived in the suburbs, had never married, and was already a professional journalist; Friedan's book did not speak to her. If she noticed anything about *The Feminine Mystique,* it was that the book failed to encompass the lives of nonwhite women. On the other hand, younger feminists, formed in the civil rights and anti-Vietnam War movements of the 1960s, also experienced their fate as women differently than did Steinem. Though she was intensely committed to both causes, she did not reach feminism through them, as did younger women.

Gloria Steinem's life is not only a study in contrasts; it is the embodiment of contrasts never before so sharply exemplified. She differs even from her most famous antecedents. Victoria Woodhull, for example, was both feminist and sexy, "a flamboyant advocate of free love," as one modern feminist historian describes her. In addition to this, however, Woodhull saw visions and held séances, traveled with her sister as a healer and clairvoyant, published a reformist journal, publicly charged the Reverend Henry Ward Beecher with having seduced one of his parishioners, and was established as a stockbroker by Cornelius Vanderbilt. As early as 1871 she maintained that women were already enfranchised by the fourteenth and fifteenth amendments to the Constitution, and in 1872 she ran for president. She was married three times, and retired to England with her third husband twenty-six years before her death in 1927. Described by the Encyclopedia Americana as "beautiful, quick-witted, and magnetic," Woodhull was, before Steinem, the only American feminist who confounded the media with what was perceived as a contrast between her politics and her looks.

Had Steinem, like Woodhull, fit more readily into the pattern of a woman using men to get ahead, and had she spoken not of the dispossessed and of subjects as unsexy as economic empowerment but of spirituality and the adulterous habits of famous men, she might have found her life less brutally assailed by the media. The most distinct contrasts of Steinem's life were perceived by the media, or by her detractors, not as contrasts but as evidence on the one hand of female ambition and on the other of sinister radicalism. A living contradiction, she worried the pigeonholers.

But it is in comparing Steinem to Victoria Woodhull's contemporary Susan B. Anthony that the inevitable discomfort produced by feminists, of whatever mien, is most evident. In 1979, when the Susan B. Anthony coin was minted, a cartoonist named Beattie produced a drawing that encapsulates the issue: From a dollar bill,

George Washington says, "They should have used Gloria Steinem, she's better looking." And Anthony is drawn on her dollar as she was always caricatured: with bun, hooked nose, and downward-turning mouth. As Kathleen Barry observes in her biography of Anthony, although a Maine newspaper had written of her that "minus her gold spectacles [she] might generally be deemed good-looking," the antifeminist press always characterized Anthony as a "strident spinster" with a "lean and cadaverous look." Barry notes: "It has been the caricatures promoted by the enemies of women's rights that have formed our contemporary image of her." Barry recognizes this as the problem faced by the "self-determined feminist of any age" whose appearance is caricatured "as a way to discredit her ideas and politics." [102]

Since she could not easily be caricatured as ugly, the press and many of her detractors trivialized Steinem as glamorous and sexy. But unlike Anthony, caught in the mores of her own time, and more like Victoria Woodhull, Steinem could simultaneously evoke indisputable sexuality and feminist courage. The notion that all feminists are homely or fat and certainly frustrated could hardly hold firm in the face of that evidence.

Institutions devoted to the education of girls and young women have only rarely and intermittently produced feminists or women ready to live outside conventional female patterns. M. Carey Thomas, modeling Bryn Mawr College closely on the pattern provided by men's colleges, graduated well-educated women, but few unconventional or feminist ones. "Only our failures marry," she famously said; but, for the most part, her successes married too— that is to say, they led lives in which they offered their talents as volunteers and as the supporting halves of their husbands' professional careers. Steinem was in important ways self-educated before she even reached Smith College. The recipient there of the best college education offered to women at that time, she was happy enough to enjoy what, in sharp contrast to her harried childhood, the college offered.

If we ask what it is, as a woman, to be truly educated, the answer for Steinem, and perhaps for all women, seems to lie in the ability to cultivate one's skeptical self and to trust what one discovers when one questions patriarchal dogma: in other words, to trust one's own and other women's experiences over social myths. While at Smith, Steinem did little to cultivate that skeptical self; she would eventually decide that her education there had not taught her anything but the history of "dead white men."

PROBABLY FEW CHILDHOODS have been so frequently remembered and recounted as Gloria Steinem's. Repeatedly asked about her girlhood in interviews, Steinem has spun and respun her family stories so that, like all "oft-told tales," they have become fixed, but not the less "true" for that. But in "Ruth's Song," written soon after her mother's death in 1981, she recreated that childhood, and for the first time transformed anecdotes into profoundly felt recollections. Even so, Steinem for some time believed that in writing "Ruth's Song" she had been writing about her mother, not about herself, and found she could not reread it for two years. Only gradually could she face the despair with which the thought of revisiting her childhood threatened her.

To compare Steinem's childhood with Charles Dickens's is to recognize a phenomenon common to both, and probably common to many. The months—they amounted to less than a year—that Dickens spent in a blacking factory reverberated throughout his life like a childhood assault, which indeed for him they were. As an adult he could hardly bring himself to speak of that experience, even to his closest friends; he was able only to transform it into the childhood adventures of his various characters. Steinem's Toledo, Ohio, years—1944–1951—were Dickens's blacking factory. But, living in a different time, she could speak of them, provided they could be encapsulated in entertaining anecdotes; fearing the danger it might hold, she walled off the pain of that time until she turned fifty. For her, Toledo explained everything, as for Dickens the blacking factory months explained everything.

Yet for Dickens's parents, as for Steinem's, and for the other members of their families, those months or years were but a small part of a whole life lived in other places and with different problems. So Steinem's mother was to be troubled by her younger daughter's anecdotes of that time, and indeed, sometimes denied or sanitized them when the press gave her the opportunity. Ruth Steinem, too, feared that if she talked about Toledo, she would return to the depression of those years.

In her fifties Steinem consulted a therapist. This was a difficult time in her life—*Ms.* magazine had taken its toll in its last desperate search for advertisers, and was now sold; she had embarked on an uncharacteristic and damaging affair with Mortimer Zuckerman, the real estate magnate; she learned she had breast cancer— a time when she was prevented from crashing only by a need to struggle on that was, in itself, equally commendable and problematic. It soon became clear to both the therapist and Steinem that she feared to look closely at the years alone with her mother, terrified that they might become an abyss of despair into which she would tumble with disastrous, even fatal, results. For Steinem also, there was the fear that the neglect might have been more disastrous than she knew. However, as she was later to remark, "If there is an elephant in your living room, it is no use pretending it is not there." Many people, of course, live with an elephant and move carefully around it, believing it to be invisible.

There were questions she had never asked herself: What would her life have been had she been homely, however spirited and brave? Perhaps in that case she would have evolved into the writer she seemed always to have wished to be. What would her life have been without middle-class roots and aspirations, without a college-educated mother—however ill that mother was—amid a working-class world? What would her life have been had she been drenched either in the Judaism of her father's family or the strict Scotch Presbyterian church of her maternal grandmother, instead of being in early childhood exposed to that grandmother's later commitment to Theosophy? What would her life have been if she had inherited, as her sister did, their father's weight problem, which no amount of discipline or dieting could ever reduce to slimness? There are, of course, numerous questions that could be asked of any person: What if . . . ? Suppose that . . . ? There is always the question of who our parents might have been and who we might meet at the crossroads. The compelling question to be asked, however, of Steinem's life is: How did it produce the committed woman she became?

When in therapy at fifty-two Steinem did look back to where she had begun, there was no elephant to be encountered, but there was nevertheless the necessity of what she had all her life avoided: introspection. It was only then that she allowed her thoughts steadily to return to her childhood, above all to the years alone with her mother in Toledo, and even before that, to the beginning of what can now be seen as the education of a woman.

FAMILY

THE TEMPTATION TO discover the heritage of previous generations and the impact of that heritage upon an individual is as
powerful as it is elusive. It is easy to look backward and pluck
from the histories of antecedents—or what can be discovered of
their histories—hints and influences that may have molded a human being, may even, happily, have adumbrated the very traits
that can be seen as most characteristic. This is an exercise well-
founded in tradition; English biographies, which have to a great
extent been the major biographical model we have had, consider
the habits, traits, and social conditions of grandparents to be essential to the understanding of any life. In the United States, where
many of us have the conviction, often accurate, that we have
largely created ourselves, as well as the knowledge that our grandparents often dwelt in another country under conditions we cannot readily imagine, this concentration upon forebears can seem
overdone. Where geneological knowledge exists, it can almost always be interpreted as predictive, influential. Where, however,
antecedents are not altogether knowable—in the event of adop-

1

tion or artificial insemination, as is ever more likely today—that very condition may suggest the danger of attributing too much causality to ancestral characteristics. In biographies of women, which have, at last, become numerous and remarkable in recent decades, grandmothers' stories, where these can be recreated with some amplitude, may significantly illuminate the eventual careers of women who have become feminists or creators of unconventional and influential female lives.

In the case of Gloria Steinem we may appease the temptation to follow ancestral clues, since we know her grandparents and the places of their birth. These four individuals, whom Steinem either did not know or did not know for long, can be seen to cast a shadow on the story of her life, mostly because of their effect on their own children, Steinem's parents. Her grandmothers' lives and struggles as women, moreover, do particularly help to explain what influenced Steinem, either negatively or positively, to become the woman she became, and no other.

Steinem's maternal grandmother, Marie Ochs Nuneviller (called "O'Momie" by her granddaughters because, as she explained to them, "I am your *old* mommy") is a woman easy to portray as controlling, punitive, and self-centered. Certainly there is evidence of this. But looked at from a slightly different angle, she can be seen as a woman full of ambition and ability that, because of the restricted lives of women in her time, manifested itself as a relentless and constant search for social and financial success.

Marie was born June 16, 1871, the third oldest of six children, two boys and four girls, into a farming family in Washington Township, Hardin County, in the small Ohio town of Dunkirk. Steinem remembers visiting only once as a child, and describes "a wooden house with a dark cellar full of vegetables, with chamber pots instead of plumbing." Marie's father, Johannes Ochs, had been born in Germany; there is little record of her mother, Louise Lins, but she seems also to have contributed to the German influence upon Marie, an influence that would be palpable when Marie became, upon occasion, a sternly disciplinary parent. Marie was named Mary Catherine but at some point changed her name to Marie, either—Steinem is uncertain which—because she thought it fancier, or because, when she married Joseph Henry Nuneviller, she wanted to avoid the Mary and Joseph combination.

As a young woman, Marie had made money first as a schoolteacher, then working in the office of the Recorder of Deeds in Dunkirk. Marie's mother, Louise, took in boarders, which is how Marie and Joseph Nuneviller met; this was thought to be not quite respectable, and treated as a family secret. Later, when they moved to the two-story house on Woodville Road in the Toledo suburbs, Marie made money writing sermons for the Scotch Presbyterian church next door, which considered dancing and music sinful, an attitude Marie regarded with cynicism. Still later in her life Marie invested in real estate, thus moving up financially if not socially. She lost most of this gain, however, in the Depression.

Marie was, by all accounts, tough and strong. Steinem remembers her as "active, sunburned around the edges of her cotton dress, out-of-doors feeding chickens, hoeing in the kitchen garden, or in the kitchen baking pies, self-willed with an edge of wildness. . . . On one occasion, she decided to burn off the fields around our house—something that was done at the beginning of the season, but usually by a team of men—and the result was nearly disastrous. After this, I was a little afraid to be alone with her, but probably didn't share this with anyone." Marie was an independent woman, traveling without her husband on the railroad passes his job provided. On a journey alone to California, Marie was caught in an earthquake in Los Angeles and did not flee with the other tourists, but stayed to watch because, she said, she had never before been in an earthquake.

Joseph, her husband, was born in Portsmouth, New Hampshire, on December 2, 1867; it was his father who, according to

family history, arrived in 1854 lashed to the mast, the survivor of a
shipwreck off the New Jersey shore in which few passengers were
left alive.[1] Joseph Nuneviller was clearly an unsatisfactory husband to a woman hoping to climb upward in the social world; he
had a blue-collar job as a railroad engineer for the Toledo and
Ohio Central, and she was more educated than he. There is a
picture of "Nunny" and his crew at the loading docks for lake
ships on the Maumee River in Toledo. He was remembered in
family lore for wearing a suit on top of his overalls and a bowler
hat to go to work (probably at his wife's suggestion), and always
eating his dessert first in order to have had the best part should he
be called in the middle of a meal. Ruth, Gloria Steinem's mother,
always preferred Joseph, remembering him as handsome and
kind; inevitably, such a father would have been cherished above a
demanding mother, ambitious for her daughters.

Ruth Nuneviller was born on August 15, 1898, in the family's
Woodville Road house. Ruth's sister, Emma Jeanette (called
"Janey" by the family), was born at home two years later, on
November 28, 1900. Ruth would long remember going to the
closed bedroom door beyond which the birth was taking place,
fearful and excluded.

Janey was always more amenable to her mother's wishes and
was, or so it seemed to Ruth, favored by her. She had golden curls
and was little, cute, appealing. After graduating from the University of Wisconsin, she taught English at the Devilbis High School
in Toledo, a school in a neighborhood where the students were
headed for college; eventually she was given charge of all the
English departments in the Toledo high school system. Childless
because, Steinem believes, she did not wish to have children until
she could have the money to bring them up "properly," with a

---

[1] (The *New York Times,* November 14–17, 1854, carried news of this event, which
Steinem would reprint in her 1963 *Beach Book*).

nanny and a fine house, Janey would also encourage her nieces to lead a middle-class life. Certainly Janey internalized the social lessons learned from Marie. Steinem remembers her mother vividly describing a trip to New York with Marie, when she and Janey were teenagers: "They walked around in the snow, with Marie showing her daughters all the hotels and other things to which they should aspire, but without enough money to go in. My mother's memory of this was bitter. She felt like a poor person 'with her nose to the glass.'" There would be moments in Steinem's precollege years when she would find a certain peace in her aunt's orderly home, but she would never feel drawn to Aunt Janey's idea of a satisfactory existence.

Janey was always bound to her mother. In 1930, after Joseph's death, Marie went to live with Janey and Robert Brand, a traveling salesman of optic glass and other ophthalmological equipment, whom Janey had married that same year. It often seemed that Brand lived with Janey and Marie, rather than Marie with them, since the house they occupied was a house Marie had bought on Maplewood Avenue. (This house was eventually left to Janey, as the Woodville Road house was eventually left to Ruth.) At the end of Marie's life, when she broke her hip and developed what was probably Alzheimer's disease, Janey still, Steinem recalls, "seemed to be in my grandmother's thrall, and was convinced she could hear and understand long after she probably could."

Ruth's childhood may have been responsible for many of the fears that would, after her first breakdown in early 1930, haunt her. To wean Ruth, her mother simply left her with a friend. Ruth's fears of being left were inevitable following her mother's habit of leaving her alone without telling her where she was going or when she would return. Marie also once, finding Ruth under the table touching herself, hit her hard enough to send her skittering across the floor. Yet none of these actions was particularly eccentric or cruel for its time; only later, in the light of revised views on child rearing, can we measure their dire effects. Gloria's memories of her still reverberate with the scent of lavender, certain kinds of purses and handkerchiefs, bus transfers—Gloria first traveled on buses and trolley cars with her—and the sound of baseball announcers. She taught Gloria to play solitaire—significantly, perhaps—a game for someone often alone.

Marie was not keen on her daughters getting married; she believed in staying single and making a living, preferably as a teacher, the only profession, Marie believed, for women. Janey, notwithstanding an often-absent husband, cooperated in this plan, which was no doubt the reason both girls attended college before that was quite as usual as it is now. In 1916 Ruth entered Oberlin College in Ohio, which her mother considered elite and for which she had saved the money; but finances forced Ruth to transfer to the University of Toledo the following year. State universities like the University of Wisconsin, which Janey attended, were not expensive at that time, and Janey worked while she was there. At the University of Toledo, Ruth began by majoring in math. Although she eventually went on to receive her M.A. in history (her thesis was a bibliography of novels that allowed the reader to learn about history without reading history books), her secret wish was to run away to New York and become a newspaperwoman. Like her daughter Gloria, she would describe writing as one of her great passions.

The transfer affected Ruth's life powerfully, for it was at the University of Toledo that Ruth met Leo Steinem. Her passion for writing had led her, almost immediately upon arriving there, to the college newspaper offices, where Leo, her future husband, was editor. She was hastened in this by his having posted a notice on the newspaper bulletin board asking Ruth Nuneviller to come for an interview. He had seen her on campus, and his aim was romance, not journalism—though when she responded to his note, he offered both. A funny, charming, feckless man, Leo Steinem must have appealed to some radical impulse in Ruth, so far was he from her mother's ideals. Here was a man guaranteed, whether or not Ruth was conscious of the fact, to *épater la maman*. Leo, for his part, seems to have loved Ruth at first sight, rather as his father had suddenly desired his mother under somewhat more awkward circumstances.

Joseph Steinem, Leo's father, was born in Germany on February 20, 1852. As a young man he came to America to make his fortune. When he had enough money to marry, gained from small rental properties and eventually a small brewery in Toledo, he went back to Germany to find a wife. He was interested in the older daughter of a cantor he knew named Hayman Perlmutter, but while he was in Perlmutter's house, awaiting him, Perlmutter's younger daughter, Pauline, came into the room, and Joseph was at once taken with her looks and manner; he asked for her hand instead. The family agreed, on the condition that he send Pauline home to Germany for frequent visits. She also agreed, on the condition that he sell his brewery, which he agreed to do. Pauline, who was born August 4, 1863 and who had graduated from the State Normal School of Bavaria, was already what would be called a teetotaler (for cooking she would use paste vanilla rather than the kind containing alcohol), and Steinem thinks it possible that she may have been an early member of the temperance movement. Pauline and Joseph were married on September 3, 1884. Their first son, Edgar, was born in Germany. They would have three more sons: Jesse, Clarence, and Leo, the youngest, born April 24, 1897.

Obviously an outstanding woman, certainly a feminist with much of the determination more familiar to us in figures like Anthony, Stanton, and Catt, Pauline was one of the few women to be included in *Who's Who* in the early twenties. She can now be seen as a forerunner of her granddaughter; she worked for women's suffrage, was the first woman elected to the Toledo board of education, organized women's groups, addressed Congress about women's suffrage, and was one of the two American delegates to the meeting of the International Council on Women in Switzerland in 1908.

Steinem, who was five when Pauline died, did not learn about her grandmother's feminist career until her own was well established. Although newspapers would continue to find something wonderfully significant in the discovery of this suffragist grandmother, Steinem has only what she calls "sense memories" of "Mama Einie."

> She was a plump, white-skinned, gray-haired woman who lived as a widow in the upper part of a two-family house. Her neat living room had oriental rugs and a ticking clock on the mantlepiece. Her kitchen was dauntingly neat. I remember having clear soup with dumplings on a table with a lace cloth, and seeing thin china cups.

Steinem's mother was closer to her mother-in-law than to her own mother, and used to quote to Gloria from the Bible the words of Ruth to Naomi, her mother-in-law: "Whither thou goest, I shall go, and thy people shall be my people." We can guess that, at the time of her marriage to Leo, and certainly in the years that followed, Ruth must have found her mother-in-law, Pauline, a particularly welcome maternal figure. It was through Pauline that Gloria would indirectly receive one of her most important inheritances: Theosophy.

Ruth came to Theosophy through her mother-in-law, and in turn converted Marie to that philosophy. They became followers of the teachings of the renowned Krishnamurti, the author of many wide-selling books on religion. As a young child Gloria was repeatedly taken to Theosophist meetings, and, while passing the time filling in coloring books, perhaps took in subliminally, as children do, the tenets of that belief. Strongly influenced by Hinduism, Theosophy encourages the living of the moral life, but in a generous, neither autocratic nor self-righteous, way. Certain of the instructions that Krishna gives to Arjuna in the Bhagavad Gita suggest its spirit: You must do your job in life, not anybody else's. Do the best you can; the fruits—rewards or punishments—are not your business. Your children are not your children; they are strangers; they are themselves, boarded out for a time in your care. Your destiny consists in living out the consequences of your acts and thoughts. Do not do evil that good may come; try to do no harm; and so forth. This kind of faith, in some ways related to what has come to be called New Age in our time, would reverberate in Ruth's daughter's life, explaining many acts that, by their generosity, bewildered Steinem's friends and seemed to have compelled her enemies to find them self-serving.

The other aspect of her grandmother that was directly significant to Steinem was that Pauline was also Jewish. But like many women before and after her, Pauline compromised; her beliefs and doubts were one part of her life, her conventional service to her husband and sons another. Steinem felt that Pauline had too sharply divided her public and private life into discrete spheres. This ambivalence about being Jewish carried over to her son Leo. He used to change his name to Standish when convenient for business reasons. He would occasionally write to his daughter under that name, jokingly. Clearly he was aware of anti-Semitism, as was Ruth, who resented religious prejudice more actively than her husband, and was always a strong fighter against racism of any sort.

Leo, as the youngest son of Joseph and Pauline Steinem, was sufficiently indulged to allow him to follow his own desires and his own often unrealistic ambitions. To him, Steinem guesses, money and food were the evidence of paternal and maternal indulgence. When Leo ran out of money, his father would first scold him and then pay up. With his mother, food may have operated in much the same way. He had been thin in college, but soon after became greatly overweight, a condition he did not inherit from his parents; his brothers were lanky. Steinem in her turn would fear becoming herself overweight because she "grew up with a father for whom food was the ultimate reward and sign of love." She believes that her father never spent an hour without thinking about food, "and he knew every restaurant with a free relish tray, every smorgasbord, and every thick malted place in the Midwest and all the way to Florida and California."

Why did Steinem's parents, two individuals markedly different and basically incompatible, marry? Theirs was a marriage perhaps no stranger than most. He was persuasive, boisterous, and, as a young man, attractive; she was female, and therefore caught, then as ever, in the youthful split between her desire to work and have adventures, and her internalized command to marry. For not to marry was to risk far more than to marry the wrong person. This was a persistent condition of young womanhood. Leo wanted to marry her, and impulsively she agreed; perhaps her immediate affection for Pauline also influenced this unwise alliance.

As though to confirm the ill-advised impulse, Ruth married Leo twice. The first time was in the spring of 1921, after she had become literary editor of the campus newspaper, and the second time in the fall of that year, in a more public ceremony boycotted by some members of both families. The spring ceremony was Leo's spur-of-the-moment idea. Once when they were out driving, Leo stopped at the offices of a justice of the peace and said: "Let's get married; it will only take a minute," a superbly characteristic Leo attitude to life. Leo always gave Ruth two anniversary presents, marked "To My First Wife" and "To My Second Wife"; October 15 was the anniversary they celebrated. Much later, when she was the mother of the now-famous Gloria Steinem, Ruth would deny being divorced; she told reporters that since she had been married twice and divorced only once, she was still married. By that time—fragile, anxious, and constantly medicated—she wanted the "normalcy" of a marriage that had cost her so dearly.

As a marriage, Ruth and Leo's was mixed in more ways than the religious. She was a gifted student; he scorned academic education. She had become a teacher to satisfy her mother's wishes. Leo had a variety of jobs after their marriage, working for his father at various real estate–connected tasks, promoting dances, freelancing as a journalist—all of which helped to support them. They also had totally different attitudes toward money. Leo had come from a wealthy family, and as a result, even when he had only a nickel and even after his family lost most of its money in the 1929 crash,[2] he felt financially secure. Ruth, on the other hand, was terrified, literally worried sick by debt.

Ruth made an agreement with her mother that after college she would teach math at the college level for a year; if she did not find that she liked teaching, she would then go into newspaper work. Inevitably, she did not enjoy teaching, and we may guess that this decision led to some resentment on the part of her mother. Ruth eventually went to work as a reporter for a Toledo paper, the *News Bee*. She also wrote some columns on local events for a small newspaper owned by a man named K. W. Kessler; for him she published her columns under a man's name, Duncan Mackenzie, a woman's byline being unacceptable at that time. The *News Bee* was soon bought by *The Toledo Blade*. There, it was Ruth's job to fill two pages of newsprint for each edition. She had realized her dream of becoming a journalist.

* * *

[2] But certainly not all: after Joseph Steinem's death in 1929, Pauline would have an income of $500 a month from rents on his properties.

IN 1925 their first child, Susanne, was born and Ruth took a year off from her job; in that same year Leo Steinem bought property at Clark Lake, Michigan, fifty miles from Toledo, a dream in which events did not cooperate. Clark Lake was in an isolated, rural area; the nearest town was Brooklyn, Michigan, population eight hundred. In 1990 [Aug. 19–25] the *Toledo Blade Magazine* ran an article on Clark Lake, mentioning that Toledoans had had a summer romance with the area since the 1890s. The article is illustrated by an engraving of the Ocean Beach Pier, which Leo Steinem built in 1928. He hoped to run a successful summer resort, with well-known bands and a toboggan run, among other attractions. The question of whether this plan would have continued to succeed had not World War II and gas rationing occurred is, like Leo and his dreams, impractical.

A decade later the original mortgage would be paid off, but Ruth subsequently discovered, to her great distress, that her husband had secretly mortgaged the pier again. Today the pier is gone, but the Hispanic-style stucco house the Steinems lived in remains. With the flat roof and arches Leo had admired in California, it was hardly suited to the Michigan climate, but that would never have been a consideration to impede Leo.

Ruth had her first breakdown—and her first stay at a sanitarium—when Susanne was five years old, in 1930, and would never again work as a journalist. One could call her illness overdetermined: she was the victim of the Depression, of accidents at the lake, of financial pressures, of isolation, and of the loss of all she had hoped for in life. Ruth's first " 'nervous breakdown,' as she and everyone else called it," Steinem later wrote, "followed five years of trying to take care of a baby, be the wife of a kind but financially irresponsible man with show-business dreams, and still keep her much-loved job as reporter and newspaper editor." Before the breakdown, Steinem continues, Ruth had been a spirited, adventurous young woman who struggled out of a working-class family and into college, who found work she loved and continued to do, even after she was married and my older sister was there to be cared for. . . . She was thirty before she gave up her own career to help my father run the Michigan summer resort that was the most practical of his many dreams, and she worked hard there as everything from bookkeeper to bar manager. [Ruth, 131]

Sometime in the 1970s, Ruth decided to set down an account of her life and all its advantages between 1920 and 1929. She listed nineteen good things from that time, among them Pa Steinem's gift of a building lot on the Maumee Bay shore near Toledo, with free rein to build "the house of their dreams." He would pay all the bills; "he did and we did." She was happily married, and had "the job of my own dreams" on the paper, "about to be made *Sunday Blade* editor, the best-paid job on the paper for any employee, male or female." Leo, always with his father's help, increased his real estate investments—more land at Clark Lake, a pecan orchard in Florida, a filling station in Valdosta, Georgia, and eight thousand acres of almost-virgin pine forest. Her own parents bought a new home, "not so large or expensive as Leo's parents', but nice." She could now buy her clothes at the most expensive shop in Toledo; Susanne went to the best private school. Aunt Soph (Marie's sister) moved into their new house on the bay as a well-paid housekeeper. The pier grossed fifty thousand dollars in its first summer. Ruth recalls Pa Steinem saying, "I now have made my first million, a dream I hardly expected to come true."

Then came the the depression of October 1929. Most if not all of the real estate remained for Leo and Pa Steinem; Ruth's mother, however, lost all and was in deep debt. "But," Ruth significantly recalls, "for Susanne's first five years she had just about everything; Gloria was born on borrowed money and never knew any of this." The disasters mounted; Pa Steinem died of shock, despair, and pneumonia after Christmas, 1929. When the market crashed, he had rushed back and forth in bad weather to read the ticker tapes as the stocks plunged. Two months later, Ruth's father died suddenly in his sleep on February 18, 1930, apparently from a heart attack. He had five dollars in his pocket as a birthday present for Susanne's fifth birthday the next day.

Only the good things, however, are here lovingly recorded, as is not uncommon among those who lost so much so suddenly in the Great Depression. But the blissful nature of everyday life for Ruth and for her marriage must be questioned. She had been a virginal bride, married to a man innocent, as his daughter would kindly put it, of a woman's pleasure. Steinem also remembers that there was a man at the *Blade* to whom her mother was attracted, but nothing came of it. Steinem and her mother never discussed sex. But once, when they were flying back from a vacation and Steinem was reading an account of genital mutilation, Ruth asked about it; Steinem, loath to show the article to her, nonetheless did. Ruth did not absorb the full horror of what she was reading, but she did notice references to the clitoris. She never used sexual terms herself, but said, euphemistically: "You know, your father didn't really know about things like that; he was always very nice, but it was over right away." In addition, Ruth had had a miscarriage in 1927 or '28, during which her mother let her bleed rather than call for help: Marie had little faith in doctors, and believed Ruth to be exaggerating.

In 1930 Ruth, Leo, and Susanne moved to Clark Lake, where it was cheaper to live than in Toledo. They sold the Maumee Bay house. Ruth gave birth to a stillborn son (named Tom) about then. There was a terrible accident on the toboggan at Clark Lake: a boy was killed riding on it when it was out of service; this upset her terribly. She became terrified to be left alone, unable to sleep

—she claimed to have gone five or six days without sleeping—she heard sounds greatly exaggerated, as the sound of the wind in the trees. She was almost continuously in a state of anxiety and dread.

Ruth returned to Clark Lake after many months in a Toledo sanitarium—a "sanitarium" that was, in fact, the house of the doctor who ran the local hospital for those suffering from "nervous breakdowns." She was much comforted by the fact that she was a resident of the doctor's house, and not of the hospital itself. While Ruth was in the sanitarium, Susanne lived with Marie— which must have caused Ruth additional anxiety, remembering her own childhood—but was often cared for by Leo, who lived in Toledo with his parents. Leo was a jolly, importunate man, kind and unrealistic, who soothed children with movies, ice-cream malteds, and what would later come to be called junk food. Steinem was to tell an interviewer: "I have a suspicion that my sister disapproved of my father more than I did. I think she resented that he wasn't more of a stable figure and providing figure. And I always felt that there may be a weight question there, because my father was extraordinarily heavy. And I think that my sister feels that living with him, by herself, all alone, while my mother was in this mental hospital, was the beginning of her weight problem, and she resents that" [Fishel, 197]. For most of her life, Susanne would continue to have a weight problem; it was not only inherited from her father, but propelled by her experience as the oldest child, bearing, as it were, the full force of her father's weight. Perhaps the fact that Susanne, after her own marriage, sustained the major responsibility for her mother was also a factor. Gloria, as the second child, would never experience her father, and his largeness, as her only parental support.

Gloria was born on March 25, 1934, nine years after Susanne. Susanne expressed an insistent demand for a little sister; certainly without Susanne's repeated wish, Ruth would not have had another child. Had Tom lived, the "little brother" might have satisfied Susanne's sibling requirements. Gloria, therefore, in a sense, owed her life to her dead brother; her name—her parents had planned to call her Cynthia—she also owed to Susanne, who had a doll of that name.

Her birth announcement proclaimed her arrival a "world premier," and the impression one gets reviewing the family pictures, in an album annotated with her mother's comments, is that the infant and child Gloria easily embodied the expectation that she would prevail in the world. This acceptance and easy admiration combined with her own inner resources as a devoted reader, dreamer, and wholesome partaker of pleasure helped to assure her of early security and comfortable adaptability. Gloria was certainly a beautiful, cheerful baby, seen in early pictures reaching out eagerly toward chickens, sheep, dogs, horses.

Summers were spent at Clark Lake, where the guests danced on a platform over the water while a child might watch until she grew sleepy and then retreat to her father's office. Steinem remembers those early summers as "a great time of running wild, catching turtles and minnows and setting them free again, looking for coins that customers at my parents' dance hall dropped in the lake, wearing a bathing suit all day long and sleeping in a little office behind the dance hall to the sounds of Gene Krupa or Wayne King or the Andrews Sisters." She was not closely cared for by her parents. Her hair would tangle; once a month, she remembered, Susanne would try to comb it out, which hurt. The bathing suit she wore all day was always red, so her mother could spot her. In reaction, she bought a black bathing suit when she was eleven, and has never worn a red one since.

Gloria was a wanted and welcome child, but she was, at the same time, not unaware of her mother's fragility. There were already intimations, which even a cheerfully occupied child could pick up, that her mother was anxious, oversensitive, and far from robust. Gloria began to have nightmares about boys spying on

Ruth in the changing rooms, or in other, albeit relatively minor, ways persecuting her. And her mother's anxieties about money were apparent: Ruth was constantly worrying about being evicted or losing the car to the finance company. Nor were her worries unrealistic, Steinem recalls: "My father often had to park the car far away to keep it from being repossessed and was also putting money 'in escrow,' or sitting in loan offices, maybe a pawnshop or two. I still can recognize the bill collector. I was trained as a three- or four-year-old to go to the door, see if it was one, and say, 'My daddy's not here.' What were they going to do to a kid?"

For Ruth, however, this way of life was not a "game," as it might have been for Leo, but a constant fear: "She never knew [Steinem recalls] when the rug was going to be—literally—pulled out from under her." Leo was constantly in debt, constantly borrowing, and mortgaging without telling Ruth. Steinem remembers her mother always keeping big commercial mustard and ketchup jars in the closet, where she put pennies and change, and Leo—catching on—depending on this small source of income as well.

Steinem recalls an incident with her parents made more poignant in that it resonates back to Ruth's own experience with Marie: "I was five or six, in Toledo, where we had come from Clark Lake to do some business errands on a hot summer day. To reward me for sitting in the car all day, they drove to some nice residential neighborhood with cool, tree-lined streets to look at the houses. In retrospect, we must have looked like Okies in our car. Anyway, she was surprised when I cried because I wanted to live there."

Every winter, escaping the cold Leo hated, the Steinems packed up and set off after Christmas in a house trailer for Florida or California. (To ensure that they would never spend the winter at Clark Lake, Leo refused to put in heating.) Sometimes the Steinems stopped at the primitive motels that were just beginning to crop up. When Gloria was a baby, Ruth carried Michigan water with her so that a change in drinking water would not cause upsets. Perhaps the most far-reaching aspect of Steinem's childhood years was that she never went to school for more than a few months at a time; some years she didn't go to school at all. Ruth's teaching certificate had armed her to deal with truant officers during the family's winter travels. The officers never got close enough to see it was for college calculus.

It was, of course, not only the cold and lack of resort business in winter that sent Leo on the road. Most fundamentally, there was always something of the gypsy in his temperament. These winter journeys pleased him, and they prepared Steinem for a life of incessant travel without a significant home base. Once, they found a movie being made on location, and Leo discovered a way in from the back of the lot. There is a picture of tiny Gloria and Gary Cooper, who was acting in the movie. Characteristically, as it was to prove, Gary Cooper is looking at her, while she looks into the distance.

LEO STEINEM is remembered with palpable affection by his younger daughter. She did not blame him for any of his irresponsible decisions, nor, even after therapy, did she view his comic gallantry with anything less than deep fondness. Most recently, she has described her father's role in her life as the readiest explanation of her ability to discover, befriend, and love amiable, unchauvinistic men. He was a dreamer whose office was his car, whose ship would one day come in. He was fun, and he was able —having no job, no office—to include a child in his life, giving her the status of a complicitous adult.

Leo Steinem had, before Gloria's birth, solidified, physically and psychologically, into the form and manner he would always display. Overweight at three hundred pounds, he was good-natured, always with plans that would make their fortune. He entered contests, inventing slogans for Old Gold cigarettes ("If you're a chain-smoker, make every link Old Gold") and ScotTissue ("You can bet your bottom dollar on ScotTissue"). He sent the latter to ScotTissue by registered mail so that no one could steal it, but he did not win that contest or any other, though he always waited for the money. His business stationary read: "It's Steinemite." He liked to dream up odd inventions: cabins with retracting roofs to enable the occupants to get a suntan; original soft drinks.

Susanne remembers that whenever she and her father returned from a jaunt he would say, "Here we are, a jolly pair." He was a show-biz type, an entrepreneur, a dance hall Sol Hurok. He was a sentimental man, full of laughter and easy tears. Steinem remembers him with spots on his suit and tie; as a sloppy dresser, whose jacket would never button. Susanne, who remembers a more serene life before Ruth's breakdown, sees him as more proper, but understands that from then on he was asked to be both parents when he was suited to be neither. For Gloria he became a pal, a peer, a companion. It is partly for these reasons that her memories of him are warmhearted and forgiving.

Many who knew Steinem in the early days when she was working in New York vividly recall her love of her father. Perhaps because he was himself childlike in many ways, he could identify with a person only three feet tall. She recalls asking him for a nickel when they were on an outing when she was four. "What for?" he asked. She replied, "You can give me the nickel or not give me the nickel, but you can't ask me what for." He said, "You're quite right," and gave her the nickel. The episode showed, Steinem observed years later (and this marked her own attitude toward children), that he respected whoever was inside that short person.

My father wasn't too interested in us until we could talk but then he was very interested. He taught me routines. In crowded elevators, he would turn to me, age five or so, and say, "So I told the man to keep his $50,000." Or he would say to me, "If you aren't good you won't go to heaven"; I was supposed to answer, "I don't want to go to heaven, Daddy, I want to go with you." And, so that we would each get the extra malted milk at the bottom of the mixer, we would go into his favorite ice cream place and order separately. I loved sitting there at age four or five with my own quarter, pretending not to know my father. He treated me like a grown-up, and I loved him for it.

When she was nine, Leo sent her alone into the store in Jackson, Michigan, the largest nearby city, to buy clothes; everything she bought, she later observed, was so cheap it no doubt shrank to the size of doilies after one washing. Though this seems more responsibility than is appropriate for a nine-year-old, Steinem early gained, along with a sense of independence, her own taste in clothes, which then and later would be eyed speculatively by many people, but which was her idea, and hers alone, of how she wanted to dress.

Writing about Leo in a 1990 essay called "The Unopposite Sex," Steinem recalled: "He treated me like a friend, asked my advice, enjoyed my company, and thus let me know that I was loved. Even in the hardest times, of which there were many, I knew with a child's unerring sense of fairness that he was treating me as well as he treated himself." It is perhaps true that had she not fitted into his life, he would probably have been unable to imagine his way into a different, more stable and parental, kind of existence. But thirty years after Leo's death, Steinem is still able to be touched by her father's efforts. "Against all he had been taught a man's life should be, against all convention for raising children and especially little girls, he loved and honored me as a unique person. And that let me know that he and I—and men and women—are not opposites at all."

If Steinem can evoke her father with such affection, and a nostalgia devoid of blame or the fear of dreadful revelations, this is also in part because Leo was, first and last, show business. Even when in later years, and to the end of his life, he took small antiques on consignment and then sold them where he could, he made the work into a kind of theater, an act the child Gloria could understand and take part in.

His wanderlust, his refusal to operate from an office, even to have a home, were all characteristics that Steinem, grown, could easily enough emulate. An attractive child, she learned to tap dance from Ruby Brown, a cigarette girl at the pier, and eventually took part in club appearances and beauty contests—all the sorts of theatrical events her father had delighted in. Steinem was certainly not the only woman to love an irresponsible father over a confined mother, but she was more unusual in modeling her adult life on his.

Ruth was, of course, someone for whom Steinem felt responsible. "For many years, I . . . never imagined my mother any way other than . . . someone to be worried about and cared for; an invalid who lay in bed with eyes closed and lips moving in occasional response to voices only she could hear." [*OAER*, 30]

In the winter of 1944, at Ruth's insistence, she and Leo separated. Apparently after leaving Leo, Ruth did not find herself able to go straight to Toledo from Clark Lake. Gloria and her mother moved to a small house in Amherst, Massachusetts, to be near Susanne, who was a junior at Smith College.[3] The following summer, while Susanne was working at Georg Jensen, a well-known

---

[3] While in Amherst, Ruth joined the Congregationalist Church, a community she found supportive. Since Gloria had never been baptized, Ruth had her baptized in this church. Susanne had been baptized in the Theosophical Lodge in Toledo.

silversmith in New York City, Gloria and her mother lived in a house in Scarsdale, New York, belonging to a college classmate of Ruth's who lent it to them during her absence; Steinem remembers this as the most miserable time of her life. Her mother, who had gained some emotional balance in Amherst, lost it and became very depressed. In the fall, Gloria and Ruth moved back to Toledo, where they intended to live in Ruth's parents' house. The house was still tenanted for the first year, so they rented a basement "apartment" in a rooming house at 551 Lincoln Avenue that consisted of one room behind the furnace. The room was close to Monroe School, where Steinem entered sixth grade. Though the rooming house was within walking distance of Maplewood, where Janey, Bob, and Marie were living, Steinem remembers seeing them only on Thanksgiving and Christmas and "once, when Janey allowed me to invite my friends there, since I couldn't have them in the basement." It was while mother and daughter were living there that Ruth and Leo were divorced.

Much attention has been focused by the media, and by Steinem herself, on how poor her family was during the following years; certainly, her experience of poverty permanently shaped her outlook on life. That her roots were middle-class is inarguable; but it was with the working class that she spent her preadolescent and adolescent years. Her only aim, and the single unrealistic dream of all her neighborhood peers, was to escape from that working-class world.

In Toledo she learned, and believed, that if you gave way to a boy, you were ruined; she determined not to be that sort of victim. She would always remember boys, bitter at having been trapped, slouching down the street with their pregnant wives, themselves barely beyond girlhood. The destiny of girls was set: They would be wives and mothers, as soon as possible. Boys would go to work in one of Toledo's three major factories: Champion Spark Plug, Libbey-Owens Glass, Willy's Jeeps. This had been their parents' destiny; they would eventually, though reluctantly, accept it as theirs. Yet even as Steinem observed and feared this constraining destiny, something in her childhood made her wary of the middle class, both when she encountered it at the house of her maternal aunt and later, when she finally became part of it at Smith College. That wariness would never vanish.

Before Gloria transformed herself into her mother's mother, she had been endowed by her father with dreams: of endless possibilities, of outwitting fortune, and of soothing pain. That endowment also devalued security and routine, and rejected the boredom inherent in an existence where what tomorrow was likely to hold was always evident, when to know what the future might hold was to limit the future's chances to astonish and beguile. Had Gloria received this philosophy only to have it washed away by a practical mother's daily struggle with poverty and thwarted wishes, its futility might have become evident. But because she became at ten, and remained until she was seventeen, the one who coped with her mother's life as well as her own, her father's disposition supported her main fantasy and hope: that one day this would all end, that perhaps it would turn out that her parents were not her parents, that these years had been a task rather like that of the youngest of the three brothers in fairy tales, and that she would escape.

But before that escape, for seven years, Steinem kept herself and her divorced mother within the bounds of a reasonable life. Those years began with a moment that would return to Steinem late in her fifties. She bent over after working hard at the computer, and a wave of nausea assaulted her. She has described the scene in *Revolution from Within:* Immediately she was back in the first day of her life alone with her mother in the dreary basement apartment furnished with bunk beds, all that the small space would allow. Gloria felt ill and she lay down in the upper bunk in the hope that someone would bring her chicken soup, cuddle her, and allow her to be sick, to be a child. But her mother was, even to an eleven-year-old's eyes, sicker than she. And so Gloria climbed down from the bunk and coped, realizing that she could not be a child anymore and was almost never sick again. As she would say in later years, "I knew that my mother loved me, but that she couldn't take care of me."

After the basement room behind the furnace, Steinem and her mother lived upstairs in the deteriorating house Ruth had grown up in and inherited from her parents; it was now converted to a three-family house with two apartments for rent. Occasionally Marie came over to clean. Steinem's impression was that "O'Momie did this in disapproval of my mother's housekeeping, but perhaps it was also in sorrow at seeing the state of what had been her house with her husband while her daughters were growing up." They lived on money from the Clark Lake property, which Ruth leased (Leo said the Indians got more for it than she), and on the rent from tenants. The downstairs was rented to two working-class families—sometimes a man in one beat his pregnant wife, the other was rented to the butcher's family. In "Ruth's Song" Steinem would recall the paper drapes she made, the books she brought home from the library to lose herself in, the cheap meals she bought for her mother.

Marcia Cohen, in *The Sisterhood,* mentions the ugly poverty. Steinem "would talk about the rats, about waking up at night and pulling her toes in under the covers in fear, about actually being bitten by one of them." Cohen reports: "Not everyone believed her." [Cohen, 45]

When these stories were told to the media, *The Toledo Blade* reported in 1972 that the city's chamber of commerce and director of public information, as well as state representative Barney Quilter, were outraged at Steinem's portrayal of East Toledo. Ruth Steinem also wished to downplay the poverty by denying it, as she denied that she and Gloria's father had been divorced.

Poverty in the United States is, of course, shame, and Ruth would later insist to reporters that things were not as bad as Gloria made them out to have been.

But Lillian Barnes Borton, who as a child lived downstairs from Gloria and her mother, wrote to *The Toledo Blade,* also in 1972, to confirm Steinem's memories:

> I have read Barney Quilter's recent comments against Gloria Steinem. While I don't agree with all her views on Women's Lib (I'm just a housewife and I love it) I have to say that everything about the house she lived in (at 747 Woodville Rd.) is true. I know because my parents and my sister and I lived downstairs in that house while Gloria and her mother Ruth lived upstairs.
>
> The house was in a bad state of disrepair and very definitely overrun with rats. The rats would even get up on our beds at night, they were in our kitchen range and sink cabinet. The only food we could keep was either canned or in the refrigerator. One night we were having dinner and our dog chased a rat from the living room and it jumped upon the table (so much for dinner). I remember when Gloria was bitten by the rats. Mrs. Steinem was so terribly upset that she cried.
>
> I can't honestly say this was a "slum" area. I don't remember that much about the rest of the neighborhood, but it wasn't real good. The church next door finally bought this house and tore it down and built an addition on the church. That is the best thing that ever happened to the house and also to Gloria and her mother. [*Toledo Blade,* Mar. 1, 1972]

Marcia Cohen interviewed Lillian Barnes Borton and learned more, some of it hard on Ruth Steinem but none of it contradicting Steinem's stories. Borton added that she longed to get close to Gloria, whom she greatly admired. When she asked why Ruth "was the way she was," Gloria would answer softly that her mother was sick, or that "my mother has a problem." She would not say more; you could never, in Lillian Borton's words, "get behind her eyes." [Cohen, 49] The young Steinem, caring for her mother, had learned to protect herself. In the seventies, when she met a high school friend named Rose Links who had also lived alone with her mother and who Steinem had, in her turn, admired, she was stunned to learn that Links was always worried about her during those years. Steinem had assumed she was successfully concealing her troubles at home: that she had never been without the fear that Ruth, finding her gone, might fail to remember what Gloria had told her of her plans and call the police, or wander unclothed into the street in search of her daughter. Today, it is likely that more sophisticated psychopharmaceuticals would have balanced Ruth's illness. But in the early 1950s the commonly prescribed drug was a chloryl hydrate cocktail called "Doc Howard's," to which Ruth was addicted. Most of the time it made her calmer. What Steinem did not reveal about her mother in "Ruth's Song," nor perhaps until recently face up to, is that her mother was, to put it bluntly, crazy.

GLORIA'S TIME at Waite High School in Toledo, and earlier at Raymer Junior High, seem to have left little impression on her teachers. When *Esquire* was preparing its antagonistic portrait of Steinem in 1971, the religion editor of the *Blade,* serving as a researcher, asked about Steinem at both schools. Little was remembered, although the French teacher recalled that Gloria had taken French to learn ballet terms. Dancing—or any form of show business, really—was, in the Toledo years, to be her way out. There is a newspaper picture of Gloria as a chorus girl in a production of *Naughty Marietta.*

What is clear about this time in Steinem's life is that getting her schoolwork done, occasionally appearing in nightclubs for ten dollars a night when she could, working as a salesgirl when she was old enough, and caring for her mother left her little time to shine in school. And she may not have chosen to shine: The pressures of behaving correctly, looking neat, buying crepe dresses and fake jewelry were pressure enough, in addition to avoiding "ruin" by a boy—that is, loss of virginity and reputation. Perhaps even worse than getting pregnant was remaining unmarried; for girls, this was a double jeopardy. Steinem remembered going to a wedding where the bride hid alone in a corner as everyone danced; Steinem went to talk to her. The bride was ashamed: At twenty-two she had still been unmarried, and a husband had to be "found," or in some way acquired.

It is possible, Steinem said forty years later, that the ethic of this blue collar neighborhood, which was so

punitive to women, terrible for women, gave me a clear feeling of "I'm not going to let them win." Toledo gave me a sense of what was at stake, of pride, one very clear motive: not to be humiliated. I don't think I was the only one in Toledo who thought that way. I did think of myself as from the working class; I didn't feel different even though my parents had gone to college; I felt poorer than the factory workers. Class was very important to me and what I became. Women were so clearly divided into victims and nice girls, and if you became a victim, not a nice girl, your life was over.

Given a choice between being a victim and being a limited fifties nice girl, I chose not to be a victim. It's very hard to convey the atmosphere of my part of Toledo to anyone who didn't experience it. Hoboken, New Jersey, is a lot like Toledo. Little tiny houses right up against the street, phony brick, screen doors with initials in the screen door, bars with Schlitz signs. There was the Eagles hall, where we used to dance; the Eagles are a lower-class Elks. Eagles were the guys on the line, whereas the Elks were maybe the foremen. We used to dance in this place, my dancing teacher put on shows, and we each made ten dollars. We came in little taffeta skirts, and we tap-danced. The wives were there, at the Eagles. We danced while the band —accordions—were out drinking; we did our little show in front of the circular bandstand. From the floor to the ceiling the bandstand was covered with chicken wire; otherwise, when the guys out front had a fight, and they always did, someone would be thrown through the bass drum. We danced in front of the chicken wire; we were earlier in the evening, it didn't get bad until midnight. At an Elks convention, I remember, I was dancing, I must have been thirteen or fourteen. The cops wanted to close it down because it was getting rowdy. They came to those of us dancing and said, "All you have to do is go out on the stage and pull your strap down as if you were going to strip, and we can close it." I was willing to do it, he may have offered me five dollars, but the dance teacher said I couldn't.

It was macho and pathetic. The guys are also such victims; most of them wouldn't have known how to open a checking account, would get their money in a pay envelope with cash. Their kids were my friends, and on payday we went to pay off what they owed for the bed, or an engagement ring. The debt was never more than five dollars. There were little stores that preyed off working-class families. We went to pay off on Saturdays before going to the movies. I remember they had these little tiny windows at the back of the shop where you handed in your five dollars' payment on the loan. When you had paid off what you owed they would ring a bell to alert salespeople to try to get you to buy something else. When I was living on Eighty-first Street when I first came to New York, it was near a black neighborhood, and I recognized it. The welfare checks came on Thursday; on Friday the prices went up, as they did on payday in Toledo. The people became human conduits, never getting out of debt. Everyone had cash. In Toledo, if someone got a rare check—pay envelopes contained cash—the check-cashing service charged a great deal just to cash it. My mother was of the class that had a checking account; even with no money, she knew about that. If my mother was in bad shape, I wrote the checks and she signed them.

And so Steinem danced for money, and eventually entered a beauty pageant. While these activities represented one of the few ways for ambitious girls to escape from the usual Toledo female destiny, they also indicate that despite Steinem's constant denial that she was unusually attractive, she must have known early that she was a "looker." In the early 1970s she would say that she was considered glamorous compared with the media's insulting picture of a feminist—butch, army-booted, hairy, fat. She is right about the media's mistaken ideas, ideas that the right wing continues to promulgate today, but wrong about denying the effect of her attractiveness. Steinem was too smart, certainly by the time she got to Smith, if not before, to want to rely on her looks. But from her first childhood years, she had the confidence of a markedly appealing and attractive creature.

Somehow the world into which Gloria Steinem was born allowed her, despite a damaged and sometimes crazy mother and an often-absent father, to construct a sustaining sense of pleasure and the chance for consoling fantasy. Steinem had early learned to read, and, like so many children, she escaped happily into books. "Louisa May Alcott was my friend. I read all her adult novels as well as her young ones, and used to fantasize endlessly that she would come back to life and I could show her all the new things in the world." She was also devoted to radio programs; she long remembered Jack Benny's voice and the comfort it brought her. She attributed her later difference from her generation of college graduates to the fact that she was never socialized as they were: she skipped both the multiplication tables and the socialization most of us undergo in our first ten years.

Above all, she continued to live in books and fantasies. From the Alcott books and elsewhere she developed extensive rescue fantasies, in which she would at the last minute save someone from a fatal situation. A man would be lynched; Gloria, arriving in the nick of time, would hold off the lynchers with a shotgun (the only weapon she had ever seen), free the prisoner, and drive away with him. These rescue fantasies were not only her escape from daily life; they were also the dramas in which she saw herself as acting upon the world, as extricating those enmeshed in the world's cruelties.

But these youthful rescue fantasies are significantly different from the usual fantasies of girls in the 1940s and the years before the effects of the current women's movement. The usual fantasies of women and girls were to *be* rescued; they were dreams of a man who would come along and carry one off, either convention-ally, into marriage, or sexually, into the fulfillment of his desire, which would, in turn, fulfill the woman who inspired it. Few girls at that time had the idea that they themselves might be rescuers; instead, their fantasies reflected the well-known fairy tales "Snow White," "Cinderella," and "Sleeping Beauty," or the sort of story still embodied in popular romance. Because of her responsibility for the household with her disturbed mother, she tended to think of herself in the active role; she saw herself as the successful last resort for people almost beyond saving. Those who knew her well in her adult years, particularly in the seventies and eighties and after, would easily understand that the rescue fantasies had be-come reality, occasionally a reality from which she herself needed to be rescued. But the signs of a revolutionary who would hardly accept the conventional female roles were, in her girlhood, already there.

As Ms. Borton mentions, the Nuneviller house was sold to the neighboring church by Ruth Steinem; the money would go for Gloria's tuition at Smith. As Gloria completed her junior year of high school, rescue came—not a minute too soon, but before it was altogether too late.

Gloria would tell the story of that rescue often; it was every bit as extraordinary, in its way, as the arrival of her "real parents," as she had so often imagined them, would have been. Now that the church had bought the house, where would Ruth and Gloria live? Susanne and Leo were visiting Toledo the summer of 1951, and Susanne suggested to Leo that he take care of Ruth for a year so that Gloria could come to Washington, D.C., and live with her sister, finishing high school there. Gloria told Susanne that Leo would not do it; after all, their parents were divorced. When, at breakfast, Susanne suggested the scheme to Leo, he refused, and Susanne walked out of the restaurant in anger. Then Leo drove Gloria to her job as a salesgirl. As she left the car, she began to weep; her hope of rescue had been too intense. Her father's sentimentality, for he had never seen her cry, was aroused. "All right," Steinem would always remember his saying, "but one year is all. We're synchronizing our watches."

Characteristically, Leo played the scene as in a movie; he was planning, with a comrade in arms, a dangerous operation. Yet however his attitude is interpreted, he did realize that Steinem, who had borne so much so bravely, could bear no more. He did return to the fragile, crazy woman from whom he was divorced, and he did take care of her for the year that allowed his daughter the necessary escape; during that year Leo and Ruth traveled around the country to California and elsewhere, as they had done during the Clark Lake winters. Had Leo ultimately refused to take Ruth, Steinem would probably have been damaged in some crippling way. Whatever his manner, he did not deny her that vital year of freedom. And thus Gloria Steinem's years of being, quite simply, mother to her mother came to an end.

* * *

CAN STEINEM be called fortunate to have been born into the troubled circumstances that surrounded her? Is it fortunate to be born into a family consisting of a nine-year-old sister, a "jolly" but irresponsible father, a life of summer fun and winter wandering into warmer climates, and a mother already addicted to "Doc Howard's" medicine? In fact, Gloria was born with every chance for disaster. Remarkably, the circumstances, though difficult, were redeeming—which is to say, that they made possible the flowering of a personality oddly but singularly suited to just such conditions. She later cast light on this by relating two contradictory but consoling childhood responses, one rational, one fantasy: She understood her parents were doing the best they could (perhaps more children understand this than is comprehended in a Freudian universe); and she believed herself to be only a guest in their lives, dropped off by her true parents, who would one day reclaim her. This provided the distance that protected.

It is likely that even as a small child, before the worst years, when Ruth was busy with the resort and Gloria was as often the companion of her father as of her mother, she was able to escape the earliest maternal pressures to conform to a conventional daughterly pattern. Those who believe that for a woman not to have babies of her own, whether born to her or adopted, is to miss an essential female destiny might consider that Steinem paid for this early experience as her mother's mother in her refusal to undergo another experience of motherhood. Some have suggested that women have children to better their own experience, or fail to have children to avoid repeating that experience. Certainly Steinem did not want to bear children, and an assessment of that decision depends on how conventional is one's view of female destiny.

Susanne, unlike Gloria, seems always to have wanted children and certainly wanted a small sister. She did not, in anyone's memory, resent Gloria, who came along when Susanne was just nine and was, indeed, Susanne's particular request. Susanne disputes some of Gloria's memories, and had trouble on her first reading of Gloria's essay "Ruth's Song," a reaction Gloria explains by the fact that during Susanne's intermittent visits to Toledo in the years when Ruth and Gloria lived there together, Ruth had always risen to the occasion. Throughout their lives, however, Susanne has been wonderfully supportive of Gloria and of their mother. She might, without exaggeration, and never herself considering any part of it as a sacrifice, be said to have made Gloria Steinem's life possible. Unlike Gloria, Susanne took daily responsibility for Ruth when they were both adults; while never quite escaping the need for maternal love and unconditional approval, Susanne had to face that need on a daily basis. She would always want her mother's love, and never, even in her adult years, feel certain that she had it.

Susanne and Gloria lived different childhoods, and remembered them in different ways. Susanne had more early years of "normality," at least until her mother's first breakdown, when she was five. Her father, offering the comfort of movies and malteds, could not finally make up for Ruth's absence. Thus Susanne, with different memories, acted out the resonance of her childhood by eventually marrying and devoting herself to a husband and six children, after abandoning an unusual career as a gemologist and diamond seller, during which she had written a history of the Hope diamond for the Smithsonian Institution. When her children were grown she became a lawyer and went to work for the Federal Trade Commission, working to regulate the franchise in jewelry industries; a profession from which she retired in 1994. But if she made herself a very different life from Gloria's, their continuing relationship exemplifies the strong family bond and the lasting affections that were their heritage.

* * *

WHEN LEO'S YEAR of caretaking was up, Ruth came to Washington to live with Susanne, and Gloria went to begin her freshman year at Smith College. There remains a thirteen-page letter from Susanne to Gloria, who was back at Smith after a skiing weekend in January of 1952. In careful, amazingly considerate detail, Susanne explains to her sister all the efforts she has made on her mother's behalf, because she assumes her sister would want to know. Clearly, the doctors all agreed, Ruth needed to be temporarily institutionalized, but Susanne did not want to commit her; she must go voluntarily. There was thought of St. Elizabeth's, the government-run mental institution near Washington where Ezra Pound had been incarcerated rather than be executed as a traitor; it was good enough diagnostically, but the living conditions seemed discouraging. Susanne visited there, and described it in detail to Gloria. Then Susanne found a Dr. Lebensohn, who didn't try to minimize the problem but seemed intelligent and sympathetic. With his help, Susanne and Gloria decided on Shepperd and Pratt, a private, much more congenial institution in Baltimore, which they paid for by selling some of their mother's property in Clark Lake. There Ruth would remain for almost two years, her condition diagnosed as chronic anxiety neurosis. She was at first in a locked ward, but was eventually allowed to make trips outside with her daughters. Steinem used to take the train and then streetcars to visit her. Steinem recalls that for the first time she recognized her mother as separate from herself, finally and simply *as* her mother, not as the distracted and needy woman for whose care Steinem had so long been too responsible too young.

After her release, Ruth would go back to Shepperd and Pratt when she needed to. When she first left the institution, she lived in an apartment, which was too lonely, then in a rooming house. Gradually she took up a life in Washington, becoming interested in various social and political groups. When Susanne, her husband, Bob Patch, and their six children moved to a larger house, they provided a separate apartment downstairs for Ruth, who never became able to live alone thereafter.

Ruth was always very fragile. Steinem would beg reporters, to no avail, not to repeat stories about their life in Toledo and her parents' divorce because of the pain these caused her mother. But when free from undue anxiety, Ruth could be charming, attractive, busy, and fond of presents. She often wrote, in her shaky but legible writing and witty style, to her friends on the staff of *Ms.* magazine, who were fond of her. She was also sufficiently sophisticated to recognize various attempts to get to Gloria through her.

Ruth had been damaged by life, but not quite fatally. Many of Steinem's friends, who knew Ruth when the symptoms from the earlier years were no longer always evident, remember her with affection and admiration. In the sixties and seventies Steinem helped her mother to live a more varied, enticing life than Ruth might otherwise have done, sending her money, buying her gifts, taking her on vacations, providing her with a rented car and driver so that she could indulge her wide-ranging interests in the Washington area without having to ride on buses, where she would often suffer panic attacks. But until her death, Ruth remained chiefly Susanne's responsibility. Gloria stayed in close touch; their mother had always said, "You are sisters and have to love each other"—remembering that her own mother had always set her and her sister Janey against each other by always praising one girl to the other—and Gloria and Susanne obeyed, gladly.

The question might arise: Why was neither sister angry, Susanne about becoming Ruth's primary caretaker after Gloria went to Smith, Gloria with Susanne for having been absent during the years in Toledo? The possibility always exists that both felt an anger they neither recognized nor admitted. It is likelier, however, that each sister had worked out her own most emotionally pragmatic solution to having had Ruth as a mother. Susanne had achieved the family life her mother had been unable to provide; Gloria pursued the journalism career that life had denied her mother. Had either sister failed in these reconstructions, they might indeed have felt and expressed deep anger.

Early in 1980 Ruth suffered a stroke, after which she went into a hospital for therapy. She returned home, but was so stubborn that she would come out of her apartment downstairs and insist upon climbing the stairs; she would get stuck halfway up, unable to continue or to go down. She returned to a nursing home, and eventually died in the hospital of a heart attack on July 15, 1981, exactly one month before her eighty-third birthday. Both her daughters were with her.

And what of Leo? He stayed in intermittent touch with his daughters but traveled a great deal, selling antiques and antique jewelry. By the time Steinem had begun her New York life in the sixties, Leo had moved to California; Steinem saw him once a year when he came east, twice a year if she visited California. She and her father exchanged occasional letters, as they had since she was ten, the year in which their annual meetings began. One year, having heard there were gems lying on the streets in South America, Leo went there and married a German-born woman who wanted to get into the United States. The marriage was short-lived; indeed, Leo warned Gloria about his wife, fearing she would ask for money.

Leo's lonely death was bizarre, yet characteristic of the negligent behavior of so many American hospitals. He didn't in those years have a permanent single residence, but stayed in rooms at different places, one of these in Arizona. The woman from whom he rented his room there wanted to go to California to meet her husband; Leo was en route to California and offered to take her. On the freeway in Orange County, they were in an accident. Probably Leo fell asleep at the wheel; Susanne had remembered him often hitting himself on the back of his neck with the flat of his hand to wake himself up when he was driving. They were taken to the Orange County hospital, but neither Susanne nor Gloria was notified, although Leo had ample identification, including the telephone numbers of both his daughters. Several days after the accident Leo's traveling companion, now released from the hospital, called Susanne at three in the morning to tell her, fearing Leo's family might not know. Susanne immediately called her father and spoke as well to his doctor, who assured her that Leo was doing well and would be moved to a convalescent hospital within a few days. While Leo was still in the hospital, Ruth wrote him cheering letters; she still felt married to him.

Susanne called Gloria, who was vacationing in the Caribbean without phone service after sundown; she reached her the next day. Together with Gloria, Susanne and Ruth decided it would be best for Gloria to go when Leo was transferred to the convalescent hospital; Susanne, with four very young children, could not go. But on April 20, 1961, the day Gloria left for the coast, the hospital called Susanne to say that Leo had unexpectedly hemorrhaged and died; it was four days before his sixty-fourth birthday. Susanne, knowing Gloria would change planes in Chicago, had her paged at the airport to give her the news of his death; Gloria continued on.

Leo's body was cremated and his ashes sent back to Washington, where Ruth, Susanne, and Gloria held a memorial service. The whole episode was painful to all three of them. For this reason it was important to Susanne and Gloria that when their mother died almost exactly twenty years after Leo they were on each side of her bed holding her hands.

WHILE LEO'S death did not have the intensity of a deep loss for his younger daughter, its suddenness was, inevitably, a shock. He had long before become a distant figure in both his daughters' lives, as Ruth had, in another way, become a secondary figure in Gloria's life. Steinem was left to sort out Leo's affairs, a laborious task. He had made no preparations. There were objects in his car, some that belonged to him, others that belonged to someone else and been given to him on consignment. This led, some years later, to a characteristically Leo-and-Gloria moment for Steinem.

She wrote to Rocky Marciano to tell him that she had discovered, in the estate of her father, "a diamond ring which must have been presented to you. It is a 3-karat diamond set in a broad gold band decorated with boxing gloves, and the inscription reads: 'To Rocky Marciano/Great Champion and Humanitarian.'" Rocky Marciano came to her house in New York, said, "How interesting that you found it," and took it away, saying he would have it appraised. But he never returned or paid for it, and Steinem could never get in touch with him again. "It shows what kind of businesswoman I turned out to be," she remarked ruefully.

IN THE 1980s much began to be heard of "dysfunctional families," families entrapped by alcoholism or sexual abuse or battering. But what, in fact, is a "functional" family? One woman, a "survivor" of a childhood with a truly dysfunctional family, faced the question: A functional family, she said, is one in which the children are believed and feel, as children, wanted.

By this definition, Gloria Steinem's family—however distant from the ideal of the nuclear family incessantly promulgated by movies, advertisers, and the politically conservative—seems to have served her well. Bertrand Russell observed the anomaly that while almost all outstanding individuals have had unhappy childhoods—that is, not "normal" childhoods—we can hardly prescribe childhood unhappiness so as to achieve accomplishment. What we can do, but probably will not, is learn that the nuclear family, functioning in the "proper" way, may well be designed to cause the maximum amount of misery to the most people, not the less so because each generation, never doubting the model, thinks that it can do better.

We might even feel challenged to redefine the "functional" family. We can, in any case, remark that Steinem's childhood, while far from easy or ideal by any known standard, served to produce a passionately engaged and loving human being. That said, we might add only that poverty, heavy responsibility when young, the companionship of a father who was unrealistic yet always a peer and always kind, and a continuing sense of being loved as opposed to being cared for, may not be so bad a recipe for the making of a responsible and contributing human being. Diane Middlebrook writes of Anne Sexton's reevaluating "her daughterhood to a strong, elusive mother, a task that occupied the rest of her life." [103] But perhaps that far-from-uncommon situation exists only where the mother is in a position to direct her daughter into the very life that failed her. Gloria Steinem's mother, during the years when Gloria lived with her, was too sick to direct her daughter into any social paths, and Gloria, in being responsible for her mother, became responsible for herself.

Yet, in a culture in which mothers are designated to take all the blame, Steinem never blamed Ruth. The significant question, in Steinem's case, remains not so much why she failed to resent her mother or why she preferred the greater ease of her irresponsible father's love and comradeship, but how she escaped, as her sister did not, the almost universal experience of daughters: the discovery that a real daughter can never satisfy the mother's desire for an ideal daughter, an image of perfect femininity who, in Diane Middlebrook's words, "reflects back to her an ideal self, equally imaginary." [88]

Middlebrook's analysis of Anne Sexton's problems as a mother help us to understand Ruth, and why Gloria escaped the usual daughterly destiny. "I, who was never quite sure / about being a girl, needed another / life, another image to remind me." This poem of Sexton's [87] captures a common motherly sentiment; perhaps Ruth, who had to give up her ambitions as a person to fulfill her role as a woman, treated her older daughter in the same way Anne Sexton (and in turn Sexton's daughters) was treated. For mothers notoriously continue the mother-daughter plot, working to entrap their daughters exactly as they have been entrapped. Sexton called the mother-daughter relationship "more poignant than Romeo and Juliet"—rightly, because it is harder to break away from, harder ever to grow free of.

How did Gloria Steinem manage to escape from what Middlebrook calls the daughterly trap that captures generation after generation? We can only surmise. If the reverse roles of Steinem's girlhood now seem to us difficult or even outrageous, we need nonetheless to ask if something in that arrangement did not make for a more successful personality than the highly touted nuclear suburban family. It is possible that a study of only daughters raised as members of the adult world, or of oldest daughters in large families where the mother was overworked—famous examples might be Margaret Sanger, Agnes Smedley, Susan B. Anthony—would reveal a life not dissimilar to the one Steinem eventually led. That is not to say that there was no price to pay for such a childhood; there is always a price. But in Steinem's case, as probably in other cases, whatever the suffering involved, the price was paid in middle age, when she could best afford it.

SAFETY

THE SMITH COLLEGE catalog declared, in the year Steinem graduated, that it had begun in a New England conscience. The money for the college was earned by a man, but it was his sister, Sophia Smith, who inherited his fortune and left it for the founding of a college. The conscience to which the catalog refers is the male conscience of Sophia Smith's minister, and Smith, like the other Seven Sisters colleges, put the male and his "natural" requirements at the center of its world. Sophia Smith was herself clear about this: "I would have the education [of women] suited to the mental and physical wants of women. . . . It is not my design to render my sex any the less feminine." Opening in 1875 on a tract of thirteen acres with fourteen students, Smith College had become by 1952—the year Steinem arrived there—one of the largest women's colleges in the world, without ever challenging Sophia Smith's conservative ideals. Not until 1975 would Smith have a woman president.

When Steinem arrived at this elegant, bucolic Northampton, Massachusetts, campus with its lake (called Paradise Pond), its

ancient, carefully tended trees, its meticulous landscaping surrounding white, colonial-style "houses," and its newer dorms like
Laura Scales (with about sixty-five students from the four classes
in each), Smith was at the height of its reputation as *the* college for
socially prominent young women—Anne Morrow Lindbergh had
begged, ineffectually, not to be sent there. The Smith girl was
known for her social skills and her athletic ability. One alumna
remembers the popular parody of the Smith girl dressed in a
strapless cocktail gown and carrying a hockey stick. For the young
women who entered the college before the 1970s, it was the place
of passage between girlhood and the inevitable marriage. If they
did not meet their future husband, attending the "right" men's
college, they were at least equipped to be the wife of such a man
when and if they met him. Smith's most famous alumnae are
Barbara Bush (who married in her sophomore year and did not
graduate) and Nancy Reagan. Smith, however, meant something
different to Steinem than to the usual college-age woman, happily
entrusted by her parents to this serene campus. For Steinem,
Smith was primarily a safe shelter, one equipped with all that she
required for a life without persistent anxiety.

In fairness, Smith must not be seen as notably more conservative and male-centered in its teachings than the other Seven Sisters colleges—Wellesley, Radcliffe, Barnard, Mount Holyoke,
Vassar, Bryn Mawr. As Liva Baker observed in her book on these
colleges, of the two significant human rights movements of the
nineteenth and twentieth centuries, the movement for Negro
rights and for women's rights, "The [Seven] Sisters were in the
vanguard of neither." [187] Congressional hearings on the Equal
Rights Amendment, from 1929 to 1956, drew no testimony from
the Seven Sisters, who have, Baker writes, not been prominent "in
pursuing women's interest politically or, equally important, in offering their considerable expertise in the education of women to
those who might use it legislatively." [188, 189] A 1971 Mount

Holyoke survey found that only 3.33 percent of those responding had ever participated in a women's liberation group. [193 fn.]

True, the young women would be urged, in Smith graduate Betty Friedan's words, "to commit your abilities to some purpose larger than yourself" [Baker 193], but that, of course, had been the stated destiny of women since the dawn of patriarchy. That they might use their talents for *women* was not to be thought of, unless of course the women were poor, disadvantaged, could be helped on a volunteer basis and with an inevitable noblesse oblige attitude. It is not that Steinem immediately drew a different lesson from this from Smith; it would, in fact, be more than a decade before she looked back critically upon her Smith education.

Sylvia Plath was a contemporary of Steinem's at Smith. Her roommate, Nancy Hunter Steiner, has described the college girls as they were in the 1950s: "In some ways," Steiner writes, "we resembled every generation of undergraduates that has ever assaulted the nation's campuses. We were scrubbed, shining, and expectant. Those of us who chose Smith were no exception. The stereotyped Smith girl of the mid-1950s was a conformist, like thousands of undergraduates there and elsewhere, before and since. She was eager to be recognized as a college girl and she was careful to wear the proper uniform, in this case Bermuda shorts, knee socks, and button-down-collar shirt. Her hair was casually but precisely styled." [35] Plath conformed to this model; Steinem, for all her contentment at Smith, did not. It is instructive to compare Plath and Steinem because, in their different ways, they confronted, both at college and after it, the same expectations and standards—Plath by fulfilling all of them better than anyone had done or, as it would turn out, could do, and Steinem by deciding, not altogether consciously, to ignore them.

Originally in a class two years ahead of Steinem, Plath, because of her first suicide attempt, did not graduate until 1955, a year before Steinem. Both were elected to Phi Beta Kappa, but from

Steinem's vantage point Plath was legendary. She had written poetry in her freshman year, the legend went, which even her professors thought good. She was beautiful, Steinem remembers, in a way that must have been especially ironic for her; she looked like a healthy cheerleader, which, Steinem now supposes, must have clashed with her inner self. By 1955, her senior year, Plath was a rare, mythical creature on the Smith campus, and for Steinem, who saw her only from afar, the drama and mystery were deepened by her suicide attempt. Steinem insists that the few who knew them both would gladly report, if asked, how pedestrian Steinem was by comparison.

At Smith, in fact, Steinem's newly found talent for fitting in with conventional expectations provided her with a temporary haven; Plath, on the other hand, while also fitting in, fought the expectations of her culture, her mother, and her college with unabated anxiety; no triumph could alleviate the essential inner struggle. According to Jacqueline Rose, she wrote in her journal her despair at her sex: "Being born a woman is my awful tragedy. From the moment I was conceived I was doomed to sprout breasts and ovaries rather than penis and scrotum; to have my whole circle of action, thought and feeling rigidly circumscribed by my inescapable femininity." [116] As Pat McPherson, currently president of Bryn Mawr, wrote of the dilemma of womanhood in 1991, "In the early 1950s it was no laughing matter for Sylvia Plath in her journal to try to come to terms with the either/or-ness of motherhood and career, purity and sexuality, domesticity and education. . . . Plath—along with the rest of educated American womanhood since World War II—was determined to exempt herself from such punishing choice. Her solution is manic over-achievement. The structural problem of separate spheres remains." [48]

Both the Steinem girls, but especially Susanne, had been subtly directed to Smith by their mother's sister, Janey, who had aspirations for them; she studied the society pages and had noted how many society women had gone to Smith. Janey wanted her nieces above all to become "ladies"; Steinem remembers her as admiring the Ford family and hoping Gloria would marry "the right person" and live in Grosse Point, the elegant Detroit suburb. She would buy Gloria clothes from Best and Company (the store of that generation's childhood, known for the subdued taste and quiet quality of its clothes) when it came to Toledo once a year to sell its wares in a local hotel room; Gloria always wished she could have the money instead. While she was at Smith, her aunt and uncle bought her a dress for one hundred dollars, an immense sum then; again she wished she could have had the money. But her classmates remembered that dress thirty-five years later; it was black and sophisticated.

Stanford and Cornell had turned Steinem down, doubtless because neither her high school grades from Toledo and Washington nor her performance on the S.A.T.—a test she was destined vehemently to criticize in future years—were sufficiently outstanding to get her into those colleges. But at Smith, her high school adviser argued successfully on her behalf and that college, in any case, seemed the natural choice; she remembered Susanne's stories of the college, wanted to go there, and asked to live in Laura Scales, her sister's house.

To Steinem, coming from East Toledo via Washington, D.C., Smith was a revelation. It was the first time she was in the company of a group of well-to-do young women with strict codes of behavior wholly unlike any she had known. It was the first place where she could be away from her family and all of the worries about her mother that had become the staple of her life. It was an amazing place of safety, with all the pleasant amenities and ease that she had not until then experienced.

In 1964, five years before her "conversion" to feminism, in an article for *Glamour* magazine, "College and What I Learned

There," Steinem wrote that she had loved college from the moment she got there; she had found a home. She was amazed by the girls who left such a comfortable place to marry. Smith gave you a quiet place to live; Smith let you read books and fed you scheduled meals. She had not previously known that other people, rather than standing around the refrigerator, regularly sat down to eat. She had, as she wrote, brought to Smith "a childhood indiscriminately bookish, during which I did not go to school but worked my way through the entirety of Nancy Drew, Godey's Lady's Books, and the Theosophical Library; a show business adolescence spent dancing in variety shows and coming in second in beauty contests in Toledo, Ohio; and more than enough time among Midwestern, Heart-of-America fundamentalists to form a bad accent and a totally unworkable set of moral principles." [148]

Before going to Smith, middle-class rectitude and ease had been her aim, and her mother's, during the struggling, poverty-stricken time in Toledo. At Smith, however, Steinem saw ladyhood embodied and evident in all its trappings, which was enough to turn her against "proper" dress. Well-to-do college students of those years wore cashmere sweaters and skirts and what Steinem would always refer to as "Peck and Peck and Peck and Peck." She longed for the rhinestones and chiffon scarves that had meant dressing up in her Toledo life.

Yet because the social mores of college in those years forbade talk about any but the allowed subjects—weekends away at the men's colleges, clothes, makeup, marriage, bridge—and certainly forbade any profound revelations about one's family, Steinem could appear eccentric in only superficial ways. And unlike other women from poorer families, on scholarship or living in the cooperative houses where they did all their own housework, Steinem did not express resentment nor decline the companionship of her classmates. At Smith, she had reached a womblike, protected place where even her lack of money, and nostalgia for the "wrong" clothes, could not prevent her basking in the amenities of this new life.

Steinem's classmates remember only funny stories of her family, of the family's winter trips to Florida or California in a house trailer; they would remember a particular story of which the punch line was "We've just finished washing last year's dishes." The family had left in a hurry one year, Steinem recalled, with dirty dishes in the sink. After they returned, she and Susanne scraped away at them, leading to the final triumphant announcement. These were characteristic, jaunty tales; anecdotes that hid the pain, the poverty, and the craziness of her mother, and revealed none of the anguish of that time in her life. There were at Smith no stories of poverty or the mother's illness, or even of the facts of working-class Toledo life.[1] Stories of brutality, racism, sexism, and poverty would only become public much later when Steinem's classmates read interviews or articles by or about her, or when "Ruth's Song" was published.

When they remember how she looked in those college years, her classmates chiefly recall her very long fingers, with their long, manicured nails, her makeup (she had taught one of them to put on eye shadow), and that her customary clothes were jeans and a gray sweatshirt; they wore Bermuda shorts and cashmere sweaters, and wished they looked as she did in a sweatshirt. They remember her dressed for a show at Amherst, with net stockings, new to them, and her hair in a ponytail, then far from usual.

---

[1] By the time of the 1968 Democratic convention, however, Kate Millett could report that when the Chicago police, to everyone's horror, were beating up the students outside the convention, "Gloria looked at violence from both sides." By then Steinem could tell Millett how her "own ideas of violence were formed in the Toledo slums, a whole society built upon brutality. You bowled on Tuesday, played pinochle on Wednesday. And beat up your wife or the nearest available black on Saturday. The ordinary way of expressing your masculinity. The Chicago police were really the boys I went to high school with." [Flying, 503] The Smith classmates, for whom Steinem carefully tailored her renditions of Toledo life, had heard nothing like this.

Though at least twenty pounds heavier than she would be in the sixties and thereafter, she moved, they thought, like a sexual woman, they like awkward girls.

And what else do her classmates from Laura Scales remember of her? They remember her as not only a fine storyteller but as a great listener, and something rarer even than that, an attentive listener even amid distractions. "When you spoke to her, she looked at you"; she did not let her eyes wander, as is so commonly the practice at cocktail parties or other gatherings. Many confided their college problems; she counseled and was helpful and under-standing. The twelve Laura Scales seniors gave one another back rubs, but hers were the best; she had learned on her mother. At Smith, Steinem perfected the skill of writing under pressure, so her classmates remembered her crouched on her bed just before her senior thesis was due, turning her notes over, riffling the pages, as though she were absorbing the material through her hands. Everything they remember has to do with the topics that were properly accepted for discussion.

If they wondered about her lack of money and what her real financial situation might be, they never asked. Money, of course, remained an issue for Steinem all through college. She was ineli-gible for any first-year scholarship because her high school grades were not good enough. The greater part of the money for her education came from what she, her sister, and her mother referred to as her "trust fund"—the money Ruth Steinem had received for the house in which she and Steinem had lived in Toledo.[2] Throughout college, Steinem earned what she could, waiting on table for banquets (she no longer danced in clubs; a strictly Toledo enterprise), while Ruth scraped up money for her from the slen-

---

[2] In her sophomore year, she did receive a small scholarship and borrowed money from the college; neither the scholarship nor the student aid came to more than a thousand dollars.

der lease money paid by those who had built cottages on the remaining Michigan property. Her father's irregularity in the matter even of occasional donations added to her financial pressures, as did the need to keep money matters straight between her divorced, if amiable, parents. Leo's help was unpredictable: he would suddenly promise money, and it would arrive, but not always at the moment when it was needed, to pay college fees, for example, or just living expenses.

Even while Steinem worried about money, and turned her childhood anecdotes into amusing stories, she did not abandon the independence of judgment and the habits of social analysis she had learned in her earlier years. She was, for example, disturbed to discover at Smith that being Jewish was not to belong to just another religion, like Episcopalians and Baptists, as her mother had told her, but a whole way of life—one that included trying to meet Jewish men at Grossinger's and spending hours on the phone with one's mother planning the pursuit. For Gloria and her sister Jewishness had never seemed to loom as a problem; growing up in Toledo, Steinem herself encountered little anti-Semitism. As she remembers it, there were "Polacks, and Honkies, and Colored People, and 'Americans.' " No one assumed anyone could be anything else. It became evident to Steinem at Smith that Jewishness was a culture into which one was born, a realization not as attractive to her as being able to choose one's religion. Her comment to an interviewer in the 1980s would sum up her views on the question: "I don't believe in either religion. When I'm around Jews who feel there's something good about being exclusively Jewish, I emphasize the non-Jewish side of the family. When I'm around Protestants who think there's something good about being Protestant, then I emphasize the Jewish side." [Cohen, 41–2]

When she volunteered to work at the state mental hospital in Northampton, she was shocked by the revelation of how the indigent and suffering were treated; there were twelve hundred patients, and only two doctors. This experience aroused her feelings about the dark side of Smith, its unconsciousness of anything unpleasant, which included even the condition of so many individuals abandoned just beyond the bucolic graciousness of the college campus. Primarily, however, these feelings adumbrated her future attentions to the conditions of the poor in the world's richest country. It is, at the same time, striking that she could not then allow herself to connect this mental hospital experience to her mother. "I was just trying to keep myself from dissolving into my mother," she recalls—a successful attempt that neatly separated the social implications of the state mental hospital from any personal maternal resonance. Successful in maintaining this separation, Steinem flourished at Smith.

INTERESTED EVEN then in politics and the condition of the governed, Steinem majored in government—though in later years, when her admiration for her Smith education had somewhat abated, she was to remark that all she learned about women at Smith was that they had been "given" the vote in 1920. During her freshman year came the first of Joseph McCarthy's witchhunts for communists. William and James Buckley's sisters Aloïse and Priscilla had gone to Smith; at this time Aloïse wrote to the twenty-eight thousand Smith graduates not to contribute to Smith until it fired the communists on its faculty, "communists" defined as those whose politics were even slightly to the left of her brothers'. (The result was the largest annual alumni contribution ever to Smith.) To Smith's credit, nothing was done, but Steinem's government professor Vera Micheles Dean was one of those named, and Steinem, like the majority of Smith students, was appalled by the Buckley onslaught. McCarthy and the Buckleys strengthened her youthful defenses against the extreme right and made Steinem take a year or two more than she might otherwise have done to see through Marxism. Her response to this particular brouhaha reveals Steinem's essential liberalism as already in place, even while she would refine her views as she grew older.

During her freshman year Steinem was feeling her way; her marks were not especially good as she delved into philosophy and literature, although then as later she was saved by her writing. (Fortunately, Smith did not count first-year marks when electing students to Phi Beta Kappa.) By her sophomore year, Steinem had figured Smith out. She took a number of courses on international politics. E. M. Forster became one of her favorite authors, understandably: his is a gentle voice, and his novels contain strong women characters. The only courses Steinem still remembers from Smith are those on international relations taught by Vera Micheles Dean, especially one on contemporary, postindependence India (clearly memorable in light of Steinem's later trip to and lifelong fascination with India). Whenever she was asked during the decade following her graduation to write about her education at Smith, she almost never wrote of the courses, but rather of the social revolution her college education was for her. Only later would doubts about the efficacy of that education for women obtrude. Meanwhile, Steinem reported on the memories of her Smith experience in the same underplayed anecdotal vein in which she had regaled her classmates with carefully contrived tales of her "amusing" childhood:

> I understood dimly, even before I arrived at college, that my background was not quite what Sophia Smith had had in mind for her seminarians, but I had so little experience with the agonies of social difference (I had never heard, for instance, of John O'Hara) that I simply didn't worry about it. Once there, I discovered that my experience could be put to use because it did not duplicate the experiences of the others. My French, for instance, which I had learned in a classful of Korean veterans

returning to high school on the G.I. Bill and which had been taught by the assistant backfield coach [this was in Washington, D.C.], was not good. I made an arrangement with a freshman who had been raised by an English nanny and tutored by a mademoiselle. She helped me with my French grammar and translations. In return, I made her up each time she went out with her New York fiancé (a little training in stage makeup can work wonders), explained the Eastern semester of her course in comparative religion (all that Theosophy had left me mystically inclined), and taught her how to iron, a skill with which she was so delighted that she ironed my dresses, too. This cheerful bargain was the beginning of an important lesson: Don't worry about your background; whether it's odd or ordinary, use it, build on it. [148]

Steinem went on to say that she had learned to think abstractly, learned that it was all right to be moody for no reason, and that she could read Plato and Russian novels and modern plays with as much intelligence as the plays required.

While at college, Steinem wrote an essay about fame—other unfinished stories, articles, poems still remain—which, she related, was a goal in life that her mother, working as a newspaper-woman, had learned no proper lady must ever seek: a lady's name could properly appear in a newspaper only at her birth, death, and marriage. In her essay Steinem challenges this decree, asserts that she will seek to have her name in a newspaper, and remembers weeping, as a small child, because she could not *be* Shirley Temple. She believed that fame (as Toledo understood it) would come only from show business. With such a father, who could one be except Shirley Temple or a grown-up equivalent?[3]

---

[3] Her father's faith in show business, and refusal to admit any other road to success, is neatly embodied in an article he sent her after she graduated. The article reported a troupe of showgirls in Las Vegas, all of whom were members of Phi Beta Kappa and over five feet seven: they were known as the High Beta Kappas. Gloria should apply to

This fragment is worth noting only because it shows that Steinem had her dreams and fantasies, though she would live to wonder at her hope of appearing in newspapers. What is significant is that her fantasies were not and would never be of a male redeemer claiming her for his own; they were of her own fame.

AS ONE DRAWN to international politics, and believing that she might never get another chance to visit Europe, it was natural that Steinem would want to take her junior year abroad; she could not imagine that her future would contain another chance to see Europe. In almost every way, Steinem's junior year abroad was characteristic of a young woman's first encounter with Europe. Despite the superficial pleasures she took in being a tourist, however, she felt a simultaneous sense of deprivation and isolation. She kept eating chocolates, and ended up weighing 150 pounds, a gain that raises the specter of her father. In any case, whatever sense of estrangement (a sense that would be remarkably absent in her future trip to India) may have caused this bingeing, unhappiness of any sort would never in the future lead her to gain noticeable weight.

Twelve Smith "girls" (as young women were always called at that time) and about twelve from other colleges sailed together for a short stay in Paris to polish up their French en route to Geneva in the fall of 1954. Under the aegis of the college planners, Steinem settled into a routine in Paris—classes each morning from nine to twelve-thirty in phonetics, grammar, and literature, then home to lunch with "her" French family. (Because she was always interested in people, and perhaps because it was cheaper, Steinem stayed with a French family rather than, like the other

---

join them; Leo knew she needed to earn a living, and what other use could there be for a college education or a Phi Beta Kappa key?

girls, in a hotel.) There were lectures on medieval art, she wrote her mother, while thanking her for her letters and encouraging Ruth about her new apartment in Washington, D.C., to which Ruth had just moved after emerging from months in the Quaker halfway house that had followed her stay in Shepperd and Pratt.

Steinem's ease and openness in writing to her mother throughout the year in Geneva are notable, and arose partly from sympathy for her and, in all probability, from a combination of guilt and pity at Ruth's life as compared with her own. They write as old companions; the mother of her daily life, the daughter of her adventures. The warmth and naturalness of the letters, saved by both of them, suggest an exchange between equals, and on Steinem's part, a strong compulsion to share her life with a deprived parent.

From these one learns exactly what she studied in Geneva: courses that range from international law with a Professor Bourquin ("perhaps the most worthwhile course at the University") to international migrations, modern French literature, comparative constitutional law, history of European civilization, and "Questions of International History." She assured her mother that on the whole the curriculum was not on a par with American universities; Geneva had some courses so specialized as to be ridiculous, such as "a whole semester on the sexual cycle of the mushroom."

Steinem also studied communism in Geneva and wrote a paper on communism in India, a movement largely discredited there for having supported the colonial British during World War II when England and the USSR were allies. Harish Kapur, a professor at the Graduate Institute of International Studies in Geneva, had a great deal to do with Steinem's changing perspective on Marxism, though his teachings did not finally take until she went to India after her graduation and experienced the negative feelings of many Gandhians and other independence fighters toward Indian communists.

While Steinem was studying in Geneva, she was nominated in absentia for the presidency of her Smith house, Laura Scales. She did not want the nomination because, while she was hoping for a scholarship to help pay for her senior year, if it didn't come through she might have to live in a special house where students, in order to pay their board, did all their own housework. The telegram asking her if she wanted to run did not arrive in time for her to decline before the election was held. She therefore won despite the fact that, as her classmate who was eventually elected dryly comments, the freshman and sophomore classes in the house were aware of her as a personality and didn't actually know her.

As it turned out, Smith had initially refused her request for the scholarship, and Steinem thought the decision unfair. Her alternative was to borrow money from the Smith Students Aid Society, Inc., which was lent without interest for amounts up to $900. A letter arrived for Steinem in Geneva on June 17, 1955, refusing her a scholarship on the grounds of her "financial situation as well as her academic standing." Steinem's anger, rarely evident in her letters—or, indeed, in anyone's memory—surfaced. She wrote to her mother:

> Mrs. Kafka [in charge of the junior-year-abroad group] says I have the highest average in the group, and here we come to the part about the scholarship. It seems to me, and Kafka says so too, that this business about not having enough money to give me a scholarship is hogwash on Smith's part. Supposing this were the case, they could have three other reasons for saying no: my grades, my recommendations and my need. As far as the first one is concerned, they did not even *have* my grades for this year at all . . . and even if they went on last year's, I still had an A average and no C's and they give full scholarships to girls with B minus averages and sometimes even less. As for the second, I have recommendations from everybody . . . and

Mrs. Kafka says she'll give me the highest one she knows how to give. Also, I can always point out the fact that I refused House Presidency partly because of my honors program, but also because I thought I might be in a scholarship house and/or have scholarship jobs to do. The third one can be no problem if they look at our income. . . . There are three girls in the Geneva group alone who have had some sort of scholarship straight through, two of them with trunks full of cashmere sweaters and not two brain cells to rub together and make a fire. [Furthermore, Steinem adds, now thoroughly worked up, one of them was given a free Cunard fare, apparently by lot.] Her average is, incidentally, wavering around between a C plus and a B minus. All of this makes me just a little angry, especially in the light of Smith's "generous" offer to loan me the 900 and let me pay it back after I graduate. How Smith can encourage me to apply for all kinds of graduate fellowships and then tie a $900 millstone around my neck is beyond me. And I most certainly am not going to let you live on potato soup and work in hotels to pay it back for me. [Ruth Steinem was now working a few hours a day at a minimum wage in the newsstand and gift shop of the hotel next door to where she was living.]

Steinem finishes by saying she will tell Smith she will have to drop out and go to George Washington University in Washington, D.C.

This paragraph, uniquely indignant among what remains of Steinem's extensive, lifelong correspondence with her mother, and taking up only half a page in a nine-page typewritten letter, is compelling for its acute sense of unfairness and also because of the anguish she must have felt about her mother's sacrifices at the same time that Steinem was hoping to attend summer school in England to avoid having to spend the summer at home.

At the end of the summer, however, her grades and recommendations had arrived, and Smith had sensibly changed its mind. Steinem was relieved she had not sent any angry letters directly to the scholarship office. It is tempting to surmise that this lesson of *not* acting out her anger, and having justice nonetheless finally prevail, supported Steinem's passive tendency not to fight but to rely on the good instincts of others—a pattern that would reemerge many times in later years.

As the Geneva trip drew to a close, Steinem succeeded in getting an Oxford scholarship to St. Anthony's College, and so escaped to relish her summer in England rather than having to endure it in Washington.

STEINEM RETURNED to Smith in the fall of 1955 to begin her senior year at the college and at Laura Scales. In those days at Smith one tended to know well the people in one's house and best of all the people in one's class. Twelve of the women in the class of '56 had jokingly formed a group called the Twelve Foolish Virgins, as a mark of which each member received a charm on her twenty-first birthday marked with the initials *TFV:* most of them still have it. Steinem, like several of the others in the group was not, in fact, a virgin. During the early days of her senior year, Steinem met Blair Chotzinoff, with whom she went to bed and to whom she soon became engaged. Though he was not technically her first sexual partner, Steinem always looked upon him as her first lover in any meaningful sense of the word. Blair was the son of Samuel Chotzinoff, the NBC music director who created the NBC Orchestra for Toscanini and arranged for him to do his famous televised concerts, and of Pauline Heifetz, the sister of Jascha. When she met Blair, he was a pilot for the Air National Guard in Purchase, New York.

There had been earlier boyfriends. Between her junior and senior years in high school, she had gone out with one Mickey

Heller, a wonderful dancer ("I'm always a sucker for this") who took her dancing on the roof of a local hotel, where to her it seemed the movies had come to life. Later there was another man to whom she was attracted—by his working-class background and status as a veteran—and still one other whom she found sympathetic, with a background similar to her own; with him she had a hardly satisfactory affair. There was, however, nothing that could be called a complete sexual experience until she met Chotzinoff in her senior year.

What is most significant about Steinem is, from Chotzinoff on, the conjunction of likable, loving men with enjoyable sex. Although she long persuaded herself that her love affairs must inevitably lead to marriage, her ultimate behavior indicates this to have been a delusion. Unlike the majority of her contemporaries, Steinem fled rather than sought marriage, fearing to be left with a child and again to become a primary caregiver before she was able freely to pursue a profession. If it took her a while to face up to this disinclination for marriage, her ability to enjoy sex for its own sake, and for the companionship of thoughtful, gentle men, was unusual for her time. Before the current women's movement (and before the threat of AIDS), such a nonobsessive appetite for heterosexual sex apart from commitment was exceptional.

STEINEM, UNDER considerable protest, was a blind date brought home to Westchester by Nancy Gary, a classmate at Smith, and her husband Sam; from the moment Chotzinoff saw Steinem get off the train on her way to Nancy's house, he was smitten. When it came time for her to go back to college, he offered to fly her there and rented a little Piper Tripacer, which could land on a croquet field, for the trip. Chotzinoff reports that they both laughed all the way to Northampton in that tiny plane; it was instant chemistry.

The next weekend she visited his family in Ridgefield, Connecticut. As it turned out, the Chotzinoffs would come to disapprove of Steinem—her intellectual stances, her daring to argue with his father (apparently about everything), perhaps her being poor and "not sufficiently Jewish"; Samuel Chotzinoff had been poor himself, but had become a snob. Blair likes to claim that his father ruined his engagement to Steinem by saying that he would buy the best set of pots and pans for Gloria when they married so that she could make his, the father's, favorite stew. "It may just be that in reaction against me she started feminism," Blair says now, a statement with enough truth to be intriguing. Blair's letters to her from that time demonstrate how, like his father, he saw her unquestioningly as a wife and "the mother of my progeny." Nonetheless, he was, as she appreciated at the time, the perfect "first lover": infatuated, kind, considerate, and nurturing.

Chotzinoff, of course, met Steinem's family, and he remembers them, except for her mother, as tough going. He particularly remembers, with some amusement, Leo driving with his handkerchief over his stomach, which was big enough to be brushed by the steering wheel; the handkerchief kept his pants clean.

By the next summer Chotzinoff was altogether in love. He was still flying for the Air National Guard, piloting a small jet that had an afterburner and could reach altitudes of 40,000 feet. In it he flew to Northampton and wrote *Gloria* in the sky, dotting the troublesome *i* by diving from 2000 feet and leaving just a puff of smoke. "Gloria thought it was pretty Philistine," he remembers; "I had embarrassed her." But Steinem, remembering, says she was also pleased. And, if she gave Chotzinoff the feeling that he was not as advanced a thinker as the Smith girls, she nevertheless thought that he was marvelous enough to accept his engagement ring.

* * *

IN HER SENIOR year Steinem was awarded a fellowship for a year's postgraduate travel in India. Although Steinem, studying in Geneva, was already interested in India, she would go to that country the year after college for entirely practical reasons. The first, and most obvious, since it provided the financial opportunity, was the fellowship, which unexpectedly materialized at Smith during her senior year: Chester Bowles, who had been the U.S. Ambassador to India, had come to speak at Smith the year before; his speaking fee, which he declined, was to be used for the fellowship. Two students in Steinem's year, she and Kayla Achter, each received one thousand dollars; a third and last fellowship went to Margaret Harrison in 1957. (In any event, Steinem, who had fallen in love with India, stayed on for some months beyond her fellowship year.)

The second practical reason was to put as much distance as possible—and India was certainly distant—between herself and Washington life with her mother; Steinem's decision to study at Oxford the summer after Geneva had arisen entirely, as she frankly admitted to herself, from her reluctance to return to the life offered by another summer in Washington. (She would, as it happened, return there immediately after her graduation to live with her mother and sister and work, as she had before, at the municipal swimming pool for blacks.)

Steinem's mother, father, and sister watched her graduate magna cum laude in June 1956. They also heard—and expected to hear—another in the long line of patronizing speeches by avuncular if famous men. As a woman from the class of 1954 vividly remembers and continues all these years later to be angry about, Alistair Cooke had delivered a commencement address to her class with a pomposity and arrogance close to parodic:

> At this moment [he assured the young women], ridiculous though it may seem, the fortune of you here is being decided by

anonymous young men who are packing their bags in New Haven, Connecticut, in Cambridge, Massachusetts, Princeton, New Jersey, Williamstown, *even perhaps* in Grinnell, Iowa. . . . It may not be the proper thing for a commencement speaker to begin this way by wishing you a happy marriage. But . . . since it is the supreme role which all of you will sooner or later hanker after, even the art students and sociologists among you, it seems to me realistic to start by recognizing, on this spring morning, the main direction in which your fancies turn. [Smith Alum Bull, Aug. 1954. Grace Knowlton; emphasis added]

When Adlai Stevenson addressed the graduating class in 1955, the year Plath finished her Smith career, he stated the reality of what was expected of them even more harshly. Steinem remembers the violence of disillusionment she felt at Stevenson's advice that they move, as Steinem puts it, "back into second-class citizenship and second-hand achievement." But with Plath she applauded politely, and said nothing. The commencement address in Steinem's year was so little different that by the 1990s no one could recall who had delivered it. Questioning half a dozen 1956 graduates evoked only blankness. After being unable to remember, a classmate was sent her commencement program by her mother, revealing that the speaker was Archibald MacLeish, a characteristic choice of the time.

After this uninspirational ending to her college career, Steinem, in Washington, began the long process of talking TWA into giving her her passage money in advance payment for a pamphlet she proposed to write on India. Here, as later, Steinem needed to earn the money for the life she chose to live, wherever that might be. After her "brain deadener of a job as a swimming teacher," she worked for a while, "not much and not paid," in Adlai Stevenson's presidential campaign—he was, after all, a Democrat, however condescending to women. She was also waiting for a visa to visit India as a student, without which she could not enter the country. The delay in her visa, not uncommon due to India's general inefficiency, was further extended by the fact that no one in India had heard of this Chester Bowles Fellowship. India always worried, in any case, that student visitors would become charges of the state.

ONE MORNING IN November 1956 Blair, who was living in the New York apartment of his sister and brother-in-law, awoke to find the ring he had given Steinem on the table together with a note calling the engagement off. He was devastated and never quite resigned; it took him many years to get over a feeling of worthlessness. When, in the early sixties, Steinem began seeing Tom Guinzberg, publisher of the Viking Press, which his late father had owned, Chotzinoff's parents said he would see that they had been right: she would marry Guinzberg because he was so rich; she had only been waiting for a truly rich man. No, she won't, Chotzinoff said; and right he was.

The whole starry-eyed, storybook romance with Blair embodies the perfect account of "true love" in the 1950s, and even thereafter for many people. He was well connected, attractive, and willing to play the role movies had made familiar, that of the resourceful pursuer. It is in this context that Steinem's rejection of so glamorous a courtship must be seen; for almost any other college woman of that time, it was the ideal, the hoped-for eventuality. Steinem was close to unique in rejecting it, even if she did so without understanding her profound impulse toward rejection—not of Blair but of the future he so gallantly represented. Benita Eisler wrote of a woman who had been in college in the fifties: "It's the wasted years that make her bitter. 'All that time when I could have been looking for me, instead of for him.' " [14] Steinem did not find "me" immediately—not, in fact, until she became a feminist many years later, but while enjoying "him," she did not mistake him for her future life. To have been that wise in the fifties was a gift of her childhood, and a gift of the working-class neighborhood and school that had inoculated her against female servitude and against the middle-class assumptions of many men she would encounter, during her college years and thereafter, that the women they married would be conventional wives.

Much as Aunt Janey had hoped that her niece would be one of those conventional wives, she had not approved of Chotzinoff as a husband: he had not gone to the right college, or any college. She was even more upset by her niece's decision to go to India. "You will one day turn down a perfectly eligible man," Steinem remembers her saying, "just because he hasn't been to India."

Why was Steinem not caught in the same dilemma as Sylvia Plath, not torn apart by the same terrible conflict of female talent and the pressures of the acceptable female destiny? Surely there were no books she could read to guide her on her exceptional way; no stories existed of the life she would choose. Barbara Ehrenreich, in her book *Fear of Falling,* has noted that all of the important books published in the 1950s, like David Riesman's much-discussed *The Lonely Crowd,* turned out to be "entries into the swelling biography of the middle class." [4] Most of these books ignored women altogether. As Benita Eisler also observed: "To critic Paul Goodman [who wrote *Growing Up Absurd*], the oppressive cynicism and conformity of fifties culture was a problem for boys only; girls didn't even get to grow up absurd. They got married, which, in his view, was the natural order of things." [14–15] Ehrenreich concludes: "There is a reason why America produced the most vigorous feminist movement in the world. We were one of the only countries in which the middle class (which is wealthy by world standards) customarily employed its own women as domestic servants." [40]

Then there was the problem of the relation of ambitious daughters to their mothers, a problem from which Steinem's "dysfunctional" childhood protected her. Steinem had seen and early reflected upon the effects of maternal fulfillment long before her Smith days. No book about Plath, on the other hand, and there are many, fails to mention, indeed to emphasize, her conflict with her mother, her fear of living her mother's conventional life, her need to be free of her once and for all. As Adrienne Rich wrote in *Of Woman Born*, "In a desperate attempt to know where mother ends and daughter begins, we perform radical surgery." Steinem's particular childhood had, for all its terrors, allowed her to perform that radical surgery long since, while continuing to take care of her mother because her mother needed care. She would, in future times, be overcaring where such care was unwise —as in the dying days of *Ms.* magazine, before it was sold—but she would never conceive herself in the position of the mother, not in any aspect.

Steinem herself, indeed, chose not to be a mother, as Plath might have done for a longer time at least, if her mother's destiny had not seemed to Plath, however violently she fought it, also to be hers. But, as Pat McPherson observed, the subordinated wife and mother was defined as femininity itself in the 1950s: "The absence of maternal fulfillment is the pathology itself in the Freudian court." So Plath went for all-around perfection, which meant appealing to the standards of everyone in the society, from her mother to magazine editors. (In fact, as she later wrote in *The Bell Jar:* "My mother kept telling me nobody wanted a plain English major. But an English major who knew shorthand was something else again. Everybody would want her."[4]) By the time

---

[4] Steinem, for her part, as she related in her 1971 Smith commencement address, was asked by a vocational adviser when she brought up the subject of law school, "Why study three extra years and end up in the back room of some law firm doing research

Plath had worked her way through to an understanding of this impossible struggle, it was too late to be of use; she killed herself soon after. Perhaps because Steinem's idea of "all-around perfection" had not yet crystallized, she was able to reject immediate marriage and leave her options open. At the conclusion of her Smith years, the avoidance of a return to any version of her earlier life was paramount.

DID SHE EVER really intend to marry Chotzinoff? She was later to remark that a third reason for going to India was the fear —still lurking, however emphatic her rejection of Chotzinoff— that if she stayed in the United States she would end up marrying him. Now, we can only know that by the time her classmates gave her a shower, she knew the marriage was off: the shower, however, hardly seemed the perfect moment to mention it. To her Smith classmates, of course, her engagement at that time seemed the most logical, ordinary step for any woman to take—despite the fact that several of Steinem's classmates, and two besides Steinem of the Twelve Foolish Virgins, did remain unmarried, an impressive record for a group of college women from those years. The question remains: Why did Steinem change her mind? She was very depressed by the shower; unable really to imagine getting married, but she had discovered love and sex, and was confused. Her decision was not because of any failing, sudden or newly perceived, on Chotzinoff's part. Rather, she was enacting the first of many escapes from marriage, postponing for the first time the moment of recognition that marriage, any marriage, was not what she wanted. That recognition would be a long time coming.

---

and typing, when you can graduate from Smith and do research and typing right away?"

If Steinem's view of her Smith education would change in time, her later realization of what her Smith education had *not* given her is irrelevant to the importance of Smith in those four years. Steinem was, perhaps as much as any student of her time, ready for what Smith had to offer, and she accepted it, indeed relished it; she allowed the college to provide her with a comfortable and (by male standards) vigorous education, to let her consort with upper-class women and observe their habits, and to discover her own social graces beyond those useful in Toledo and Washington. Smith did not train her to be a feminist or encourage many thoughts of social revolution. The college simply nurtured her, allowed her to escape from her family, and gave her an interim of safety that would make possible all that followed.

INDIA: THE
TRANSFORMING
INTERLUDE

AT THE END of the summer Steinem went to London, there to await her India visa. The visa did not come for three months, during which time Steinem worked illegally as a waitress at a coffee shop and spent a lonely Christmas. But a lonely Christmas was the least of it.

She had not been long in London when she discovered that she was pregnant. At the time she told no one, not even Jane Bird Nissen, the Smith classmate in whose home in Chelsea she was living. She did not tell Blair, who learned of the pregnancy only many years later. Certainly she did not tell her mother—with whom, in any case, she did not discuss her sex life—until sixteen years later, when she was about to sign her name to a list in *Ms.* magazine of those who declared they had had abortions. Desperate, but clearly intent on dealing with the matter alone, she even for a time, and uniquely in her life, contemplated suicide.

After falling in love with Chotzinoff, Steinem had gotten a diaphragm in Northampton by telling the doctor she was going to be married. (Contraceptives were still difficult to acquire in Mas-

sachusetts, a state politically dominated by the Catholic Church.)
When she broke the engagement, she discarded the diaphragm.
She slept with Blair again, however, in the fall of that year, for
reasons of long-standing sexual attraction.

In London she went to a G.P., Dr. John E. Sharpe, a man she
has always remembered with gratitude. She later discovered he
was the Sitwells' doctor, but she had picked his name out of the
telephone directory only because he was near the home of her
hosts, the Nissens. Dr. Sharpe seemed quite old, at least to her at
that time, and his office was one room filled with books, old
carpets, and a gas grate you put pennies into. He was kind, and
gave her a prescription to bring on her period if she was not
pregnant, but of course she was.

After many terrifying weeks, Steinem met "a very egocentric
and aggressive American playwright at a party who, just in passing, was complaining about how many of the actresses in his play
he had to get abortions for. That was how I learned it was possible in England with the written permission of two doctors saying
something like this would be bad for one's health."

So she went back to Dr. Sharpe, who, after some hesitation,
agreed to be one of the two and reluctantly enlisted another doctor, a Harley Street woman surgeon, to perform the abortion. The
surgeon was rather brusque and made it clear that she was partici-
pating only because of Dr. Sharpe. From this Steinem concluded
that he was the one taking the risk, which increased her gratitude
to him. The woman surgeon, whose name Steinem has forgotten,
was memorable for her person, if not for her kindness. She wore a
fashionable suit and smoked a cigarette in a long cigarette holder;
not friendly, she said she hoped Steinem would use birth control
in the future, especially in India. Nonetheless, she was good at her
job, and Steinem, after a few days in bed taking pills for the
bleeding, and telling her classmate she'd hurt her back, was fine.
Dr. Sharpe, compassionate as the woman surgeon was not, asked

of Steinem, as he signed the necessary paper, only that she never tell anyone and that she promise to do what she really wanted with her life. She promised that she would, and did not tell until after his death. The abortion, done at the last possible moment because of the difficulty in finding another doctor, cost Steinem almost half of the thousand dollars she had accumulated for her arrival in India.

Without question, the abortion, and the decision to take charge of her own life and to speak of the matter to no one, indicated a newfound self-sufficiency, a sense that her destiny could be in her own hands. It is tempting, in the light of her mother's Theosophy, to wonder at the apparent evidence of karma in providing Steinem not only with this, at that time, extremely unusual opportunity to travel throughout India and crystallize her emerging social convictions, but also with the chance to take upon herself total responsibility for her own actions. As she was later to observe, this was "the first time I stopped passively accepting whatever happened to me and took responsibility." It seems clear that this sharp need for responsibility and sense of commitment made even more significant the Indian adventure and its consequences. She would write, in a 1989 article for *Ms.:* "My own [abortion] had taken place in a time of such isolation, illegality, and fear that afterward, I did my best to just forget," but to deal with what must be dealt with and then to put it behind one are maneuvers indicative of maturity.

In January the visa came and she was off. At the time, of course, the decision to spend the greater part of a year in India had been a long and agonizing one, "all the time praying it wasn't a slow-boat-to-China, escape-type decision," as she wrote to David Shaber, a theater instructor from Smith who had become a friend. As it turned out, she would discover in India the political focus of her life; she would also learn that neither marriage nor the romantic plot was for her, although none of these discoveries would become palpable for some years.

Steinem set off across Europe, with a brief stop in Paris, a return visit to Geneva, and a hectic stop in Athens. On February 4, 1957, she stepped out of the plane in Bombay, as she put in a letter to Shaber, "all wool-clad and uncertain, to find sultry moonlight and staggering whiffs of jasmine and India." From that first whiff, she was entranced.

From Bombay she flew to New Delhi, where she joined Kayla Achter. They were enrolled in the University of Delhi for three months, during which time they became acclimated and agreed that they liked each other better occasionally than as constant companions; Steinem had already sensed that it would not be with other Westerners that she would discover India. On her own, she learned to wear a sari—"more a way of life than a dress"—and attended classes. From New Delhi she and Achter took one last shared trip to Mussoorie, a hill station in the Himalayas for two weeks of, as she put it in a letter to Shaber, "being still and just being." Then she went on alone to Calcutta.

By this time she was already struggling with a lack of money and the difficulty of dealing with what money she could earn in India. TWA, for example, for which she had written a travel brochure, paid her with a check, but she didn't have a checking account, and the check couldn't be paid over to any other person. And so it went. Except for news of India, money would continue to be the principal subject in letters to her family—how she earned it, how much they were sending, even the need to wash new clothes before sending them to India, because new clothes would be subject to tariff.

Steinem's preoccupation with money was due in the first place to the plain fact that she hadn't enough to get along on. She also indulged it in part to satisfy her mother, whose obsession with money began in a working-class family, intensified after her mar-

1. Marie Ochs Nuneviller, Steinem's maternal grandmother. Steinem several times used "Marie Ochs" as a pseudonym.

2. Steinem's paternal grandmother, Pauline Perlmutter Steinem. She was a suffragist and active in community affairs; she died when Steinem was five.

3. Steinem's parents, Leo and Ruth, at the time of their two wedding ceremonies

5. Leo with baby Gloria

4. Susanne Steinem, nine years old, with baby Gloria, whose birth she had requested

6. Ruth and Gloria in the trailer going south for the winter

7. The family,
before Susanne left
for Smith College.
Ruth, Leo, Susanne,
Gloria, about nine

8. Gloria, dancing in Toledo

9. A picture taken by
Leo of Gloria in front
of their house at Clark
Lake, just before Leo
and Ruth separated

10. Gloria's high school graduation picture, Western High School in Washington, D.C.

11. Steinem in India, modeling a sari, which she always wore, together with her hair darkened

12. Steinem with classmate at her Smith graduation

13. Steinem, with one of the signs she hoped to introduce at her twenty-fifth Smith reunion

riage to Leo, and only became greater with time. Money was scarce both at home and in India, and Steinem was constantly aware of the financial struggles of her family. It is certainly likely that the way of life Steinem adopted after she returned to the United States and went to work—a way exactly like her father's, without a regular nine-to-five job, a regular place of work, a budget, savings, or the payment of taxes—was an unconscious rejection of her mother's unabated if realistic anxiety about money.

To support herself, Steinem helped an Indian man design sandals for export, and she posed in a few advertisements for saris, toothpaste, shampoo, and cold cream, for which she was paid in rupees. She also wrote "The Thousand Indias" for the tourist bureau of the Indian government, which they later published as individual essays though never, as was originally proposed, as a book.

Steinem found it difficult to write her fellowship reports, however, because they were supposed to be for a Western audience about the "mysterious East," and she didn't find India mysterious; she felt oddly at home there.[1] She had been warned by author Santha Rama Rau, whom she had visited in New York, to stay away from the Westernized parts of India, from the country clubs, café society, the well-to-do, the sophisticated those, in short, who took no part in the Indian life she sought—a warning that was

---

[1] The first four of these fellowship reports are still in the files at Smith; the later ones, covering the period when Steinem was more at home in India, are apparently missing. Reading them nearly four decades later, Steinem found equally intriguing both what she did *not* say and what she did manage to say. She did not, of course, mention her relief after the abortion or the difficulties of the Smith classmate who was also in India on a Chester Bowles Fellowship and who seemed to have had a minibreakdown and to have failed to communicate with her parents. As Steinem would long do in journalism, she did not admit emotion or use a personal voice in the reports. She did, however, note her attraction to the villages, to Indian tradition, and to the workings of grassroots democracy there, as well as her aversion to the excesses of Westernization and the imposition of industrial values.

hardly necessary. During her time in New Delhi she darkened her brown hair to go with the saris that young Indian women at the university would bring her to wear. Putting on the Bermuda shorts she had been given by her classmates at Smith (to wear instead of her cut-off jeans) had been like joining the enemy; putting on the saris was like joining friends. Since she had always identified with the least privileged, she found herself easily at home in India. By the 1980s, India seemed to have become a necessary stop on the itinerary of the diligent traveler, but that was far from true three decades earlier. In the 1950s there were few tourists interested in the non-Westernized parts of the country. For weeks at a time Steinem often saw no Westerners at all.

STEINEM HAD, on arriving in India, "revirginated" herself, as she would later put it. Her practice of revirgination in India—that is, of allowing the assumption that she was a virgin—had to do both with the protection virginity offered and with the Toledo knowledge that once a woman "lost" her virginity—or let it be known that her virginity was lost—she was ruined, or at least fair game. Steinem was not without a number of pursuing men, met and remet in India, but she consummated love affairs with none of them. ("Nick," a journalism student, one of the men in love with her, as his many letters testify, was, like Harish Kapur—also attracted to her sexually—conventional and would not sleep with a virgin.) Perhaps most important, however, was the conviction that, whether or not she felt that what she was experiencing was a kind of novitiate, sexual activity was not supposed to be part of a single woman's life in India.

After Calcutta, where she stayed about a month, Steinem set off southward to Madras, having been told by Indians that this was the "real India." She made her third-class way by railroad through the South, savoring it all. Women were still taken care of in India, she wrote, meaning that women were given their own third-class car on the railroads, so that they could be safe from male attentions. During her trips in these cars, Steinem was repeatedly asked how many children she had, and when she said none, the immediate response would be: How do you manage it? Indira Gandhi reported the same experience to Steinem when they met years later. Asked how many children she had, Indira Gandhi would say "two," and poor women in similar railroad cars would ask her how she had limited herself to that number. Except for some handing down of traditional methods, women in India had little access to birth control, or could use it only if they could discover a method their husbands would be unaware of.

Steinem came finally to Gandhigram, where, as she had hoped, she met up with a group of Gandhi's followers, who were preparing to walk through the Ramnad area to try to stop the caste riots, in which villages were burned and people killed because of caste tensions and the politicians who took advantage of them. The riots went largely unreported in the American papers; and news of them was also embargoed in India.

Gandhi had been campaigning, as Steinem reported in *Revolution from Within,* for all castes "to be respected as one, all religions as one. He literally turned the hierarchy on its head, not by giving orders but by himself making the bottom rung his standard of living. He led by example."

Teams walked through the villages and invited people to come to meetings and to make peace. There were too few women for the teams; women in the Hindu villages wouldn't come to meetings unless a woman was present, so at least one woman was needed with each team. That woman could also go into the women's quarters to invite them to the meeting. Steinem discovered an Indian from Delhi was as foreign in this area as a white person, so she was taken along.

Steinem had been told, upon joining the teams, that she could walk many miles a day with a sari, a towel, a cup, and a comb. She found a freedom in having so few possessions, a freedom that would be for many years reflected in her style of living amid boxes and inadequate furnishings. Only with her inner revolution at fifty did this attitude change. But even then, she did not feel protective of her possessions, and would share them or give them away with ease.

And so in India she lived on what the villagers gave her, slept on mats in the women's quarters, washed in streams, and let her wet sari dry on her. The team set out, walking from five to eleven in the morning, sleeping through the midday heat, and then continuing from four to eleven at night. Each time they got to a village that had been burned and silenced, they held a meeting to say that people knew and cared about the village's plight, and to allow a place to talk about fears and discover facts instead of rumors, thus interrupting the chain of revenge. Steinem, as one of the speakers, developed a "sort of speech" on these subjects— speechifying was something she would not take up again for over ten years, and then with trepidation—that was simultaneously translated into a kind of Tamil. Then they would sing songs, and the team would be on its way again.

Women whose children had been tortured before their eyes brought Steinem rice and said they "had never thought anyone outside knew or cared." Steinem wrote this to David Shaber; it reads now as a prophecy of what she would be doing for most of the seventies and eighties, in grassroots America. As she herself later phrased it, she remembered India as the first time in her life when she lived completely in the present, when neither the past nor the future impeded her enchantment with "now." "My sandals were tied on with thongs, I was bathed in streams and rubbed in coconut oil like an Indian girl, and I was hopelessly lost in caring for these people, those ageless, suffering, dignified people."

At last, her feet gave out. Blisters had become sores and the sores had become infected. When she reached a village with a doctor, he took one look, gave her penicillin, and told her to stay put. The others left her behind to stay with the doctor and his family, to sleep on clean straw and recover. She went back, finally, the way she had come, but this time by ox cart and bus, to Madurai. Then she traveled through the mountains to Trivandrum on the Malabar coast of Kerala, the only Indian state to vote the communists in, as well as the most literate, egalitarian, and matrilineal, though "entirely too beautiful to worry about politics, definitely Gauguin territory." She found she could live very well for fifty cents a day.

Thanks to assignments to write a brochure for a documentary film company and to do some travel pamphlets and newspaper supplements, she avoided carrying out an earlier decision to borrow money in order to get home. Some of these projects worked out; most did not. And she was past her first year in India.

Throughout the greater part of her Indian adventure Steinem was alone, in the sense of not having a constant or even intermittent Western traveling companion. She found her way among people who, when she returned to the United States, would seem less strange to her than the segregated, bourgeois, consumer-oriented citizens of her own country. In India she had seen much of the huge subcontinent, met many people who would remain her friends, tried many jobs, had many adventures. As she reported in the Smith College *Sophian,* with that characteristic dullness apparently endemic to academic newspapers, "The longer I was in India, the more grateful I was for the first advantage of a small, personally administered fellowship such as mine: I was not confined for nine months of the year to one university in one part of a vast subcontinent. India, almost as much as Europe, is many countries in one, and I spent three or four months in several areas and several universities to get a realistic picture of the whole as well as to do research on my own project and special interests."

The truth was far more profound, indeed pivotal. As Steinem recognized at the time of her sixtieth birthday, India was the event that marked "before" and "after" for her. And by the time she was sixty, she would find herself ready, as she had not been nearly forty years before, to report the radical advice, encapsulated in sayings she had learned from followers of Gandhi, and from the leader of her Gandhian team as it moved among the villagers:

"If you do something the people care about, the people will take care of you."

"If you want people to listen to you, you have to listen to them."

"If you hope people will change how they live, you have to know how they live."

She remembered another aphorism from that time: "If you want people to see you, you have to sit down with them eye-to-eye."

IN DELHI, Steinem found an Indian woman companion with whom she shared interests, met a social group of Gandhians, and enjoyed Indian festivals. Devaki Jain (named Devaki Shrinavesen when Steinem met her in India in 1957) was a Gandhian economist who became a close friend. Their mutual attraction was immediate and lasting. For an unmarried young female in Delhi in those years, escapades were improvident, but together Jain and Steinem could gallivant more unrestrainedly than either could alone. After 1958 they lost touch, but starting in 1974, Jain, who had become a feminist while writing a book on women in India, came to the States every year either for a U.N. meeting or a meeting of one of many international women's groups; from that year on she always stayed with Steinem.

Jain had long wanted Steinem to revisit India, and Steinem anticipated such a visit with equal fervor. The visit, however, given Steinem's schedule and commitments, had always, until February of 1976, had to be postponed, and even then it had to be curtailed. In 1976 Steinem returned to India, in a trip arranged by Jain, to visit Indian women's groups in Bombay, New Delhi, and Ahmedabad.

This later visit to India is worth mentioning because Steinem would find confirmed what she had surmised in her original visit: that the large, populist women's movement in India in Gandhi's time and before had had a great influence on Gandhi. In Delhi, she and Jain interviewed Kamila Devi Chattopaphaya, one of the few surviving women who had worked with Gandhi; she had later helped to found the handicraft movement. This movement had mitigated the Western trend of building steel mills and creating huge urban centers, and had as well given value to women's hereditary skills. Chattopaphaya was, for Steinem and Jain, the most genuine of Gandhi's followers in India, accomplishing what Gandhi had hoped Indians would do: she turned beautiful Indian handicrafts into consumer goods, a unique achievement. Formerly, and elsewhere, such handicrafts had been bought by tourists or acquired as decorations, if at all. Chattopaphaya converted these artworks into utility goods by encouraging Indians to use the traditional tablecloths, leaf plates, and other useful goods in their daily lives, thus ensuring employment and generating secure jobs. From her and from other Third World women's groups, Steinem learned the methods of what these groups taught her to call "economic empowerment" when adopted by poor women in the United States.

Jain and Steinem sat with Chattopaphaya on her verandah, explaining their project of distilling Gandhi's tactics for use by women's movements in other countries. Being nonviolent, those tactics were well-suited to women. Finally Chattopaphaya said: "Well, my dear, we taught him everything we knew." It was no wonder that women had found Gandhi's methods useful; women had invented many of them. Jain and Steinem encouraged Chattopaphaya to write all this down, but when she did so, she had only recorded statistics and facts, with nothing conceptual and not having given herself any credit at all.

Steinem enjoyed herself enormously in India in 1976, more she felt than she had on her visit as a recent college graduate nearly twenty years before. Much of that earlier stay in India had been, she decided upon reflection in 1993, aimless: She had not known what she would do with her life, she was disappearing into, falling in love with, another culture. On the later trip, she had a sense of purpose. Characteristically, in her introspective mode of recent years, she remembered the sense of having seen, on that second visit to India, her former self, poignant, walking down the same streets. Whether what she saw in India was indeed that different former self, or only her recent reinterpretation, is open to question. Doubtless the younger Steinem in India was aimless, but aimless and open to all impressions was what she needed to be at that time. Looking back and seeing herself as lost was to assume that she could, later, rightly judge the young woman she had been.

Steinem's devotion to Gandhi was confirmed by the later trip; this devotion did not, however, differ from her original comprehension two decades earlier of his essential qualities. According to Jain, Steinem not only found Gandhi a rich source of ideas and of theories about political economy, but she also shared his belief that human beings are essentially good, rather than born in original sin, as the Christian religions would have it. Steinem has never lost this profound belief in inherent human goodness.

Gandhi influenced Steinem all her life—as would be manifested, for example, by her support of Cesar Chavez and Dolores Huerta in their efforts on behalf of the farmworkers. Some of the phrases she used when discussing Gandhi in *Revolution from Within* describe her own philosophy: "His hope and his heart were with average people and ordinary actions." She wrote of Gandhi what another might have written of her: "He did become a leader who was known for his ability to bring people together and negotiate with the powerful." As Gandhi had, Steinem believed that no person should be turned into an inferior as a servant. Like Gandhi, she had "learned to find out the better side of human nature and to enter [people's] hearts." And Gandhi provided a major theme of her book, that of "giving up a false self and learning to trust a true one." For he, too, had once tried to adopt colonial values, and enter a hierarchy not his own. In India and in Gandhi's teachings, Steinem found a culture and way of life that exactly matched her nature and encouraged it, both sooner and later, to flourish; her 1976 visit to India confirmed this. An ironic echo remained, however, from her first visit. Steinem had never believed in reincarnation, but in 1957 she had been persuaded in Bengal to have her horoscope cast. The astrologer informed her that she had lived in Bengal in a previous incarnation, and that she had done something disastrous to have been born in the United States.

IN 1958, when Steinem returned to the United States, the ideas she had learned in India would not seem "very portable." In fact, she found herself unable to put into practice any of the ideas of social reform honed there. Whenever she mentioned India in conversation, a dull silence "indicating zero curiosity" answered her. Her early attempts to enact what she had discovered included a determination to ride in the front seat with taxi drivers—this in response to the deep discomfort she had felt in India being pulled in a tonga by a man running between the staves. She had loathed being pulled by another human being; the extension of this loathing to New York taxis however, eventually struck even her as excessive. As she later wrote, "I must have been a terrible pain in the ass."

The one social reform that did, in time, become practically transferable from India to the United States was student politics. It was in this area that Steinem found her first position in the United States after her return.

India affected her profoundly because she came already prepared to appreciate what it had to offer, and because she was determined (however much the sixties life of a freelance journalist might, in the next decade, camouflage her determination) to avoid the effects of socialization that would so clearly determine the careers and adventures of the majority of her college classmates. Her later reflections notwithstanding, she had arrived in India at age twenty-two ready for what it could teach her, and for what she could learn of herself; she had prepared herself by the course taken in Geneva and, in a more general way, by the government courses at Smith; principally, she had already heard India anticipated in the tenets of the Theosophy her mother and grandmothers had practiced. The words she had taken in as a small child at Theosophy meetings while she colored in a book on the floor had presaged India, as had her mother's openness to the sacredness of all human beings. Ruth Steinem was probably as devoid of prejudice, in the sense of judging persons according to a previous, condemned identification, as it is possible to be. Theosophy as a religious conviction, or even as a guide to living, is open to a good deal of skepticism and even ridicule, and it has received both. But in the lives of those who were exposed to it when young, it may continue to reverberate, and ultimately to reinforce an adventure such as Steinem underwent in India.

Why does an experience become pivotal in a person's life? Or, more accurately, why can an experience be clearly identifiable in hindsight as the division in a life of "before" and "after"? In Steinem's case, the answer seems to be that India became pivotal because she had already acquired what is essential to a woman who will be ready to undertake both the criticism and the transformation of her own culture. That one essential—which Steinem's childhood encouraged—is the ability to resist socialization. It was this that enabled Steinem to allow India its powerful impact.

Obviously, no child can resist socialization altogether. But the ability simply to refuse, as a young child, the standards of one's social milieu appears to be either inherent or encouraged by an unconventional family life: For Steinem it was both. A woman who will become an effective leader and purveyor of radical ideas may rest quiescent, for a time, as Steinem did at Smith. (And women who have been socially resistant as girls and who have gone on to live conventional lives well beyond their college years may find that it requires courage in middle age to reactivate, as some in Steinem's generation have done, their early unconventionality. Yet despite the calm years at Smith, Steinem's own early escape from socialization made her uniquely ready for what India offered her.

Steinem did not approach India with a camera or the stance of an observer, a commentator on an alien culture. She let India take her over and she learned what it could offer. There was born, or at any rate defined, in the person she became in India, the essential individual Steinem would continue to be, or endeavor to be, ever after. Romance, in fairy tales and in most women's lives, assured a "happily ever after" of marriage that no one was inclined to question or examine closely. If Steinem, however, had a romance, it was with India, with its people, its struggles—its life free, as she saw it, of Western obsessions with property. India came as close to being Steinem's "happily ever after" as any other period or event in her life. Life in Toledo had been arduous, but to Steinem in India, Toledo must have seemed like the lengthy preparation for a vocation that now became a lifelong commitment.

On a level less high-flown, India demonstrated to Steinem that her ability to earn money lay mainly in two talents: writing and advocating. Although she would always deny that her looks were a major part of what she wanted to be or do, those looks were, all the same, essential to her mission. As her life in the sixties would demonstrate, her writing and her ability to persuade and to captivate—however much she might scorn these latter talents—would become, as they were in India, the ways by which she achieved what was necessary or desirable, or both.

The next decade or more of her life would be so unlike India as to suggest the ultimate contrast in cultures and values. But as Theosophy and Hinduism teach, the spirit is not interested in time. A moment may ramify through a whole life, and years of uncontemplative practicality may leave little residue. India nudged Steinem toward the cause of the farmworkers, toward the civil rights movement, toward the anti–Vietnam War crusade. Only with her discovery of feminism would what India had taught, coupled with the media skills she had learned during the sixties, be enacted into what might be called a destiny. Meanwhile, the transition to a life of journalism, and her transformation into what columnist Liz Smith would call "a butterfly," began on her return to New York in 1958.

After many months spent in an unsuccessful search for a job that could use her India experience, and trying to inspire friends to share this interest, the deep experience of India appeared to fade for a time; surely, one would have thought in the sixties, India bore little relation to the intriguing and much photographed young woman whose "glamorous" life and career were frequently depicted in magazine and newspaper articles—while suburban women fretted. Steinem had never bought the "feminine mystique." Instead, she had "bought" India. But for many years, it would seem that she also lost it.

N E W Y O R K

STEINEM RETURNED from India in 1958 by way of Burma, Hong Kong, and Japan. She arrived in San Francisco; from there she went to Washington to see her family, then on to New York to look for work.

New York appealed to Steinem for the same reason it appealed to women in general and to gay men: it epitomized freedom and diversity and excitement and choice in a way no other city did; no other city even occurred to her as a possible destination. Washington was out of the question—her mother was living with her sister there—and while at Smith, she had read the *New York Times* and concluded there was a world in New York full of possibility. She also came to New York because, through Blair, she had had a taste of what the city was like: frightening but infinitely alluring, as it had been for Susanne, who came to New York to work during the summers in her college years.

Life for women in 1958, even amid New York's promised freedom, was extremely constricted. If feminism was anywhere in sight at all then, its presence was far from obvious. None of the feminists who later became famous—from Kate Millett to Shirley Chisholm—had yet been heard from. Eisenhower was president, and would be until 1961; Nixon was vice president, and Robert Wagner was mayor of New York City. Most upper-middle-class women, following what was not yet called the "feminine mystique," had fled the city for the suburbs, where their lives centered around their homes and children; husbands commuted. Four years earlier, school segregation had been ruled unconstitutional; three years earlier, Rosa Parks had refused to give up her seat in a bus to a white man, thus setting off the Montgomery bus boycott. By 1958, the civil rights movement was in its earliest, most perilous years, and desegregation was being greeted either with outright opposition or dragging feet. To some, looking back on the 1950s two or three decades later, they may have appeared, in Ann Snitow's words, "by contrast, safe. But for me, as for every feminist who lived through them, the 1950s were not safe . . . and they don't become so with hindsight." [61]

It is not surprising then, that when Steinem arrived, ready to change the world, the city was at first unreceptive. She hoped to find a job with someone or some organization that would allow her to extend the kind of work with struggling peoples she had done in India. She applied to the India Committee of the Asia Society in the hope they would hire her as a writer or for public relations work. She had several interviews with Norman Cousins, who, as editor of the *Saturday Review* and head of the World Federalists, seemed a sympathetic person to work for, but he turned her down, telling her she wouldn't be happy with the job he had to offer. The Cousins rejection was to prove paradigmatic. In the fifties, women weren't hired for "important" jobs, and college graduates appeared overqualified for the "unimportant"— i.e. secretarial—ones. She wrote a letter to the *Ed Sullivan Show:* "I'm just back from two years in South Asia, mostly India, on writing assignments and have been talking to Eric Sevareid, Ir-

ving Gitlin, Sig Mickelsons and others about the possibility of a
job with CBS. In the process, I heard that Ed Sullivan was planning an international series and that the first show is to originate
in India. This is exactly the sort of series on which I would like to
work. I think I could be of use to you. . . ." This sortie also led
nowhere, as did all her other attempts to land a job that could
involve her in the political and social ideas that she now found so
compelling.

Although she progressed further than most at a time when
journalism was not an easy path for a woman, the struggle to find
meaningful work in the world was not to end until the founding
of *Ms.* magazine in 1972. Meanwhile, during the endless and fruit-
less search for jobs, Steinem was sleeping on the floor in the living
rooms of two married classmates from Smith and trying to sell
sandals made by her Indian friends to Bloomingdale's and other
department stores whose indifference to her wares matched that
of her prospective employers to her.

She did answer an ad to share an apartment on West Fifty-
seventh Street. It turned out to be a very odd apartment indeed,
shared with three women, one of whom had posed for a large
nude painting that was displayed across the wall; there was also a
pay phone in the kitchen. Steinem suspected they led rather unconventional lives, an impression reinforced when one of the
women asked to borrow her ratty thirty-year-old fur coat, a hand-
me-down from Aunt Janey, in the hope that wearing it would
induce her "boyfriend" to buy her a new one. Steinem remembers
this as a checkered period in her life.

In 1959, as the decade drew to a close, no job of any sort
became available to Steinem in New York. She therefore reluctantly moved to Cambridge, Massachusetts, to direct the Independent Research Service, a nonprofit educational foundation concerned with encouraging young Americans to attend International
Communist Youth Festivals in spite of the Stalinist era and Mc-

Carthyism. A man doing his Ph.D. in India, who had also been part of the U.S. National Association, recommended Steinem for the job. It was her task not only to encourage young Americans to attend the festivals, to meet Third World students, and to show the diversity of political opinion here—unlike in the Soviet Union —but also to raise money to help pay passage for those who couldn't afford it.

Tom Hayden, in *Reunion,* wrote of Steinem at this time: "There also was a woman who interviewed potential applicants, including myself, to participate in an international youth festival, where her task force was planning to offset communist influence. It was tempting, partly because the travel to Europe was paid for by her committee, and partly because I was curious to meet her." [37]

In the light of the 1975 accusations by the Redstockings of Steinem's alleged connections with the CIA and assumptions about the nature of American participation at the Youth Festivals themselves, these events must be placed in their historical context. Anticommunism was then, and for some years thereafter, virtually the only acceptable political attitude in the United States. Senator McCarthy had finally gone down in defeat, but the postwar atmosphere had succeeded in confusing communism with the left in the public mind. When Steinem was told by former National Student Association leaders that the CIA was funding foundations that in turn were supporting American attendance at the Youth Festivals, she remembers feeling relief that someone understood the importance of the noncommunist left in general, and students in particular. As she had learned in India, students had been a crucial force in the independence struggle, and their organizations received government support; yet in this country, students were generally trivialized and ignored. Though she also raised money from other foundations, none of it, as far as she knew, from CIA-funded sources, some young people feared the personal consequences of being seen at a Communist Youth Festival, and she told them that participation was CIA backed and supported. Ironically, it was this that sometimes persuaded them to attend, though a few still refused out of fear of the anticommunist atmosphere.

Years later, in a conversation with Arthur Schlesinger, Jr., Steinem was given a further explanation of this CIA program—a program that was later revealed to include socialist and Christian unions in Europe as well as intellectual groups like the Congress for Cultural Freedom and student organizations. In those years, the Soviet Union was subsidizing pro-Stalinist unions, journals, and intellectual fronts in other countries, and it did not seem unreasonable for the United States to give corresponding support to proven friends of democracy in labor movements and intellectual circles. But in the atmosphere generated by Joe McCarthy in the 1950s, disclosure of government support for the European noncommunist left would have been inconceivable. In addition, the CIA was one of the few government agencies that protected liberal employees against the scattershot accusations of the Mc-Carthyites.

Steinem herself went to the 1959 Youth Festival in Vienna. As the first one to be held outside a communist country, it attracted many more students from the Third World. (Steinem had tried to attend the previous festival, held in Moscow in 1957 while she was in India, but the Indian students with whom she would have gone were denied travel documents by their government; the memory of communist support of the British, plus other reasons for anticommunism, was strong.) After she returned, she wrote of it to her aunt Janey and uncle Bob in a letter, only part of which survives:

In the past few weeks I've talked so much into the dictating machine (200 pages of post-Festival booklet from ten crates full of research stuff) that I greeted Mother with "hello exclamation point how is everybody question mark." [The European trip] was far more hectic, worthwhile and eye-opening than I had ever imagined. I really had a Europe-1937 sense of urgency once I got there and saw how much there was to do and how few people there were to do it. I think it struck a lot of us the same way. It's a realization that, pretty often, the men who run Everything are just guys with gravy on their vests and not too much between the ears and that you (one) can do something toward putting monkey wrenches in the totalitarian works and convincing the uncommitted that it's smarter to stay that way than to trade Western colonialism for Communist imperialism.

Everybody who was anybody was there. If Vienna had blown up, the Kremlin would have been pretty short-handed. When we arrived and discovered how shorthanded the Austrians and others were in their efforts to counteract the Festival, we hatched plans with them and ended up by opening three Vienna offices instead of one and doing press and coordinating type things for all the non-Communist groups instead of just the Americans. It was fun, in a deadly sort of way ("In one hour, we could take Berlin, in six days, Paris!" said K's [Khrushchev's] son-in-law also editor of *Izvestia* over brandy) and there was lots of activity: smuggling the Dalai Lama's brother out of India and into Vienna, setting up a trilingual press bureau from which came all but three of the stories about the Festival (the Festival organizers wouldn't let non-Communist journalists in much of anywhere—sometimes they even did bodily harm—so we got the news out through some of the American and other independent delegates), working all day, holding meetings all night and living on stay awake pills. . . . I suppose that this was my small world equivalent of going off to join the Spanish Revolution.

Steinem felt more isolated in Cambridge than at any time before or since. She was traveling to campuses to encourage people to go to the festival, and she felt intimidated and ignored by the Harvard community as well as discouraged by the fact that if Cambridge folks with three Ph.D.'s couldn't get interesting jobs, how could she? In Cambridge, however, she had observed Susan Wood, a photographer who, wearing her hair tied back with a shoestring while photographing in Harvard Yard on assignment from *Esquire,* seemed to Steinem to have the ideal job and presence. Wood provided a rare and proleptic vision of an attractive professional woman intent on her work—a unique role model for Steinem.

After the festival she was glad to leave Cambridge, glad to return to New York. In 1962 she would work part-time for the Ninth Youth Festival in Helsinki. The organization had an office in downtown New York, where she took part in the festival's planning; she then went to the festival itself as a volunteer, working mainly on a daily newspaper published by Finnish student groups to counter the festival newspaper, whose issues had been printed in advance. She also reported on the event coolly, almost statistically, for the October 1962 *Show* magazine, declaring it a failure.

But that was after she had returned to New York and was continuing her life as a struggling freelance journalist. While fate had apparently offered no opportunities for a young woman of talent and equivocal ambition in 1958 and 1959, it now demonstrated that the Cambridge adventure had not been without its hidden benefits.

In Cambridge, through Walter Freidenberg, whom she had known in India, Steinem met Harold Hayes, a Neiman fellow, and his then-wife, Susan. Hayes was an editor at *Esquire* and would soon replace Arnold Gingrich as the magazine's editor in chief. Through him, Steinem met Robert Benton, the first man in her life who would give her a sense of her promise and open up the world, not only of marriage and love, which others had offered, but of professional possibilities and encouragement. Benton, who was then an art director of *Esquire,* was "the first man I had ever met who was a real emotional professional companion."

Benton, who came from Texas, had friends from there known as New York's "Texas Mafia"—Liz Smith, Tom Jones, and Harvey Schmidt. Schmidt did the lyrics and book for *The Fantasticks.* Steinem was at the time blind to the show's politics—it had a song romanticizing rape—but she immediately felt at home with this group, perhaps the first time she had felt at home since India, because they felt themselves to be outsiders in New York. Apart from Benton's personal and professional influence, she felt herself lucky to have run into a group of smart, creative people who didn't "separate the head and their hearts in that New York way as so many do."

In addition to Benton and friends, she met Clay Felker, then also an editor at *Esquire,* and started doing brief, unsigned pieces for that magazine. It was Felker who six years later would provide Steinem, at the founding of *New York* magazine, with her long-hoped-for opportunity to write political journalism. Through *Esquire,* Steinem would meet all those who would help to shape her career in the next few years. Meanwhile, Harold Hayes knew that Harvey Kurtzman, the brilliant creator of *Mad* magazine, was looking for an assistant. Hayes recommended Steinem, and Steinem went to work for Kurtzman in 1960 as an assistant on his new satirical magazine, *Help! For Tired Minds.*

"We had a big staff," Kurtzman told a reporter, Barbara Nachman of *Suburban People* in 1989, "me and Gloria, that was it." The account continues:

> "She was on her way up and very talented," [Kurtzman] remembers, adding that the now famous writer and feminist was a big asset even back when she was unknown.
>
> What Kurtzman remembers best about Steinem is her

"chutzpah" and her good looks. "The world is used to seeing Gloria in straight hair and glasses and blue jeans," says Kurtzman. "But I remember Gloria when she wore gowns and had hairdos."

Kurtzman also recalls how Steinem would go anywhere or ask anyone for freebies whether it be appearances or props. At the time *Help!* was running *fumetti,* a feature invented by Fellini that used photographs and word balloons.[1] Steinem brought in such free talent as Sid Caesar, Dick Van Dyke, Jackie Gleason, and Jerry Lewis.

Steinem and Kurtzman had in common a deep doubt about the efficiency of war, particularly the war in Indochina that would become the Vietnam War, and a deep though humorous cynicism about politics. In November of 1960, a newspaper in Oklahoma City picked up on a wire-service story by writer Betty Reef about Steinem working on *Help!* and featured it, together with a picture of her over a caption that said she intended to send Mort Sahl to the next presidential summit conference. Reef went on to say: "It's hard to believe, looking at cool Miss Steinem across a desk at *Help!*'s crowded little Madison Avenue office, that so much I.Q. buzzes way behind those big brown eyes." When questioned by Reef for the interview, Steinem was still talking about India, where "you face problems like starvation, like life and death . . . not whether firemen should get more pay."

Reef's article and interview, the earliest on Steinem aside from notices in the Toledo paper about high school events and local theatrical performances—together with its photograph of Steinem sitting on a desk—is a gentler precursor to many articles that would follow. Describing her as a "willowy beauty, 34-24-34," five

---

[1] There remains a *fumetto* of an office Christmas party in which Steinem posed as an office worker; Milt Kamen was the villainous sexual harasser *(avant la lettre)*. Steinem, though looking seductive, was not the object of his attentions.

feet seven inches and a Phi Beta Kappa graduate of Smith, this early article is distinguished by one factor that would change: Steinem is allowed to make statements on U.S. and world politics. The balance between references to her looks and to her ideas would not often be quite achieved again.

IN THOSE DAYS Steinem, like every other aspiring writer, loved the *New Yorker* and faithfully, hopefully, read all the short stories published there. None was ever about a childhood remotely like hers. Her reading up to that time had convinced her that her childhood and the Toledo ambience could not provide material suitable for a writer, so the best plan was to forget them. In all the novels of that time, only Saul Bellow's character Augie March seemed to have a socially mobile life similar to hers. But then came Benton, who would say, "Tell me a Toledo story." He in turn told her about his childhood in Waxahachie, Texas. Steinem thought her years in Toledo were certainly painful and preferably ignored, but Benton found them compelling. He went to Toledo with her when she did a story for *Show* on tap-dancing classes there. "She took me to the club where she used to dance on Saturday nights," he recalls, "a Lion's Club sort of place; I really got a chance to see her life."

Together they collaborated on pieces for *Esquire,* including an article called "The Student Prince: Or How to Seize Power Though an Undergraduate." Steinem wrote text for a men's fashion piece for young people around New York, and other such tidbits. She and Benton sat in endless hamburger places over endless cups of coffee devising movies. He now, of course, writes and directs them, but at that time his first movie was still to come. Steinem still finds his encouragement a crucial gift. Perhaps from their interchanges came the courage necessary to enable both of them not only to speak now of their childhoods but later to use their own ongoing experiences in their careers. Steinem would rely on her personal experiences in her journalism, while Benton would recreate Waxahachie in the movie *Places in the Heart,* and set his most recent and highly successful *Nobody's Fool* in a small town in upper New York state.

Benton gives Steinem the same credit she gives him. He loved her and he knew a good thing when he saw it, he says. Moreover, Steinem could write, while he had taken one creative-writing course at college and had flunked it; screenplays were his mode. Until he met Steinem, he was not even sure that he could write those. "She gave me for the first time a sense of myself," he remembers. "I had no faith I could write before Gloria; whatever she says I did for her, she gave me more. She was the first woman I really trusted. We would talk about all these things, and inevitably she left me with the sense that I could write. Within a year after we broke apart, David Newman and I started writing *Bonnie and Clyde*."

In addition to presenting an unusually equal pair of lovers, *Bonnie and Clyde* is set during the Depression, with Bonnie and Clyde robbing the banks that have taken away poor people's farms—a concept congenial to Steinem's ideas about the Depression, as to Benton's. Benton senses that there was something in the relationship between him and Steinem that was like the relationship between Bonnie and Clyde: a professional love affair, between two people who could deal with each other at their most intimate level in terms of work, with no part hidden. "Steinem educated me in a profound way," Benton recalls, "about two people being together, what we should expect and what we shouldn't. She was wiser than I was."

During this time, Steinem wrote to Benton on a visit to Toledo, telling him about her family and visits to her great-aunt Mame, still drinking Bacardis at ninety-three; describing how very up-to-date and well run a Midwest TV station is; and saying: "I did all these things, but all of them in a haze of love and fatigue and remembering words, touches, imagining those to come, wondering what-it-all-meant and would-it-last, always only half doing what I was doing and half still under your hands, in your arms; all the time pre-occupied with love. . . . Because of you, everything is alive and sensual and very very beautiful." Steinem's love letters, to Benton and later to other men, are provocative and a bit like the popular songs of the day. (She wrote to a later man that she would always remember the first time he kissed her—a memory she eventually, however, failed to recover.) She was still following a romantic script.

Benton and Steinem were together for only a year and a half, until 1963, but both see their time together as one that transformed their lives. They have remained friends, and she has always been grateful to him as the man who set her on her professional, if not her feminist, path. In 1962 she took an *Esquire* assignment from Felker to write about the effects of the Pill on the behavior of college women. He realized that Steinem, as a recent college graduate, would be in a unique position to understand the problems, including that of young women encouraged by peer pressure to have sex before they were ready. This was her first big byline, and she thinks Benton found her solo flight difficult. Benton thinks it was probably obvious to her early on that they wouldn't stay together, but "she treated me well." Their breakup was gradual. She quietly edged away and began seeing publisher Tom Guinzberg, in the characteristic Steinem hope of avoiding conflict and confrontation.

When Steinem first came to know it, *Esquire* still had the Fitzgerald-Hemingway flavor editor Arnold Gingrich had long ago given it. Tom Morgan, a writer of that era, was selected by Gingrich to follow him as editor, but Morgan wanted to write, not edit. As Steinem remembers the situation, Gingrich then hired three smart junior editors and let them fight it out. One was Harold

Hayes, one was Ralph Ginsburg, and the other was Clay Felker. Felker and Hayes were played off against each other; in Steinem's opinion Felker "was the more creative and intelligent and interesting editor, but Hayes got there every morning on time." Hayes became editor in chief and Felker left the magazine. Steinem by then did not care for Hayes, who seemed extremely insecure, sending portraits back to art editor Benton five times "because they didn't make the Marine general look heroic enough, the sort of repressed man who has a hard time talking to women. From the beginning Harold probably viewed me with misgiving." His then-wife Susan, however, has remained Steinem's lifelong friend.

Esquire was then an invigorating place to be, full of intellectual fun. There were no editorial meetings, and no women editors, but there were some women writers like Helen Lawrence, who, unlike Steinem, never came into the office. Gay Talese was beginning to write then, as were Tom Wolfe, Gary Wills, James Baldwin, and Gore Vidal. They invented something they called double dactyls, a form that had to contain a nonsense double dactyl and a name and words that were double dactyls. Steinem remembers several she wrote, including one that was inspired by a current novel about Christ by Nikos Kazantzakis: "Hipriot, Skipriot, Judas Iscariot / Hell-bound in a chariot beautifully made. / Is it that secretly, extra-terrestrially / Christ had requested the role that you played?" *Esquire* had been particularly fortunate in its art directors; Henry Wolf had preceded Benton, and, together with Milton Glaser, they mentored Steinem. Henry Wolf is a man for whom Steinem still holds great affection; she describes him as a "Viennese person who talks very slowly, and is very creative, gifted, and so kind that you don't mind that his lady friends are always the same age as he gets older; I always say to him that I was too old for him the moment I met him."

Henry Wolf moved from *Esquire* to *Show,* a handsome arts and culture magazine financed by the A & P heir Huntington Hartford, "one of the more sad and rootless 'rich people,'" in Steinem's words. Wolf gave Steinem her first *Show* assignment, which was to report on those who worked behind the scenes to create the actors and actresses as they appeared on stage and screen. Wolf told her she could have any photographer she wanted for the piece, and she, laughingly, named Cartier-Bresson. To her astonishment, Wolf hired him for the job.

Steinem's detractors have suggested she was a collector of famous people, but one might also consider that she met many of them before they became famous—as they met her.

WHILE SHE WAS still living in Cambridge, Steinem had visited New York to search for an apartment and finally found one on West Eighty-first Street, opposite the planetarium. It was a studio with an alcove bedroom. She hung curtains, bought secondhand furniture, and began to live in the first of the New York apartments in which she would throw papers into grocery cartons, change her clothes, and, after wide-ranging research, write her articles. The apartment cost $150 a month, a fortune to her at that time. She stayed there until 1961, when the rent was raised beyond her reach and she moved into a small studio apartment on East Seventy-first Street with Barbara Nessim, an artist she had met through Henry Wolf. Twenty-two to Steinem's twenty-six when they met, Nessim felt noticeably younger, but she never found Steinem other than agreeable and easygoing.

Nessim, a successful artist today, was then struggling to establish herself in the art world as Steinem worked to become a writer; they both sought freelance assignments to pay the rent at a time when few women undertook such careers or were willing to face such risks. Like Steinem, Nessim came from what might later be called a dysfunctional family, but neither realized it at the time. They thought of their families as fine and didn't talk much about them. Nessim does remember Steinem speaking of her father, however, recalling his two points of pride: that he didn't wear a hat, and that he didn't have a job.

Together with Steinem, Nessim recognized that women in those days lived only in the male gaze and she drew sketches in her daybook of women pinioned in that gaze. They seem apposite and easily understood today, but they were unusual for that time. Both women, in short, were feminists before that word was again current. Whenever Steinem needed any art done, or any special accoutrements for an assignment, Nessim would provide them. She made the white mask Steinem wore to Truman Capote's famous 1966 Black and White Party at the Plaza; in 1970 she made the sign, featuring a photograph of the massacre at My Lai, that Steinem carried in the New York march to celebrate the fiftieth anniversary of women's getting the vote.

Nessim's single awkward moment with Steinem would come as a result of a vicious portrait of Steinem by Leonard Levitt for *Esquire* in 1971. Levitt, digging for dirt, asked Nessim if she and Steinem ever slept together. Nessim, horrified (as she would not be today, but lesbianism was less easily discussed or accepted then), answered that no, in fact they often spent their nights out with men. Steinem was annoyed when this news was published, since she had gone to considerable trouble to keep from her mother the fact that she had a sexually active life; when Ruth Steinem stayed with her and Nessim, as she often did, they hid the birth control pills; Nessim was so upset by what Levitt had done that she didn't talk to a reporter for the next ten years.

Several months after Steinem and Nessim became roommates, they found a nicer apartment on West Fifty-sixth Street, still one room, but bigger, with more privacy for each. It was on the third floor above Steak Pommes Frites, a French bistro, and cost one hundred and twenty-five dollars a month. There was a weird square bathtub and two beds, unassigned; whoever went to sleep first slept in the corner. There was a brick fireplace, and a kind of bookcase with 13- by 13-inch squares that could hold the records of the day, as well as books, shoes, and jewelry. Steinem worked in a corner, where she had a desk and files.

It was while Steinem was living here that she had a brief but haunting interlude with Paul Desmond. Desmond also lived in the neighborhood, on West Fifty-fifth Street, and they used to run into one another. A great musician who played alto saxophone with the Dave Brubeck Quartet, Desmond was, she recalled, a wonderful, shy, talented person, in an odd way doomed. Herb Sargent, who was a writer for *That Was the Week That Was,* and soon to be a lover of Steinem's calls him "one of the world's greatest musicians, one of the smartest, funniest people I've ever known." Steinem identified with Desmond because "he was a good writer who never wrote," who was always "about to begin on a book called 'How Many of You Are There in a Quartet?' "

When she had stopped seeing Benton, Desmond told Steinem he felt he was only her transitional man, and that when she found someone new, she wouldn't need to see him anymore; but they stayed friends. Years later a woman told Steinem that that wasn't what Desmond had meant at all, that he hadn't wanted to be transitional, but had resigned himself to an ephemeral role.

Desmond died at fifty-two, an indelible memory to many who still listen to his saxophone recordings. He remains, too, a ghostly figure in Steinem's life, one of those passing ships, recalled, as other men are not, because of his genius and his personality. He is not an "event" in her life but rather a reminder of the impression she almost inadvertently left on others.

In 1966, Steinem found a two-room apartment on the second floor of a brownstone on East Seventy-third Street and she and Nessim moved again. They acquired a new couch that was a daybed, and built a sleeping loft; Steinem, as she would for many years, used a rolltop desk on loan from Herb Sargent. She and

Nessim worked in one room and slept in the other. What little cooking there was to be done in either place, Nessim did. They were both, perpetually and inevitably, trying not to eat too much. (Steinem, neither then or later, ever had any food in her house because she believed she had inherited from her father a compulsion to overeat. He too had begun thin and, unlike him, she was determined to remain so.)

In 1968 Nessim had the chance to acquire an apartment especially suitable for an artist and decided to move out. But they remained friends and Nessim continued to contribute, as she had always done, whatever artwork Steinem needed, even for political causes with which she herself was unconcerned. Nessim knew Steinem as only someone who has lived with another person six years can; still, as with so many of her friends, while Steinem was easy to get on with and a good companion, the deeply personal intimacy of close friends was not then, or perhaps ever, what she was about.

WITH THE ADVENT of Robert Benton and his friends, Steinem's 1960s may be said to have begun, and with them the life she would lead before the women's movement focused it, before she recognized the idea of feminism, and, most importantly, before there was any available "story" about a woman like her. After several years of struggling and being published only rarely, she gradually—in her desires, her accomplishments, her life as "The World's Most Beautiful Byline" (as *Newsday* billed her in 1965)— became a more public person, if not perhaps in the way she would have chosen. Her life inevitably divided into two: on the one hand, efforts on behalf of farmworkers, for civil rights, against the Vietnam War, all done privately; on the other hand, the slick but elegant articles she did for magazines on everything from hairdressers and textured stockings to the mayor's wife, Mrs. John

Lindsay—as she was then inevitably called. Occasionally the two worlds came closer together—as in an exposé of a Lefrak Housing project for the *New York Times Magazine*—but that was rare.

A chronological account of those years cannot easily capture either their development or their accomplishment. She was living the peripatetic life of a freelance writer in a small apartment with a roommate, wearing what clothes she could afford to buy whole-sale or could acquire after a fashion shoot (accounting for the Pucci dresses in which she was often photographed). She also had a Jacques Kaplan mink coat she was buying from the furrier on her block, pelt by pelt, on the model of the tiny necklaces given to middle-class young girls pearl by pearl. A fur coat was an object of significance in those early years when she was living up to Toledo's idea of success; however, she subsequently gave the mink coat to her cousin and lost interest in furs altogether. Meanwhile, her furs and showy rings from her father's wholesale antique jewelry trade convinced hovering journalists she was living proof that "A Writer's Life Can Be Glorious and Beautiful." [*Washington Post,* December 1967] Much of her time was spent researching and writing articles, but to judge from the press's rendition of her life, she did nothing but sweep in and out of elegant parties and meet the "in" people. This confusion may, to some extent, have existed in Steinem herself as well. The Toledo urge toward the middle class, and her own disaffection from that class, had not yet been resolved.

The 1960s—Steinem's 1960s—can be grasped under three headings: the articles she wrote, the men in her life, and the causes she gave her time and money to but was unable to publicize through the press as she would have wished. The three inevitably interlock and interact. But the essential transformation took place in the early New York years, when Steinem ceased to be "a mousy, unassuming person who didn't say anything," in Liz Smith's description—someone in Smith's memory, who, immediately after her return from India, talked, if at all, of India. Some time after she had met the "mousy" person in glasses through Benton, Liz Smith was astonished when, as she covered a benefit fashion show, a gorgeous creature, one of the volunteers modeling dresses, leaned down nearsightedly from the runway calling, "Liz, Liz, don't you remember me? It's Gloria!"

"We remained friends," Smith remembers, although Steinem was always trying to get Smith to do "serious things," while Smith was trying to make a living and have a good time. Knowing Steinem in those days, Smith says, was like knowing Mother Teresa or Gandhi; she was a living rebuke to those who hadn't her dedication. If Liz Smith felt annoyed with her through the years, it was because she felt "inadequate to live up to Steinem's ideals for me; she has been a devoted friend to me, and I have disappointed her." This is a disappointment Steinem denies; she always speaks of Liz Smith with admiration, particularly as one who always checks her facts, and is always fair to women.

IT IS WORTH noting that Felker and Steinem established a professional association in 1962, one year before the publication of Betty Friedan's *The Feminine Mystique,* a book that primarily revolutionized the upper-middle-class suburban world of educated women who led lives centered on their homes. In 1963 Steinem had no personal need of Friedan's revelations, which, moreover, didn't address the inequality she was experiencing. Many years later, however, Steinem would recognize that women rich from inheritance or marriage can themselves be as impoverished as the materially dispossessed, if differently; but that was still far in the future. Though these women had the material means to rescue themselves, they were imprisoned in conventional ideas about womanhood; they required a kind of revelation to discover that the door to their prison was, in fact, unlocked. But in the year *The*

Feminine Mystique was published, Steinem had already embarked on a career of a kind that Friedan's primary audience still only dreamed about.

As women in the suburbs were reading Friedan, younger women were working in radical student movements and in the civil rights movement; they soon began to notice that the male leaders rarely included women in their drives for equality. Two other women had, in 1961 and 1962 respectively, published books that would, in time, be recognized as transformative: Jane Jacobs's *The Death and Life of Great American Cities* and Rachel Carson's *Silent Spring.* While the books were widely noticed, argued with, and commented upon, the profound influence their authors would have was still, like the difference that Steinem herself would make in the destiny of American women, potential. The evidence was there; the words had been written; but it would take until the end of the sixties, and beyond, for the full effect to become manifest. Meanwhile, Steinem's own sixties went on; she was a successful journalist, unmarried, glamorous, an internal radical and some-time worker for the downtrodden—in short, still a woman whose particular way of life appeared anomalous.

THE HISTORY OF Steinem's journalism career must be considered on its own. "The Moral Disarmament of Betty Coed" was published in *Esquire* in September 1962. From then, until she wrote the Playboy Bunny article and published *The Beach Book* in 1963, she worked tirelessly to get assignments. She began to write regularly for *Glamour* in 1963, and by the middle of 1964 she was also writing for the *Ladies' Home Journal, Vogue,* the *Herald Trib-une,* and the *New York Times Magazine.* Having abandoned all hopes of combining her deepest interests, confirmed in India, with her need to earn a living, she worked hard at developing her reputation as a reliable and gifted freelance journalist. She was a careful, thorough researcher, and—what she came to recognize after considerably more experience—"a publishable writer." What she handed in was what was published; she didn't remember any trouble. Only when she became an editor at *Ms.* in the seventies did she fully understand what had made her so publishable: "I did come to realize that my ability to make a living as a freelancer was not that I was good, but that I was good enough; I was publishable. How valuable that was I learned later, when as an editor you assign twenty pages and it comes in forty pages; you assign this subject and it comes in that subject. It was amazing to find out how 'good enough' I was."

Later in the sixties, when asked by *Harper's Magazine* why she wrote, Steinem found three reasons that could be extended to all parts of her life: "When I'm doing it, I don't feel that I should be doing something else instead; it produces a sense of accomplishment and, once in a while, pride; it's frightening." She went on to explain further that she liked to get paid for learning; that she liked the freedom, or the illusion of it; that she liked to see her name in print; that writing prevented her from believing everything she saw in print; and that, women's lives being what they were, "when the double chins begin to form," she might have something to be judged on other than her looks. [November 1965] Much of this was the sort of thing writers write for publication in response to unanswerable questions. The passage is of interest not because it was all ever literally true, but because it suggests the justification for her life as a writer that she was beginning to formulate in place of the hopes she had brought back from India.

Steinem's going undercover in 1963 as a Playboy Bunny for "A Bunny's Tale: *Show*'s 'First Exposé for Intelligent People,' " came about not, she remembers, as an idea but as spontaneous combustion. She was sitting around in an editorial meeting—*Show,* unlike *Esquire,* had editorial meetings—and a staff member mentioned that a New York Playboy Club was about to open. Steinem, an ardent admirer of Lillian Ross, then an acclaimed writer for the *New Yorker,* suggested that they send Ross to be a Bunny; not a practical idea given Ross's age, but Steinem could just imagine Ross's lethal description. There was a little silence, and then the guys said: You go. Steinem at first said no, but then finally agreed to go only for an audition. Certainly, she thought, they wouldn't hire her since, applying under her grandmother Marie Ochs's name and social security number, Steinem had no proof of age, which would be legally required to serve liquor, or any other necessary credentials. "I went," Steinem says, "and the thing took on a life of its own."

Going undercover had a tradition, established by the first female journalist, Nellie Bly, who in 1887 feigned insanity to gain admittance to a city hospital. In fact, Gael Greene, now the food writer for *New York* magazine, had written a series of undercover reports when she worked for the *New York Post.* She had, for example, pretended to be a nurse's aide and exposed a hospital and had gone on diets and reported how they worked. Steinem went to the Playboy Bunny audition in the spirit of Greene's adventures.

To read the dark article that Steinem wrote in 1963 is to wonder again why it took her until 1969 to understand and name as "feminist" her recognition of this symbol of the condition of women in our society. The article's surprising insights, particularly that "all women are Playboy Bunnies," so clearly echoes the declarations of the women's movement then and in the years to follow.

"Only if the club was uncrowded, and the coats were not fur, was the Hat Check Room available to women." [*OAER,* 48] "I tried to categorize the customers as I checked their coats. With the exception of a few teenage couples, the majority seemed to be middle-aged businessmen. Less than half had women with them, and the rest came in large all-male bunches that seemed entirely subsidized by expense accounts. . . . The least-confident wives of the businessmen didn't measure themselves against us, but seemed to assume that their husbands would be attracted to us and stood aside, looking timid and embarrassed. There were a few customers, a very few, either men or women (I counted ten), who looked at us not as objects but smiled and nodded as if we might be human beings." [49] "The men call colored girls chocolate bunnies." [46] "[Bunnies] eat on the run from communal plates of food swiped from the customers' buffet." [59] One could quote indefinitely. When one places these observations in the context of a situation, indeed a national attitude, in which women are worth something only as Bunnies, and Bunnies are worth little, Steinem's point of view and the accuracy of her reporting are notable.

With the publication of the Bunny article, Steinem leapt into instant fame, not all of it welcome. She always claimed that the piece led not to serious assignments, only to more offers to go undercover as a sex object. Once, she managed, against the rules, to sneak the minuscule Bunny costume out for the delectation of Barbara Nessim; friends remember that even when her heart was going out to the Bunnies, she could be hilarious about the Bunny life. But the whole experience was exhausting, and this concentrated vision of how women are treated and perceived never left her. Her immediate reaction was not only that she never wanted to repeat the experience, but that she profoundly regretted it, because it seemed to force her even further into becoming the kind of woman and reporter she did not want to be. She was sure she had lost serious journalistic assignments because of the "Bunny's Tale," and perhaps she had. Reprinting the article in *Outrageous Acts and Everyday Rebellions* twenty years later, she admitted, finally, to the benefits of the undertaking, seeing it now through her own eyes instead of a patriarchal lens. She realized "that all women are Bunnies. Since feminism, I've finally stopped regretting that I wrote this article."

The article had a number of unpleasant consequences: She was sued, as she reported to writer Mel Shestack, "not for the Bunny article itself, but for a statement I supposedly made to the *Brooklyn Eagle* about the Club manager. The statement wasn't in quotes and I was involved, I guess, only because of resentment of the *Show* article, but there it was nonetheless. I counter-sued the newspaper and won court costs. The *Eagle* settled out of court. I must say, it was very unpleasant for a year or so: threatening phone calls, etc."

Astonishingly, Steinem had letters from women asking for help in becoming Bunnies themselves. For example, a young woman from Brooklyn wrote: "Dear Miss Steinem: I happen to be a great admirer of yours, and although this request is probably unusual, I do hope you will answer my questions. At some time in the past, I read that you had been a 'Playboy Bunny.' I am interested in becoming one but I don't know how to go about it." Steinem wrote back:

> I'm afraid I can't honestly encourage your interest in becoming a Playboy Bunny. I worked under another name and only as research for an article. . . . In making up what I thought to be a logical background for a potential Bunny, I said I had worked as a secretary. The "Bunny Mother"—who turned out to be a twenty-four-year-old ex-Playmate—asked me what I wanted to be a Bunny for if I knew how to type. That turned out to be a revealing comment. The experience of Bunnydom was all downhill after that, and not a bit what the brochure said. At best, you are a glorified waitress, and at worst a sort of Pop geisha who is encouraged to go out with anybody who could do the club any good. Although I didn't go to the after-hours parties or out with the customers—there's only so far one

can go with research—it was still one of the two or three most depressing experiences of my life.

Far from finding a long waiting list of applicants for Bunny jobs, the management seemed to have difficulty getting girls and keeping them once they were hired. About half the staff left and had to be replaced, even during the month that I was there.

Although the Bunny experience had, as Steinem saw it at the time, so many bad repercussions—including being frequently introduced as a former Bunny—she at first was interested when she heard that David Merrick wanted to turn it into a musical; nothing came of it.

In the meantime, Steinem had returned an advance from New American Library for turning the article into a paperback book. Unlike a fictionalized musical, she later realized that a book would memorialize this unhappy identification further by putting her on the cover with a title like "I Was a Playboy Bunny." In 1983, years after feminism had made her revalue this project, however, a TV film was made of "A Bunny's Tale," directed by a rare woman director, Karen Arthur, and with Kirstie Alley in the Steinem role. Because of the lawsuits from Playboy and Hugh Hefner, the core of the story had to be exactly that of the original, but a love affair with a playwright was added as fictional filling to the writer's private life.

By this time, Steinem's network of friends on magazines had expanded. Mary Ellin Barrett, for example—whose husband, Marvin Barrett, was an editor at *Show*—was an editor at *Glamour;* another woman at *Glamour,* Marilyn Mercer, had previously been at the *Herald Tribune;* Steinem had met her through Felker. These connections helped, and Mercer invited Steinem to attend editorial meetings as a contributing editor.

Many remember her willingness to help women gain connections while trying to get started as journalists in New York. Jane O'Reilly, now a well-known feminist journalist, remembers that it was two years after she had gone to Washington and had a baby that she returned to New York to live with Steinem and Nessim in the Seventy-third Street flat and break into the writing game. Steinem introduced her to editors, lent her clothes, gave her a place to live. "And I, the guest from hell," O'Reilly remembers, "was staying there and staying there and staying there." It was Nessim, says O'Reilly, who finally asked her to leave.

By the end of 1963 Steinem was well launched in the magazine world, if not as the serious writer she had hoped to be. No one meeting her then could have foretold the Steinem of the seventies, or even the Steinem of *New York* magazine, soon to be founded, where she would be allowed to write regular political articles, and where, even if she still followed celebrities around, they were political persons rather than just "jazzy folks."

It was Tom Guinzberg—at his father's sudden death he had taken over at the Viking Press—who further introduced Steinem to New York's glitterati. Steinem remembers Guinzberg, the lover for whom she left Benton, as the first person she thought of as really rich. Guinzberg's version is slightly different: He says he was more potentially rich than rich, but was certainly able to live a life that seemed fairly glamorous to Steinem. He widened her scope in many ways and, on a more mundane level, put her in touch with an accountant who helped her file returns for past years; she had, of course, continued to live the life her father had embodied for her: no regular source of income, no office routine, no thought of paying taxes. In Guinzberg's memory, Steinem accommodated to his life perfectly: "She could handle absolutely anything." Interestingly, he remembers her in those early years as having had to make no special effort to fit into his world, including the elegance of Southampton, Long Island. She always seemed to have the right dress, always looked good. She, on the other hand, remembers that when he took her to her first black-tie party she was alternately full of anticipation and dread: She didn't have a long dress, didn't know what such parties were like. In the end, Barbara Nessim's mother made her a dress, and all was well. Significantly, however, Steinem was sharply aware of being an outsider, of not belonging in Guinzberg's world. This dissonance, long unexpressed, perhaps even unenunciated, is nonetheless her prevailing memory of the sixties: always feeling an outsider, even though none of the insiders, or anybody else, noticed.

To Guinzberg, he and Steinem are still family, a sense he shares with most of the men she has loved or known well. When they were separating as lovers in 1964, Steinem wrote him about how she would remember him: "I remember a rainy night in the little East River park, and a fair night in the library on Sutton Place with the breeze blowing in the window. When I am eighty and rocking-chaired and supposedly beyond such things, I will re-member all of that. . . . Whether or not I see you for a while or at all, I'll be walking around with a piece of you inside me, and it will always be there." She herself recognized that she often wrote to lovers more directly than she could speak to them, particularly when the affair was tapering off. But however familiar these words may sound, they were both true and without rancor—she was ready for the relationship to end.

Guinzberg now jokes, as does Benton, that it is always fun to hear from Steinem, but that if she wants something, it is always for someone else. Reminded that some have thought Steinem fell for the glittery life, Guinzberg says it is they who have fallen for it, not she. He remembers that he was not serious enough in his reactions to political disasters for her taste; it was one of the things they quarreled about. He was slower than she to condemn the Vietnam War—which Steinem opposed from the beginning—be-cause he believed what he had heard from John Steinbeck, who was both a friend and a Viking author. President Johnson (Lady

Bird Johnson was a classmate of Steinbeck's wife) had sent Steinbeck to Vietnam to report back to him on conditions there; Steinbeck was shown what the generals wanted him to see, and his report was favorable. Steinbeck died in 1968 never knowing that he had been wrong. But Steinem and Guinzberg did not have many serious conversations; they had fun. And he remembers her as loving, bright, "a very zesty lady; in no way inhibited; there was no one else like her."

It was certainly Guinzberg the man in love and not Guinzberg the publisher who in 1963 went forward with the publication of *The Beach Book*, a project Steinem began with Benton and gained custody over, so to speak, when they split up. (Guinzberg still jokingly claims that Benton owes him a book.) Indeed, Guinzberg asked Steinem to meet with her editor in Schrafft's restaurant, housed in the same building as the Viking Press. *The Beach Book* was clearly not a book any serious publisher in his right mind would have agreed to—it was an exercise in flirtatious frivolity, coffee-table size, with a sun reflector on the inside of the jacket—but it was a witty frivolity. Steinem wrote a number of the entries, but does not take credit for them, although the anthology is "by" her. The introduction was by John Kenneth Galbraith, who admitted in its first sentence that he was writing the introduction to the book because he liked "the girl who put it together."

Vogue mentioned the book in its "People Are Talking About" column, describing it as stuffing "prose, poetry, games, pop art, and Charles B. Slackman sketches into one grand design for sunning." [August 15, 1963] The book includes, among others, these Fantasies to Have: "Cary Grant is walking down the beach toward you. He is carrying a shaker of martinis. He is smiling." "You are on a planet exactly like this one except they have never heard of Cole Porter and you just happen to know all his songs." "You have just dealt a crushing defeat in public debate to (choose one) William Buckley, Jr., Hugh Hefner, David Susskind, Ayn

Rand, who is being laughed off the stage." Even in fun Steinem's early 1960s politics bubbled to the surface.

STEINEM DID NOT marry Guinzberg, as she did not marry Blair Chotzinoff or Robert Benton. (Though with Benton she had gone so far as to apply for a marriage license; they let it lapse.) It was not that she intended never to get married. In the sixties Steinem was still planning to marry and have children, but not yet. Both the social atmosphere around her, and her harsh memories of Toledo, had persuaded her that marriage was the end of a woman's life; afterward only the husband's life counted. And Steinem was not yet ready to end her life. She finally accepted the fact sometime in the late seventies that she would never marry, when she looked up for a moment from the magazine and the women's movement that had the ultimate claim on her.

With the hindsight of three decades, one can ask, What did she need to marry for? She had what she called her "little marriages"; there was no lack of desirable—and, more important, kind—men. She liked her work. She liked the freedom to work for the causes gripping her; she was having fun. Inevitably, she had visions of herself as a single mother with a child. When she was most depressed, she would say, "Oh, well, I can always get married"; but marrying meant giving up.

Jane O'Reilly married someone she met on a double date at the beach with Steinem. When Steinem heard of this some years later, she was dismayed: "You married that man? I would have stopped you; he's another conservative central European." And she was right, O'Reilly says. Yet O'Reilly, like many others, was nearer to the almost-inevitable destiny of women in the late fifties and early sixties than was Steinem.

That Steinem did not want to repeat her parents' miserable marriage is likely enough, but many products of miserable marriages have married, planning to do better themselves. It is possible that she is one of those who consents to be loved, rather than one of those who love, as the French epigram has it. Clearly, she was never the victim of obsessive love, never hung around the phone pleading with it to ring, never wanted to move in with any man. Although she left changes of clothes for her next day's work at the homes of many she was involved with, and they lived together on weekends and vacations, the thought of merging her collection of books with anyone else's struck her as beyond serious contemplation: a significant symbol for an unconscious decision. Apart from Steinem's views on the matter, conscious or unconscious, the most obvious fact is that she did not need to marry to assure herself of loving and highly agreeable male companionship whenever and wherever she wanted it. For Steinem, in those years, short-term intimacy sufficed.

In 1963, Barbara Nessim asked Steinem for a quotation around which to make a portrait of her; Nessim liked making such portraits. Although it was never made, the quotation Steinem produced, about unmarried sisters in Isak Dinesen's story "The Supper at Elsinore," is still framed on Steinem's wall, and in 1963 captured the attitude she was as yet unable to formulate in her own words:

> It was another curious phenomenon about them that they, to whom so very little had happened, should talk of their married friends who had husbands, children, and grandchildren with pity and slight contempt, as of poor timid creatures whose lives had been dull and uneventful. That they themselves had had no husbands, children, or lovers did not restrain them from feeling that they had chosen the more romantic and adventurous part. The explanation was that to them only possibilities had any interest; realities carried no weight. They had themselves had all possibilities in hand, and had never given them away in

order to make a definite choice and come down to a limited reality. They might still take part in elopements by rope-ladder, and in secret marriages, if it came to that. No one could stop them. Thus their only intimate friends were old maids like themselves, or unhappily married women, dames of the round table of possibilities. For their happily married friends, fattened on realities, they had, with much kindness, a different language, as if these had been a slightly lower caste, with whom intercourse had to be carried on with the assistance of interpreters.

As her relationship with Guinzberg faded, Herb Sargent, who had met her on double dates with Guinzberg, was, so to speak, waiting in the wings. Sargent had been a writer for many television specials and eventually went to work at *Saturday Night Live*. When Steinem met him, however, he had become the producer and head writer of *That Was the Week That Was,* and asked Steinem to write for it. She went on to write a department of the program called "Surrealism in Everyday Life," collecting odd and diverse facts and figures, and putting them together to come up with hilarious results.[2] Jane O'Reilly, remembering Sargent from that time, calls him "the sexiest man who ever lived."

Today Herb Sargent, still a friend, speaks of Steinem with warm affection. "I was in love with her," he says. "Ask me anything." He remembers that she didn't seem prefeminist as far as using the word *feminist* goes, but she was. She would say things that turned up later in her presentations of feminism, as in "female Uncle Toming": You ask a man the time and then you say to him, "Aren't you clever to know what time it is!" But Sargent says Steinem wasn't yet aware that sending a woman for coffee was not only irritating but part of a system.

[2] These very funny programs can still be viewed at the Museum of Broadcasting in New York City.

Liz Smith, an old friend of Herb's, was pleased when Steinem started going out with him. She described him accurately. "He's a sweet guy, but not a great talker," Liz says. "He's great with one woman, but you have a hard time making social conversation with him. Gloria was great for him. She had to be a person of substance and quality and sweetness or these men wouldn't have been interested in her." Her involvement with Herb continued for years, through all her efforts on behalf of everything but feminism, a term she did not yet understand or use. He was one of her little marriages—although, once again, she never moved into his house. Steinem's mother liked Herb too. Writing to Gloria about this time, she said, "Speaking of sandwiches [she had been describing a woman who made her think of watercress sandwiches] what you are, Honey, is a date and nut bread charmer, with cheese cake filling. Herb, however, is a toasted rye, with Bermuda onion, lots of sweet butter . . . because it makes me feel pretty good to be around him." Sargent, like Benton, feels Steinem opened up a lot of things for him, especially politically. She was a great teacher, a natural teacher. "She is one of the smartest people I know," he says.

This is a judgment repeated by all the people Steinem knew in the sixties, most of whom still see her from time to time. And they respond indignantly to the idea that the men in her life helped her along. "What did she ever get out of these men she went with?" Liz Smith asks. "She was one incredible-looking woman. People wanted to know her. What if Tom Guinzberg published *The Beach Book* because he was in love with her? We all did things like *The Beach Book*. I did a map for *Esquire* of where famous people lived. We needed the money and we needed to get published. . . . She's intelligent," Smith sums up; "smarter than everyone else, but she never puts her intellect forward, doesn't try to overcome you."

Clay Felker, asked about her now, says that Steinem got on

with so many people so well because she wasn't threatening. Why she was not threatening is, like so many questions about Steinem, a complex one. Part of the answer lies in the indifference to most of life's ordinary anxieties that she inherited or learned from her father, somehow bypassing her high-strung mother's inescapable and constant anxieties. It is always possible that her mother, given a different life at a different time, would have been less anxious; as it was, she represented, as many miserable mothers do, an example of what Steinem would never let herself become. This determination, in Steinem as in many women, not to be like her mother, played a major part in the development of Steinem's temper and invariably calm demeanor. Passive in part, she avoided the assertiveness that many are too quick to find discomforting in other feminists.

FOR STEINEM as for most of America, 1963 closed in the terrible aftermath of President Kennedy's assassination. She had, some months earlier, met Ted Sorensen, a speechwriter for Kennedy; Steinem would offer suggestions for the speeches from time to time. It was ironically Ruth Steinem who created the bond that Steinem felt with Sorenson—she fell in love with him, as she reports in *Outrageous Acts* (without identifying him),

> only because we both belonged to that large and secret club of children who had "crazy mothers." We traded stories of the shameful homes to which we could never invite our friends. Before he was born, his mother had gone to jail for her pacifist convictions. Then she married the politically ambitious young lawyer who had defended her, stayed home, and raised many sons. I fell out of love when he confessed that he wished I wouldn't smoke or swear, and he hoped I wouldn't go on

working. His mother's plight had taught him self-pity, nothing else. [144]

David Halberstam, in *The Unfinished Odyssey of Robert Kennedy,* takes a compatible view of Sorensen: "Heralded in the press as a great liberal who had taught Jack Kennedy his liberalism, and had masterminded the great victory, he had gained an insider's reputation during the White House years, of being the most pragmatic politician of all, far removed from his liberalism. Following the assassination he did not plunge himself into the social issues with which the administration had been so concerned, but rather became just one more wealthy lawyer." [47]

Almost thirty years later, Steinem had a letter from a professor of history who was about to publish a book on John F. Kennedy. He was, he told her, the first researcher to use the Secret Service White House Police Gate Logs, which record visitors to the White House. The gate logs showed that she had been in the White House four times in October 1963 and also on November 2 and that Theodore Sorensen had authorized the visits. Steinem answered him:

Ted Sorensen was a friend whom I knew through either Ken Galbraith or David Schoenbrun. On those days, I must have been in Washington (I was living in New York) and either meeting Ted for dinner, or helping him to add a little humor to Presidential speeches—though I'm not sure that any of my suggestions were used—or both.

If my memory is right . . . I was in the White House on a date later than November 2nd. I remember Ted finishing a speech for which I had tried to help think of witticisms, and then running it out to the President as he left by helicopter for that Texas trip. I watched through French doors—I think in the Oval office the President had just left—as Kennedy walked toward [the helicopter] across the lawn. That was, of course, the last time I saw him alive. (I had never actually met him, but he was a President who made me and so many others feel connected to our government for the first time in our lives.) His figure walking away from the White House on the lawn, blown by the helicopter's gusts, is still an indelible image in my mind.

She went on to say that Kennedy's administration was the first and last time when writers could feel that what they wrote might be read and taken seriously in the White House. Later, when she was writing about Nixon's campaign for *New York* magazine, it seemed to her that ungenerous hearts might be in power for a long time to come.

Even while Steinem continued to write to Sorensen in the frightful period just after the assassination, offering him what comfort she could, she had come to see him as puritanical and to realize that a steady relationship, once undertaken, would not last. Sorensen married quickly after the assassination, but the marriage endured for only a few months. Much of Steinem's life and of everyone else's seemed frozen in that moment with the President on the White House lawn, assailed by gusts from the helicopter and by so much else.

MIKE NICHOLS and Steinem became lovers sometime after she had begun meeting him at dinners and parties to which Tom Guinzberg had taken her. With Nichols she came to know people like Betty Comden and Adolph Green, a very theater-based social group. Again, Steinem felt "like the outsider in the audience; I wasn't creating [she always dreamed of writing novels and plays] and they were," but she much admired their talent. When she met him, Nichols was already well-known for his skits with Elaine May, although they were no longer performing together. He had yet to make the films for which he would become famous, and was preparing to do his first Broadway play, *Luv*. Steinem felt, as she would continue to feel, that although he was immensely talented, she never found enough heart in his work. They spent time with a number of people, like Julie Andrews, who were just at the start of their careers: Andrews had a youthful success in *The Boyfriend,* and was then married to Tony Walton, also at the start of his career. Steinem still remembers watching them late at night doing charades in the middle of the empty street; they were immensely gifted. Steinem and Nichols also saw a good deal of Sybil Burton, already separated from Richard, and Stephen Sondheim and Jerome Robbins.

If Tom Guinzberg had introduced her to the world of artists, intellectuals, and elegance, with Mike Nichols came even more glamour, and the renewed threat of marriage and a conventional woman's life, albeit with someone of great talent and increasing position in the entertainment world. Nichols was the only man in Steinem's life whom she felt she treated very badly. Again the question of marriage had been raised, more forcefully than ever, and Steinem panicked.

Leonard and Felicia Bernstein (Steinem felt that Felicia wanted her to make the compromise Felicia had made—that is, give up her own identity to marry a famous man and become part of his world), John Kenneth Galbraith, and many others urged her to marry Nichols: He was talented, clearly headed for immense success, and she liked him. She would, however, sit with him at dinner parties feeling she had no identity, while he had so definite a one. But wasn't that what one was supposed to want in a husband, someone who represented the life you as a woman could never have? So at the time when Steinem's life could be described as the height of success for a woman, she felt miserable. She was not writing what she wished to write; she did not want to live a husband's life instead of her own.

Matters came to a head when she and Nichols, together with Elaine May and her husband, went to Washington for Johnson's inauguration in 1965. Julie Andrews and Carol Burnett were there too. Soon after arriving, Steinem, using the phone in the hotel room she shared with Nichols, tried to order room service. She could not make the clerk taking the order understand that, yes, her name was Steinem, and, yes, she was entitled to be in the room. Finally, to get the food, she had to agree to being called Mrs. Nichols; the room service man said "Congratulations," conspiratorially, as though she'd caught a big fish—all of which she found very depressing. She saw that she was "the girlfriend," not a person in her own right.

Steinem was unfair to Nichols, she now believes, because she could not tell him her true feelings: that she shouldn't be involved with him, because she didn't want to marry him or anyone. But she had not yet admitted to herself that she would never marry at all, and so rather than discussing this with Nichols directly, she started blatantly seeing other men. For a long time Nichols felt a justifiable resentment.

In the late 1980s, Steinem took him to lunch and apologized. Still later, returning from the dentist, she came upon him in front of a pet shop on Lexington Avenue, shooting a scene from *Regarding Henry* with Harrison Ford. Nichols told Steinem that the title character was going into the pet shop to buy a dog. "Why don't you have him get it at the Humane Society?" Steinem asked. And they were back in the same sort of conversation they used to have twenty-five years before, on different sides of what were, essentially, social and political questions.

Clay Felker has said of Steinem that she came into and out of the sixties without anyone knowing how to describe her; that is the simple truth. He also believes she invented being a professional woman; there were few enough of them at that time to make the claim plausible. Felker, however, is not all praise. He recognizes Steinem's fear of confrontation and her decision not to marry, which he connects and considers weaknesses. "The famous men who have wept on my shoulder: My advice has always been just to cut your losses. She decides to move on, she doesn't want confrontation, and she hurts them more." Perhaps Felker's view of Steinem would be of even more value if he were not convinced that marriage and children are the most important events in life for a woman. "In the end," he says, "she couldn't give herself to one man." What Felker considered a defect, however, can be seen as a discovery, or a way of life destined, despite right-wing anguish, to become even more common than it is today.

In February of 1964 Steinem was featured in a *Glamour* article as "New York's Newest Young Wit." After mentioning the Bunny piece, the article went on to discuss Steinem's fashionable clothes and the history of her makeup. To the reader, Steinem's hope is almost palpable—as it is in all the articles about her at this time—that her looks might be dismissed and her ability to write about politics and other serious questions might be recognized. Until Clay Felker and the advent of *New York* magazine, however, this hope did not materialize. Her talent and ambition seemed irrelevant after her looks had made their impression.

Nonetheless, the significance of Steinem's attractiveness is certainly greater than she likes to believe. Once she was identified as a feminist in the media's eyes, her looks might play their part in her feminist career but they would not be more significant than her ideas. In the sixties, however, she had not yet found her life's work but had met the people whose encouragement was essential to her development as a woman and a journalist (though not as a political activist); the importance in those days of her attractiveness must not be underestimated, even if this myth that women's power is tied to their looks is, as usual, overestimated. When the first reporter to interview Steinem as a "talking dog," a pretty girl who writes, arrived from *Newsday* in the early 1960s, he told her with such forcefulness that looks got assignments that even Steinem agreed. It was only the next day she realized that nearly all her own editors were women.

More than a hundred years earlier, a young and talented woman had come to London to be a writer and an assistant editor for the *Westminster Review,* edited by John Chapman. Her ambition and her moral vision were, like Steinem's, intense. We know her as George Eliot. While working on the *Review* she met, in addition to Chapman, the philosopher Herbert Spencer; both recognized her intellectuality and her ardor. But, as Sally Beauman wrote in the *New Yorker,* neither Chapman nor Spencer "was physically attracted to her; Chapman remarked in his diary on her 'want of beauty'; Spencer liked her, but seems to have found her too morbidly intellectual. Had Eliot been beautiful—and she bestows the gift of beauty on every one of her heroines—the reactions of Chapman and Spencer might have been different. . . . [F]ew minced their words that she was *ugly.*" [April 10, 1994, p. 90] True, Eliot's fate in regard to men, as Beauman puts it, was to be happy. But that came much later in life.

Would Benton, Guinzberg, Desmond, Sargent, Sorensen, Nichols, and the other men who were to follow, have responded to Steinem initially with such enthusiasm had she looked like George Eliot? Certainly, once they got to know her, they were further attracted by her brains and her charm. But there can be little question that the opportunity to discover who she was would probably not have revealed itself had she not possessed an animated, close-to-beautiful face and perfect body. This is to take nothing from her accomplishments or talents; it does suggest, however, that her looks didn't hurt. When she had become a spokeswoman for feminism, the reassurance her appearance offered to women that, contrary to the impression given by the media, not all feminists resembled male truck drivers in boots and fatigues, was profound.

Back in the sixties, however, Steinem must have welcomed, in however ambivalent a manner, the publicity her looks and talent brought her. There can be little question that, in addition to being a journalist herself, she had an instinct from the outset about how to use the press. In the following decades she would regret a great deal of this publicity—she had, as with the Bunny article, already regretted some of it—but what she learned from that publicity would serve the feminist movement well. Although nothing and no one, not even Steinem, could prevent the media from misrepresenting feminism for their own ends, or from exploiting the fact that bad news about women is always exciting news, she certainly handled the media most of the time with skill and finesse. She learned much of this the hard way in the sixties and early seventies, but she did learn it.

The most visible articles Steinem was allowed to write in the sixties were on celebrities, some of whom actually interested her. For example, in 1965 *Glamour* arranged for Steinem to spend "A Day in Chicago with Saul Bellow." [April 1965] Would Bellow have spent the whole day with her, and included Professor Richard Stern from the University of Chicago, if Steinem had looked "pudding-plain," as she later described Bernadette Devlin? [*Glamour,* Dec. 1969] Although her article meticulously describes Bellow, their wanderings around Chicago, his looks, and his ideas, it is permeated by the sense that he is happily in the presence of a beautiful woman. For Steinem, of course, who had admired him since *The Adventures of Augie March,* the assignment seemed better than her usual ones. If she was aware that Bellow's attitudes toward women were less than acceptable to her, she did not mention it.

James Baldwin was a celebrity she had admired since *Giovanni's Room.* The article she did about him for *Vogue* in 1964 suggests much of what would emerge in her writing once she was given the chance.

In repose, James Baldwin is an ugly man. He has been told so all his life. Long before he knew that being a Negro could be considered ugly in itself (that is, long before he was ten years old) . . . he had grown used to the cruel mirror held before him by his friends and by his father. At school, he learned that being darker than many of his classmates and smaller—and smarter—than any of them was no advantage. They called him "Frog Eyes" and beat him often. From his father, a fundamentalist Christian minister and implacably stern, he learned that his ugliness was the ugliness of sin, that the intelligence shining from his strange, prominent eyes was the knowledge of the devil: "You always," he now says sadly, "take your estimate of yourself from what the world says about you." . . .

Moving through a restaurant during a break in rehearsals of *Blues for Mister Charlie,* his Broadway play, it seemed that the vitality of his gaze had infected the whole of his tiny, wiry body. Even sitting dead still and thoughtful, he gave the impression of movement, of an energy barely controlled. He is a Presence, and in that presence it is suddenly difficult to know whether he is ugly or something close to beautiful.

Later in the article Steinem observes that "somewhere, through all his work, there walk, like repertory players, the clearly recognizable figures of his family, and of the people who have influenced him in the four stages of his life: Harlem, the Village, Paris, and, now, the struggle for civil rights." It couldn't yet occur to Steinem that these four stages also describe her own life: Toledo, India, New York, and, eventually, the struggle for women's rights.

And then there was Truman Capote. Steinem interviewed and wrote him up twice, in 1966 for *Glamour* and in 1967 for *McCall's,* and did not speak with him outside of these interviews, but his writing had influenced her long before that. In 1961 she saw the movie—she had already read the story—*Breakfast at Tiffany's,* and

Holly Golightly would seem to speak for her in many ways. When she decided to add blond streaks to her dark brown hair, it was to imitate the rebelliousness of Holly. (From then on she would streak her hair.) But more important than the way Holly Golightly looked was how she left home. As Doc describes it in the story: "Reading dreams. That's what started her walking down the road. Every day she'd walk a little further: a mile, and come home. Two miles, and come home. One day she just kept on." For some reason, that way of leaving home spoke to Steinem. (It was, of course, also the way she left men—Steinem and Holly shared an unwillingness to commit.) Her great enjoyment of two sixties Broadway productions, *A Taste of Honey* and *Gypsy* echoed this theme. She said she liked them because they were about women and their mothers, about leaving home. Yet each of these heroines' stories ends with the protagonist following a life Steinem would never even contemplate. It was their breaking away she responded to.

As one reads the story today, other touches from *Breakfast at Tiffany's* resonate: Holly saying, "I want to still be me when I wake up one fine morning and have breakfast at Tiffany's." She has cards that read "Holly Golightly, Travelling." She answers, when asked about it: "After all, how do I know where I'll be living tomorrow?" Holly Golightly has a cat with no name. " 'Poor slob,' she said, tickling his head, 'poor slob without a name. It's a little inconvenient, his not having a name. But I haven't any right to give him one: he'll have to wait until he belongs to somebody.' " In fact, in the 1970s there arrived at Steinem's apartment a stray cat named Crazy Alice, which, although named, came for only a few years.

Steinem, like Holly, traveled too much. Holly's room, like Steinem's, had a "camping-out atmosphere; crates and suitcases." Steinem's did not look as though everything was "packed and ready to go," but certainly, with its boxes of papers and piles of books, it could not be called "decorated," or substantial, or done up. Gerald Clarke, Capote's biographer, thought that Holly Golightly was based not so much on any woman Capote had known as on Capote himself. This seems likely, and illuminates the ready understanding between Steinem and Capote.

IN MAY of 1965 an article appeared in *Newsweek* that can be usefully chosen to mark a shift in the way the media treated Steinem: the addition of innuendo, sneer, and envy to a kind of astonished admiration that Steinem, by the end of the decade, learned to characterize as "It walks, it talks, it's a feminist." Her looks were never beyond consideration (most of the reporters then were male), but whether those looks would ever allow her to be taken seriously as a person fell into a new, nastier, political kind of doubt. The *Newsweek* article, titled "News Girl," offered, in its first two paragraphs, the following:

> Usually the journalist remembers his [sic] place—on the edge of the action recording the news made by others. But Gloria Steinem, a striking brunette of 30, is as much a celebrity as a reporter and often generates news in her own right. . . . She has dated Ted Sorensen and Mike Nichols, discussed the poverty program at lunch at the White House, and makes opening nights (and the women's pages the next day).
>
> Miss Steinem is a magazine writer and her subjects often become her most vociferous fans. "She's the smartest, funniest, and most serious person I know," says Nichols, "and she looks great." . . . Says Julie Andrews, "I think I'd like to be her if I weren't me."

The picture, even more than the article, carried the message. Steinem is seated, cigarette held aloft, her legs in a short skirt facing the camera. The caption reads: "Steinem: Easier than you think." Steinem herself was profoundly hurt by that caption, and the writer of the article (a man), who was not bylined, wrote to her apologetically, claiming he had gone on vacation leaving the shaping of the article and the writing of the caption in the hands of other editors.

This was the beginning of a kind of media treatment of Steinem that, as far as mainstream publications were concerned, would not change for the better. Indeed, there was worse to come. No doubt they kept writing about her because they couldn't quite decide who or what she was. The seeming conflict between her politics and her looks would continue all her life, but for the first years after the feminist movement got under way, when her fame reached to the covers of *Esquire* and *Newsweek*, the conflicting aspects of her life would continue to inspire denigration and admiration in varying proportions.

But in 1966 she might still have hoped for more measured treatment; she herself had not yet become provocative as a feminist. That year, as her Smith class prepared for its tenth reunion, she and a classmate sent out the usual questionnaire (husband, children, politics, pets, hobbies, weight) and wrote up the results. Only five years ahead lay the Smith commencement address that would certainly, at the very least, startle her listeners and mark her wholly new persona as a rebellious, revolutionary, outspoken woman. But here she was still doing as she was told, responding as a Smith graduate should properly respond to such a task.

Yet Steinem's gifts—and perhaps her irony—show through the report. "To give you a general picture of the results [of the questionnaire] we put together the most typical answer to create a kind of Class Personality. And, in a fit of nostalgia, we named her Lydia Glutz. Remember Lydia Glutz? Our mythical classmate? Well, here she is ten years later."

Mrs. Glutz is married and is somewhere between ecstatic and

content. Her husband went to Yale (but almost Harvard) and is a businessman; she does not hold a job but keeps busy with her children in her suburban house. "Lydia herself is overwhelmingly in favor of integration, but has no close Negro friends. And though she hasn't lived abroad, she would like to. She has moved leftward since her Republican undergraduate days at Smith, but not very far." And so on. Where Steinem found herself in all this is unclear. She was still, in 1966, reporting on the world around her, aware that she had an unusual place in it, still hoping, but with less confidence, that her chance to be a political and meaningful writer was not far off.

At the same time Steinem was being locked into celebrity status by her peers, she was still, like her father, powerfully drawn to show business, particularly to writing films. A man named Robbie Wald had inherited a property called "High Heels" from his father, the movie producer Jerry Wald, and Steinem was hired to write a modernized treatment of a story that had originally featured a dance hall girl. William Friedkin, then an unknown director of documentaries, was hired to direct. She renamed it "Cally" and changed the setting to a topless bar. (She spent depressing days in Los Angeles interviewing topless dancers, all of whom seemed to be single mothers supporting kids.) Steinem's treatment of the subject would reflect her growing if still unnamed feminist ideas. Robbie Wald wanted to produce it himself, but he was unknown, and the project came to nothing.

All through the sixties, Steinem fell in love with books and would think how they would make great plays. To this day, she considers that *Out of Africa* could be a wonderful one-woman show. She also wanted to dramatize Elie Wiesel's *Town Beyond the Wall,* and dreamed of Wonder Woman, with whom she had grown up, as a musical. (Wonder Woman appeared on the cover of the first independent issue of *Ms.* magazine.) Though she tried to get the rights to Wonder Woman and *Out of Africa,* nobody wanted to sell them to a novice playwright.

In 1966 producer Ray Stark was making *Reflections in a Golden Eye,* from the novel by Carson McCullers, and had approached Steinem to write additional dialogue. Only one of her suggestions, and that without dialogue, was used: Marlon Brando, playing an army officer who has a crush on a young soldier, picks up a candy wrapper the soldier has just tossed onto the sidewalk, smoothes it out, and puts it in his pocket. Stark also hired Steinem to scout out plays for possible movies; she went to little off-Broadway plays on his behalf. By 1968, when Steinem was raising money for McGovern's first presidential campaign, Stark said he would give her a contribution if she would ghost an article he had been asked to write for the Sunday *New York Times* about his experiences as Fanny Brice's son-in-law (Stark had produced *Funny Girl*). Steinem remembers it as one of the more surrealistic moments in a life scarcely devoid of them. She interviewed Stark and wrote the article, which did appear in the *Times* under Stark's name. She thinks that in the end he may have felt a little contrite about making her do this in order to get a political contribution, because in addition to giving her the contribution for McGovern he insisted she accept a gaudy enamel ring, which she tried to return for the money, but could only exchange. The episode is vintage Steinem, not least in that this was all in aid of a political cause.

In 1967 Ralph Ginsburg, one of the original *Esquire* editors and publisher of the short-lived *Fact* magazine, was starting a new magazine, *Avant Garde,* and wrote to Steinem to ask her if she would become a staff writer. Answering him, she described her life:

[H]ere's my problem. I seem to have signed too many contracts —articles and editorial advising for Condé Nast and McCall's, plus a movie script that I haven't the faintest idea how to do—and I'm now in a fit of over-obligation. Scarcely does a telephone call go by without some justifiably angry editor saying "where-the-hell-is-it." I have promised myself, my agent, and anybody else who would listen to cool it for a while, at least six months to a year so I can get caught up. (After all, I started this freelance business so that I wouldn't know what tomorrow might bring, and now I know.)

Some of this was exaggerated, no doubt, to provide a tactful refusal. But in addition to overcommitting herself—as she would continue to do—she was now being offered slightly better assignments, and even the *New York Times Magazine* was giving her more challenging subjects to write about than textured stockings and fashion. The piece she did on Samuel Lefrak, the builder of a huge middle-class housing development called Lefrak City, had a hard edge and was subtly critical.

Her tendency toward overcommitment was also encouraged by the many requests she was receiving to undertake political activities. She was, for example, asked by the president of the Lexington Democratic Club to serve on the county committee as an emissary from the West Fifties. She informed him that she had moved to the East Seventies; she was ashamed, "but the rent was cheaper." She added: "If there is anything I can do from here, please let me know. Going out of town frequently to do articles makes me a little undependable, and, on a scale of 100, I have minus 10 points of sympathy left for the Johnson-Humphrey team, but with those two qualifications, I would be happy to do anything I can." She volunteered to write releases, if needed.

She was also asked to join a Washington delegation from an organization called Negotiation Now. She answered: "I got discouraged after a Washington trip with Women Strike for Peace because they somehow ended up speaking only to more-or-less friends (Robert Kennedy, Jacob Javits) about the uselessness of the war, and booing *them*." She offered to help, however, adding: "One of the pleasures of being a freelance writer is that there are no organizational ties to restrain one's action. (Of course, there's no regular paycheck either, but I'm so far gone that I even enjoy that!) Please call me if there's anything I can do."

Steinem's life in New York in the sixties was a compromise between her ambitions and her political passions. Like so many women of that time, she tried to live and find her way in the culture she knew, consciously or unconsciously trading inner life and sense of self for the comfort of the known restrictions of a man's world. What is distinctive in her case is that she made this trade-off work for her. In a certain sense, her personality and her attractiveness may have been handicaps; they certainly slowed her realization of her needs as a woman, her need for feminism—matters more obvious, and obvious sooner, to women without her attributes.

1968

NINETEEN SIXTY-EIGHT was the year the anti–Vietnam War movement came to a head, the year of the violent Democratic Convention in Chicago; of the student uprisings at Columbia and elsewhere; of Cesar Chavez's organization of the farmworkers in California; of the first of the Miss America Pageant disruptions that, quite inaccurately, gave the term "bra-burner" to feminists. It was the year the women's liberation movement got under way and consciousness-raising groups became widespread. Steinem, however, deep into the anti-war movement and soon to be intimately involved in the farmworkers movement, was, if aware of burgeoning feminist actions, forced to miss them because of other journalism assignments. It was also the year Clay Felker founded *New York* magazine as an independent enterprise, an endeavor in which Steinem had a significant role and for which she was to cover these and related events.

Felker had left *Esquire* in 1962, and when Steinem was preparing for the World Youth Festival in Helsinki, she asked him to edit one of the English editions of the daily newspapers produced by the Finnish socialists. Felker didn't have much money at that time; he was eager for an adventure, and his girlfriend (soon to be wife), actress Pamela Tiffin, was making a movie in Paris and London. Editing the newspaper provided a way to get to Europe to be with her.

Felker gained a keen appreciation of Steinem's political instincts during their Helsinki adventure, and his admiration for her grew after their return. Considerably later, when he was in need of a job, Steinem arranged with Tom Guinzberg for the Viking Press to hire him as a consultant. What struck Felker about Steinem, as it has since struck others, is that she knew he was in need of a job and, without consultation, helped to find him one. Suddenly, as he puts it, "there was this offer from Viking." This in turn led to another consulting job. In time he was hired by James G. Bellows to become a consultant for the new magazine section of the Sunday edition of the *Herald Tribune*. The magazine was named *New York*.

Richard Kluger, who wrote a history of the *Herald Tribune,* describes Felker as "a rapid-fire talker . . . with an eclectic intellect adept at making connections between ideas and their manifestations. . . . As an editor, he was remarkably good at conceptualizing stories and then putting the idea together with a writer who could fashion it well and on time." [680–1]

In Kluger's opinion, shared by many, the freshness and excitement of *New York* magazine, even as a newspaper supplement, were direct results of Felker's personality and of the fact that he was "perpetually overstimulated by the city." Felker was on the *Herald Tribune* only two years, but "he helped reshape New York journalism and redefined what was news." [703–4] Among those who wrote for *New York* when it was still part of the *Herald Tribune* were Tom Wolfe, Jimmy Breslin, Langston Hughes, Nat Hentoff, Liz Smith, Walt Kelly, Peter Maas, Walter Kerr, Judith

Crist, Walter Terry, and Jerry Goodman (now better known as the economic analyst Adam Smith).

Felker's gratitude to Steinem, in addition to her natural talent as a journalist, made him want to include her in the adventure of *New York* magazine. Significantly, even in the early sixties when the magazine was still in the future, they did not have a romantic or even a social relationship; theirs was a professional partnership. Felker was the first not so much to enable Steinem (as Benton did), or to turn her into a butterfly at home in all social worlds (as Guinzberg did), but to identify her, beyond her brains and beauty, as a smart woman with whom he could work. He recognized talents in her that were not then recognized in women because they were not supposed to be present in women.

By 1966 Felker's magazine was the au courant publication in New York. But the *Herald Tribune* was failing under the constraints of union demands, and with the help of Steinem, Breslin, and Peter Maas, among others, Felker began looking for the money to finance *New York* as an independent magazine. Steinem remembers going to many lunches at which she was the only woman, as they tried to raise the initial investment. When, finally, several contributors were put together, and the first investment collected, Steinem got some stock in return for having helped to raise the money.[1] At first they were not at all sure that they would continue to call the magazine *New York*. Steinem wanted to name it "New York Moon," so that trucks could drive around the city bearing signs that read "The *Moon* is out." She thinks, however, that it may have been Tom Wolfe who thought of the trucks.

---

[1] Rupert Murdoch, on acquiring the magazine in 1977, paid for her stock; characteristically, Steinem can't remember how much, but "certainly less than ten thousand dollars." She lent the proceeds to the struggling *Ms*. Steinem had also—to Felker's considerable annoyance—used her *New York* magazine stock as collateral through bondswoman Ida Shankman to get bail for prisoners at the New York Women's Prison who needed leave in order to get abortions that the prison refused to provide. The women, let out on bail, had their abortions, and returned.

(Steinem eventually lost her affection for Wolfe after the publication of his notorious article "Radical Chic," about Leonard Bernstein and friends entertaining the Black Panthers. For years afterward, she recalled, it was impossible to get anyone to do a benefit for anything; people will undertake many generous fund-raising efforts, but not, she found, if the result is ridicule.) Although she saw little of drama critic John Simon in the office, she found his articles offensive also, and suggested to Felker that if Simon ever admired any theatrical production, they announce it on the cover of the magazine as "John Simon Likes Something."

The staff of the new publication rented a floor in the big old whitestone building on East Thirty-second Street that housed Milton Glaser's Push Pin Studios. Steinem remembers working endlessly on the first issue [April 8, 1968], which was a disaster: The design didn't work, and everyone's piece had to be cut. She herself contributed the article "Ho Chi Minh in New York," which she does not now regard as one of her better efforts (it, too, was cut drastically). Steinem named the regular departments—an undertaking she found particularly appealing, so she continued to suggest new ones. One day, for example, as Felker tells it, "She came and said: 'I don't know much about food and I'm afraid to have food around the house for fear I'll eat it, but I've been listening on TV to this woman every morning telling us where you can get bargains in vegetables and fruit. Why don't we do something and call it "The Passionate Shopper" '? So we hired Joan Hamburg, took the idea and ran with it. We had the idea that one of the main activities of the modern reader was as a consumer. . . . [Steinem] and I sparked each other a lot." The column proved a success, employing many writers over the years.

Steinem recruited composer Stephen Sondheim, a double-crostic aficionado, to construct the puzzles in the back of the magazine, a duty later taken over by Mary Ann Madden. *New York* had women working on the magazine in all capacities, even as salespeople, which was then almost unknown. The circulation director, Ruth Bower, was an essential factor in the magazine's success and a woman who Steinem would, one day, woo over to *Ms.*

Felker gave Steinem her first chance to write on politics. Kluger, as is characteristic of male historians, writing of Felker's gifts and achievements, fails to mention one of his most striking attributes: that he matter-of-factly hired women to write what women had not been allowed to write before. Felker attributes his lack of professional sexism to his mother, who, he says, "preconditioned" him. She was a journalist who stopped working when he was born and was never happy about it. She had been a competent professional who held a responsible job as the women's editor of a St. Louis newspaper. When asked what she had done for the cause of women's liberation, she said she had a son who gave women opportunities. (Neither Felker nor Steinem seems to have noticed that both their mothers had, and abandoned, careers in journalism.)

As Felker discovered, "when you get Gloria, you get this array of talent." Jane O'Reilly, for example, was brought to *New York* by Steinem; Felker also offers this story: When Ali MacGraw was staying with Gloria and Barbara, she got the starring role in the movie *Goodbye, Columbus.* "One day, Gloria came in and said, 'You know, Ali keeps this diary; she kept it during the making of *Goodbye, Columbus.* We could pick up that story.' " MacGraw was by then a big movie personality, and the diary with both her words and drawings was a success.

Felker recognized the "enormous political instincts" that others didn't know Steinem had. As he puts it, "I had other writers to do other things, some of which she did too, but I didn't have any good political writers; it was as simple as that. She showed that she knew what she was doing immediately." By the end of the year Steinem was writing a regular column, "The City Politic," which still continues with other writers. The days of being the glamorous jet-set kid who wrote about celebrities were over; she was on her way to becoming a serious journalist, reporting events affecting women, as well as other dispossessed groups, but not noticing that she was noticing women in any special way.

If one follows Steinem through her articles and "City Politic" columns, they reveal the scope of her reportage as well as her populist instincts. She reported on the nature of the major events then holding the attention of informed New York City readers. The presidential campaign was under way, and Steinem interpreted it for her readers. In her October 1968 article, "In Your Heart You Know He's Nixon," she noted that the reporters who traveled with him "don't like Richard Nixon." She reported their lack of interest in Nixon's rallies and speeches—an attitude so different from that on other campaign tours with Kennedy and even with McCarthy and Rockefeller. Steinem remembers that Nixon would periodically walk back through the plane to talk to the press, but he was so inept that he could remember only one thing to say to each reporter, and it was always the wrong thing. If he decided that one reporter's house had burned down, for example, he would cleave to the subject, even though it was the wrong reporter and the wrong fire.

Steinem, the only woman on the plane, was once late in returning, and Nixon shook her hand as though she were part of a group seeing him off. She was, of course, acutely aware that there were no black faces in Nixon's entourage, just white men with ties and briefcases and state-of-the-art electronics. There was no heart; everyone agreed on that.[2]

Excerpts from her columns about the Nixon campaign were reprinted in *Outrageous Acts and Everyday Rebellions.* In her piece

---

[2] In 1992, when Pat Buchanan sounded, at the Republican National Convention, like the most extreme proponent of the radical right, Steinem remembered that he was so disliked on Nixon's plane that no member of the press would sit next to him, although such proximity to campaigners was just what the reporters sought.

titled "Campaigning," for example, she reported on a Nixon rally in Tampa, Florida: "A banner read REGISTER COMMIES NOT GUNS. It suddenly seemed that we were surrounded by anti-life, conserving, neighbor-fearing people . . . and that the enemy was going to win. . . . It was the death of the future, and of our youth, because we might be rather old before the conservers left and compassionate men came back." [*OAER,* p. 112]

Also reprinted there is the interview Steinem did with Pat Nixon. Steinem had asked for an individual interview with Richard Nixon, a privilege traditionally afforded reporters with the campaign, but was given Pat Nixon instead. The interview became famous because of Pat Nixon's uncharacteristic frankness about her childhood, and Steinem always regretted that she hadn't been able to say in her *New York* article that she liked Pat Nixon much better after the interview, and that she understood her subject's resentment of her early life, a life not unlike Steinem's. Steinem also regretted that her attempts to further break down Pat Nixon's wall didn't work; a failure that makes Pat Nixon close to unique, and suggests how rigid was the defense life had forced her to erect. Pat Nixon was, in fact, furious at Steinem; she shouted at her that "other people had it easy," and she had not had it so. The interview is a scream of anguish.[3]

The 1968 Democratic Convention in Chicago was a watershed for Steinem: It was almost the last time that she would try to work through male-run institutions. With *New York* under way, Steinem went to Chicago to try to prevent Hubert Humphrey from winning on the first ballot, to promote George McGovern's peace candidacy as a way of picking up delegates who were disillusioned with Eugene McCarthy, to distribute farmworker literature, and above all to work for the end of the Vietnam War. Four

[3] An account of this interview, and of the harsh experiences of Pat Nixon during Nixon's political career, can be found in David Halberstam's *The Fifties.*

years later, at the 1972 Democratic Convention, Steinem's efforts would be on behalf of the women's caucus, campaigning for women's rights and representation. Her experiences in 1968 had proved to her what she was already coming to suspect: that working through hierarchical male institutions did not serve women.

Steinem was passionately opposed to the Vietnam War; she took a major part in organizing writers to withhold that portion of their personal income taxes likely to support the war. The anti-Vietnam tax movement began in 1967; in February 1968 over four hundred writers and editors signed an advertisement, "Writers and Editors War Tax Protest," declaring their intention to withhold 10 percent of their taxes. This amount corresponded to the proportion of the national budget being spent to prosecute the war. Together with Alice Mayhew (who became her editor in 1987), John Leonard, and others, Steinem had organized the ad. She reported in her *New York* column of February 10, 1969, that they weren't dragged off to jail as many of them had feared: The government, so their banks had informed them, simply removed the tax money out of their bank accounts.

> This was the anti-climax to long months of discussion. Would some of us lose our jobs? (The *New York Times* had refused to print our advertisement, though the idea for the group had started among its own employees.) Were our phones tapped? Worst of all, would the IRS subject us to punitive audits? Well, nothing happened. (At least in this case. The War Resisters League [has collected] a wide variety of personal experiences with tax non-payment.)

Steinem, though she had earlier had some fleeting hope for the possible effectiveness of the anti-war movement, knew by the time Humphrey had been nominated that "the protest couldn't work inside the structure, and I couldn't even work inside the protest."

As writer and professor of sociology Todd Gitlin expressed it, in writing about his feelings after Robert Kennedy's assassination less than three months before the convention, "I think many of us were divided, . . . but in a way we refused to acknowledge. We still wanted the system to work, and hated it for failing us." [310] After the 1968 Democratic Convention, many besides Steinem would recognize that failure. She continued to take part in the political process, but never again within a political party; the pressure she exerted would come from without.

Steinem's efforts to prevent the first ballot for Humphrey at the convention involved lobbying the delegates who had been Bobby Kennedy's and were uncommitted because of his death. Eugene McCarthy was, of course, the nominal antiwar candidate; as Steinem discovered when she worked for him before the convention, he carried the antiwar banner in a way that seemed admirable if you didn't happen to believe it was insincere. She and other writers who were preparing his speeches went to see him before he went to New Hampshire, and he told them not to mention the war because New Hampshire was a "hawk state." They finally persuaded him to speak out against the war by agreeing to put that statement next to his mention of veterans' benefits. Gitlin's version of McCarthy's behavior concurs with Steinem's: "With Kennedy dead, the life went out of McCarthy. During the following weeks, McCarthy's antiwar staffers looked on disgusted as their hero proceeded to take leave of his own campaign. What McCarthy's devotees didn't know was that, three days after the assassination, McCarthy had gone to Humphrey and met with him secretly for an hour, fishing for a policy change that would justify his dropping out." [311]

As Steinem puts it: "It became more and more clear that McCarthy's main motive was that he hated the Kennedys because they were bad Catholics. Perhaps it was more complex than that," she admits, "but he did not inspire you when you were in his presence. In addition to his questionable attitude toward the war, he was very proud of the fact that well-educated people supported him and uneducated people didn't. He would never go to Harlem. The old-time street demonstrators knew McCarthy was not their friend, and they were right." In fact, everything about McCarthy was beginning to make Steinem uncomfortable. She felt that he was less open to difficult questions by the press than any other candidate. As she explained in a letter to an interviewer from *Time:*

> Questions are turned aside by his use of a) moral superiority, b) very negative and sometimes insulting wit, c) refusing to admit there is an issue (especially in civil rights where he just says he won't address remarks to any "racial or other special interest groups"), d) repeating the same high-sounding but non-specific and unnewsworthy remarks over and over again. When all else fails, he just bores the press to death. In three days, there wasn't one question on gun control, concrete plans for [the] Paris [peace talks] or his peculiar voting record on everything from the Subversive Activities Control Board and the DAR to NASA and federal subsidies for rifle practice, all of which he voted for increasing.

Many of the young people who had been followers of Robert Kennedy wanted to stay in electoral politics so as to back a candidate who was against the war. Like Steinem, though, they already had their doubts about McCarthy's sincerity.

Steinem had met George McGovern through John Kenneth Galbraith and believed him to be the "real" Eugene McCarthy, because he had given the first-ever speech on the Senate floor against the war, saying that the war was going to haunt the United States all over the world for years to come. Steinem uttered this opinion on a late-night radio show, thinking she was talking to dead air, but one of the young Kennedy followers who was now doubting McCarthy called her up to say that some of them were interested in supporting McGovern and wanted to start a "New York for McGovern" group to try to help him prevent the first-ballot nomination of Humphrey. And so, with Steinem's encouragement, the McGovern campaign in New York began.

THE VIOLENCE AT the 1968 Democratic National Convention and the actions of Mayor Daley and his police have been widely described, though from different points of view. Theodore White, in his *The Making of the President 1968,* takes a pro-Daley stance. He believed the protest to be communist-inspired and communist-directed, a common conservative opinion of the time; had it not been for the unprovoked attacks by the Chicago police on Eugene McCarthy's young supporters, one of which White happened to witness, he probably would have criticized the police even less than he did. White, of course, does not mention Steinem, although she was in the room with him when he tried to persuade McGovern to back Humphrey. But he does report that Dan Rather, "a reporter whose high competence is matched by his good manners and ever-gentleness, ha[d] been slugged and beaten to the floor by a security agent." [285] Steinem inadvertently got too close to Daley while passing out literature on behalf of Cesar Chavez and the farmworkers, a cause she had taken up with passion; his security guards shoved her roughly and broke her glasses.

Few of those in Chicago that day forgot the sight of the police and national guard wading into the crowds of antiwar protesters and bystanders. Members of the press, too, were manhandled, Mike Wallace and Walter Cronkite as well as Dan Rather. Steinem, watching from Frank Mankiewicz's hotel room—the center of McGovern's press operation—saw police pursuing demonstrators, saw the blood on Michigan Avenue, saw bystanders being pushed through plate-glass windows as the police forced the crowds back. Jimmy Breslin called the event a police riot.

White reports the violence but not the provocative behavior of the Chicago police, under Daley's explicit orders. A comparison between White's account of events and that by Todd Gitlin in his book *The Sixties* is instructive. White observes that Abraham Ribicoff "occupies screen attention as he denounces Daley and the Gestapo of the streets of Chicago." [302] But Gitlin reports what Steinem and many others remember: "Abraham Ribicoff of Connecticut denounced the police's 'Gestapo tactics' and Mayor Daley yelled something which the TV sound couldn't pick up but lip-readers later decoded as 'Fuck you you Jew son of a bitch you lousy motherfucker go home.'" [334] At this time, Steinem and Frank Mankiewicz were backstage, having helped with Ribicoff's speech nominating McGovern, and they were startled and gratified to hear Ribicoff spontaneously attacking Daley.

Gitlin writes: "To our innocent eyes, it defied common sense that people could watch even the sliver of the onslaught that got onto television and side with the cops—which in fact was precisely what polls showed. As unpopular as the war had become, the antiwar movement was detested still more." [335] Television news, rapidly changing its point of view, ceased criticizing Daley and his handling of the convention. Few who had been in Chicago failed to learn another lesson: that, as Gitlin put it, the establishment media were part of the establishment. That time was a watershed for others as well as Steinem, even though many of them either returned eventually to take part in the political system, or dropped out altogether.

* * *

RIBICOFF'S ROLE in the convention greatly helped his later run
for the Senate in Connecticut. McGovern, however, was not
helped in his Senate race in the much more conservative state of
South Dakota. Steinem and others who had supported and encouraged McGovern's role in the convention went to South Dakota to help his campaign; they felt a responsibility, because he
had done so much for the antiwar movement. For the only time
in her life, Steinem conformed to a dress code; in South Dakota
she tried "to look ladylike for George."

Her ultimate disillusionment with male-run politics came by
way of Ribicoff and McGovern: At Ribicoff's invitation, McGovern supporters decided to meet in Connecticut to organize Mc-
Govern's run for the presidency in 1972. McGovern invited his
staff to attend, including Steinem, but then he told Steinem that
Ribicoff had said: "No broads." Ribicoff has since denied he said
this, but it was not a remark Steinem was likely to forget or
overlook. What shocked was not only the fact that Ribicoff might
issue such an edict; it was also McGovern's acquiescence. Steinem
was forced to realize that if Ribicoff had said no blacks, no Asians,
no Native Americans, or no Jews, McGovern would have objected; but "No broads" was acceptable.

So while McGovern remained, for Steinem, the only sincere
anti–Vietnam War candidate, by the time he came to run again in
1972 she was working not only for McGovern but for women. By
1972 the "broads" were in evidence and fighting for their own
causes.

At the time of the convention, the media was still viewing
Steinem in the old, confused, uncertain way, unable to fit her into
any of their available stereotypes. A *Washington Post* column of
August 28, 1968, by Maxine Cheshire illustrates the point neatly:

Writer Gloria Steinem, the mini-skirted pin-up girl of the intelligentsia, was being congratulated in the Sheraton-Blackstone

today because Sen. McGovern's staff picked up one of her quotes to use for a button that may become the collector's item of this convention.

It reads: "McGovern: He's the REAL McCarthy."

"Shhh!" said Miss Steinem: "Those buttons aren't supposed to be released until after the first ballot. Until then, we're all for unity."

Miss Steinem went to work for McGovern two weeks ago. Today, she was sneaking up the back stairs loaded with two enormous brown paper bags. They were filled with hamburgers to feed herself, Frank Mankiewicz and other hungry McGovern staffers who found room service impossibly slow.

Miss Steinem was dressed for her intramural car hopping in a brief, clinging brown jersey mini, belted with a chain that ended in an ivory molar that looked like a tooth from a man-eating lioness.

The whole column is a put-down characteristic of the time. "Miss Steinem" is the "pin-up girl of the intelligentsia"—never a member of it; her clothes, like her role as a carhop, get more attention than her political contributions. "I remember," Steinem recalled twenty-five years later, "that none of us had slept for nights and nights; I remember the skirt and top they describe; I kept it on for five days because there was no place to change. The 'ivory molar' was the claw of an Indian tiger I got in India." There was, and would long be, a large gap between what Steinem was doing and what the media represented her as doing.

STEINEM MET Rafer Johnson at the 1968 convention; this was the first of her "romantic friendships" with a black man. Many of the activist black men she met were, she found, more sensitive to the dangers and oppressions of sexism than their white male counterparts. Rafer Johnson, an outstanding athlete who won the gold medal in the decathlon in the 1960 Olympics, was a case in point. A friend of Robert Kennedy's, he was present at the assassination and helped capture Sirhan Sirhan, the assassin. Probably it was Johnson's gentleness and their mutual admiration for Robert Kennedy's antiwar stand that brought him and Steinem together for a short time—their lives on opposite coasts precluded frequent meetings.

Steinem was, however, to learn from the football player-turned-actor Jim Brown that not all black men are sympathetic to women's sense of unfairness. James Toback, in *Jim,* his book on Brown, argues that Brown introduced a new dimension to football as its first black hero [6], but was as sexist as most football heroes. (Toback believes that football is so popular because it is the most violent, warlike, masculine—and therefore essentially satisfying—game. [5–6])

Steinem met Jim Brown in October of 1968. She had gone to Arizona to interview him—he was shooting a movie there—for a *New York* magazine article. They had a short affair, but Steinem soon discovered that, while he treated her well, Brown was often accused of behaving differently with women he didn't see as equals. In her article, "The Black John Wayne," she celebrates his refusal to play Hollywood-type "Negroes"—"handy human indicators of white status"—and insistence on playing what all viewers will recognize as "a Negro hero for Everyman." She admired his insistence on black economic independence—what he called Green Power—but, as she also wrote, "being a male chauvinist, he has low standards for women, and always seems surrounded by squadrons of manicurists, salesgirls and that international breed of models who don't model and actresses who don't act."

Brown seems not to have changed for the better since Steinem wrote about him. A *Washington Post* reviewer called his 1989 autobiography "sex-stuffed." It includes an account of his affair with Gloria Steinem.

STEINEM'S IMMEDIATE sense of empathy with out groups, including individuals who have suffered from racism, is, perhaps, unusual for a white person. She has, in fact, had an exceptionally happy history of friendship with African Americans. Two decades after she met Rafer Johnson, she was asked by *Ebony* to contribute an article; though she never wrote it, she made some notes of stories she might have told about her many black friends and how she had met them.

When she was in high school, Steinem attended a ballet class where she met a black girl, her first black friend of those years. (Waite High School in Toledo was integrated, but not socially.) This ballet student was better educated than Steinem, more classically cultured, better dressed, and from a nicer home, and she had attendant relatives she called "aunties" who were certainly more elegant than anyone from Steinem's neighborhood. She helped Steinem see that not all black people were poor and helped her to articulate the difference between race and class. The girl in the ballet school marked the beginning of Steinem's education in racial consciousness. Steinem clearly had an early inclination to question any society that chose her friends for her.

When Steinem moved to Washington, D.C., for her senior year, she attended an all-white school. During that year, Smith College held a tea for all prospective Smith students; any Washington, D.C., girl with college aspirations was invited. There were many black girls at the tea, but when Steinem got to Smith, she found there wasn't a single black student in her class. The young black women who'd attended the tea were able to afford college and had the necessary academic qualifications. Finding none of them at Smith when she arrived, Steinem asked someone on the admissions committee why there was not a single black woman in her class. His unforgettable and unforgivable answer was that you had to be careful what Negro girls you admitted to college because there weren't enough Negro college men to go around.

Soon after Steinem heard the response, she became better fortified against the characteristic racism of this answer. The summers during college when she worked as a lifeguard and swimming instructor at one of Washington's two segregated city pools were pivotal. When she first arrived at the pool she was the only white person there, but the black children, the other lifeguards, and the two full-time recreation department employees gradually accepted her. They taught her Southern card games, "bid whist," and "coon can," and on rainy days they repaired to the changing room where the lockers were; Steinem learned how to "do bones, which the little kids did. You sit hunched over and do rhythm on your arms and legs, using your body as a percussion instrument."

Sometimes they all went out for a Coke in the neighborhood, the all-black community of Rosedale. Steinem remembered a classic teenage redneck who responded with fury to the sight of a white girl with all those "niggers." One tall young lifeguard from Howard University put his hand on the white teenager's shoulder. Then he pointed at Steinem: "You see that girl over there? That girl is just one big recessive gene." When Steinem was late, she would take a taxi to the swimming pool. Sometimes drivers refused to take her to Rosedale; one said, "Why are you going there? You'll give them ideas; you'll make trouble." She got out and walked.

These early encounters with black people would make even sharper than it might otherwise have been the barrenness Steinem later felt returning from India to find herself in a world of only whites and the uniform culture of the 1950s. Although she could not find work that would allow her to use her Indian experiences, her determination not to let racism limit her life and her friendships was already established. Thus, when she decided, despite her fears of public speaking to go on the road on behalf of feminism, she went with a black woman, Dorothy Pitman Hughes, whom she already knew. And the story she selected for *Revolution from Within* to exemplify love, not just romance, was a slightly fictionalized version of her long friendship with Franklin Thomas, until the summer of 1995 the president of the Ford Foundation, whom she met toward the end of 1969.

STEINEM'S SUPPORT of Cesar Chavez and *la causa*—the movement on behalf of the farmworkers—began with a woman named Marion Moses. Chavez was, as a product of his own culture, a male chauvinist who took for granted men's right to control women and their bodies, even though he defied much of male culture by espousing nonviolence; it was therefore perhaps inevitable that the story of Steinem's commitment to Chavez and the farmworkers began not with him but with the woman he had sent to New York as a fund-raiser with little money to live on and no connections.

Her commitment to the farmworkers' movement, both in 1968 when she embraced the cause and in 1969 when her full-time efforts turned into part-time ones, was emblematic of Steinem's beliefs. Chavez, despite his misogyny, was the sort of leader to appeal to her. Born in 1927, he had grown up in migrant labor camps in Arizona and California. He became the general director of the Community Service Organization in San Jose, California, in 1952 and left in 1958 when the organization refused to create a farmworkers union. By 1965 he had enrolled 1,700 families in his National Farm Workers Association; that year his union joined migrant Filipino grape pickers in a strike against the grape growers that would last for several years.

Marion Moses, who grew up poor and Catholic in the South,

was the first of her family to go to college. She started working as a volunteer for the farmworkers' union in the summer of 1966, moving to Delano, California, where Cesar Chavez had his headquarters, and serving as a nurse full-time in the farmworkers' clinic. In 1968 she was one of those sent to New York City by the union to organize the boycott of table grapes, which began in January of that year.

The farmworkers in California, almost all Mexicans at the time when Chavez formed his National Farm Workers Association, labored under the most oppressive conditions imaginable. Forced to work long hours in the fields of agribusiness farms, without toilet facilities, medical care, or decent housing, paid less than the minimum wage, they had to live in company-owned shacks and were sold food and other necessities at elevated prices. Lacking transportation, they were being slowly poisoned by pesticides and consequently suffered enormous health problems.

In 1960 Edward R. Murrow had drawn attention to the plight of migrant workers with his television documentary *Harvest of Shame*. But the film offered no solution to the problem; perhaps Murrow still believed that revealing the situation would be sufficient to encourage the government and shame the growers into reform. Such a hope must have seemed a mockery to those who worked on behalf of the farmworkers. In 1968 the attitudes of California's Republican governor, Ronald Reagan, and of Richard Nixon, Republican candidate for president, toward these farmworkers would clearly foreshadow the hardening of the country during the Reagan years into a nation indifferent to its poor.

Against the powerful agribusiness forces, the workers had little chance of effecting any change in their condition. They were, in addition, not well educated, had large families, and desperately needed income. Chavez decided that throughout the strike he would follow a policy of nonviolence, partly because the violence of the growers was so much more dangerous than any the farmworkers could muster, but mainly because Chavez believed that the methods Gandhi had used in India were the best model for his endeavors. By the time Marion Moses came to New York City in 1968, Chavez had determined upon two means to bring the condition of the farmworkers to the attention of America: his own fasting and the grape boycott. Steinem's willingness to join the farmworkers' cause, natural enough once she had met Marion Moses, was certainly reinforced by the knowledge that Chavez was influenced by Gandhi.

The boycott of table grapes was decided upon as a way to bring the nation's attention to the condition of the farmworkers, and to force the growers to recognize the farmworkers' union. Table grapes were chosen as the best crop to boycott because they had to be picked by hand, and because they were purchased from markets, not pressed into wine; also, they were a luxury food, suited to boycotts in that no one had an economic need to purchase them.

The outrage expressed against the boycott by the growers and the politicians to whose campaigns they contributed was as dishonest as it was frightening. Reagan, as governor, delivered a speech in defense of the "poor growers" facing adversity. This speech, author Peter Matthiessen prophetically observed in his 1969 book *Sal Si Puedes: Cesar Chavez and the New American Revolution,* "is not astonishing from a politician who still had reason to believe that a staunch defense of the haves against the have-nots might win them the Republican presidential nomination." In September 1968, "Governor Reagan delighted the growers by calling the grape strikers who picketed them 'barbarians.' On this occasion he was accompanied by Richard M. Nixon, who declared his intention to eat California grapes 'whenever I can.' Two weeks earlier, in San Francisco, Mr. Nixon had termed the grape boycott 'illegal.' " [312] As Robert Taylor explains in his book *Chavez and the Farmworkers:* "Politicians like Nixon, acting on behalf of their agribusiness constituents, had opposed the inclusion of farm labor under the National Labor Relations Board for 33 years. At the time Nixon made the San Francisco Statement [that the secondary boycott of California grapes was clearly illegal] the National Labor Relations Board had no jurisdiction over the farm workers. The UFWOC's secondary boycott actions were clearly legal." [236] This legality was constantly pointed out to Nixon by Massachusetts senator Edward W. Brooke and others, like Steinem, who traveled on the Nixon campaign plane, but he continued to make the same speech nonetheless. Though a Republican, Brooke, also one of the few blacks at that time to serve in the U.S. Senate, eventually left the plane because of Nixon's continued lying. When Nixon became president, the army bought barrels of grapes for the soldiers in Vietnam to support the growers: about one barrel per soldier, it has been estimated.

The farmworkers had decided to picket large markets in urban centers, because these sold more grapes and so would feel the boycott more, and because they received table grapes disguised in boxes as other produce from the boycotted growers. In addition, boycott supporters, posing as shoppers, were able to cause disturbances in the supermarkets, noticeably affecting their sales.

When Marion Moses first came to New York City to begin the boycott there, she lived in Brooklyn, in a building loaned to the farmworkers by the Seafarers' International Union. The union could not even afford to pay her living expenses, so she slept in a bunk, without privacy, a phone, a typewriter, or air-conditioning. And she discovered that living on five dollars a week, even in 1968, was hardly possible.

Moses recalls coming to New York because she had been told that was where the money was, but she had no idea how to raise it. "It turned out," she ruefully recalls, "that there wasn't any money walking off the trees." She hiked around the streets from one possible source of income to the other, trying to get funded;

she talked to Michael Harrington—his book on poverty, *The Other America,* had profoundly influenced President Kennedy—who helped but had no money. She followed every lead; nothing worked. While she was still in California, Fred Ross, a longtime associate of Chavez, had suggested she get in touch with Charles Silberman, who had just written *Crisis in Black and White.* Through Silberman's office she met Judy Wheeler, a Smith classmate of Steinem's then working for the Rand Corporation. Wheeler suggested she call Steinem: "I called," Moses says. "She called back. I can still hear that wonderful voice. 'How can I help?' she asked."

They met for lunch, and Moses recalls, "I couldn't believe it; she was all business: What do you need?" Steinem said she would talk to people on the *Today* show, and otherwise do what she could. "I felt," Moses said, "like I had found gold at the end of the rainbow. She was the first person I had talked to who didn't say she was real interested in what I was doing, period." Steinem began to organize some publicity, and joined in the picket lines outside supermarkets. "Why don't you come and stay with me?" Steinem asked Marion. She came in June, sleeping in the loft, and stayed until September; they worked together, often all night, and became friends.

Within the next year, Steinem and Moses got reporters from *Time* and *Life* to meet with Chavez; Steinem did an interview with him for *Look,* placed him on the *Today* show, and eventually helped to put him on the cover of *Time.* (Steinem remembers that Chavez called at the last minute, wanting to postpone the cover for a few weeks; this was characteristic of his naïveté about the media.) The main purpose of the publicity Steinem arranged was to slow down the violence of the growers, who were "accidentally" running over workers with trucks and who had threatened Chavez's life. Since local law enforcement officials were generally on the side of the growers, media attention was the migrants' only protection. Steinem, learning of these "accidents," would call the sheriff in the rural towns where they occurred and as a reporter, ask: "When are the federal marshals coming?" She had no reason to think they were coming, but the mention of the possibility may have had some future cautionary effect.

The interview with Chavez in *Look* reached publication only after a prolonged struggle. Because the publisher feared pressure from such prospective advertisers as Sunkist, the magazine at first resisted running an article on the farmworkers. A previous article on Chavez's work had been sent back for "balance." Finally, Steinem suggested to Pat Carbine, then the magazine's editor, that she publish an interview with Chavez, using his own words; "balance" would not then be in question. Years later Steinem learned, from another source, that Pat Carbine had got the interview published by threatening to quit. Plenty of editors say this, but few mean it; Carbine did, and *Look* could not afford to lose her. When the interview (unsigned) appeared, *Look* did, in fact, lose some advertisers.

Moses and Steinem decided to put on a benefit for *la causa* at Carnegie Hall. They set up a committee that included Steinem; Marietta Tree, a wealthy, public-minded New Yorker who had been an activist in Adlai Stevenson's campaign; and Amanda Burden (through Carter Burden by way of Robert Kennedy, who was an ardent supporter of the farmworkers until his death). Steinem, Moses remembers with awe, got Milton Glaser's Push Pin people to do the invitations; she found a photographer for the event, and Herb Sargent pulled in Mort Sahl (who was in those days a liberal), Lauren Bacall, George McGovern, and Peter, Paul, and Mary. Using the words of the farmworkers, Steinem wrote a script, which was read by Ann Jackson and Eli Wallach, as well as Bacall and others.

The Carnegie Hall benefit raised $30,000, according to Moses, including subsequent donations from Paul Newman, Joanne

Woodward, Jackie Kennedy, Woody Allen, and others. But even more important, it raised the visibility of the movement. Even the other labor unions were not too enthusiastic about *la causa,* because the organizing was taking place outside their influence.[4] Steinem observes that the male union people never knew how to organize the women, who couldn't go out to meetings at night and who often had demands different from those of the men. But Moses and Steinem did have the help of Local 1099, the hospital workers' union, composed mostly of women, and one of the few unions, Steinem says, with "heart and conscience."

It is ironic to realize today how little attention the historians of Cesar Chavez and the farmworkers movement have paid to women's contributions. Here is yet more evidence of how women and their accomplishments are written out of history. Although some historians are aware of boycott organizer Dolores Huerta, who was essential to Chavez's effort, she herself does not feel sufficiently recognized.[5] As for Moses and Steinem, they are not even mentioned, except for Matthiessen, who used Moses's notes and interviewed her for his book. Robert Taylor, in the manner of male historians in 1975, asserts: "Chavez spent much of his time dealing with the press, learning how to handle the various sides of the media." [182] There is no mention of Steinem's contribution to handling "the various sides of the media"—a contribution that at the time of the Carnegie Hall benefit was far from over.

---

[4] The farmworkers had, in fact, little labor support at first, except from the International Brotherhood of Teamsters, which already controlled the trucking of farm products and wanted to control the migrant workers. This was an association Chavez was disinclined to welcome, and thereafter the Teamsters opposed him.

[5] In Cathleen Rountree's book *On Women Turning Fifty,* Dolores Huerta says: "Many years ago I organized the first grape boycott, but nobody ever says I did. Then I came back and wrote and negotiated the contracts. Later, some young lawyers came in and wanted to change the history to his-story. Again, I was on the humble side of everything: you don't necessarily want the credit or to have your name mentioned—that's not why you do the work. Still, it's a shock when you see the reverse happening—you are not only unrecognized for what you do, but you are *denigrated* for it." [130]

Steinem did consider turning Chavez's words into a book, going so far as to take a politically aware expert in book publishing, Bob Gutwillig, to Delano to meet Chavez, but Gutwillig was ambivalent, and in 1970 Peter Matthiessen produced *Sal Si Puedes*.

Steinem's last major project for Chavez and *la causa* came in May 1969, when she helped him to get publicity for a march from Delano to Calexico, California, on the Mexican border. Chavez had developed a grand plan: The poor of Mexico would march to the border, there to meet the poor of the United States; they would have a celebration and agree never to work against each other. There would be speeches from flatbed trucks that bore images of the Virgin of Guadalupe, and the publicity would help draw attention to the plight of the farmworkers.

While the workers wended their way across the desert, carrying a figure of the Virgin in 110 degree heat, Steinem drove to Calexico with a lawyer who worked for the farmworkers and who became sexually fixated on her. If being sexually fixated upon was not an unusual experience for Steinem, being enclosed with the fixated one in a small and battered car, crossing the more deserted reaches of southern California, certainly was. To complicate the situation even further, the man wore leg braces, which made her fear he might mistake the reason for her refusal. Eventually, however, they reached a tiny motel near Calexico; there they set up headquarters and were able at last to have separate rooms rather than sleeping on oily garage floors, as they had been doing along the way. Now Steinem had a phone to call the press, and the celebrities and political leaders who would attract the press. She ultimately put all the charges for motel rooms for the press, for food, and for phone calls on her American Express card, to the deep unhappiness of that company, which reacted by canceling her card for nonpayment.

She succeeded in attracting some celebrities and a good deal of press attention. Ted Kennedy came; John Tunney, the congressman from the district, who had been warned not to come because he did not support the boycott, came anyway. He was booed by the farmworkers, and also by Ted Kennedy, who enjoyed booing Tunney, his roommate at Harvard. Jerry Brown, then an unknown son of the governor of California, Pat Brown, came as well, although no one had invited him. The event was a big success, to Chavez's admiration. When the marchers met at the border, the rally on flatbed trucks was satisfactorily dramatic.

Chavez wrote to Steinem: "I want to thank you for all your hard work for us during the march from Coachella to Calexico. [I am told] that you did a fantastic job of press relations. . . . Our financial situation is very precarious and it is coming at a good time." Marion Moses recalled that Cesar could not get over what Steinem had accomplished all alone.

Steinem has continued to help the farmworkers, planning rallies and benefits; she joined Chavez in a benefit as late as 1992 and spoke at the grant rallies after his death in 1993. But Calexico was her last full-time effort on their behalf.

Moses, like Steinem, eventually burned out, though for different reasons. Although brought up a Catholic, and theoretically opposed to contraception and abortion, Moses saw the farmworker women bearing child after child. When a diabetic woman who had seven children and was suffering from hypertension begged for contraceptive pills, Marion gave them to her, acquiring the prescription from a doctor. She monitored the woman carefully, giving her the pills one month at a time. The woman's husband was outraged that she was having no more babies. Characteristically, so was Chavez when he heard about it; he had already objected to Moses having a doctor talk to the women about birth control. Moses stood her ground: To deny the woman birth control was not medicine but dogma. She told Chavez that either she used her judgment or she quit. She stayed.

But after five years as a nurse for the migrant workers, Moses was also exhausted, appalled at the effects of pesticides on her patients and at the lack of authority she had as a nurse rather than a doctor. She decided, at the age of thirty-six, to go to medical school; she had, in fact, always wanted to be a doctor, but her father had pressured her into nursing. In 1971 she went to Berkeley to take premed courses, and eventually became an M.D. Although she was, and remains, a friend and admirer of Steinem, Moses will not call herself a feminist. She has many reasons, among them her distaste for abortion (although she believes women should make their own choices in the matter) and her sense that housewives are ignored by the feminist movement. She had found Steinem's feminism "kind of extreme, likely to alienate people like me." While nursing for the farmworkers she didn't feel that the women had a worse time than the men; life was so bad for everybody. Fighting specifically for women's rights does not seem a large enough cause for Moses. This perspective is not an uncommon one among women who avoid identification as feminists.

Moses's feminist consciousness, however labeled, took a gigantic leap when she attended medical school. Here she found that the professor showed porno movies in class and made jokes about women. Moses complained to the professor, who said it lessened tension. She argued, but to no avail. She got up a petition, signed by the women students, objecting to this sort of behavior. The professor said Moses had to get men to sign, so she did. The battle was won.

Then, during the lectures on gynecology, the professor brought in a prostitute on whom to demonstrate gynecological examinations. His behavior was offensively salacious; Moses got up and walked out. She and four other women went to the dean's office. "Everyone was up in arms," Moses remembers. "I called Gloria, asking her to come and rescue me." Moses asked her to give a talk, legitimizing what the women had done. Everyone knew of Steinem, and the place was packed.

Moses has, like all of us, changed in many ways. "I used to think there was such a thing as sin," she says now. Because she saw the effects of pesticides on farmworkers, she has made it her lifework to disseminate information about pesticides and their impact on our lives. She now runs a private consultancy for environmental and occupational medicine in San Francisco, where she continues her vital fight.

Dolores Huerta, who was so valuable to the farmworkers and Chavez, had to contend with his disapproval of her personal life: She had eleven children with several different fathers and was not subordinate to one man. But she wholly subordinated herself to the cause and didn't change her views against feminism until the First National Women's Conference at Houston in 1977. She and her contingent of farmworkers went to demonstrate in support of the "right-to-lifers"; when she saw the extreme right-wingers who were supporting them, she changed her position, although she and Chavez had long supported the "right-to-life" movement. Huerta took a leave from the union to work for the Fund for the Feminist Majority office in California, fielding Chicana women candidates for state legislature. Huerta says it was Steinem's use of the term "reproductive freedom" that converted her, but Steinem believes it was Huerta's finding herself on the same side as the Klan and others that achieved her conversion. Both Moses and Huerta represent paths different from Steinem's to populism and feminism, whether or not they accepted—sooner, later, or never—that latter identification, as Huerta now does. After Chavez's death, Huerta went back to work for the union—this time as a feminist.

Peter Matthiessen, writing, of course, in the not-yet-enlightened 1960s, quotes Chavez on the subject of sugar beets: " '[They are] one crop I'm glad is automated. That was work for an animal, not a man. Stooping and digging all day, and the beets are *heavy*—oh that's brutal work. And then to go home to some little place, with all those kids, and hot and dirty—*that* is how a man is crucified, *Cru*-cified.' " [228] As the years went on and his union grew, Chavez changed his attitude toward feminists, fighters for choice, and homosexuals. By the late seventies it had become clear that these were the groups most willing to support his cause. But at the time of the march to Calexico, Steinem became impatient with his attitude toward women and came to realize that in helping him she was working for only the male half of Chavez's followers.

In the late 1960s her feminism caused Steinem to question raising money for a clinic to which women were forced to come on their knees begging for contraceptives, and to begin to aid the women directly instead. Her increasing intolerance of male attitudes, her disillusionment with Chavez's ignorance of women farmworkers' needs, her frustration with McGovern, Ribicoff, and the Democratic National Convention, culminated in the Mailer-Breslin mayoral contest, which would be the last of her male-centered campaigns.

AWAKENING

HOW DID GLORIA STEINEM evolve from a political columnist for *New York* magazine to the most famous feminist in the country, if not the world; and how was she so suddenly, as she thought, transformed into a feminist, and one who would never desert that cause? There are two strands to this question. One, biographical: What, at this late point, finally brought her to feminism? One, historical: What was feminism when she became, as it seemed, its instant media embodiment, and why did this happen?

History first.

A comprehensive history of so-called second-wave feminism in the last half of the twentieth century has yet to be written. The summary offered here relies almost entirely on those women who have recorded their experiences in or reflections on the development of feminism between the middle 1960s and 1972. This account is far from being even a synoptic history of the movement; yet, as an examination of the most thoughtful books and articles on the subject, it may nonetheless be useful in marking the state of feminism at the point where Steinem found herself cast as its "instant" spokeswoman.

From the beginning, there were two movements within the second wave. On the left was a group that coalesced during the civil rights and student antiwar movements of the 1960s. These movements were both entirely male-run and largely uninterested in the role of the women in their midst. As the early feminist Robin Morgan, editor of the influential anthology *Sisterhood Is Powerful,* summarized it, the line used against women was that if they were unsatisfied with their role, it was because something was wrong with *them.* This was, of course, the view of classical psychoanalysis and of its founder, Freud. When, as Morgan records, "women began to form caucuses within the Movement organizations where they worked, men's reactions ranged from fury to derision." When women demanded a plank on women in the SDS (Students for a Democratic Society) resolution, they were "pelted with tomatoes and thrown out of the convention." [xxi] Eventually, the women in SDS and in civil rights groups withdrew to form their own organizations, from which emerged what we might call the radical branch of the women's movement.

At about the same time, in 1966, a more moderate, centrist group came into being with the establishment of the National Organization for Women (NOW). Betty Friedan, who had published the powerful *The Feminine Mystique* three years earlier, was one of its founders. NOW was a largely upper-middle-class organization of women and men (it was the only early women's organization to have male members), working to bring women into the mainstream of American society on equal terms with men. In its early years NOW did much important work, especially in combating job discrimination. Aileen Hernandez, a member of the EEOC, resigned from that commission in protest against its failure to fight cases of sex discrimination. NOW backed Hernandez and elected her as its executive vice president; she became NOW's second president, succeeding Friedan.

Both groups of feminists supported consciousness-raising groups, although Friedan personally disapproved of them and NOW therefore supported them only much later after overwhelming demand. These intimate assemblies, in which women discovered that their problems were not singular but ubiquitous and widely shared, were the brushfires through which the conflagration of feminism spread with enormous speed. Consciousness-raising groups were first developed by the radical women, notably by Redstocking Kathie Sarachild, but they spread rapidly to less overtly political women as well, who were anything but radical—if "radical" means wishing profoundly to change society. Professional women, NOW, and Friedan wanted to enter American mainstream culture, not transform it.

The writer Ellen Willis, who joined a group called New York Radical Women in 1968, the key group involved in the historic Miss America demonstration of that year, describes their aims: "We argued that male supremacy was in itself a systemic form of domination—a set of material, institutionalized relations, not just bad attitudes. Men had power and privilege and like any other ruling class would defend their interest; challenging that power required a revolutionary movement of women." [*Sixties,* 93] Together with other radical women, Willis, who wrote for *Ms.* magazine for a time, later became a vociferous critic of Steinem.

Steinem did not take part in the radical women's movement until she attended the Redstockings speakout on abortion in 1969. It is important to note here that the Redstockings were an off-shoot of the New York Radical Women. When the Redstockings later reconstituted in 1975, led by Carol Hanisch and Kathie Sarachild, they would cause Steinem much grief. But in 1969, long out of college, Steinem was not active in any student group, and while she strongly supported the civil rights movement, most of her activism was on behalf of the farmworkers and the movement to end the war in Vietnam. Had she been earlier called upon to choose between the two branches of the emerging women's movement, doubtless she would have joined the radicals. But as it happened, while all these groups were in formation, she was earning a living and trying to find a voice in the almost wholly male-directed world of magazine publishing. Having nothing in common with the suburban college graduates of whom Friedan wrote, Steinem struggled on alone, not yet conscious of the pattern of oppression that would reveal itself to her in 1969.

In the eyes of the historian Alice Echols, "one of the most striking characteristics of 60s radicalism was its aversion to liberalism," [15] which radicals saw as being insufficiently strong on civil rights and opposition to the Vietnam War. Unfortunately, again to quote Echols, "the opposition to centralized organizations and hierarchy impeded organizational efficacy and efficiency." [17] Early radical feminism's major inefficiency arose from the attempt to counter the hierarchies it recognized as essential to the patriarchy. Jobs in any organization were assigned by lot, and any individual woman catching the attention of the media was denounced. As the political scientist Jo Freeman later explained, "because the movement had not chosen women to speak for it, believing that no one could, the media had done the choosing instead." A good example of this, Freeman points out, is Kate Millett, author of *Sexual Politics:*

> She and Shulamith Firestone [author of *The Dialectic of Sex*] both published the first new feminist theoretical books within a month of each other (September 1970). Through a combination of Millett's publisher (Doubleday), her own personal predisposition, and *Time* magazine's plan for a special movement issue to coincide with Women's Strike Day (August 26, 1970) her picture appeared on *Time*'s cover. This "established" her as the

first feminist spokeswoman after Friedan, and subjected her to very severe criticism from the movement. When she subsequently, at a feminist conference, publicly declared herself to be bisexual, *Time* announced that she was now discredited as a movement leader. No movement group had a role in either her ascendancy or dismissal. [*Time,* Dec. 14, 1970, p. 50] [120]

After the media attack on Millett for declaring her bisexuality, Steinem and others held a famous press conference in Millett's defense, throughout which Steinem held Millett's hand in support.

Freeman subsequently wrote two significant articles for *Ms.* on the problem the radical feminist movement had with allowing individual leadership to develop: "The Tyranny of Structurelessness," [July 1973] and "Trashing." [April 1976] Sara Evans, writing later, observed that "the lack of structure and responsible leadership led to a loss of internal coherence" [223] in the radical women's movement. In addition, by the early seventies, a further split had developed between the lesbian and heterosexual women in these groups.

NOW, under the direction of Friedan, had become notoriously antilesbian. As Freeman reports, in 1969 and 1970 Betty Friedan was trying to " 'purge' NOW of what she called the 'lavender menace.' " [99] Although Friedan, having driven many lesbians out of NOW, would later try to defuse this split, the sense persisted that NOW was antilesbian, white, upper-middle-class professional women, and fearful of antagonizing men. At this time also, Susan Brownmiller reported in a 1970 article for the *New York Times,* Friedan, after having tried to exclude lesbians, made another substantial mistake. Without question, the consciousness-raising group was the means by which feminism was catching on. But Friedan, who had attended by invitation one of the small group meetings, "went away," in Brownmiller's words, "convinced that her approach—and NOW's—was more valid. 'As far as I'm concerned, we're *still* the radicals,' she said emphatically. 'We raised our consciousness a long time ago. . . . The name of the game is confrontation and action.' " Friedan's intransigence early made a reconciliation with the radical side of the women's movement impossible. Of course, it might have been impossible in any case, but an important point was missed: consciousness-raising and the need for small support groups is a continuous process, not a one-time event.

Alice Echols has perceived another split: "In the terminology of today," she wrote in 1989, "radical feminists were typically social constructionists who wanted to render gender irrelevant, while cultural feminists were generally essentialists who sought to celebrate femaleness."[1][6] The split had been seen differently by Robin Morgan almost two decades earlier:

> NOW is essentially an organization that wants reform about the second-class citizenship of women—and this is where it differs drastically from the rest of the Women's Liberation Movement. Its composite membership (and remember the men) determines, of course, its politics, which are not radical. An ecumenical view (which I hold on alternate Tuesdays and Fridays) would see that such an organization is extremely valid and important; it reaches a certain constituency that is never going to be reached by [radical groups] and it does valuable work, as well. On certain Mondays and Thursdays, however, I fear for the women's movement's falling into precisely the same

---

[1] This "difference" has continued to this day in a slightly altered form. The so-called essentialists believe that women are inherently different from men and have much to offer society precisely because of their femaleness. Those opposing this view believe that women can never gain equality if they are regarded as essentially different from men. The middle ground sees women as different only in relation to reproduction and suggests that "female" characteristics are to a great extent those learned in the experience of oppression.

14. Clay Felker in 1977. He had started *New York* as an independent magazine and in 1972 helped to launch *Ms.* as an insert in *New York*.

15. Robert Benton, the first one to say: "Tell me a Toledo story."

16. A picture of the girlfriends of the *Esquire* editors, taken in the early sixties. Steinem is in the middle.

17. Jimmy Breslin, left, and Norman Mailer, conceding defeat in New York City's primary election for City Council candidate and mayor, June 18, 1969

18. Steinem speaking with Kate Millett at a meeting answering charges against Millett as a lesbian

19. Steinem at home with the cat Crazy Alice in the 1970s

20. Frank Thomas

21. Cesar Chavez and the farm workers, one of Steinem's major causes in the sixties

22. Steinem, on the road speaking with Dorothy Pittman Hughes

23. On the road with Margaret Sloan

24. On the road with Flo Kennedy

trap as did our foremothers, the suffragists: creating a bourgeois feminist movement that never quite dared enough, never questioned enough, never really reached out beyond its own class and race. [xxii]

History professor Hester Eisenstein, responding to Echols at the Berkshire Conference of Women Historians in 1990, suggested the importance, in talking about the legacy of radical feminism, of distinguishing between their "feminist analysis and their strategic contribution." Eisenstein feels that the attack of radical feminists on the family, marriage, love, normative heterosexuality, and American bourgeois values may turn out to be more significant than their failure to build a mass base for radical feminism.

It is also important to remember Jo Freeman's admonition that "it is a common mistake to try to place the various feminist organizations on the traditional left-right spectrum." Structure and style rather than ideology "more accurately differentiate the two groups. . . . Intramovement differences are often perceived by the participants as conflicting, but it is their essential complementarity that has been one of the strengths of the movement." [50, 51] Once the feminist movement was under way, women who might never have considered rebelling against their place in society became aware of their oppression. Without the movement they would not have done so; but the movement, radical or liberal, was no longer controlling or directing the awakening consciousness of such women.

The media, meanwhile, had been awakened to the women's movement by activities designed precisely to engage them: the disruption of the Miss America contest by the New York Radical Women in 1968; the invasion by Friedan and others upon the all-male Oak Room at the Plaza Hotel in 1969[2]; the women's march

---

[2] Although her feminist awakening was also acted out in the Plaza, Steinem was not there for the invasion of the Oak Room; she was put off by her own class prejudices,

in 1970 celebrating the passing of the Nineteenth Amendment, which gave women the vote.

The press sensed the gathering storm; what they lacked was a figure to represent feminism and to speak for it. Friedan was already familiar, associated with the reform movement aimed at college-educated women and men. As Brownmiller explained it in her *Times* article, "Friedan, the mother of the movement, and the organization that recruited in her image, were considered hopelessly bourgeois." Not only was Friedan bourgeois, she was only moderately appealing to stereotypical media tastes, and the radical feminists, as we have seen, had refused to allow a representative to emerge.

In Steinem's March 10, 1969 "City Politic" column, there is a final item that, within eleven days, would evolve into the single most significant moment in Steinem's life. The item reads, in full:

> Policemen resorted to the rather feminine tactic of hair-pulling today in order to get a group of very vocal women out of a meeting on Abortion Law Reform. The women, mostly under thirty, disrupted the meeting in fine style, wanting to know why there was only one woman called to testify ("and she's a *nun*"), and why the abortion laws weren't just repealed, instead of compromising on reforms.
>
> Florynce Kennedy, a lawyer and black militant at whose name strong white men shake, went into her specialty—creating a newsworthy side show to call attention to a good cause. "Listen," she said cheerfully. "Why don't we shoot a New York State legislator for every woman who dies from an abortion?"

---

finding the Oak Room too elite for feminist attentions. As she recounted in *Revolution from Within,* her own encounter with the Plaza was far from upper-class: Sometime in the late sixties, she was asked by an assistant manager to leave the Palm Court of the Plaza (where she was to interview an actor) because a woman alone was considered a prostitute; later that same year at the Plaza, she seized the opportunity to tell that assistant manager off; such was the fast-changing difference in consciousness.

The sixties were almost over before Steinem found herself, like so many others, wholly transformed by them. In 1969, Steinem attended the abortion hearing organized by the Redstockings and underwent her conversion to feminism, recognizing at last the explanation for all the attitudes toward women she had endured and witnessed.

There is clear evidence that even a year earlier Steinem was coming to understand feminism, even if she could not yet name it; certainly she revealed this in her 1968 *New York Times* review of Caroline Bird's *Born Female*. "Since I became . . . a professional writer," Steinem began,

> people have been asking me on the average of once a week if this sort of work isn't more difficult for women than for men. And once a week, I have been answering no, of course not; it's just the same. Equal rights were won by our grandmothers in a necessary, but rather quaint revolution, or so I was told in college. Besides, it seemed unfeminine to complain.
>
> Caroline Bird's very serious and heartfelt book has convinced me that I was wrong to trust self-righteous teachings of the fifties and wrong to dissemble about observations of my own. . . . In fact, women who write, like Negroes who write, are supposed to be specialists on themselves, and little else. Newspapers and magazines are generous with assignments on fashion, beauty and childbirth. (Would men like to write about hunting, shaving, and paternity?) But scientific or economic or political stories have a way of gravitating somewhere else. The rule Henry Luce invented 30 years ago still applies: . . . women research, men write.

It was at this stage in the history of the movement and in Steinem's own personal history that she was brought into a fateful, and perhaps inevitable, collision with feminism.

And so it happened that Steinem attended the speakout on

abortion organized by Redstocking leader Kathie Sarachild, an occasion, she would later say, that turned her into a feminist on the instant. As she would later write in *Outrageous Acts,* "It wasn't until I went to cover a local abortion hearing for *New York* that the politics of my own life began to explain my interests. . . . Suddenly, I was no longer learning intellectually what was wrong. I knew. Why should each of us [who had had an abortion] be made to feel criminal and alone?"

She understood the central passion of that meeting, and expressed it in her "City Politic" column: "Nobody wants to reform the abortion laws; they want to repeal them." Brownmiller, in her *New York Times* account written shortly after the abortion speakout, is again valuable in placing the speakout Steinem attended in an historical context:

> Redstockings made its first public appearance at the New York legislative hearing on abortion law reform in February, 1969, when several women sought to gain the microphone to testify about their own abortion. The hearing, set up to take testimony from 15 medical and psychiatric "experts"—14 were men—was hastily adjourned. The following month, Redstockings held its own abortion hearing at the Washington Square Methodist Church. Using the consciousness-raising technique, 12 women "testified" about abortion, from their own personal experience, before an audience of 300 men and women.

Steinem has described her feelings at the abortion speakout as "the great blinding lightbulb" that suddenly illuminated a previously dark room. Women spoke personally; they trusted those hearing them. She, who had kept her abortion, however legal, a guilty secret, now heard that she was not alone.

All the humiliations of being a woman, from political assignments lost to less-experienced male writers to "a lifetime of journalists' jokes about frigid wives, dumb blondes, and farmers' daughters that I had smiled at in order to be one of the boys" suddenly sharpened into focus, their meaning revealed. She, who considered her women friends the most stable and important element in her life—women like Barbara Nessim, Jane O'Reilly, and the wives of some of the men she worked with, like Shirley Glaser —had conversed with such friends mainly about the logistics of making their way in a difficult, male-crowded profession. Jane O'Reilly, for example, was always funny and perceptive and a good writer. But Steinem spoke with her mostly to share lists of friendly editors and to help in finishing up pieces of writing. As Steinem put it:

> That was the worst of it, of course—my own capitulation to all the small humiliations, and my own refusal to trust an emotional understanding of what was going on, or even to trust my own experience. For instance, I had believed that women couldn't get along with one another, even while my own most trusted friends were women. I had agreed that women were more "conservative" even while I identified emotionally with every discriminated-against group. I had assumed that women were sexually "masochistic" even though I knew that trust and kindness were indispensable parts of my sexual attraction to any man. It is truly amazing how long we can go on accepting myths that oppose our own lives, assuming instead that we are the odd exceptions. But once the light began to dawn, I couldn't understand why I hadn't figured out any of this before. [*OAER*, 19]

The answer, or one answer among others, is that women situated as Steinem was, in a largely male world, spoke to other women less to exchange experiences and frustrations than to help one another to negotiate with powerful men, navigate in their world, find the way among the reefs and shoals. Even though the effect of the abortion speakout was overwhelming, she did not then report either her own reactions or her own story. Still mired in the masculine reportorial ideal of the reporter who never speaks in the first person, she maintained, correctly as she thought, a cool and impersonal objectivity in her "City Politic" article:

> I researched as much as I could about reproductive issues and other wellsprings of a new feminism and wrote a respectable, objective article (not one *I* in the whole thing) called "After Black Power, Women's Liberation." It contained none of the emotions I had felt in that church basement, and certainly not the fact that I, too, had an abortion. (Though hearing those women had made me free to say it for the first time, I still thought that writers were more credible when they concealed their personal experience. I had a lot to learn.) But I did predict that if these younger, more radical women from the peace and civil rights movements could affect what were then the middle-class reformists of the National Organization for Women, and join with poor women already organizing around welfare and child care, a long-lasting and important mass movement would result.

All this, if a mite optimistic, certainly recaptures her emotions and her sense of women as a caste confined by the patriarchy to certain actions they could only pretend to condone, and feelings they could not freely express. Yet conversions do not appear out of nowhere; the light that suddenly blinds, shocking one into stunning recognition, has long been prepared for, and does not instantaneously alter one's entire life. Steinem was accurate and sincere in identifying the beginning of her conversion story: we all, in transforming our lives into narrative, seek for the beginning that will get our story properly under way. But even while we (mostly men) cherish the (always masculine) story of how a man—Gauguin, Sherwood Anderson—one day walked out the door and never came back, leaving his family to fend as best they could, the lives of women rarely contain such sudden moments of departure. Irving Howe, for example, has written a now-famous passage about Thomas Hardy's *Mayor of Casterbridge,* the novel which opens with a man selling his wife to a sailor:

> To shake loose from one's wife; to discard that drooping rag of a woman, with her mute complaints and maddening passivity; to escape her not by a slinking abandonment but through the public sale of her body to a stranger, as horses are sold at a fair; and then to wrest, through sheer amoral willfulness, a second chance out of life . . . [it is this stroke which is] so insidiously attractive to male fantasy. [Irving Howe, *Thomas Hardy.* New York: Collier Books, 1966, p. 84]

This male fantasy of abandoning an old life for a freer, more ranging existence, is, apparently, close to ubiquitous. It is notable that Howe felt no compunction about writing this terrible paragraph, nor did any male critic comment on it. It was only well into the 1980s that the "attractiveness" of this male fantasy was held up to the light by newly created feminists. The male narrative of sudden conversion and the sudden dropping of all else to follow the light—these male dreams of immediate escape must have suggested to Steinem that her conversion to feminism dropped out of nowhere, giving her a name for all the humiliations she had suffered and the deceptions of herself she had unknowingly practiced. Women's stories have been learned from male accounts. But for women, in fact, life's changes are not so sudden, nor so instantly freeing. Their commitments and relationships—even those that ought not, perhaps, to have been entered upon in the first place—continue as women, likelier than not, continue to honor them.

So, soon after that abortion speakout, after she had at last a name for what women undergo and themselves orchestrate, her life went on for a time much as before.

In those months when her feminist awareness was in its last stages of ripening, Steinem indeed seems to have allowed herself to be tossed hither and yon, to give in to her maverick impulses, almost as though to convince herself that whatever the boys dreamed up—the 1968 convention, the farmworkers' efforts—it wasn't likely to change much for the female half of the population.

And so, two weeks after the Redstockings speakout, she was still embroiled in the last of the macho radical events in which she became involved: the Mailer-Breslin primary election campaign in New York City in the spring of 1969. Norman Mailer, promoter of the view that a writer could do without anything but "balls," and Jimmy Breslin, a newspaper columnist and old acquaintance of Steinem's, had decided to shake up New York City politics by running for the Democratic nominations for mayor and president of the City Council.

Mailer was running on a ticket of making New York the fifty-first state, and wanted Jimmy Breslin as his running mate to complete the slogan "Vote the Rascals In." Breslin was reluctant and urged Steinem to keep him company in this semiserious effort by running for comptroller. This campaign, like the larger one culminating in Chicago, was a wholly male affair, but Steinem was swept up into it without, it seems, actually considering what she was getting into. In Steinem's first article on the subject, "The Making (and Unmaking) of a Comptroller," she describes her involvement in their campaign: "[H]aving got interested in the idea of running Norman Mailer for mayor and Jimmy Breslin for city council president as a way to keep rigor mortis from setting into our brains before the Democratic primary . . . I found my-self temporarily nominated to run for comptroller of the City of New York."

Steinem's lack of qualifications for the position of comptroller are so obvious as to be ludicrous, if only slightly more so than her attraction to the whole campaign in the first place. As she put it, "Standing up to give a whole speech unaided is the stuff of night-mares. As for answering hostile questions . . ." Well, her run-ning was clearly beyond consideration and it didn't take her long to extricate herself from the role of candidate. What she didn't report in *New York* is that she agreed to help with the campaign to make up for deciding not to run on the ticket, a characteristic Steinem guilt reaction: Having once said yes, however offhand-edly, she could not find the courage to say no. She says now, without too much conviction, that Mailer and Breslin's running was so unlikely a phenomenon that it appealed to her on that score alone. It was also about being smart; Mailer was a smart person. She liked their slogans: "The other guys are the bad guys"; "Make New York the 51st State." And, most important, all three knew one another from journalism. As she later explained, "I did it for Jimmy"; she was very fond of Breslin, a fondness that no doubt prevented her from completely escaping this imbroglio.

To say that the whole caper was sexist is understatement twice compounded, which makes Steinem's involvement the more astonishing. Indeed, it was partly to extricate herself from the campaign that she welcomed Chavez's predawn phone calls from California asking her to organize press coverage for the Calexico march: Committed to the march, she did not—despite the fact that she saw clearly enough that she was, in working for Chavez, working mainly for men—abandon the farmworkers. Although, by Steinem's account a lightbulb had gone on with a blinding light, it did not immediately blind her to her prelightbulb obliga-tions, and its effect was, for a short period, diffused.

Joe Flaherty, who was the manager of the campaign and who wrote an authoritative if strictly patriarchal book about it, *Managing Mailer,* ended with this triumphant howl: "Even though it was a party from which we didn't get to take home the girl, I'm glad I attended. . . . Mailer and Breslin went out and had 'a dubious fuck with that mean woman,' the city of New York." [222] Flaherty's description of an early meeting in Steinem's house neatly sets the scene:

> On Sunday evening, April 6, Steinem held a meeting at her apartment in the East Seventies. The decor of her study, where we gathered, is a mass of ideological contradictions. It is wall-papered in a black and white zebra pattern similar to the motif of that bastion of decadent capitalism, the El Morocco [in fact a blue and white old-fashioned flame stitch], interrupted by posters of Che Guevara and Cesar Chavez. . . . Above a photograph of Robert Kennedy with his unruly hair is hung a collection of matched earrings in precise flight formation. The earrings were to provide the last semblance of order I was to witness that night. The meeting then moved into her living room—large, attractive, painted a warm yellow, and furnished with those spartan chairs that are rewards for the adherents of Ry-Krisp and Metrecal.

And so on. As Flaherty recounts, it soon became clear that Mailer was scarcely satisfactory on the subject of women's rights. There were endless arguments about getting a woman or a black person—Steinem suggested African-American feminist lawyer Flo Kennedy—to run for comptroller, but in the end the attempt to have a "balanced" ticket, in the old political mode, was abandoned. As Steinem wrote in a column after the fact, she got off on the wrong foot "by trying to explain why women's political groups won't support [Mailer]. His mystical resistance to birth control and to repeal of the abortion laws seems unrealistic, especially to poor women. He thinks about that for a while. Legal abortion, he decides, is preferable to birth control. 'At least that way, women know they're murderers.' I silently write off the women's groups, and wonder if the whole thing is worth it." To anyone else it would have been obvious that it wasn't.

What, in fact, was the Mailer-Breslin platform, apart from making the city work better by giving more power to communities? Most dramatically, they proposed to make New York, and adjacent parts of New Jersey and Connecticut, into a separate state. This city-state area, Steinem reported, sent $322 billion to Washington every year, while the city staggered along on a budget of $6.6 billion, only 15 percent of which was money that had found its way back from Washington.[3] The candidates' idea for a public monorail running around the edge of Manhattan, with jitneys going across the island and (as in Venice) no cars allowed, appealed to Steinem and others. In one of her columns Steinem railed, as did Mailer and Breslin in their campaign, against the preposterous, Kafkaesque requirements for legal petitions to be on the ballot, involving "such big issues as pencil instead of pen, green ink instead of black, 'St.' instead of 'Street.' " [May 16, 1969] Like so much that the campaign wanted to change, this undemocratic device for keeping the incumbents in and the challengers out is, today, still functioning.

In order to raise money, those who worked for the Mailer-Breslin effort agreed to contribute articles to a book, the advance for which helped finance the campaign. (The book, edited by Peter Manso and entitled *Running Against the Machine,* appeared in 1969.) Even when Steinem was in California on the Calexico

[3] As recently as January 1995, Mayor Rudolph Giuliani was quoted by *New York Times* reporter Sam Roberts as saying that "from an intellectual analysis, if New York [City] were a 51st state, New York would not have a budget deficit."

march, she kept in touch with many of those contributors, particularly those women in New York who could run Mailer-Breslin fund-raisers.[4] Her sense of women as outsiders in all these processes increased daily.

Flaherty sums up Mailer's race for the mayorality thus: "It would be hard to think of any campaign, except Napoleon's last, that ended in such disaster." [199] One of the campaign buttons read "No More Bullshit," and it became clear that "bullshit" was more or less the byword of the campaign. When, for example, they finally got television time, Steinem reported to Flaherty that "CBS said they would have a lawyer in the sound booth, and at the first hint of a 'fuck' coming from Mailer's mouth he was going to pull a switch that would produce total blackness on the home screens." [209]

What Flaherty could not record, and what no one has known till now, is that Mailer had made it endlessly clear that his manhood could not survive if he didn't have sex with Steinem, in whom he had been expressing interest since taking her out for dinner on what he later confessed had been his fortieth birthday. Now, six years later, she consented, either because of fatigue or because of the nonfeminist kindness that gives out "mercy fucks." But Mailer, in this campaign as in the one for mayor, wasn't up to it. Steinem charitably suggests that his trouble may have been too much alcohol; *her* trouble, clearly, was letting herself feel sorry for a man who showed little such concern for the welfare of women. Pity for the delicate male ego is inbred and internalized even in one who would soon become outstandingly feminist. The whole campaign, in fact, could be summed up as a triumphant, failed example of the "fuck 'em" concept of life.

The ultimate irony of this altogether ironic primary campaign

---

[4] The feminist writer Linda Francke's humorous account of her part in organizing these fund-raisers appears in *Running Against the Machine*.

was that both right-wing candidates won their respective party nominations: John Marchi narrowly defeated John Lindsay for the Republican nomination, and Mario Procaccino nosed out Robert Wagner and Herman Badillo in the Democratic race. The two winners then split the conservative vote in the general election and allowed Mayor John Lindsay to be reelected on the Liberal party ticket with only 42 percent of the vote. If Mailer had not run, the 41,000 votes he received in the primary could conceivably have given either Badillo or Wagner the nomination. In that case two liberals would have been competing on the left, and the very conservative Mario Procaccino might have been elected instead of the liberal Lindsay. Flaherty discounts the possibility, but it remains one of those intriguing might-have-beens.

It is a fact that the Mailer-Breslin campaign tried to raise some important points; it may have awakened some New Yorkers to conditions they were aware of, or unaware that they could affect. No doubt there never was the hope or desire to win, but Flaherty suggests that a combination of Mailer's bad manners and lost opportunities made the result worse than it otherwise might have been. Also inevitable was Steinem's realization that she had come to the end of a road. Once the farmworkers and the Mailer-Breslin campaign were behind her, she would never again work for any group, small or large, that did not place women at the center of its revolutionary or reform aims. Men might be with women there, but women must, in all the years to follow, be at its center if Steinem was to labor on any organization's behalf.

BEFORE HER OWN final conversion to movement activism, Steinem had at last achieved the right to be a political commentator. But she was not allowed to write about feminism; not, at least without editors—and Clay Felker was one of these—insisting on running an article condemning feminism alongside so as to have both sides of the story. Sometimes editors of women's magazines would tell her they'd already published their feminist article for that year. Even the mild things Steinem published made editors angry. And when she finally started to write about overtly feminist issues, she was taken aside by her fellow reporters, all men, and told not on any account to let herself be identified with those "crazies."

One of the rewards for investing in *New York* was to have its writers at one's dinner table. Steinem recalls attending one such dinner at the home of investor Armane Erpf, chairman of the *New York* board. During this dinner anthropologist Lionel Tiger waxed on about how women couldn't be effective in political life because they couldn't bond, and journalist Gail Sheehy agreed that women had "labial personalities." Steinem felt unwilling to argue with another woman for the entertainment of the table, and her anger manifested itself as tears at the back of her throat. She left as soon as she could without making a scene; neither then or later did she welcome confrontation, but not for long would she stay at *New York* to be baited by this sort of male presumption and female division. As her feminist convictions solidified, her sense of belonging at *New York* and other male bastions began to fade; she began to feel that she had lost a home there as well. Ironically, however, it was through her "City Politic" columns that Steinem, in June 1969, would meet Dorothy Pitman, the woman with whom she would speak on feminism from 1970 on.

Steinem chose Dorothy Pitman's pioneering child-care center on the multiracial West Side of Manhattan as the subject of her column "Room at the Bottom, Boredom on Top," and produced what had become the characteristic Steinem piece: unlimited praise for all the good guys—Pitman, various New York foundations that had somehow been persuaded to give a pittance (by foundation standards) but whose stamp of respectability counted for even more; a woman from the West Side who was impressed by the center's refusal to take her two-year old because she wasn't a "working mother" (this woman eventually underwrote the mortgage for a new building, empty but in need of extensive renovation); and a man named Bob Gangi who came to the center by way of the Kennedy Action Corps, a group of young people doing community work, carrying on the spirit of the recently assassinated Robert Kennedy. Gangi, whom Steinem admired, had been let go from a city-run shelter for taking the part of the "clients"—that is, the children—against the administration. It was he who, before Steinem had met Pitman, persuaded her to cover the center. A storefront child center was news of the sort that reverberated with Steinem, and with her own column she could take it on, even though Clay Felker didn't okay the assignment.

Steinem had a good time with the city health code's twenty-page section on day-care centers. She reported that a number of prominent businessmen considered the code to be the greatest single obstacle to the development of such centers. Some regulations were necessary, of course, but the kind dreamed up by people who have never cared for a child all day were another matter. Private builders and developers bribed inspectors to evade codes; those who were both poor and honest struggled with the exaggerated demands.

While she was gathering material for her article, she, Pitman, and Gangi were all sitting on little chairs and eating peanut-butter-and-jelly sandwiches from paper plates. Gangi remarked that the woman he loved wouldn't marry him because he wouldn't let her work after they were married. "Dorothy and I," Steinem remembered, "looked at each other, and connected on this, even though we didn't know each other. We went to work on him, showing how his feelings about class could be connected to his feelings about women." They convinced him; he married the woman, she kept her job; and they are still married. Steinem's career as a persuader for the rights of women was well under way. When she received speaking invitations she was too fearful to accept alone, she thought that she and Dorothy Pitman as a team might persuade others.

Steinem helped Pitman when she organized a sit-in in order to bring attention to the mothers and children who were occupying a dilapidated welfare hotel where a child had been killed in an elevator shaft. Pitman took the occupants to the Human Resources Administration offices, where they sat-in for ten days without results. Steinem went to the HRA to interview Pitman, and during this time several busloads of policeman and three fire trucks pulled up and set off a smoke bomb in the Chemical Bank below the HRA, forcing the occupants to vacate the building. Pitman took the women and children across the street to another city building. Steinem, Jule Sugarman, one of the founders of Head Start, and Frank Thomas were able to galvanize public support, and within a few days, housing was found.

Steinem was one of the first white women Dorothy Pitman was able or willing to be friends with. Toledo sounded not unlike Pitman's hometown of Lumpkin, Georgia. "As I talked to Gloria," Dorothy Pitman Hughes remembers, "I started to see comradeship between my blackness and my femaleness, an expansion; when Gloria and I could say we think alike—she came from Toledo, I came from Georgia—I saw that connection was not tied together by race as much as by feminism. At that point I began to understand some of what was happening to children, and women's burden, through feminism. I started to organize parenting differently: a responsibility of the men as well; partners in the care of the child. Exciting to me: I understood friendship in a different way with a white female. In Georgia, I never had anything to do with being friends with a white; I would almost have to be born again, to do that in Georgia." Steinem also remembers Pitman's stories of her New York arrival, particularly of working for a woman who asked her to walk the dog. "In Georgia," Pitman told the woman, "dogs walk themselves."

IN SEPTEMBER 1969, Steinem went to Washington to speak at the Women's National Democratic Club on the subject of her column "After Civil Rights—Women's Liberation." The WNDC event was Steinem's first major speaking engagement, and she was terrified—in what she called a "catatonic state." She told Sally Quinn of the *Washington Post* that she almost offered the group a thousand dollars to let her off.

Barbara Howar, the well-known Washington hostess, threw a party in Steinem's honor after the speech, which Quinn, writing in the *Washington Post,* described as "the most diverse gathering of party-goers in town." It was at this party that Steinem was photographed with Henry Kissinger, leading to the still widely held impression that they were romantically involved. The photograph was actually taken of Steinem with Kissinger on one side of her and McGovern on the other, but McGovern was cropped when the picture appeared with Quinn's article and elsewhere. (Kissinger later told Steinem that when the Nixons saw the photograph, Pat Nixon said with some disapproval, "Henry, can't you do better than that?") A reporter from the *New York Times* called to ask her if the picture meant she and Kissinger were an item, and Steinem, hoping to be witty, said: "I am not now nor have I ever been a girlfriend of Henry Kissinger." She was astonished, upon opening the *Times* the next morning, to see that this remark was the "Quote of the Day." That picture and the rumors it produced would haunt Steinem ever after. As late as 1992, for

example, a letter to the *Women's Review of Books* criticized
Steinem for "dating" Kissinger.

While Steinem and Kissinger never dated, the story of their
acquaintance is an amusing one. After Steinem wrote "In Your
Heart You Know He's Nixon," [Oct. 28, 1968] Kissinger, whom
Steinem knew by reputation only, called to praise it, and told her
that Robert Kennedy was his political hero. (The question of why
Kissinger changed is an apposite one. The two possibilities offered
are either that he grew more right-wing, or that he always told
people what he thought they wanted to hear.) At this time he was
still a professor at Harvard, and so, he told Steinem, he was in-
trigued by the question of who from Harvard could go to work
for the Nixon administration. Schlesinger clearly could not, as it
would be seen as a betrayal of his constituency. Others might go,
but Kissinger would not unless his mentor Nelson Rockefeller
did; he could consider going to help Rockefeller, but that was the
only situation under which he could imagine going to Washington, and he would, in any case, stay no more than a year or two to
help get Rockefeller established in what he assumed would be his
important Nixon-appointed job. As he put it, the basic question
was the well-known dilemma of whether you went to make a bad
regime better, or whether you stayed away and didn't cosmeticize
the regime, but didn't get anything done. Kissinger described this
as the collaborationist's problem, a phrase that captured Steinem's
imagination.

She asked him, therefore, to write an article called "The Collaborationist's Problem" for *New York*. He accepted the assignment, and as far as Steinem knew was still working on it when he
called her up to say that he didn't know how to tell her, but he
had after all decided to work for Nixon.

Steinem went to dinner once in Washington with Kissinger,
and visited him in his White House office after a peace demonstration, hoping that she might be able to influence his thinking

about the war.[5] It was at this dinner that he told her about Pat Nixon's reaction to the picture. Later Kissinger himself, in response to a coy note from a colleague, wrote that he had always admired Gloria Steinem. She was not his girlfriend.

Steinem now says of Kissinger that those rumors flew about him in part because he was the only single man in Nixon's cabinet or in Washington's upper reaches. Her final analysis of him is that, as a refugee, he was overly grateful to this country—thus not willing to criticize it—and even more, he was too respectful of authority.

AT THE END of 1969, Steinem wrote an article for *Look* entitled "Why We Need a Woman President in 1976," which appeared on January 13, 1970. Her optimism was extraordinary, reflecting the way feminists felt in the early years of commitment. "Surely a woman in the White House is not an impossible feminist cause," Steinem concluded in her *Look* article. "It's only a small step in the feminist revolution." Such naïveté seems remarkable now, but the hope was palpable then, and for much of the seventies. For the first time in print, Steinem spoke for all the women she had known who hadn't been allowed to become what they had in them to become. She mentions the overwhelming sense of waste, the unfairness, the ubiquity of the discrimination. Writing wasn't enough. Like Paul after his vision on the road to Damascus, but like him in no other way, she decided to go forth and speak, to spread the message. Her paralyzing fear of speaking would have to be overcome.

It would help, of course, if she could speak with another

---

[5] Steinem took a rather long time to understand that some people could not be influenced on such matters; the war was then on everybody's mind, and she would always be, perhaps naively, hopeful.

woman. And the woman she chose to speak with, and who chose to speak with her, was black. Steinem, learning fast after her conversion, observed that the movement was in danger of becoming, or solidifying as, a white, upper-middle-class movement, given the composition of both NOW and the consciousness-raising groups of radical women in New York, where the media was focusing. That white women in Toledo factories and black welfare women were also organizing was getting lost. She did her best to counter that danger, while claiming only that she needed someone to speak with if she was to overcome her terror. She admired Pitman. And, after all, together they had convinced Bob Gangi. In early 1970, they set out on the road.

Steinem, now a committed feminist, was working at full throttle for what she would always call "the movement." She and Dorothy Pitman, soon Hughes, began to speak all over the country about women and their rights and problems. Reflecting their own racism, reporters would ask Steinem about feminism and Hughes about civil rights, as if the latter were not also a woman, and the former had no concern with civil rights. Though the two objected to this pattern, it often turned up in news stories. Part of their motive in speaking around the country was to reach people not yet awakened to feminism, or unaware of how that new movement might affect their lives, and also to attract diverse audiences outside New York, especially in the South. Steinem tried to avoid being identified as feminism's spokeswoman, but the media knew news when they saw it, particularly if the news looked like her.

Clay Felker and *New York* provide a useful barometer of the shifting attitudes within the popular media. Felker remembers that in 1968 Abby Rockefeller and others around Cambridge, Massachusetts, were sponsoring a weekend devoted to teaching women self-defense skills. This was well before "women's lib" had been noticed as a movement in Felker's world. He says he asked Steinem if she wanted to go cover the story and that she refused; Steinem has no memory of being asked. In any case Julie Baumgold, who Felker recalls as a rather conservative person, was sent instead. Baumgold wrote a hostile article, which was featured on the cover of the magazine, with a trick photograph of a woman model with long hair and a man's muscular arm. The caption read, "You've come a long way, baby," a slogan that was to cause Steinem grief during the *Ms.* years. But in spite of this ridicule, in Felker's world, as he would later observe, the idea of feminism was simply too powerful not to be effective. "I watched women become radicalized," he says; "our consciousness was raised very rapidly."

For those women who were coming out of the left to organize the feminist movement, and to Betty Friedan, Steinem seemed, as she was and has always admitted to being, a late arrival on the scene. That she was also the one the media anointed because she was "feminine"—an adjective Steinem had used in her column on the abortion hearing to describe policemen pulling hair, but would never use again—glamorous, and, as Felker emphasized, nonthreatening was to cause a good deal of ill feeling among feminists who had arrived earlier, pledging their lives, their fortunes, and their sacred honor when the movement was young. These women certainly didn't have a Steinem in mind when they set out to attract media attention.

Whether, in time, feminists came to consider Steinem a good or bad thing depended, to a large extent, on where they came from and where they hoped to go. The aura of frivolity would never leave her, no matter how fundamental her allegiance. But that same aura would reassure millions of women teetering on the edge of feminism that one did not have to eschew elegance or "femininity," or, above all, men, to be for "women's lib." The fear of lesbianism had already taken hold. The number of intelligent women who harbored that fear is greater than most of us like to imagine. Steinem's very existence, although she fought as ardently for gay rights as for the rights of any other oppressed group, still assuaged the fear of lesbianism when it threatened the wider movement. This was not her aim; quite the contrary. But it was the result. She did a great deal more than that for the movement, but her appeal to the media, however much it compromised structureless feminism on the one hand, and challenged Friedan's upper-middle-class feminism on the other, went a long way toward keeping the feminist cause in the forefront of the national consciousness.

Steinem never deserted feminism, never betrayed it, never suggested it needed to backpedal, never let anyone in the media get away with jeering at it. She remained, as everyone noticed, full of allure. She also remained, through long, hard, slogging years, an outspoken, uncompromising, boundary-crossing feminist.

M S .

UNTIL 1970, Steinem was seen as an intriguing combination: a career girl, a journalist—she actually had a byline (sometimes even wrote about serious subjects!) and met famous people. Cute, isn't she? It writes articles, it earns its living, it's a girl! By the end of 1971, the "girl" had become a representative of the women's movement and was speaking about the rights of all women, regardless of race, class, national origin, or sexual preference. The tone of the articles on Steinem changed.

An *Esquire* article in October of that year was characteristic of the response of the press. Entitled "She"—perhaps after the famous Victorian novel by H. Rider Haggard—the purpose of Leonard Levitt's article was to account for Steinem's fame by an analysis of her effect on men. He tried to transform her from a successful feminist activist to a "femme fatale"—"No man who seeks to know how the wind blows can afford to ignore Gloria, the intellectuals' pinup. . . ." Indeed, to him she appeared fatal.

While Clay Felker had told Levitt, as he told many others, that Steinem's appeal lay in the simple fact that she was not "threatening," to Levitt she was clearly fearsome, because to her allure, brains, and magnetism she had added a monstrous factor: power. When Felker spoke of Steinem as nonthreatening, he meant that in the context of the then acceptable and expected male-female relations, she didn't argue unduly; didn't frighten men with her brains; didn't disturb their sense of their own masculinity, however firmly or unfirmly established. She wasn't, in the lingo of the day, a "ball-breaker" or a "penis-envier." It was one thing to have been nonthreatening to individual men before the women's movement; once the movement was under way, it was quite another to suggest that men as a group move over and share their power with women.

But in truth, Steinem threatened the patriarchy more than New York congresswoman Bella Abzug or Betty Friedan ever could. These two, married and mothers though they were, could be undermined by the oldest patriarchal trick: to challenge their dominion as sex objects. As for early black feminists, from Celestine Ware—author of *Woman Power: The Movement for Women's Liberation* (Tower, 1970) one of the earliest books to discuss the connections between the current women's movement and Black Power—to Shirley Chisholm, they were lumped together with the civil rights movement as threatening, but in a different way: not everyone had one at home or next door—as all men had women. That didn't work with Steinem. She became, like Haggard's She, a terrifying spectacle. Indeed, Levitt's article is subtitled "The Awesome Power of Gloria Steinem."

Susan Gubar and Sandra Gilbert, in their groundbreaking three-volume study of modernism and gender, *No Man's Land,* describe She as also the possessor of awesome power: "She Herself, therefore, turns out to be an interesting cross between Venus and Persephone. As Venus, for instance, She commands the absolute erotic devotion of any man who looks upon Her unveiled. . . . But even swathed in ghostly white, She has the Circean power of transforming human males into animals." [15] In this study of male fear of females' growing power at the turn of the twentieth century, Gilbert and Gubar illuminate the extent to which a sexually vibrant woman, claiming power, becomes threatening in just the way Levitt's article illustrates. But the article succeeded, as was Levitt's intention, in causing a good deal of misery to Steinem and others. It also marked the culmination of Steinem's transformation from a smart, sexy woman journalist to a media symbol of feminism and women's demand for change.

In August of that year *Newsweek* had featured her on its cover for a special report entitled "The New Woman." Steinem, trying to draw attention away from herself and to the movement, refused to pose for a cover photo: *Newsweek*'s photographer had to shoot the picture secretly through a telephoto lens at a welfare rights rally. In addition to her career, the *Newsweek* article merely continued to emphasize her looks and her men: Guinzberg, Desmond, Nichols; there was a picture of her with Rafer Johnson. It is worth recalling that in those years when the press ignored the sexual activity of the president of the United States—every newsman knew about John Kennedy's compulsive womanizing—and years before Gary Hart, running for president in 1988, would be caught out as an unrepentant philanderer, women's sex lives were open season. Similarly their bodies. The man in charge of the *Newsweek* article—who, like many journalists knew and admired Steinem—wrote to apologize, just as the *Time* writer had a few years earlier.

The three young women "researchers" who worked on the *Newsweek* article—all the writing was done by men—leave a rare picture in their notes of the impression she made at that time. These three were sent out to cover what their magazine referred to as "the amorphous, revolutionary state of mind known as women's liberation" and its "unlikely guru, journalist Gloria Steinem, who is pursuing that role against the handicaps of her own beauty, chic, celebrity and professional success." [Aug. 16, 1971] Looking back, one is tempted to conclude that between August and October, when the *Esquire* article appeared, the "handicaps" of Steinem's beauty had turned into the threat of Steinem's beauty, as Haggard understood it.

Betty Friedan was not yet taking overt swipes at Steinem, but her comments to the researchers were emblematic of the way she and her followers would characterize Steinem from then on. "Gloria has not advanced any new ideas in the women's movement—but she's an outstanding publicist." Decades later, Friedan's friends still refer to Steinem as the "missionary" of the women's movement, with Friedan as its "founder." This judgment is based on the fact that Friedan had written a highly influential book, while Steinem had later gone about speaking. Friedan's nomenclature was probably adopted in an attempt to minimize Steinem's importance to the movement, even as that importance swelled. The word "missionary" is, however, ill-conceived, since missionaries spread the teaching of their church, and Friedan's teachings were far removed from Steinem's message. In addition, Steinem did understand that sexism and racism were related caste systems, that heterosexism is part of the patriarchy as well as a critique of the patriarchy itself. Steinem's recognition of the necessity of unity with African-American women and lesbians in the movement was certainly a new idea to Friedan; also Steinem's understanding of class, learned in East Toledo, was not that of the *Feminine Mystique,* learned in the suburbs.

Flo Kennedy was the second of Steinem's African-American speaking partners (Dorothy Pitman Hughes had a baby and decided not to continue to travel). Kennedy was considered so outrageous that Steinem was warned against speaking with her, but she was a big success. It was Kennedy who nicknamed the speaking duo "Little Eva teams" and summed up for the *Newsweek* researchers Steinem's attractiveness and its importance to women:

"Unfortunately, her principal value may be that she is so glamorous. That's what she would like least, but that's the package part and we are a package-oriented society. . . . I think it is important for the girls on the campuses to know that you can be beautiful, graceful, gracious, strong, daring, and committed and like black people and like farmworkers and you don't have to suck and still come out smelling like a rose." But talk-show host David Susskind, one of the very few people Steinem admits to disliking, commented to one of the *Newsweek* researchers in true Haggard form. "I just wish Gloria would find a good chap and relax. . . . What Gloria needs is a man. . . . The whole thing is so boring —and ridiculous. Gloria comes on with that flat Ohio accent and goes on and on about women's oppression—you feel like either kissing her or hitting her. I can't decide which."

Nor was it only men who had problems with Steinem's new image. Helen Gurley Brown, the editor of *Cosmopolitan,* turned down a portrait of Steinem by Liz Smith as a "fan magazine piece." But critical reporting apparently wasn't a *Cosmo* requirement: Smith recalled that all unflattering facts had been excised from an earlier piece she did about some people close to the magazine's owners. Her impression was that Brown rejected the Steinem piece because she rejected what Steinem stood for. All that interested *Cosmopolitan* was Steinem's love affairs. Women's magazines at that time catered to the same patriarchy that men protect, but in catering to the women defenders of that patriarchy, they were even more circumspect and fearful and, as Smith puts it, materialistic. (As it happened, however, Smith's piece appeared that year in *Vogue.*)

Yet, despite such doubters as Susskind and Brown, Steinem was able instantly to create a bridge to feminism when she revealed, simply by appearing, that one did not need to be man-hating or "shrill"—the media presentation of a feminist—to be a feminist. Though a combination of beauty and power threatened men, it reassured women. One of Steinem's most notable and useful traits was her consummate unflappability: She always remained calm. (Steinem said this was due to "a difficulty in getting angry" that she criticized in herself, but was nonetheless helpful.) Women to whom she spoke throughout the country loved her because she inspired them and proved that they had the right to assume power without sacrificing sexuality. The media loved her, too; but, wholly male, they feared her as well. Here was a woman who looked good enough to be one of *Esquire*'s sexy dolls, but who threatened to take away their rights to those dolls. Rider Haggard hadn't known the half of it.

The media were then presenting the women's movement as a few scattered bra-burners and others who were unattractive and "obviously" sex-starved: nothing worth noticing, certainly not in the heartland of America. But when in the early 1970s Steinem and Pitman Hughes arrived in Wichita, Kansas, almost the exact middle of the United States, they found three thousand women waiting to hear them. Steinem learned that in speaking about the movement she and Pitman fulfilled a passion these women had, both to know about the very movement that the media had assumed was marginal and to hear women's experiences spoken in public and taken seriously for the first time. What was more, Steinem welcomed responses from the audience; she listened and, listening, discovered the desperation of the women who came to hear her. More important, her audience listened to stories of each other's lives and discovered they were neither crazy nor alone. She learned, too, how many women wanted to write about being a woman in our culture but had not supposed that anyone would welcome what they had to say.

As so often happened, Steinem's instincts led her in the right direction. Once enlightened, she knew there must be many women all over the United States who had been as unable or unwilling as she had been to recognize the limitations of their lives as part of a deliberate structure: patriarchy.

Nowhere was this more evident than in her commencement speech delivered to the Smith graduating class of 1971, the first year when Steinem's somewhat ambiguous sixties fame overlapped with her new role as an eminent figure in the feminist movement. In this instance, she spoke alone.[1] Thomas C. Mendenhall, president of Smith, wrote to Steinem on behalf of the class of 1971, and Steinem accepted—with more than her usual trepidation. She wrote and rewrote the speech in her room beforehand, just as her classmates remembered her having done with her senior thesis, working against a deadline. In hindsight, it was President Mendenhall who should have felt the trepidation. In an address called "The Politics of Women," Steinem lashed out at Smith with a directness that surprises even today; the romance with Smith was over.

She began by telling them how strange it was to come back to her own college as a commencement speaker. "Speaking at commencements is for other people," she had thought while at Smith. "And in my head, I would have pictured a man behind this podium—a man probably old and definitely white—because I had internalized, without conscious thought or formal instruction, the racist and sexist values around me."

She went on to commend Smith's "change in consciousness" in recent years, from the abandonment of the rules demanding that students be in their rooms by 10:15 P.M. to the introduction of black studies. She also spoke of the "myths of feminine inferiority

---

[1] Steinem was not the class of 1971's first choice—indeed, she was not even on their original list, which included men ranging from Canadian Prime Minister Pierre Trudeau (their first choice) through psychoanalyst Erik Erikson, who declined because of illness, to Paul Newman, William F. Buckley, Jr., and Edmund Muskie, all of whom either declined or weren't asked. Such a list of prominent and unobtainable persons, as deans and college presidents know to their sorrow, is far from atypical.

[that] have been used to suppress the talents and strengths of half the human race." And then, we must assume to the discomfort of many, she quoted a remark of Flo Kennedy's that "there are only a few jobs that actually require a penis or vagina."

The heart of her address was simple and clear: "Let me say to you some of the things that I wish so desperately someone had said to me. It would have saved me so much time and so much heartache." She mentioned women in history ignored by Smith historians. She talked about how middle-class women's primary unpaid job was housework, which "is after all the only work that is only noticed if you don't do it. It is the definition of women's work, which is shit work." Leaving some of her audience, one assumes, reeling at these unexpected declarations, she went on to discuss the illegality of abortion as "the number one health problem among women." She questioned whether courses in political science shouldn't discuss "the problem of the masculine mystique." She questioned the politics of religion. Perhaps most offensively for that particular audience, she attacked volunteerism, which she saw as the result of men being unable to stand the challenge to their ego of a wage-earning wife. "I suggest that we volunteer to change the system, not to perpetuate it," she offered, also asking Smith to become "a feminist institution, a radicalizing institution," in the knowledge that no women's college had ever done anything of the sort. "I am one of five women commencement speakers in the history of Smith College," she concluded, the last woman speaker being "a captain in the WAVES," because it "was during World War II and I believe they couldn't find a man."

As a lesson in the indeterminacy of history, disagreement about the immediate reaction to Steinem's speech serves nicely. Steinem herself says that she had just taken up political speaking around the country, and did not sufficiently tailor her remarks to this genteel audience and occasion. A woman who was then a student at Smith remembers the speech with pleasure, and that all the students were grateful to Steinem for speaking out on reproductive rights. At that time, no contraceptive advice was offered at Smith (or probably at any other women's college), and, indeed, such advice had been illegal in Massachusetts.[2] The same student remembers that the students rose to their feet in appreciation after the speech; the faculty did not. Half the parents walked out. Others deny all this as unlikely. The paper evidence is slight, but a letter from an outraged relative, "the provider of the funds" for one graduate's education, is indicative:

> To Smith College students, as well as their families, their graduation and the related Commencement Exercises are among the major experiences of their lives. Traditionally, such exercises are serious affairs, conducted in a religious atmosphere, and highlighted by an inspirational address by a highly respected person designed to guide the graduates in the difficult transition from a sojourn in a world of fantasy to a life-time in one of stark realism.
>
> In that light, the 1971 "commencement address" was inexcusably shallow in its contents and crude in its language. To me it seemed as if it represented the bleatings of an over-sexed, frustrated spinster forced to seek her sexual experiences where and when she could find them, and around which her mind revolved.
>
> That Smith College would take advantage of a captive audience and force them to listen to such filthy drivel . . . sandwiched between the Lord's Prayer and the Benediction by the College Chaplain was astounding to me, to put it mildly. Filth is filth.

[2] Most of what Steinem said on this subject was expunged from the Smith Alumnae Quarterly, which, in justice, always printed commencement speeches "in part," including Alistair Cooke's.

This letter is, in its way, a model of prophecy, adumbrating the stance of the far right that would constitute the backlash to feminism in particular and the sixties in general. What is most poignant is that in speaking of the necessary transition commencements represented, the letter writer and Steinem were in total agreement: They differed only in their definitions of fantasy and stark realism.

There was more, and one wonders that the writer didn't expire on the spot, rather than bravely survive to write this letter. There was far too much in the speech; all Steinem's new and overwhelming discoveries found their way into it. Yet we can see nothing there that anyone but a member of the radical right would today find objectionable. Certainly the later Steinem, as she honed her talent for public speaking, would have put it all a little less defiantly. It is not, therefore, surprising that Smith waited until 1988 to give Steinem an honorary degree.[3]

And some of their complaints were, certainly, justified. It appears that Steinem sent the president's office one advance speech and delivered another. Steinem remembers this less as premeditated and more the effect of overwork. At the time they asked, she sent a speech she had; at the last minute she determined to write a different speech, into which, through the long previous night, she put everything she now wanted to say. To compare this speech to the commencement speech she had given a year earlier at Vassar is informative. Although the same myths about blacks and women are addressed—"Patriotism means obedience, age means wisdom, woman means submission, black means inferior: these are perceptions buried so deeply in our thinking that we honestly may not know that they are there"—the emotion with which one addresses one's family, as opposed to strangers, is evident in the

---

[3] Time, however, brings perspective and forgetfulness; Steinem, again in Smith's good graces, was its commencement speaker in 1995.

barely contained anger still palpable in the Smith commencement address. Steinem would never speak in quite that way again; the Smith administration found it difficult to be grateful for this unique occasion.

If the students of the seventies responded to the content of Steinem's message, indeed all that Steinem had come to stand for, her own class, the class of '56, did not. Steinem's classmates had watched her in the media, and many, of course, had met her again after college. Some of their opinions of her were now more critical, and came to a head after a sign-carrying caper at their twenty-fifth reunion in 1981 (about which Steinem herself wrote in *Outrageous Acts*).

She and classmate and fellow writer for *Ms.* Phyllis Rosser had made and brought several signs to the reunion in the hope of getting some of their classmates to carry them as they marched in the procession. The signs read: THE SECOND WAVE OF FEMINISM SALUTES THE FIRST. WE SURVIVED JOE MCCARTHY—WE CAN SURVIVE REAGAN AND THE MORAL MAJORITY. '56 REMEMBERS OUR SISTERS WHO DIED OF ILLEGAL ABORTIONS. DON'T LET IT HAPPEN AGAIN! WOMEN GET MORE RADICAL WITH AGE.

It appeared that Smith women did *not* get more radical with age. Steinem had been hoping to bridge the years between her class and older and younger marchers, although since the majority of the class had voted against Reagan, and 98 percent favored legalized abortion, she had expected no trouble from the signs. It transpired, however, that Smith women like to organize things, and they had organized this reunion around the theme "Focus '56," a pun on middle age and bifocals. Steinem and Rosser thought more deliberate political statements would be appropriate; they were wrong. The whole class had not voted on them, although they had, one was to assume, voted on the placard: NOW OUR AGE IS THE SAME AS OUR BUSTLINE. In the end those classmates carrying Steinem's signs were told to march at the end of the whole procession, but the class of 1966 (there to celebrate their fifteenth reunion), one of whose members had died of a botched abortion, took the sign-bearers into their ranks. They had, they reported, been wondering about the wisdom of carrying political signs at the commencement, and this incident had given them courage. "You should have let us know," Steinem reported their saying; "we never dreamed alumnae would do *anything*."

Where, Steinem's classmates wondered—even as she considered Smith, so they felt, "stuck-up"—would she be without the Smith experience? One of Steinem's classmates believed that Steinem was insufficiently grateful to Smith, without whose education she would have been a housewife in Toledo. Gratitude and praise in the face of error are middle-class female characteristics Steinem is not prepared to honor above all; Steinem had reconsidered her Smith experience. Some of her classmates had not only failed to do this, seeing no reason for it, but had also found her actions discourteous and an affront. They felt, moreover, that Smith had been the only traditional event in her life, and that it had given her something essential to her development. Steinem would not have denied this, but though Smith had, in many ways, acted more as a parent to her than had her actual parents, she felt toward the college as she might have felt toward a family that had raised her to be a dutiful daughter and nothing else: a reexamination of the principles involved was, she thought, obviously incumbent upon her.

Steinem's fame inevitably caused resentment: How could it not? Some from her class felt she had become famous through powerful men. The publicity of the sixties did her little good with Smith alumnae, or indeed with many others. There was a sense that Steinem had somehow dined out on stories about teaching Smith women to iron. In looking back, of course, the classmates realized how little they had actually confided in one another: Steinem was not the only classmate with a crazy mother, though the only one with an experience of poverty. But they all felt that they were expected to be happy, never to complain or speak of family troubles.

There was another point the classmates implied, this one the least openly expressed, perhaps the most important. Steinem had deserted them, they may have felt, not out of snobbishness or ambition or ill-feeling, but because they were what they were: privileged, college-educated women. Was it not true that this group was less easy to revolutionize, the results of the attempt less immediate, less satisfying than work done among her Toledo schoolmates, or among the dispossessed, the battered, the abused? It is possible that, unfairly critical as she was of *The Feminine Mystique* for addressing itself exclusively to this group of white, upper-middle-class, college-educated women, she had herself turned away from that very group of women. Barbara Ehrenreich later observed, in praise of Friedan's book: "The home, that sink-hole of consumerism, had become a 'comfortable concentration camp,' producing children capable only of an inmate's muffled existence. A class that was half working professionals and half domestics, half strivers and half shoppers, could not reproduce itself. Affluence, abetted by the ancient tradition of gender in-equality, was reducing the middle class to a race of sleepwalkers." [*F of F,* 41]

This race of sleepwalkers needed further awakening and en-couragement, especially from someone like Steinem who knew them and yet had known another life. But their impression was that she told them what she thought and left them to get on with doing something about it. She was not so demanding of the dis-possessed, listening to them with loving care, offering them help without domination, learning from them. It seemed to many that Steinem had decided she had nothing to teach her Smith class-mates and their peers, and nothing to learn from them. Those who do much always bear the burden of blame for not doing more, but Steinem could not avoid giving the impression of having benefitted from middle-class advantages even while she disdained the middle class.

Steinem's classmates saw much wrong with the world, and the place of women in it. Perhaps they had been reluctant to act politically, however much they agreed. Certainly those in the corporate and business world, and the few who had not married, felt the burden of women's failure to bond with other women and to treasure their friendship above their personal ambitions and the support and companionship of men. They felt the need of a new wave of feminism, or a revival of the old one. The fact was, if Steinem had not provided leadership, neither had anyone else. Many women worked hard and long at the grassroots level, for example, beginning the process of introducing women into the political scene at all levels. But after Friedan's book, no single woman with Steinem's universal recognition had devoted her efforts to the struggles of highly educated, well-to-do women. Partly there would always be the argument that while a welfare mother of five was starving with her family in Detroit, worry about the well-off seemed inappropriate. But beyond even that lay the fact that educated women can be, as Steinem found, slow to change, slow to take fundamental risks. Ironically, and not uniquely in Steinem's life, she was simultaneously resented for deserting women like her Smith classmates while living a social life that certainly appeared, as the media presented it, to contain all the middle-class comforts. Steinem seemed to have had it both ways, ever a source of disquiet if not envy.

The apparently sharp contrast in Steinem's life between her devotion to, for example, Native Americans—the first American victims of imperialism, colonialism, and commercial conquest—and her place in New York City, meeting the rich and famous and attending their dazzling social events, has been seen both crudely and inaccurately. What is true, however, is that she has, like it or not, had the best of both worlds. If she has used her connections on behalf of others, nonetheless, those connections are available to her. If she can sleep happily on the ground in the badlands of North Dakota, and help poor women there to purchase their own portion of that inexpensive land, she returns to a comfortable home and the company of movers and shakers. It is this anomaly that most frets those who, from a distance, have followed her career largely through reports in newspapers and magazines.

There is something grating, and perhaps Steinem's classmates felt this, about Steinem's brilliant use of the benefits of a privileged life and her apparent scorn of it. It may be commendable to feel you are going snow-blind when confronted with a sea of white faces, but to the owners of the white faces with their particular deep and painful struggles, it may well seem that Steinem has become a kind of missionary, if not Friedan's kind, setting forth from the embattled at home to comfort those who seem to her profoundly deprived and deserving. Even those close to her who recognize her mission as selfless, brave, and hugely strenuous must concede that few will understand, and some will not forgive, anyone's simultaneously enjoying the benefits of success while idolizing the poor.

The fact remains that poor women, Toledo women, African-American women, Native American women, and working-class women do not feel the need of theory or of complex explanations. Steinem, like them, honors experience over male-authored theories. College-educated women seemed to Steinem to be, in many cases, the prisoners of Plato, Aristotle, Freud, and Marx, rather than the observers of their own experience and pain, and enactors of their own justifiable rage.

* * *

MEANWHILE, the 1971 Smith commencement speech behind her, Steinem and Pitman were still on the road. The brilliance of insisting always on speaking with a woman of color is palpable now, but Steinem denies race was the major reason. She encountered Pitman, Kennedy, and later the writer Margaret Sloan in the course of her work; these women were as galvanizing to her as they were to the audience. She was always, in any case, continually interested in countering the idea that feminism was a movement of only upper-middle-class white women.

Inevitably, Steinem and her partner were accused of being lesbians. It was Flo Kennedy who, characteristically, came up with the right response, neither appeasing nor betraying, when an angry man in the audience so accused them: "Are you my alternative?"

Steinem and her partners toured the country with an exhaustiveness that makes the early traveling theatrical companies look stationary. As Steinem writes in *Outrageous Acts:* "Though we tried to focus on parts of the country that were most removed from the little feminist activity that then existed, there were so few feminist speakers that we ended by going to almost every kind of community and, I think, every state but Alaska. There were times when we felt like some combination of Susan B. Anthony and a lost company of Blossom Time."

Although those who heard her would have found it hard to believe, Steinem's fear of speaking was acute and receded only slowly. In earlier days, she had gained such a reputation for copping out of television and radio shows at the last minute that she was blacklisted. In time the fear, to some extent, faded, partly, as she explains, because she learned that "you do not die from it, however awful it feels." In fact, she became more comfortable speaking outside of New York than she was on her home ground. But even as late as 1992, addressing a formal ceremony at the Waldorf-Astoria, her mouth went dry and her teeth, as she describes it, grew "angora sweaters." And she would always remember being asked by Kay Graham in 1982 to talk to the editorial board of the *Washington Post,* urging them to support an extension of the ratification deadline for the Equal Rights Amendment. The members, apart from Kay Graham and Meg Greenfield, were all men insensitive to feminism; Steinem was so nervous at the combination of responsibility and hostility she can remember nothing but how dreadful she felt.

Margaret Sloan, the third of Steinem's speaking companions in the early seventies, was only twenty-four when they began. They had met in 1972 when Steinem was snowed in at the Chicago airport, and Sloan spoke in her place at a Midwestern woman's conference. She was a gifted speaker and writer who also appeared on radio and television as a representative of civil rights and feminism. She had marched with Martin Luther King, and, along with Flo Kennedy, had been selected to serve on the jury during a "people's trial" of Edward Hanrahan organized by the Black Panthers after the murders of Fred Hampton, leader of the Black Panther party in Illinois, and twenty-two-year-old Panther member Matt Clark in Chicago.[4] She wanted to get to New York and went to work for *Ms.;* she wrote well, but was something less than efficient as an editor.

All three of the women who spoke with Steinem report that she would stay up for hours after the talks to help local groups with organizing, even after her partner dropped with exhaustion. Steinem was always able to survive on little sleep, an ability made possible by her capacity to sleep anywhere at a moment's notice.

[4] According to Michael J. Arden's *An American Verdict* (Doubleday, 1973), Edward Hanrahan, State's Attorney of Cook County, was believed by the Black Panthers to have been responsible for the death of the two men during a raid to search their apartment for illegal weapons. Despite ballistic evidence to the contrary, the judge found insufficient evidence to "establish or prove any conspiracy against any defendant." Hanrahan et al. were acquitted.

Those who know her have often suspected that, like a horse, she could sleep standing up. Her gift for falling immediately asleep in an airplane is legendary.

As the women's movement gathered momentum, Steinem was occasionally asked to write for the mainstream press on feminist issues. When in August 1970 she wrote the article "What It Would Be Like if Women Win," for the issue of *Time* magazine that had Kate Millett on the cover, she was paid less, as she later discovered, than male journalists who had written similar essays.

There now began a deluge—of mail, and of media coverage of the speaking tours—that never diminished. In part, the many requests for help, for information, for guidance led to the founding first of the Women's Action Alliance in 1970 and then of *Ms.* magazine in 1971. The birth of *Ms.* was also partly a consequence of a new friendship Steinem made in 1970; one of the salient and exciting facts about the early women's movement was how women ignited each other toward accomplishment. Brenda Feigen had seethed through Harvard Law School, beginning with the convocation for entering students in 1966, when Dean Irwin Griswold told the women students that they were taking the place of men who would be breadwinners. The sole eating club at Harvard Law School was Lincoln's Inn, open only to faculty (white males all) and to male law students. The squash courts allowed only men; firms that announced they would never hire women were allowed to interview on campus. At this time also the Harvard Club in New York would not admit women, except as guests entering by a side door.

It is worth noting that in Scott Turow's now famous book *One L,* about his first year at Harvard Law (1974), he reports that for the first time a woman (Susan Estrich) had become president of the *Harvard Law Review*. He then records, with apparent approval of the humor, that the April Fool's issue of the law school newspaper carried an article reporting that "a second campus publication noting the *Law Review*'s choice of a female head, had taken affirmative action one step further and installed a dog as editor in chief. Streaky woofed, 'My species had nothing to do with my being elected.' "

Like so many women who seethed inwardly, and they thought, uniquely, Feigen discovered that she was not alone—in 1969, the year of Steinem's similar discovery. Back in Cambridge after her marriage to Marc Fasteau, she happened to be watching the *David Susskind Show*. She had never heard of Gloria Steinem, but there on the screen was an "obviously intelligent, glamorous woman, thirty-something, spouting facts and statistics about injustices of all kinds against women. This was [my] first realization that what [I'd] been fighting for during those three long years in Cambridge had broader repercussions in the rest of the world."

Soon after this, Feigen called NOW's national office in Chicago and asked to join. When the NOW leaders discovered that she was a lawyer working for the city of Boston, they recruited her to run for national vice president for legislation. At the annual NOW convention in New Orleans that year she was elected.

By 1970, the congressional Equal Rights Amendment hearings were being prepared. Subcommittee chairman Birch Bayh, for whom Feigen had worked between her junior and senior years at Vassar, asked her to coordinate the favorable testimony. Feigen remembered the woman she had seen on the *David Susskind Show;* she called Steinem and asked her to testify before the subcommittee. Steinem agreed and a fruitful friendship and collaboration began.

Steinem's testimony, and the work she and Feigen did on behalf of the ERA, immediately distanced her from the "radical" feminists, who thought in terms of "inside" or "outside" the system, and spurned, at that time, any electoral activity. Steinem and Feigen agreed with them about the need for fundamental changes, but felt that some "reformist" short-term tactics could have transforming long-term results. In fact, in later years, many of these radical women joined the fight for such reformist causes as the ERA, as well as the rights of lesbians to adopt children.

Steinem and Feigen complemented each other in essential ways. Most importantly, Feigen was outspoken, forceful, ready to take on conflict. Steinem hated conflict. In those days her distaste for confrontation was so great that, as Feigen puts it, "I was so often called on to do the wars. When Gloria was asked to debate the ERA on television, she wouldn't do it, she referred it to me; I debated Phyllis Schlafly, Marabel Morgan, all these people on television."

By the fall of 1970 Feigen had come to realize that NOW was only prepared to deal with large, national issues such as the ERA. In November 1970, then, Steinem and Feigen began discussing the idea for the Women's Action Alliance (WAA), an organization to help women at the grassroots level fight for relief from the many problems that, as women, they experienced in their daily lives: job opportunities closed to women, sexist textbooks, marital abuse and desertion, the need to fight for nonsexist, multiracial child-care centers. By early 1971, the organization was formed.

The Women's Action Alliance was where Feigen put her energies. The postman delivered so many inquiries from women to their office on Lexington Avenue (letters addressed to "Women's Lib" arrived despite the many tenants in their building) that he soon decided it was best to thrust the sack of mail in through the door and then run. Because of this overwhelming response, Steinem was convinced that the WAA needed a simple newsletter to keep its members informed and also to be a source of income; she took upon herself the task of starting one.[5] Feigen, who was running the day-to-day operations of WAA, felt the idea of a

[5] At this time, few foundations even had a category for women's projects, and the WAA was running largely on hope, a few small contributions, and Steinem's speaking fees.

newsletter should be taken one step further. If a newsletter, why not a glossy magazine? Feigen and Steinem would investigate this possibility over the next twelve months.

Letters to and from Steinem at this time indicate how often she spoke, in how many places, and how important she had become as the prevailing spokesperson for feminism. A member of the New York Bar Association wrote to thank her for her appearance in a symposium entitled "Has 'Women's Liberation' Liberated Anyone?" Steinem, like Betty Friedan and Eleanor Holmes Norton, had been invited to speak, but she became aware in advance that the women members of the association had not been given time to state their internal complaints, and turned over her time to them; she was subsequently thanked for having "served as a smashing 'Trojan Horse.' " The letter writer also reported having been told that "there are a lot of male New York lawyers walking around today with their consciousness substantially raised."

But in Cambridge, alas, this was not the case. In 1971 Feigen supported Steinem when she accepted an invitation to give the *Harvard Law Review* banquet address, which would make her the first woman ever to do so. To give the address was a high honor; the banquet was attended by past and present members of the review's staff and the (still all male) Harvard Law School faculty. Exactly why the school asked Steinem is mysterious; perhaps they considered only her fame, her attractiveness, and her reputation for a certain "feminine" mildness. Whatever the reason, Steinem turned down the invitation: She wasn't a lawyer, and she was uncomfortable at the prospect of any audience, especially such a critical one. But Harvard's women law students insisted that she accept, that she was the first woman "they've" ever asked, and they probably wouldn't ask another. In addition, Feigen urged Steinem to name the faculty members offensive to women, and to mention specific injustices suffered by women at what Feigen referred to as "that elite white male bastion of superiority." The law school students confirmed Feigen's stories and added a few others. In a gesture of generosity, or caution, they decided at the last minute not to mention names, but to the insiders, those were doubtless recognizable by category.

The black-tie *Harvard Law Review* banquet might well be near the top of the list of "outrageous acts" in Steinem's life. A summary of the speech was released finally into the Congressional Record, and the rest can be more or less reconstructed from Steinem's notes and other reports.

Steinem began by mentioning that she had wished, upon graduation from Smith, to go to law school, but had been discouraged by her professors and by a job counselor. At that time, she said, both Harvard and Columbia law schools, though they had begun to admit women a few years previously, regarded them as freaks. Not having thought about law schools from that time to this, Steinem had been reluctant to accept this invitation, she said, but she had decided to do so for two reasons. First, she had learned that the other speakers proposed were William Buckley, Jr., J. Edgar Hoover, and Vice President Agnew. Second, Brenda Feigen had argued that "I might be useful to the law school alumnae, to the one hundred and twenty sisters now feeling alone and somewhat aberrant among fifteen hundred and fifty male students, and to some future versions of myself, the aspiring lawyer." She then announced that she was there that night to talk about the half of the human race that is women, the necessity of feminism as a path to humanism, and the areas "in which Harvard Law School is showing no leadership at all."

She spoke about men and women in our society, and then pointed out that while there was a course called "Racism and American Law" at Harvard, there was no course on sexism. "In fact," she added, having been well instructed by the women who had persuaded her to give the speech, there is everything from "The Chinese Attitude Toward International Law" to "Law and Social Change in Africa" and "The Uses of the Ocean," but nothing for, by, or about American women. In the internal description of courses, special mention is made of such problems as "The Conservation of Whales, Seals, and Fish," "The Allocation of Radio Frequencies," "The Rights of Servicemen," "The Implications of 'Socialist Transformation' of the Economy in China," and "The Production of Fish Protein Concentrate." But in the course on constitutional law, there is no mention of the Equal Rights Amendment. The "Family Law" description offers no hint that women lose many of their civil rights by marrying.

And so on, through many courses. Steinem mentioned a securities-law expert who "used descriptions of stupid widows and wives to explain sample cases of stock loss and the like," that other professors described rape as "a very small assault." She listed many of the affronts women students suffered directly from the professors and male students (apart from the subject matter of the courses) and ended by suggesting remedies that must have seemed radical (such as nearly 50 percent women students) at the time, but that have, in fact, been brought to pass. What is notable about her speech is that it does not deal in generalities or abstract aims; it describes wrongs and explains how they may be corrected. And that was exactly why the Harvard establishment took offense. Even the liberal Richard Goodwin, the speaker from the year before, had played the game by speaking about problems that were far away. The men's applause was polite, though restrained, but the few women in the room, including Feigen, clapped and cheered wildly. Then something even more unusual than Steinem's addressing such an audience occurred: An eminent professor of the law school, red-faced and sputtering, according to Feigen, tried to rebut the speech. To Feigen he seemed in a state of hysteria, and the audience was embarrassed. It is perhaps unnecessary to point out that Steinem was the first person ever to have a speech rebutted at the banquet. She held her ground, and some changes in the treatment of women began to occur at the Harvard Law School.

TO LIST THE colleges and universities at which Steinem and her partners spoke would take many pages, perhaps more than to list those at which they did not speak. She was also in demand to argue on behalf of the women's movement on television. On one occasion, October 2, 1971, *Eyewitness News* ran an "exclusive" with Steinem. The announcer described her as "a virtual superstar in the field of women's rights." There followed a "comprehensive interview" with Jim Bouton, Bill Beutel, Melba Tolliver, and Roger Grimsby. The entire transcript of the interview (at which Steinem remembers sitting on a chair in the center, as at a bullfight) is a valuable document in the history of the women's movement. For example:

> *Bouton:* Is there a paradox between women's attitudes toward, you know, the fact that they don't want to be treated as sex objects and the fact that you dress very sexily?
>
> *Steinem [who is wearing blue jeans, a leotard, and glasses]:* Do you think I'm dressing very sexily?
>
> *Bouton:* That's a pretty sexy outfit, I'd say.
>
> *Steinem:* Well, I mean that my pants are sort of about the same price, et cetera as your pants. You know, that's a kind of a stock question?
>
> *Beutel [at the end]:* I hope you forgive our masculine notion that you're an absolutely stunning sex object.
>
> *Steinem:* Well, I should comment on your appearance, but I don't have time.

In much the same vein, Steinem responded to a letter from Ron Dorfman, editor of the *Chicago Journalism Review,* who wanted to bill Steinem vs. Mailer as "the real fight of the century":

I'd do almost anything for the Chicago Journalism Review, which I read regularly, but the offer of debating Norman Mailer is one which I (and Kate Millett and Flo Kennedy and almost everyone else) had already received from the Theater of Ideas here and turned down. For one thing, it would be a bear-baiting. People would come to see the hostility fly and that doesn't seem very constructive. In fact, this is one of the situations where debating may be a male hangup: it's what intellectuals do after they're too sophisticated to beat each other up in bars. For another, I think Norman is trying to change, and that any opposition would only shove him back in his male chauvinist corner.

Steinem's characteristic suspicion of intellectuals did not lessen over the years, although it is generic and rarely directed at individual intellectuals, some of whom, like Galbraith and Michael Harrington, were her friends. The refusal to fight Mailer head-on is also characteristic as a reflection of her belief that the movement would not be furthered by such confrontations.

IN AN ATTEMPT to turn the convergence of radical and mainstream demands into political clout, the National Women's Political Caucus was formed in 1971. Among its founders were Brenda Feigen; Steinem; Bella Abzug, who had been elected to Congress the previous year and had made a startlingly vivid impression on her fellow representatives, the public, and the media; Shirley Chisholm, who in 1968 had become the first black woman elected to the House of Representatives; Betty Friedan; Patsy Mink, congresswoman from Hawaii; and Kay Clarenbach, a leader in the women's movement from Wisconsin.

Clarenbach described the founding of the NWPC for Marcia Cohen's *The Sisterhood* [315]: "It was really thrilling. A whole new collection of people. There were political women—both Democrats and Republican—who never thought of themselves as feminists; there were civil libertarians, members of the League of Women Voters, some who wouldn't touch NOW[6] with a ten-foot pole . . . and there was a wonderful representation of women of color." Cohen goes on to present an account of the debates that followed:

> Fannie Lou Hamer, the longtime civil rights leader, rose to announce, as Shirley Chisholm already had done, that she had suffered more discrimination as a woman than as a Black. . . . Betty [Friedan], siding with Hamer and Chisholm, once again pressed for her concept of uniting across political lines to elect women and focus attention on *women's issues,* which in their view, wouldn't include welfare, abortion, or racism. Bella, pumping for her feminist coalition, for what Betty would call "the outs," took the more radical line, announcing that it was "certainly not my purpose to replace or supplement a white, male, middle-class elite with a white, female, middle-class elite in the position of power in the nation."
>
> "Our aim should be to humanize society," Steinem agreed with Bella at the plenary session, "by bringing the values of women's culture into it, not simply to put individual women in men's places. . . ."
>
> "I think I was drafted to chair the Caucus," Kay [Clarenbach] would remember, "because I could get along with both Betty and Bella. They were both talking about the need

[6] NOW hadn't yet turned its attention to electoral activity; the position of the NWPC was to elect feminists. As Abzug said: "We're not trying to elect Phyllis Schlafly."

for women in politics, but they each had little private gatherings and invited people separately, independently, to their hotel rooms. Each of them thought she was going to be the keynote speaker and kept sending lieutenants to me to ask how she was going to be introduced."

And though Kay believed that she had solved the problem by avoiding the announcement of a keynote speaker entirely and creating instead a nonpartisan panel, this hardly satisfied Betty. Something—or someone—was loosening her hold on the reins of the women's movement.[7] [316–17]

Friedan suspected, from that moment on, that the something or someone was Steinem. Steinem had become a force, and called for new leaders and spokeswomen: "I'm tired of seeing your face and yours," she said, pointing at Friedan and Abzug, "and I'm tired of seeing my own." [Cohen, 117] She was not half as tired of seeing her own as Friedan was.

Bella Abzug, whose brusquerie had initially put off Steinem, as it had so many other women and men, soon became an object of Steinem's steady admiration. Steinem has admitted that the first time she heard Abzug speak, she recoiled. Abzug was forthright, downright, with a loud, demanding voice that overturned every concept of the appropriate in women, whether that concept was

---

[7] Since the cast of characters involved in the first founding meeting seems to vary with every history, it is worthwhile to list those who took part in the opening session of the first NWPC national convention in February of 1973, which was chaired by Liz Carpenter: Present, among others, were Bella Abzug; Shirley Chisholm; Pat Schroeder, already a Congresswoman; Helen Delich Bentley, the chairwoman of the Federal Maritime Commission; Mary Coleman, a justice of the Michigan State Supreme Court; Ethel Allen, a Philadelphia City Councilwoman; Barbara Mikulski, then a City Councilwoman in Baltimore; Rhea Mejica Hammer, a La Raza Unida Party activist from Chicago; Steinem; and Jill Ruckelshaus, assistant to the co-chairman of the Republican National Committee. Sissy Farenthold from Texas (of whom Walter Cronkite said: "A lady named Farenthold wants to be Vice President") would open the convention's first plenary session on the next day. It is notable how familiar many of these names are more than two decades later.

held consciously or not. Steinem may have rejected the idea of middle-class ladyhood, but she had not yet ceased taking for granted the expectation that even political women would speak quietly, gently, and with a certain graciousness. Indeed, she had first met Abzug in the late sixties, before feminism made her examine her own reactions to other women's styles, ladylike or otherwise. Many male politicians had spoken as Abzug did, though often in less generous causes, but what was acceptable and even attractive in men was jeered at, resented, and mocked in women. It took Steinem time to recognize that these criteria were patriarchal, and that Bella was, in fact, a gutsy, forceful woman with little resemblance to men's idea of a lady. The two remained friends and comrades in arms. Sometimes Steinem would advise Abzug never again to submit herself to the terrible public malignings, gleefully reported by the media, that she took when running for various offices, but once Abzug had decided to run, Steinem was with her all the way, up to and including Abzug's unsuccessful 1992 try for the seat left vacant by the death of New York congressman Ted Weiss.

With Friedan, the matter was quite different. Many in the media, delighted as always with the spectacle of women fighting each other, or appearing to, characterized the Steinem-Friedan conflict—which became marked after the founding of *Ms.*—as the expected catfight. This always felt to Steinem as though, while she had been standing waiting for a bus, a woman had come up and hit her with a two-by-four, and a crowd had said: "Why are you two dames fighting?" But it seems clear that Friedan's identification of Steinem as an enemy began with the struggle growing out of the founding of the National Women's Political Caucus, and the decisions about what directions it would take.

According to Brenda Feigen, one of these decisions involved the representation of younger women on the advisory committee of the NWPC. There were many young women about Feigen's

age (she was twenty-six) who had worked hard in the organization and felt it was unfair that no one under thirty-five was about
to be elected to the committee. Together with Barbara Lamont, a
black newscaster from New York, Feigen organized the younger
women and demanded a seat. She explained the extent and reasons for the youthful outrage at doing the work but not being
represented; as a result, Feigen and Lamont were elected to the
committee and were thus part of the NWPC's representation at
the Democratic National Convention in 1972.

THE FEMINIST MESSAGE was beginning to get across, although Steinem's looks rarely went unmentioned when her name
came up. An article in the *Miami Herald* in May 1971 was typical.
Headlined "Feminine Qualities? Gloria Scorns Them," it went on
to report that Steinem, "blessed with a hard-to-beat combination
of brains, beauty, and charm," was an outspoken advocate of
women's liberation "who believes her good looks have been more
of a hindrance than a help in her success . . . and feels that
women are more interested than men in sex." Although reporters
were still picking out the salacious bits to report, as they would
ever do with Steinem and others, the fact that she was speaking
out on feminism emerged at last as the dominant theme.

Writing was still primary in Steinem's hopes, however inadequate the time she was able to devote to it. Sterling Lord, then her
agent, had negotiated two contracts: first, for an expansion of the
Playboy Bunny article (she eventually returned the advance) and
then for a collection of her essays, for Random House. In the
event, this early collection would never see the light of day and
Steinem returned the money to the publisher. Meanwhile, the
concept of a magazine by, for, and about women had percolated
long enough in Steinem's and Feigen's minds for them to take
further explorative steps. While the idea of such a magazine was

tempting, Steinem thought, surely no one would advertise in a feminist publication. From the beginning she doubted the viability of a successful marriage between feminism and advertising, and though she became persuaded of the possibility, time was to prove her correct. Feigen, who was more optimistic, sought the opinion of Jane Trahey, a rare female advertising power at this time, who headed her own agency and thought it would be possible for a slick feminist magazine to succeed.

Early in 1971, the energy of feminist women provided enough momentum to overturn most doubts—particularly Steinem's. Before committing herself totally to such a magazine, Steinem wanted to hear directly from women themselves that there would be enough support to make a go of it. She reached out to women editors, journalists, and opinion makers in the magazine world of the time to attend a meeting at her apartment to discuss the idea. Two meetings were held, one at Feigen's, one at Steinem's. Susan Brownmiller, Adrienne Rich, Robin Morgan, Susan Braudy, Jill Johnson (who objected when Yoko Ono brought John Lennon to one of the meetings), and Vivian Gornick were among the many, bylined and nonbylined, women writers who came together in agreement. They wanted to write for a women-owned and feminist-run magazine, had been unable to get women as subjects into the general press, and knew they hadn't been able to write about their real interests in traditional women's magazines; there, they felt, they had been muzzled. Steinem, who herself knew how hard it was to write feminist pieces in a hostile environment, had often wondered if this experience was widely shared; now that question was answered.

Might Jane O'Reilly, for example, have written her instantly famous "Click" piece—about the "clicks" in women's minds when they hear sexist remarks and assumptions, particularly from husbands, which had previously passed unnoticed—before the founding of such a magazine? Unlikely; it would not have occurred to her that anyone would publish the piece, so it would not occur to her to write it. Steinem now believed the magazine they were contemplating would provide a place for all the feminist writing no other magazine would publish, let alone assign or inspire. Susan Braudy told Mary Thom that, after a meeting where everyone was arguing and carrying on, she had written Steinem a note telling her that "the only person I could see really heading it was her, even if she kept saying she didn't want to. . . . She was very level-headed and calm, she would be a great person to be in charge of the magazine and she shouldn't shirk that."

Feigen's notion of an expanded version of the WAA newsletter, plus ad hoc meetings of writers, editors, and movement people, had led to many months of unsuccessful efforts to raise money with a mock-up. Then came Clay Felker's offer to publish a piece of a sample issue in *New York* magazine, which always did a double issue at the end of the year. Felker and Steinem therefore determined to include in the December 20, 1971, year-end issue a thirty-page section that allowed women to write on the ideas and experiences giving rise to what Felker called "the contagion of feminism." A preview issue with an additional one hundred pages would then be published nationally as a one-shot test. In return, *New York* would take all the advertising profits from both the insert and the preview issue; the editors would have no control over the advertisers, who would get to be in two publications for the price of one, an additional inducement. *New York* would have half the newsstand profits from the one-hundred-thirty-page preview issue, but would have no continuing interest in or ownership of the new feminist magazine thereafter. It seemed a generous offer at the time and still does.

Felker recalls deciding which among a long list of articles would be best for the *New York* insert. He used many of the *New York* staff, including art directors, Ruth Bower, Nancy Newhouse (now a top editor at the *New York Times*), and Rochelle Udell (now president of CondéNet, but then assistant to Milton Glaser). Steinem and the other editors worked on the first issue for nothing except writing fees. In addition to Steinem, editors of the first issue were journalist Bina Bernard; Joanne Edgar, a political activist and experienced editor; Nina Finkelstein, a book editor with many years experience; journalists Nancy Newhouse and Mary Peacock; and journalist and author Letty Cottin Pogrebin. It was a confluence of the right talent at the right time. Felker insisted on two conditions: that he have the final say on what was in the thirty-page *New York* insert, and that there be a limit on obscene language. The second condition sounds odd today, but Felker remembers the sudden use of obscene language by the newly energized women's movement, and he had already lost advertising for publishing photos of a woman with unshaved armpits.

Mary Thom is writing a full account of the extraordinary birth of *Ms.* and its subsequent history. Its naming, however, is worth recalling here. The name *Ms.* seemed a natural. This form of address for women, which did not require a knowledge of their marital status, was beginning to be widely used (although the *New York Times* did not allow the term until 1986), and, further, Steinem had discovered that the U.S. Printing Office, as early as the 1950s, had allowed use of the form when necessary. Before the name *Ms.* was agreed upon, Steinem had announced her wish to call the new feminist magazine "Sisters"; but the last important woman to come on board, Pat Carbine, was emphatic that, for someone like herself raised in Catholic schools, such a title would be a complete turnoff.

Pat Carbine had moved from being executive editor of *Look* to become, in 1971, editor in chief of *McCall's*. She was the first woman to join the Magazine Publishers board, and for a long time the only woman on the Advertising Council board. At this moment in *Ms.*'s history, however, Carbine was a silent partner in the enterprise, still seeking advice about leaving the position that made her the highest-ranked editorial woman in the magazine business. She had just had a tremendous internal fight at *McCall's* about putting Steinem on the cover as the Woman of the Year. *McCall's* was outraged at the idea of putting a self-declared feminist on the cover; the year before they had featured Katharine Hepburn, the right kind of woman, feisty but no feminist. Carbine threatened to quit; Steinem stayed on the cover. The idea of helping to run a feminist magazine, with radical ideas, was a powerful draw, but she would be giving up a good deal. During this time Carbine went to California and found herself next to Robert Redford at dinner. When she told him her dilemma, he said, "Do it."

James Marshall, an independent investment adviser, helped *Ms.* from the beginning, not by giving money but by volunteering invaluable financial counsel. He did advise Steinem and Carbine to try for a truly mainstream magazine that would make money; they did not take this advice. The actual financial setup of the magazine was arranged by lawyer Philip Mandel and accountant Arthur Tarlow, who remained *Ms.*'s accountant through all its history. Marshall, however, continued to help Steinem and Carbine over the years with contracts and other matters. He says today: "I've always loved Gloria," a simple statement one hears repeated often by men who have known her intermittently, casually, or intensely over the years.

Another who became involved in the early organization of the magazine was Elizabeth Forsling Harris, one of Steinem's few enemies, but her most constant one, who would ultimately cause Steinem and *Ms.* much grief in 1975 when she sued the magazine in a ludicrous action that the media nevertheless covered with glee. Details of the suit and its emotional effect on Steinem will be taken up in the chapter "Trashing."

Steinem and Betty Harris began talking about working together when Harris came to New York from California, where she had hoped to launch a women's newsletter. Brenda Feigen, who would shortly extricate herself from the fund-raising process because of WAA demands, had asked her to come because she claimed to know the business side of magazine publishing and to have important money contacts; she came immediately, which should, perhaps, have suggested some caution. Pat Carbine also met her at this time.

From the beginning Clay Felker found Harris difficult and refused to work with her. As he describes it:

> She had nothing to do with the first issue of *Ms.* magazine. As I remember, she just got in the way, tried to throw her weight around, and frankly, we were putting the magazine out with the *New York* magazine staff and we had hired just a few people. We had Rochelle Udell and Nancy Newhouse working on it; very experienced people. She was coming in there and trying to tell us what to do. I said, in effect, "Don't come around anymore."
>
> I had met her on a weekend in a house party; at first she's kind of plausible. She was there, and it was a friendly thing. Then she started throwing her weight around and I had nothing to do with getting involved with *Ms.* It was Gloria and Pat, and I thought, Well, they must know what they're doing, and I accepted her until she tried to run things and we put a stop to that immediately. Ruth Bower was our first line of defense there; she knows how to deal with something like this.
>
> We heard she was throwing things at Gloria on the promotion tour, and we never could figure out what she was doing on it in the first place, except that Gloria's not a spotlight monger; one of the reasons we wanted Gloria in this project, we didn't have a lot of money, she'd be a wonderful person to promote this. Every once in a while [Betty Harris would] start these wild attacks on Pat and Gloria, and we had to stand by them. Other-

wise, I had nothing to do with her. I frankly was so appalled by this woman that I cut off any more contact as soon as I could. She had nothing to offer. She wasn't a journalist, she wasn't an author, I didn't know what she was doing. She thought she had a role as publisher . . . I wasn't going to let our magazine be run by someone I didn't have any faith in, a stranger. We were putting up all the money for this thing, we weren't all that wealthy, and after all, Gloria and I had worked harmoniously for a long time together; that wasn't really an issue.

Harris is and apparently always was a person who makes an excellent initial impression. She is attractive and calm, and she appears efficient and knowledgeable. Many of those with and for whom she has worked have learned, however, that there is another side to her, which they have described as out-of-control, demanding, and sometimes self-destructive. As this side became evident to Steinem and Carbine, they realized—although it probably took Steinem longer than it would have taken most people—that they could not work with her. Steinem's mishandling of the situation, or at the very least her allowing it to go on so long, suggests that her fear of confrontation and her dislike of personal conflict cost her dearly in this case. Moreover, she had suspended her own discomfort with Harris for a poor reason: Harris was supposed to know about money, and Steinem thought this put her in a different and less compatible group.

Jim Marshall remembers Harris as distraught and unbalanced; the latter is the term that many apply to her. He had found her in their original conversations to be effective, organized, directed, an intelligent person with obvious skills. But she seemed unable to keep herself on track. At the time Harris began arguing with Carbine and Steinem, Marshall thought her self-destructive and scary, and he continues to think she was her own worst enemy. He recognized that Harris was smart and could have been a fine business entrepreneur, were it not for what he viewed as her unbalanced behavior.

As Carbine remembers it, when the three joined forces at the beginning, they each put up $146 as an entry fee. Harris had decided that they should create a corporation with three equal stockholders, Harris, Steinem, and Carbine. She said they needed to have a corporation, to have bylaws, etc., even before they went out to raise money. Carbine recalls that Harris was supposed to be the one to find funds and venture capital.

> Betty spent a lot of time around Wall Street [Carbine recalls]. This was the early 70s, a very go-go time, magazines were attractive as investments, they had an aura of glamour. The idea of investing in a feminist magazine, however, left every- body ice cold. Ice cold! Betty was getting nowhere. I was a silent partner. I was slightly uncomfortable signing the corpora- tion papers, because I was still sitting there as editor of *McCall's,* which it would never be competitive with. Betty and I got on all right, I bought her dinner frequently and cooked dinner for her at home. We talked a lot about how she was going to get this done. We had no money at all; Joanne [Edgar] was work- ing for Gloria then, and when Joanne needed to pay the rent, Gloria would write her a check.

In these financial doldrums, the idea was hatched of going to Katharine Graham, owner of the *Washington Post,* to see if she would like to be a supporter. Steinem, Carbine, and Harris had lunch with Graham at the Newsweek building in October 1971. Carbine again: "It was a great experience to see her response; she was very tentative on the one hand about not committing herself as to whether a magazine like ours could have a viable place, but she felt the idea was intriguing, the timing was appropriate, and the talent seemed promising." As a result of that lunch Graham wrote a personal check for twenty thousand dollars as walking-around money, to see if the three could get their act together, thus becoming a stockholder in a corporation that had no value.

Carbine remembers that "the real Betty Harris began to emerge" as time went on. She didn't handle pressure well. She would call Carbine frequently at night to tell her all that was wrong with the magazine. Simultaneously, Steinem used to call Carbine at night to tell her that Betty was a problem. Carbine recalls that major clues began to make clear "that Harris was not a partner one wanted to grow old with. She was a holy terror." The people at *New York* were finding her intolerable.

The sworn depositions of Joanne Edgar and Clay Felker at the time of the 1975 suit suggest some of the problems they were facing. Edgar reported: "Her behavior was beyond any norm of executive conduct or human courtesy. She treated some of the staff members like dirt, ordering them around and yelling at them. . . . She called me names, yelled at me, and raised her hand and threatened to slap me. . . . She did not hit me but she was out of control. [S]he became furious about something somebody did and she began to throw things at the wall." Clay Felker testified that "she engaged in hostile, screaming tantrums and insults."

It is worth emphasizing that none of this would have become public if Harris had not brought her suit in 1975. But the publicity she achieved, and has continued to achieve in her many newspaper attacks on Steinem, most prominently in the *New York Post,* has of course had far broader circulation than these legal records.

Perhaps, not surprisingly, Harris thought Steinem would be a perfect figurehead, who could get media attention but shouldn't be making decisions. It was clear that Harris wanted major credit for the new magazine, beginning with the insert. She is remembered as instructing those doing the promotion that Steinem was not to appear on any television program without her; whenever there was any publicity, Harris had to have equal access to the microphone. Steinem complicated matters by insisting on Harris's presence out of guilt about the older woman's state of mind. When they eventually toured to publicize the magazine, there was a huge blowup because Harris said *Ms.* magazine hadn't been visible enough. It turned out that she considered herself as synonymous with the magazine. She came home determined to make trouble.

It was clear to Marshall that Steinem and Harris had to separate. An agreement was worked out under which Harris got Majority Productions, a firm she had established, and Steinem got *Ms.,* though each retained 10 percent of the other's organization. Steinem, in her typical way that might, indeed, be seen as abnormally forgiving, wrote Harris a kind letter, sent her flowers, and insisted upon paying her a more than fair sum, as Marshall saw it. Steinem's unsuitable graciousness toward Harris is characteristic and seems preposterous: She always hoped, even in desperate situations like this one, to part amicably.

After the Marshall division in 1972 and the first issue of *Ms.* appeared on newsstands throughout the country, Carbine and Steinem offered Harris a price for her stock if she agreed to sign off on a separation rather than launch a lawsuit, hold a press conference, or commit suicide, all of which she had threatened. At that point, Carbine quit *McCall's* and went to *Ms.* The only funds available were from *New York* magazine's preliminary settlement for the insert; there was no other money. So, when it came time to settle with Harris, Carbine and Steinem made an agreement that she would get half of the revenues from the spring 1972 issue (the first complete issue of *Ms.)* or ten thousand dollars, whichever was greater. In the end she got about thirteen thousand dollars, and they also agreed to pay her two thousand dollars a month for fourteen months. Although Harris was supposed to be the one with contacts for raising money for the magazine, almost all the money contacts were in fact Steinem's, and Steinem recalls that Harris had raised only five thousand dollars. Thus, Harris became the only person to profit from the magazine, and she profited still more when her stock was eventually purchased.

Jim Marshall reports that Steinem and Carbine were adamant from the start about retaining financial control over the magazine. On their initial search for investors, Steinem and Carbine had been turned down once by Warner Communications, but Letty Cottin Pogrebin introduced them to its president, Steve Ross. Although Steinem's enemies later pilloried her because the magazine did ultimately receive one million dollars from Warner's in return for a 25 percent stake in the company, the original offer had been for half again as much money and a one-third interest. That, however, would have been a sufficiently large portion to give Warner the potential to assume control if the magazine ever needed refinancing. Steinem and Carbine resolutely refused the bigger offer, a refusal that Marshall thought greatly impressed Warner. And they did finally retain control, a fact made possible by Warner's ability to understand the need for this women's magazine to be women-controlled. In many ways, of course, Warner's money might have been considered more of a public relations gesture than a serious investment, since it came from an enterprise so rich it had just invested more than four million dollars for a contract with Pelé, a Brazilian soccer player. At a time when the industry minimum for starting even a small magazine was, Carbine recalls, approximately four million dollars, one million dollars was hardly a sufficient sum; the magazine remained woefully underfinanced by industry standards.

THERE WAS A great sense of camaraderie, and no hierarchy, in the one-room office at Forty-first Street and Lexington Avenue where this small group of women had produced the preview issue.

But there was apprehension also. "Could there possibly be even 100,000 women in the country who wanted this unconventional magazine?" Steinem recalls their worrying. She had learned when she went out speaking that feminist doomsayers were wrong: There were many potential feminists around the country. But if you listen to doomsayers long enough you begin to believe them; the magazine might sell in New York, but what about the Midwest, the Southwest? History has shown that they need not have worried. The preview issue sold out in eight days (though its cover was dated *Spring* so that it would remain on the stands if it didn't sell) and complaints about its scarcity became insistent.

Few women who were grown and feminist at that time can forget the first appearance of *Ms.* The cover of the December 20, 1971, *New York* shows two hands holding the cover of the 130-page preview issue. The cover picture is of a woman with eight arms holding in each hand one of the implements essential to a housewife: a frying pan, an iron, a feather duster, a typewriter, a steering wheel, a telephone, a mirror, and a clock. She's weeping from overwork, and the homunculus she is carrying is visible.

Headlines on the cover characterize the articles within: Gloria Steinem's on "Sisterhood"; Letty Pogrebin's on "Raising Kids Without Sex Roles"; Jane O'Reilly's on "The Housewife's Moment of Truth"; "Sylvia Plath's Last Major Work *(Three Women: A Play for Three Voices)*"; and Barbara Lee Diamonstein's "Women Tell the Truth About Their Abortions." Inside could be found "My Mother the Dentist" (by Nicholas von Hoffman); "Why Women Fear Success" by Vivian Gornick; "Can Women Love Women?" by Anne Koedt; "I Want a Wife" by Judy Syfers; and "Welfare Is a Woman's Issue," by Johnnie Tillman. That subjects such as these, still viable and debatable today, appeared in this new feminist magazine is certainly astonishing. For women throughout the country, it was mind-blowing. Here was, written down, what they had not yet admitted they felt, had always feared to say out loud, and could not believe was now before their eyes, in public, for all to read.

When the preview issue came out, David Frost turned over his television show to Steinem, with whom he had worked on *That Was the Week That Was,* allowing her to devote the program to feminism and the new magazine. The tape, seen today, reveals that in those days it was possible, if one was given time on television, to develop an idea without the feverish pressure characteristic of today's broadcasting. Jeannette Rankin, the antiwar activist and first woman to serve in Congress, was on the program, together with singer Judy Collins, Jane O'Reilly, Eleanor Holmes Norton, Margaret Sloan, and Betty Harris. Dorothy Pitman Hughes and her sisters closed the program with a song they had written for the occasion. (In addition to her uniform of a turtleneck leotard, jeans, and boots, Steinem wore aviator glasses and very long hair, from behind which she seemed to peer. The earpieces of her glasses went over rather than under her hair, holding it forward, perhaps to make it function as a curtain. Carbine's mother kept saying to her, "I don't know why you left *McCall's,* because every time I see your partner on television, she looks as though she ought to cut her hair.")

Long, enthusiastic letters, more than 20,000 of them, came in from women all over the country.[8] The issue of *New York* with the insert sold so well that Ruth Bower, the business manager of *New York* and subsequently of *Ms.,* said that they couldn't include the figure on their ABC statement: it would have skewed their circulation numbers for the following year. As Clay Felker put it, if *New York*'s average sale of an issue was 40,000, this issue sold 120,000. It is worth noting at this point that from the moment of its triumphant birth *Ms.* has lacked neither readers nor critics.

---

[8] The editors discovered that a typical women's magazine, with a circulation of, say, seven million, received fewer than two thousand letters an issue.

Advertisers would cause the greatest problem, both because of their dictatorial attitudes toward the editorial content of women's magazines and because of their inability to understand the kind of market the new magazine represented. In addition, *Ms.* wouldn't provide the pages of recipes, beauty copy, and fashion spreads that "complement" ads.

But it is the critics who, throughout the history of *Ms.,* present the greatest puzzle. Not that the magazine did not deserve criticism; not that the editors did not make mistakes, and recognize them. Rather, the critics seemed to comprise ardent groups of feminists from the left and the right who vehemently felt that *Ms.* was not the magazine it should be. NOW objected that its efforts and accomplishments were insufficiently reported. Those on the left scorned *Ms.* for many reasons, most of which resulted from the original determination to create a slick, widely distributed magazine, which looked quite unlike left-wing publications (even though it shared their principles). Steinem herself was the major target of most of this criticism, a great part of which was made by people who either wished for another sort of magazine altogether or were wholly unaware of the practical problems involved in editing any magazine, let alone a feminist one. Feminist author Vivian Gornick, who wrote for *Ms.* from the beginning, was the only critic of the magazine who, in an article written for the *Village Voice* in 1975, recognized the futility of blame. "Gloria Steinem and *Ms.* are not the enemy," she wrote. "The enemy is sexism."

Gornick did not claim to admire the magazine or its editors. "Their view of the world is not my view of the world." She was politically to the left of *Ms.* and certainly had little sympathy for a glossy mass-distributed publication. For all that, however, she concluded, its producers were feminists, and her allies in a larger cause.

The first regular issue of *Ms.* was published in July of 1972, with Steinem and Pat Carbine its leading figures, despite the alphabetical listing of all editors in an effort to avoid any replication of the typical male hierarchical structure. The editors were those who had produced the *Ms.* insert, plus Suzanne Braun Levine, Harriet Lyons, Margaret Sloan, and Ruth Sullivan. Carbine became the individual responsible for the business end of the magazine. Steinem, whatever she preferred to believe, was clearly the dominant figure. Although she would spend more time on the road than in the office—still speaking on behalf of feminism and trying to raise money, and obtain advertisements and publicity for *Ms.,* there was never any question whose name was most widely associated with the magazine, or who was its star. However, Suzanne Braun Levine became the only editor through whose hands every article published in the magazine sooner or later passed; among others who worked for the magazine from its beginning to its sale in 1987 were Joanne Edgar, Letty Cottin Pogrebin, and Mary Thom. Editors came, and some of them went. Steinem herself was ambivalent for quite a while whether she would remain.

Clay Felker remembered leaving Steinem at the new *Ms.* office after lunch one day. She paused at the entrance to say to him: "This is something I've always wanted to do, but it is coming at the wrong time in my life." Twenty years later Steinem would confirm Felker's recollections: "The magazine was something I wanted to happen; I wanted there to be a feminist magazine, but I didn't want to do it. I remember saying to Clay, 'I'll do this for two years, no longer.' "

DISSONANCE
AT CLOSE
QUARTERS

THE YEAR *Ms.* magazine was launched, the Vietnam War was tearing the country apart. Nixon was president and would be reelected at the end of 1972. By that year, U.S. feminism was establishing itself, despite being dubbed "a passing fad" by the *New York Times,* which also announced that "in small town USA, Women's liberation is either a joke or a bore"; Harry Reasoner gave *Ms.* "six months before it ran out of things to say." *Ms.* magazine, on the other hand, was preparing for the future. The *Ms.* Foundation was established in 1972 because no foundations then extant gave money to women's causes; the Foundation was to receive the profits of the magazine, if any.[1] Gloria Steinem's face was on the cover of *McCall's,* who called her "Woman of the Year," and on the cover of *New Woman* as well. She was photographed for newspapers throughout the country, speaking, sup-

---

[1] In 1973, the NBC-TV special *Free to Be . . . You and Me* was created by Marlo Thomas to benefit the *Ms.* Foundation. It won an Emmy, and continued to sell as a book and recording.

porting political women. Liz Smith interviewed her in *Redbook* talking about sex, politics, and marriage in a long article offering over many pages a history of the women's movement. Earlier, in Washington, Steinem became the first woman to address the National Press Club (they gave her a tie). On the radio, Steinem could be heard on the Barry Gray show together with Brenda Feigen and Richard Reeves, the political writer, discussing the coming election, war, violence, and masculinity, among other topics.

The media had decided that the women's movement was not a fad likely to fade immediately away, so they made the best of an uncomfortable revolution by identifying it with a woman attractive in their eyes. Naturally enough, this annoyed quite a few people, including many women from the early days of feminism, who had originally risen up against the male-centeredness of the student and civil rights organizations. Had they demonstrated against Miss America only to have someone else anointed as a true representative of *their* movement? Her appearance was not, however, the only reason she was chosen: She was also the only feminist who happened at that time to be working in the media while also working full-time for the movement.[2] The resentment of Steinem's media coverage was both understandable and forgivable, although less so some years later when it would take the form of a real vendetta. The scorn of the left was logical; they had early hoped to bring about an anticonsumer, anti–woman-as-sexobject revolution, and they regretted, with reason, those heady days.

The new magazine promised to be successful, but Steinem's wish to work on it for only two years seemed less likely to be

---

[2] By then, Abzug was in Congress, Friedan was no longer president of NOW, and the media disqualified all women of color, wrongly assuming all feminists were white.

fulfilled; it was becoming increasingly clear that the needs of *Ms.* would bind her well beyond her hopes for a shorter commitment.

In addition to her work at *Ms.,* Steinem's strong political alliances were continuing their demands, the Democratic National Convention loomed, and she still had her own journalism projects and her hopes of writing.

India had been the first and last time for Steinem, up to this point, when an awareness of the pleasures of "now," of the present, had been possible. Until the combination of the magazine's sale in 1987 and her own exhaustion forced her to stop and reflect, in her fifties, on the experiences that led to *Revolution from Within,* her ability to savor the present moment would not return; the knowledge that she was urgently, constantly needed was always palpable, and she drove herself accordingly. But at least she had learned, as long ago as the 1968 Democratic Convention, the lesson that experience had to teach, and when she returned to politics in 1972 at the Democratic Convention in Miami she worked only for women—their platform, and their demands. She worked through no male candidate.

At the very beginning of 1972, Hubert Humphrey wrote to Steinem, informing her of the imminent announcement of his candidacy, asking for her advice and help, and hoping that he would soon be working with her. But, of course, it was South Dakota Senator George McGovern, who had been the first to speak out against the Vietnam War on the floor of the Senate, who received the Democratic nomination. Nixon, the opposing Republican candidate, represented, as Steinem's articles on him for *New York* magazine made clear, everything she and the political forces she worked with most feared.

Women at the convention, widely condemned by party regulars for what were considered their unrealistic demands, struggled in an atmosphere of what often seemed like betrayal; their demands were always, it appeared, the first to go under pressure. Steinem and the NWPC had been there from the beginning during the reform of the delegates selection process, and had also urged the inclusion of women's reproductive rights in the Democratic platform. They were demanding, unsuccessfully as it turned out, that those delegations subject to challenge on inclusiveness not be seated. Because of the reform rules, many women were seated, but the politicians themselves were still at the stage of displaying one white movie star and one black athlete. As NWPC member Donna Brunstadt reported to the Connecticut Women's Political Caucus: "I don't think anyone sat out in the trailer and said, 'How can we let the women down on these issues?' They figured, 'They'll follow McGovern to hell and back.' " As she later reflected at that point, "most of us would have. I no longer would do that for any man." Steinem had made that very decision four years earlier.

The situation of women in politics up to and in the few years following the 1972 Democratic National Convention is cogently analyzed in Susan and Martin Tolchin's book *Clout* (about how women don't have it, politically), from which the Brunstadt quote is taken. The Tolchins open their book with a question from a woman television reporter to Mayor John Lindsay about why there were no women commissioners in his administration. "Honey," he answered, "whatever women do, they do best after dark."

This was one typical response. Another, also recorded by the Tolchins, was delivered by New York Representative Emmanuel Celler, who was then dean of the House and chairman of its Judiciary Committee. He said he opposed the Equal Rights Amendment; after all, he told Bella Abzug, there were no women at the Last Supper. She responded: "But there will be at the next." One rejoices to remember that Celler was unseated in the next election by Liz Holtzman.

The Tolchins report Steinem's dismay at the way feminists

were being covered by the media, a dismay there has since been no reason to abate. Six hundred women had attended a day-long meeting in 1972 of the Manhattan Women's Political Caucus. "About a third of them were black and Puerto Rican," Steinem points out. "It actually represented the city. It is the only political meeting I have ever been to in my life which racially represented the city. And the press reported it as mostly white middle-class. They do not go into the NDC [New Democratic Coalition] and report that, or the Republican party where you can go snow-blind, as mostly white middle-class."

At the convention itself Steinem became so upset and angry at the floor fight over women's reproductive rights being included in the platform that she "wept with rage," according to Nora Ephron, reporting on the events in Miami. ("I cry when I get angry," Steinem says.) She attacked Gary Hart, at the time McGovern's campaign manager, of whom Jean Westwood, one of McGovern's earliest advisers, said to the Tolchins: "I think Gary Hart did not like women in politics, even though he liked me. He once made a remark that there were no women involved. Somebody took him to task about it, and he said, 'I didn't mean Jean; I never think of her as a woman.' "[3]

It is well to remember that in 1972, during an extremely fraught convention, the feminists were living under hardly ideal conditions. Theodore H. White, however unsympathetic to

[3] Hart, who of course, ultimately lost his chance at the Presidency through flaunting his womanizing, was, like Celler, not quite prepared for the changing tides in the affairs of men. Nor, after he was elected, was Bill Clinton. In December of 1992, Clinton lashed out at women's groups, who had done so much to assure his election, for "playing quota games and male games" about his selection of Cabinet posts. The women had hoped that Clinton would keep his promise and appoint more women to his Cabinet than his Republican predecessors. The article on this in the *New York Times* (Dec. 23, 1992, p. A15) was the more remarkable for staunch Republican Jeane Kirkpatrick's confirmation of the fact that "successive Presidents find so many different reasons not to appoint specific women to specific positions in specific Cabinets," and, she added, they "always get irritable if they get pressed about this."

women and Democrats, reports this best, observing that the NWPC

> had taken over as headquarters the third floor of the derelict, sea-sprayed Betsy Ross Hotel. One might be amused by the high-octave span of women's voices gathered together, or the rooms with the unmade beds, half-unpacked suitcases, yogurt cartons, chests covered with blue-jeans and bras—but only briefly. The Betsy Ross Hotel was a power center. Mimeograph and Xerox machines spewed out leaflets in thousands of pink, yellow, green, blue sheets; the switchboard at the Betsy Ross Hotel jammed; fuses blew; and each night, after dark, couriers boarded the buses to travel north on Collins Avenue and persuade night clerks of the forty or more major hotels to stuff mailboxes or let them slip leaflets under delegates' doors. "Women Power 1972" remained stained on the Betsy Ross's third-floor carpet, in faded red paint, when the convention broke up; women power 1972 was real. [168]

Two women named Shirley were responsible for much of the struggle that rocked the women in Miami at that time: Congresswoman Shirley Chisholm and actress Shirley MacLaine. Shirley MacLaine defended McGovern against the demands of his women supporters and succeeded in having women's right to choose abortion removed from the platform.[4] Throughout the convention, MacLaine made clear her conviction that were McGovern to accede to women's demands, he would weaken his chance for nomination. About Shirley Chisholm there is more to say. The struggle that ensued after she was nominated and ran for president serves

---

[4] The Tolchins, like Ephron, make good reading on the subject of Shirley MacLaine at this time. Certainly no biography of George McGovern will be complete without an account of MacLaine's part in his 1972 campaign.

as an example of how history—and biography—picks and chooses its evidence.

Chisholm was the first black woman to run for president, and Steinem backed her in every state where she was on the ticket. In states where Chisholm was not on the ticket, Steinem continued to back McGovern, saying he was the best of the male candidates. This was particularly confusing in New York state, where Steinem had backed McGovern before Chisholm entered the race, and where Steinem was running as a delegate. McGovern forces feared, with some reason, that voters would assume that a vote for Steinem as delegate would be a vote for McGovern. Shirley Chisholm herself records in her book *The Good Fight* that on television programs Steinem would say, "I'm for Shirley Chisholm—but I think that George McGovern is the best of the *male* candidates." Chisholm reports that she told Gloria: "You're supporting either George McGovern or Shirley Chisholm . . . don't do me any favors by giving me this semiendorsement. I don't need that kind of help." Paula Giddings, in her book *When and Where I Enter: The Impact of Black Women on Race and Sex in America,* repeats this story, adding that Steinem was "coy." [338]

To some, it might seem that Steinem was trying to have a foot in both camps, to avoid saying no to either. Like all politicians, she was balancing the need to accomplish her aims with the need to please those in power, and in this case she displeased both McGovern and Chisholm. When this is done in Congress, we understand even if we condemn it. But since Steinem was not an elected politician, it inevitably appeared to her critics that she was unable to commit herself, and thus she antagonized those she admired and who had long counted on her. But Steinem wrote Chisholm's major TV speech, which Chisholm delivered almost word for word; in addition to running as a Chisholm delegate, Steinem also supported her for vice president until Chisholm bowed out in favor of Sissy Farenthold, a political feminist from Texas who later headed the NWPC.

Betty Friedan was another matter. It was at the convention that Friedan threw the gauntlet at Steinem in earnest. As Nora Ephron would observe later that year, reporting on the Miami convention, Betty Friedan believed the women's movement was her movement. "Is she supposed to sit still and let a beautiful, thin lady run off with it?" Ephron asked. Ephron estimated clearly enough the absolute importance of appearance. In addition there is no question that Ephron understood the position in which Steinem now found herself: "Gloria," she wrote,

has become dedicated in a way that is a little frightening and almost awe-inspiring. She is demanding to be taken seriously— and it is the one demand her detractors, who prefer to lump her in with all the other radical-chic beautiful people, cannot bear to grant her. Once the glamour girl, all legs and short skirts and long painted nails, David Webb rings, Pucci, Gucci, you-name- it-she-had-it, once a fixture in gossip columns, which linked her to one attractive man after another, she has managed to trans- form herself almost totally. She now wears Levi's and simple T-shirts—and often the same outfit two days running. The nails are as long as ever, but they are unpolished, and her fingers bare. She has managed to keep whatever private life she still has out of the papers. Most important, she projects a calm, peaceful, subdued quality; her humor is gentle, understated. Every so often, someone suggests that Gloria Steinem is only into the women's movement because it is currently the chic place to be; it always makes me smile, because she is about the only remotely chic thing connected with the movement. [43–44]

What Ephron recognized in Miami, not uniquely, but more wittily and more analytically than most, was Betty Friedan's dis- may over all the women who were taking attention and, as she thought of it, *her* movement, away from her. Ephron observed that one year earlier, Friedan had resigned from the national board of NOW because of her disagreements with it, and had run and lost as a Chisholm delegate to the convention, during which campaign she had issued a press release announcing that she would appear in Harlem with a "Traveling Watermelon Feast." Regardless of her support of Chisholm, sensitivity toward blacks was not Friedan's strong suit. The truth was, as Ephron observed, that Friedan's influence in the movement had waned.

It is quite simply regrettable—indeed sad—that Friedan could not learn to share the limelight. Intimations of this came when an election was held for the steering committee of the NWPC the previous July. Many women were elected, but Friedan, one of the founders of the NWPC, was not one of them. Friedan felt cheated, and demanded a recount of the ballots. She even went so far as to send a lawyer to Washington to look through the organization's books, promising that if all looked in order she would drop the issue. She dropped the issue.

But the worst jolt came two weeks before the convention, when the NWPC chose Steinem as the spokesperson for the Democratic Convention over Friedan, even though Steinem wasn't even there at the time and didn't want the honor. The spokesperson's duties included speaking for group decisions and representing the NWPC at morning roundtable meetings of all the other out groups, from the Black Congressional Caucus to the informal Poor People's Conference—duties they didn't believe Friedan could perform well. As a result, as Ephron reported it, Friedan accused Steinem of "ripping off the movement," of being "a tool of George McGovern," of being "part of a racist clique that would not support" Chisholm.

"Every day," Ephron continued, "Friedan would call the Betsy Ross Hotel downtown and threaten to call a press conference to expose the caucus. Every day, at the meetings the NWPC held for press and female delegates, movement leaders would watch with a kind of horrified fascination to see what Betty Friedan would do next." [43]

For Steinem the convention was a kind of nightmare, which combined public speaking and the fear of confrontation she always avoided with the responsibility for presenting the first-ever organized women's electoral pressure as a well-organized success. But there was one reward: jointly nominating (with Fannie Lou Hamer and a representative of the Chicano Caucus) a female vice president, Sissy Farenthold, and seeing the convention's support. Great strides were made, but nonetheless, a week after the convention Friedan attacked Steinem again, in an article in *McCall's,* quoting her out of context and calling her antimale, an accusation Ephron and all the others naturally found preposterous. The article's main thrust was to defend men who criticized the women's movement as having gone too far, to talk about a husband's "pain and loneliness," and to use phrases such as "If we make men the enemy, they will surely lash back at us," (neatly twisting the fact that the women she condemned had not made men "the enemy," but were criticizing a system that placed the needs of men at its center). Friedan condemned what she called "female chauvinism," and concluded: "Brooding on the danger signs of corruption and backlash, I feel that the women's liberation movement has had enough of sexual politics. . . . It's time to leave behind as dinosaurs, or isolate as lethal freaks, male chauvinist pigs and female chauvinist boors alike."[5] When she collected articles for her 1976 book *It Changed My Life,* Friedan notably did not include this ill-judged piece from *McCall's,* although her next book, *The Second Stage* (1981), was to make many of the same points. What remained in *It Changed My Life* is, however, replete with unflatter-

---

[5] Significantly, this accusation that early feminists were "man-haters" would be repeated in the 1990s by third-wave feminists such as Naomi Wolf and Katie Roiphe.

ing remarks aimed at Steinem. Steinem, the "beautiful thin lady," was clearly the most resented of all.

By 1972, Friedan's hatred of Steinem had come to public attention; the legend of this one-sided feud between two leaders of the women's movement became a part of the lore of feminism. "Trashing," as it had come to be called, was a recognized danger in the women's movement. Probably no feminist of any prominence has not been attacked by some woman in the same line of work who resented the publicity and attention she received. In this regard, Friedan did the movement some damage—first, by wishing to retain her central position as "mother"; and second, by trying to keep the movement from taking up such causes as abortion, lesbian rights, and welfare, which she regarded as so much unnecessary baggage in the struggle to give middle-class women their rightful place beside men in the mainstream. Her distrust and dislike of other women leaders, of whom she seemed to hate Steinem the most, never abated. Friedan never understood that a little reform, like a little pregnancy, will not continue in the same stage for long.

It is most frequently assumed that Friedan's resentment of Steinem stems from simple envy of Steinem's looks. On the other hand, Friedan was getting enough publicity on her own. The *New York Times* for many years seemed to consider her the only—or at least the representative—feminist. She was featured in that paper more often than any other feminist, and considerably more often than Steinem. For example, on November 29, 1970, Paul Wilkes wrote an article for the *New York Times Magazine* on Friedan, entitled "The Mother Superior to Women's Lib." Many feminists must have thought that an arguable assertion. In it, Friedan damned the "man-hating radicals" with her usual ferocity.[6]

---

[6] When *Life* magazine ran an issue in the fall of 1990 covering "The 100 Most Important Americans of the 20th Century," it included Friedan as the only feminist, calling

But every time Steinem, to her own dismay, was portrayed as the spokeswoman for the movement, Friedan suffered the reopening of a deep wound. It is certainly true that without the presence of Steinem, Friedan would still have fought lesbians and others more radical than she, would still have attacked Bella Abzug, Kate Millett, and others, and would certainly have always been a difficult person, even to her most ardent admirers. As Paul Wilkes reported in the *New York Times Magazine,* "Jacqui Ceballos [Friedan's close, longtime friend] won't gloss over Betty's faults. 'She's a terror to deal with, and there is an overpowering ego at work.' "

But Ceballos and many others, including younger women, are willing to credit Friedan with changing their lives with *The Feminine Mystique.* For that book, even if its message was limited to an audience of middle-class, educated women in the suburbs, did entice millions of mainstream, suburban women into feminism. And with the creation of NOW, Friedan brought together a group of women who were able to exert pressure on federal regulatory agencies to enforce the laws against sex discrimination, and who accomplished much else that continued to reverberate until the first Reagan administration.

Friedan and some of those who did important work in NOW and the NOW Legal Defense Fund feel bitter that *Ms.* never gave their important efforts sufficient coverage or credit. But the differences between Friedan's and Steinem's feminist philosophies had long since revealed themselves. As early as 1970, for example, Friedan told a reporter from the *Palo Alto Times:* "I think the movement has been infiltrated and the lesbian issue has been pushed forward for divisive purposes. We must not let ourselves

---

her "The Housewife Who Liberated Everywoman." All of those named were widely influential, for better or worse (such as Joe McCarthy), and her place among them marked the fact that the mainstream press continued to recognize Friedan as the founder of the women's movement, however inaccurately. It had no single founder.

be used." This was an opinion with which Steinem profoundly disagreed. Similarly, Friedan and Aileen Hernandez, the second president of NOW, who was to become Steinem's close friend and companion in arms, disagreed over the necessity of including minority women in the publications and ads put out by NOW. The inclusion of minority women, essential to Hernandez, was also essential to Steinem.

In the midst of all this fervid activity, a figure of reassurance, crucial sympathy, and rapport entered Steinem's life. By 1971 Frank Thomas had become the most important and intensely cherished of her lovers. It would be only partly true to say that he provided a sea of calm in her turbulent life; he was himself preparing for a difficult divorce when Steinem met him.

Franklin Thomas, the longtime head of the Ford Foundation until his retirement in 1995, was directing the Bedford-Stuyvesant Development Corporation. He and Steinem met when both were appearing on a panel discussing urban justice issues at Brooklyn College. His mother, born in Barbados, had been a maid, and was a woman of great wisdom and calm. Thomas worked his way through college, and then through law school after a stint as a navigator in the Air Force. He was on Robert Morgenthau's staff in the Manhattan D.A.'s office, and then went on to direct the Bedford-Stuyvesant restoration. As chief officer, he was known to hire women for unstereotypical positions, including as construction workers—and to include them as neighborhood leaders.

Steinem had always believed that sympathetic black men had special insight into the problems of women of all races because, unlike white men, they understood on a visceral level what being treated like a stereotype was like. It is certain that Thomas confirmed and still confirms that observation. He seemed, like Rafer Johnson (though she had a far more profound relationship with Thomas), to comprehend on a visceral level the constant denigration women face, the frequent parallels between racism and sexism. (Both men also benefited from heroic and wise mothers.) Once, Steinem and Thomas were at a fund-raiser for the Women's Action Alliance, of which both were board members; one of the corporate executives attending came up to them, said something of a lecherous nature to Steinem, and punched Frank playfully in the stomach, asking if he played basketball. Each knew instantly how the other felt, and each understood that such attitudes came together for a reason.

Steinem and Thomas have remained close friends who speak to each other every week, offering encouragement in the conduct of their eventful lives. Each considers the other an essential support and consultant, without whom life would be considerably less livable. The question arises among Steinem's friends: Why didn't she marry Thomas? Again, from her point of view, if they did stay together they would probably have to get married; and Steinem was still avoiding marriage. But as she came to recognize as she turned forty, her avoidance of marriage had become rational and positive rather than negative: Her fears of having her professional life end, or of being unable to extricate herself from an unhappy relationship, were no longer operative. She was ready to admit to herself that she wanted to live alone and function as an individual human being. She recognized also that her vague intentions to one day get married and have children—but not yet —were evasions of her now-clear decision and were no longer necessary.

Beyond all this—and most importantly—both she and Thomas recognized that they would be better off retaining their friendship but having a central relationship with someone less like themselves. They were simply too much alike. They shared not only painful experiences of racism and sexism and their admiration for each other's intellect and generosity, but above all a certain calm acquiescence in the face of life's assaults. Two people so inclined to be laid-back each needed someone with a higher level of emotional energy. Both of them did find such people (in Steinem's case it was Stan Pottinger, the next beneficent man in her life), who could firmly and convincingly talk them out of their languor.

Changing her relationship with Thomas was a long and painful process for Steinem. She thinks in retrospect that because Thomas was having a hard time with his divorce and its effect on his children, the emotional demands on her forced her into what she calls her "taking-care-of-my-mother groove." This was her problem, not his; but she reacted as she had with her mother: She did everything she was expected to do, but she was turned off emotionally.

Frank Thomas and Gloria Steinem remained lovers from about the time of the founding of *Ms.* until 1975. When that part of their relationship ended, Thomas became the central figure, and one of the few men, in Steinem's devoted chosen family. George Bernard Shaw said, as have others, that the best friendships between men and women are between those no longer lovers. It is a wise observation.

CLEARLY TENSIONS would define Steinem's early years at *Ms.,* particularly the tension between the mission to provide a forum for new feminist ideas and the impetus to bring basic women's issues to as many readers as possible, and between Steinem's innate reluctance to offend anyone, where offensiveness would be essential against the tough imperatives of a business operation dependent on advertising.

These tensions arose, furthermore, from that most difficult and paradigmatic task facing feminists: the dangerous and perplexing undertaking of operating within established patriarchal institutions, whether journalistic, commercial, governmental, academic, or religious. Though running an alternative, woman-controlled publication like *Ms.* was not the same as having to operate within a traditional magazine or publishing company, in the media world the need to acquire sufficient funding for feminist endeavors provides perhaps the most formidable of all such challenges.

During the *Ms.* years, the price Steinem paid for her appearance never lessened; it is not clear that she recognized that cost. Steinem was the woman moneyed men would meet with, often only to patronize her. Steinem's closest associates were always aware of how useful she was in fund-raising, and how relentlessly she was used for that purpose by organizations she wished to help. By the time of the 1990s adless *Ms.,* Steinem's books as premiums to new subscribers were the absolutely most effective attraction, even while she wished it could be otherwise.

For Steinem, taking on the magazine was an expression of her decision not to work any longer in male-dominated organizations. Yet she did not take the opposite tack and align herself with the usual small, volunteer, counterculture newsprint magazine, such as *off our backs*. Because she wished above all else to appeal to working women and to those with little money who were attracted to "real" magazines, and because she did not see her ideal audience as composed either of intellectuals or those who were already members of feminist organizations, she understood the advantage of producing a glossy, inviting magazine that was available nationwide.

A contradiction emerges here. If Steinem was all her life critical of the middle class and uninspired by its standards, why did she, as her many critics would ask, make her magazine one that would appeal to this very group? The answer is complex, and has to do with the difference between image and reality. Glossy paper is not only necessary to sell advertising, it is also cheaper. Moreover, neither working-class nor lower-middle-class women are likely to pore over the fuzzy mimeographed sheets of feminist organizations. That her feminist message became instantly attractive to middle-class women tells us more about the sudden appeal of feminism than about Steinem's intentions. It is also notable that women of color made up a larger percentage of *Ms.*'s readers than of any other women's magazine except *Essence.* Yet it cannot be denied that, standing as she did between the working class and the upper middle class, Steinem was able, aiming at one, to reach both. To this must be added that, inevitably, many of the writers for *Ms.* magazine, even if radical in their beliefs, were themselves upper-middle-class, by education if not by origin.

Many believed at the time, and believe still, that a magazine both glossy and absolutely feminist is an oxymoron. To the challenge of this combination, Steinem, with the other early editors, added another: the determination to run a communal, cooperative, nonhierarchical, democratic organization, in the tradition of the strict structurelessness of the early radical women's movement, with its rejection of spokespersons and its assignment of duties by lot. They felt that this came naturally to women weary of male hierarchies.

A further problem is subtler, less easily enunciated: that of the voice of the magazine. One reason Steinem was able always to meet new people with eagerness and mutual satisfaction was her ability to sustain a conversation, often repeated, with those who were just discovering feminism. She was also ever ready to expound first principles, and to encourage newly born excitements, even as she herself continued to absorb new ideas and possibilities. For intellectuals, for radical theorists, and certainly for academics, the excitement of new ideas rapidly faded; they came to prefer the detailed examination of texts, theories, and discourse. Indeed, the *Ms.* staff assumed they were providing an in-take mechanism for the movement, which people would read for a few years and then move on, but this meant an added expense of always replacing a certain number of subscribers. Nonetheless, they did not want to be, in Steinem's words, "like *Commentary,* where people grew old along with Norman Podhoretz."[7] In fact, the reading pattern that developed was composed of three groups: new readers, a few who never left, and many who left for a while but came back because there were always some issues and information they could find nowhere else.

Even Steinem's most devoted friends have found difficulty in understanding how she could repeat the same ideas, differently formulated and with great enthusiasm, in speech after speech and listen with genuine eagerness to the responses of her audience. She had a way of sticking to fundamentals that was beyond the comprehension of some of those who worked with her on the magazine and wanted to refine and question those fundamentals. Paradoxically, her talent for tolerating restatement and for making it exciting would, by the time she reached her sixties, run the risk of imprisoning her in concepts too little reconsidered.

To Steinem and the other founding editors, the magazine's first priority was to speak to an ever wider audience, and its ability to return to first principles in new ways was then its significant strength. The *Ms.* staff were less interested in producing an "elite" magazine featuring professional writers than in publishing as many women as they could—some 530 different writers in the magazine's first years—and in giving a voice to the thousands of letter writers who, whether they praised or attacked, were the extraordinary and unique expression of *Ms.*'s success.[8]

It is also important to remember that the preview issue and

---

[7] In May of this year Podhoretz stepped down from his thirty-five-year term as editor in chief of *Commentary* magazine.

[8] Amy Erdman Farrell's 1991 dissertation for the department of history at the University of Minnesota, *Feminism in the Mass Media: Ms. Magazine, 1972–1989,* presents, with clarity and balance, the history of the magazine and its prominent complexities. Farrell's work is of particular value because she understands that while *Ms.* faced many problems, the response of its readers and their belief in the magazine provide an indication of its success that an account of the more obvious financial and editorial problems might ignore.

additional material sold out in eight days. In spite of the antifeminist, male-gaze advertising *New York* magazine had accepted for the preview issue, this phenomenal response indicated a
hunger among American women that no one had completely anticipated.

More rigorously feminist publications like *off our backs* were
sharply restricted in their circulation and tended to be read by the
already converted, relatively few in number. As early as 1921,
Frieda Kirshwey, longtime editor of *The Nation,* had felt that a
"new sort of women's magazine," one that would work to "spread
the feminist revolution" was called for. [34] Fifty years later, *Ms.*
magazine answered that call. Of course, it was precisely the mass-
circulation aspect of the magazine and its glossy mass-media look
that caused most of the defections within the feminist community.

Inevitably, in appearing on newsstands next to the *Ladies'
Home Journal* and *Cosmopolitan,* and with these as the only available models of women's magazines, *Ms.* ran the danger of resembling them too closely; this was a real threat to the new magazine's integrity. Neither Mary Thom nor Steinem believes that it
ever competed with other women's magazines for readers or advertisers. But newsstands are segregated by sex, and *Ms.* could not
get placed next to *Time, Newsweek, Rolling Stone,* or other magazines its readers were most likely to seek out. To the continuing
distress of Steinem and Carbine, advertisers didn't differentiate
among women readers, and never believed that *Ms.* readers were
different from the readers of standard women's magazines.

Ms. felt enormous pressure from all sides on every question; for
example, many letter writers were offended by articles on lesbianism, or couldn't identify with women of color, while others complained that the magazine's audience was too clearly white, middle class, and heterosexual. But from the beginning, and especially
at the beginning, *Ms.* was clearly part of a new way for women to

look at the world around them: It was distinctly feminist, and remained so. In a world where the media often misrepresents the movement and almost never depicts feminism fairly or without also offering an antifeminist counter, *Ms.* spoke directly and unapologetically for a clear, feminist point of view.

As the years went on, the problems of finding enough advertisers to offset rising production and postal costs became increasingly acute. Advertisers of traditional women's products who did not demand complementary copy about their product remained scarce, as did those who could be convinced that feminists had money and would spend it on such nontraditional items as, cars and sound equipment. (Steinem was fond of observing that shaving cream was advertised in men's magazines without the advertisers insisting upon an article about how to shave.) And after ten years of publication, it would be *Ms.*'s failure to appeal to advertisers that caused it to lose money despite its many readers. By the eighties this problem would become a highly destructive force in Steinem's life.

The spirit of those early days at *Ms.* can best be recaptured by the memories of Mary Peacock, who left the magazine in March of 1977. Peacock had been with *Ms.* from the beginning, editing the regular columns in the front of the magazine. She recalls,

> I was there early enough so that I had enough territory. When I started there were only four people in the tiny office, and my desk was a cardboard box. I was one of the few people there who felt that they did have enough power, except about the covers. Harriet Lyons and I didn't really have a say in the covers although we had ideas. I felt heard in editorial meetings and in my comments on articles, but the covers weren't discussed in editorial meetings.
>
> There was always the question of whether *Ms.* was a feminist magazine speaking to the converted, or a general woman's

magazine having a feminist base. It was never resolved. This
push and pull made for a lot of editorial flattening; neither side
could win, but they should have let the authentic voices come
out.

The problem of the magazine, in my reading, was not so
much political, as not wanting to show any warts on women.
"Is it good for the women's movement?" All the feminist voices
had to be perfect. It was about making women look good because we were so vulnerable. This was going to prove that
women were not all these bad things. We had to say "M, S" for
the first few years, because you couldn't say "Ms," no one understood it, they pretended it was a buzz. That was a different
time, it was all best foot forward.

If many of the editors had hopes of turning more women to
feminism, there were others who early scorned the particular feminism *Ms.* promulgated; yet for all its difficulties, the magazine
provided new and unusual editorial challenges. Everyone on the
staff was welcome at the editorial meetings, which took place in a
room furnished only with carpeted steps to sit upon, so there were
no privileged positions. Everyone, theoretically, had an equal
chance to talk, and those who have reported on the meetings
describe them as freewheeling, often including accounts of personal experiences or decisions. Each person could offer ideas or
comment on those already presented. Many felt, however, that
despite the democratic editorial exchange, certain individuals, like
Steinem and Levine, were more equal than others. They tried
various remedies such as meeting before the general session with
the younger or newer staff members who had difficulty speaking
out.

The absence of the usual masthead was another aspect of this
antihierarchical arrangement. The editors were listed in alphabetical order, as were the members of other departments. Pat Car-

bine, who had the most publishing experience, was made publisher, but even she was listed alphabetically with her staff.

This masthead form was to cause difficulties later. Some of the women came to require and demand, for professional reasons, public expression of their responsibilities. Others, like Levine, learned, after the magazine was sold, that without the masthead declaration of editorship, to find an equivalent position was more difficult. But the absence of barriers in the masthead did reflect an openness among the staff. Ellen Sweet, for many years an editor at *Ms.,* discovered as she went on to other magazines that friendly interchange of ideas was not the general rule and that she missed it.[9]

After the first few months, most of the staff was paid—but to a great extent they could, more realistically, be viewed as volunteers. No one was ever *not* paid, although during the two years before the sale of the magazine, in a period of especially acute financial difficulty, Carbine and Steinem declined to draw their salaries. Certainly most of the staff received less money than they deserved, or than they might have earned elsewhere. They were, however, paid, and many others working for the movement were not paid at all. In exchange for low pay they found new experiences and new responsibilities that were at that time unavailable to them elsewhere. They also had the satisfaction of believing wholeheartedly in what they were doing.

In these days when Steinem was not in a plane or speaking around the country, she worked in the *Ms.* office, her desk pushed against a wall that she faced but otherwise open to the whole room, to the roving children and the crowded group of editors and staff. Sometimes she stayed working late into the night,

---

[9] When the new *Ms.* was created in 1990, the customary masthead, in order of precedence, was used by Robin Morgan, then editor in chief. Suzanne Braun Levine is now editor of the *Columbia Journalism Review.*

searching for sweets, engaged in more editorial work than, in later years, she would have time for. Alice Walker, who worked for the magazine two days a week, found it impossible to concentrate in the midst of this melee, and was given first a large room and then, at her own request, a small cozy room somewhere in the back.

Walker brought in many stories that were offbeat, and she and Steinem often agreed. If she liked the story Walker had recommended and the majority did not, Steinem would prevail. But for the most part the office, like the editorial meetings, was open, democratic, and run on altogether different grounds than other magazines. Walker, happily ensconced in her small room, found it "difficult to work in an open room with other people, and impossible to think. Phones were always ringing." To others, too, it may have seemed confusion twice confounded. To Steinem, it was the natural way to run a magazine, it was women's space and echoed with women's voices. The fact that Steinem was with everyone else, as in a city room, and her assistant, Darcy Gilpin, was in a private office probably indicated that each of the women had picked the work space that suited her; hierarchy was not the principle by which office space was allocated.

Steinem and Carbine had insisted from the beginning that the magazine be controlled financially by women and run entirely by women; that never changed. But as the years went on, objections to many of the magazine's operating habits developed; inevitably, some personal conflicts removed from the magazine's rosters a number of writers and editors, some of them highly talented and effective individuals. And, despite the nonhierarchical process of eliciting editorial opinion, bitter controversies inevitably arose: how to present political division within the feminist movement, particularly regarding abortion, pornography, lesbianism, men; and whether to print critical reviews and discussion of feminist authors.

Problems about one particular aspect of *Ms.* crystallized by

1974. In a mock lawsuit, *Lesbian Nation* (plaintiff) v. Ms. *Magazine* (defendant), a group of lesbians instituted an "indykement" charging *Ms.* with "gross neglect and Psychic genocide against Lesbian women; sexist and heterosexist representation of women; perpetuating antifeminist attitudes and politics: elitism, professionalism, classism, superstarism, and dollarism."

In fact, *Ms.* was running more articles on lesbianism than did any other magazine not exclusively gay, and paying a price for it in advertising. Journalistic wisdom warned them not to include an article discussing lesbianism in the preview issue, and so, of course, they included it. Steinem always believed strongly in the importance of lesbianism to the women's movement. Ivy Bottini, a fighter on behalf of lesbians in the early New York NOW, for example, remembers that when everyone in the 1970 march celebrating the fiftieth anniversary of women's suffrage was asked to wear a lavender armband, Betty Friedan threw hers onto the ground and stamped on it. Steinem wore hers. She was frequently asked by the press if she was a lesbian, and out of solidarity—refusing to answer the question with a direct negative—she often said something like "Not yet." It is ironic that while on the one hand Steinem was often accused of using men to get ahead, on the other hand she was assumed to be a lesbian. She herself was told more than once by men in the media that had she in fact been a lesbian, they would have found her feminism easier to cope with.

So the "indykement" demonstrates the bind *Ms.* and its editors were in, caught between those who wanted to write about men and other more "mainstream" topics that would have wide appeal, and radical lesbians and others who wanted a feminist magazine to look more at the internal problems of the movement. It is clear now, as it certainly became clear to Steinem, that no one magazine could straddle this divide. And while *Ms.* fulfilled its purpose in the seventies, of bringing many women to feminism and awakening them to the real conditions under which they lived, it also never fully satisfied anyone already part of feminism and certain of her attitude toward it. It is, however, essential to note that it was not the division between lesbians and heterosexuals that brought *Ms.* down, but the pressure of the advertisers and their retreat in the face of outspoken feminism.

The first of those to leave *Ms.* for what she said were political reasons was Ellen Willis, who with Kathie Sarachild was among those who founded the Redstockings, the group whose abortion hearing had been Steinem's original awakening, and some members of which would later accuse Steinem of subverting the movement for the CIA. Steinem had invited Willis onto the *Ms.* staff, out of gratitude for her role in that awakening and against the advice of others who found Willis abrasive and often antiwomen. As can be seen, from this example, Harris, and others, Steinem has a gift for opening the door to her adversaries.

Speaking in 1991, Willis, a brilliant writer ("Are men bad, women good? Or are men human beings who've had too much power?") who had long been rock critic for the *New Yorker,* elaborated her criticisms of the early *Ms.*

> It was a magazine where the idea was, This is the voice of responsible feminism, and everything has to be vetted and edited by fifty people, and by committees, and it drove writers completely mad. . . . I remember when Elinor Langer wrote a piece hating Kate Millett's book—I think it may have been *Flying;* she wrote a scathing critique of it, and of confessional writing. . . . A really good piece, and people didn't want to run it because it might hurt Kate Millett's feelings. I don't remember the whole story. Finally, there was a confrontation in a meeting, with cuts I couldn't go along with; someone said Kate might have a nervous breakdown if she reads this; I remember saying, I certainly don't want to be the cause of any-

body's nervous breakdown, but I feel, Hey, she's a grown-up. That's the kind of problem.

Steinem, in fact, gradually came to consider Willis, despite her claim to be radical, the token conservative on the magazine, and found her difficult to work with; in Steinem's view Willis wanted not *more* news but *her* news. One of their fiercest arguments was over whether or not to include an article on the Rolling Stones, a rock group hardly known for its feminist lyrics. The disagreement about rock groups was not confined to Willis.[10]

Harriet Lyons, who left *Ms.* after eight years, went first to the *Daily News* and is now at *Redbook*. She had criticisms of the magazine, but also praise for what it accomplished.

We raised the consciousness of Madison Avenue by what we were editorially, a very different package from anything between two covers calling itself a woman's magazine. It was clear who we were; we were an idea whose time had come. Each issue was awaited, had urgency, each issue might have been the last, everyone always predicting our demise, so we were revolutionary in terms of publishing procedures. This was the magazine that first exposed the extent of the problem of battered wives, sexual harassment—we broke it first.

I left *Ms.* in 1980. The intense political fight was between Ellen Willis as the house radical and Robin Morgan, who

[10] An October 1974 *Ms.* piece by Karen Durbin, entitled "Can a Feminist Love the World's Greatest Rock and Roll Band?" defended the Rolling Stones because of their great musical talent. Letters in response, appearing the following February, were vehement. While Pauline Bart wrote that a Jew cannot love the Nazis, however artistic their performances, and most felt self-respecting women cannot love the Rolling Stones, Willis insisted that an equal number of letters be published that praised the article. The discussion remained open; a later article by Barbara Ehrenreich in 1982 mentioned that "Billboards for the Rolling Stones album 'Black and Blue' showed a scantily dressed woman, bruised, bound, and 'loving it.'" That billboard became the subject of a nation-wide boycott of the Rolling Stones and their record company, showing where populist women's opinions were.

helped shape Gloria's political views; there was division on almost every major feminist issue.[11] The view of Susan Braudy and Barbara Grizzuti Harrison [who came to the magazine after its inception] and me at that point was to cover the waterfront: to have many divergent views and be more reportorial. One of our most intense debates occurred over the issue of abortion. While there was a rock-bottom conviction for *Roe* v. *Wade*, there was an emotional argument going on among feminists; there was a lot of ambivalence. It took *Ms.* a long time to get to that for fear that admitting [abortion] was sometimes emotionally difficult for women would be grist to the right. There was a tug of war.

On complex, debatable issues, it pulled punches or delayed or consumed itself in pedantic debate. Steinem and her people and Carbine had very definite opinions. As to *Ms.* being nonhierarchical, none of us had any voice in the true business decision-making at *Ms.* [which was handled by Carbine]. We were not included in that process. My mother expressed it best: She said, "I saw your boss on television." What I wanted was to get some really lively journalism in the magazine.

Harriet Lyons left because she came to realize that she had to make more money—she was a single mother—had to advance her own career, needed a place on a masthead and a position in which she could rise. "I had decided that my career was important to me, and my career was defined by promotion, recognition, and reward. I realized that they couldn't implement what I wanted

---

[11] Robin Morgan did not, in fact, come to work at the magazine until 1977, and Willis had left in 1975. Morgan had been powerfully influential through her widely read anthology *Sisterhood Is Powerful: Writings from the Women's Liberation Movement* (Vintage, 1970). Her introduction described how women had been radicalized by their treatment in the civil rights and student activist movements. Morgan's view, like Steinem's, has been to put the needs of feminism before practical considerations that might compromise the movement. An excerpt from Morgan's *Going Too Far* was published in *Ms.* in 1975, but her views had undoubtedly impressed Steinem before that.

without alienating too many people; I realized my future was not at *Ms.* I wanted a more professional structure, and I wanted male colleagues. My ideas weren't registering."

Lyons also became impatient with the incessant arguments over politics. What would she have done had she been in charge? "I would have made it more reportorial, I would have approached feminism as a thinking woman's editor, from the point of view of where the various debates were, where the liveliest people were; I believe in people, that's where the stories are for difficult messages."

But Lyons never lost her affection for Steinem. Speaking in November 1991, when she was still working for the *Daily News,* Lyons said: "I still adore Gloria. She had a valid point about wanting to publish what no one else would publish; but some of us wanted to put the whole culture through the filter of feminism."

One of the most intense arguments centered around the heated discussion of pornography. As Lyons says, "Pornography was one of the subjects on which there were divergent opinions; *Ms.* either shied away from them or burned itself out giving diverse opinions. *Ms.* was late a lot [in examining] issues, and because of this, not just because of lead time." Even more intense than the debate over whether admitting that some women felt ambivalence about having had abortions would buttress the right was the question of whether to support ordinances that would make legal action possible where violent pornography could be shown to have caused a sexual crime, and the ordinances that would allow the possibility of civil damages in that case. Steinem, like law professor Catharine MacKinnon and writer Andrea Dworkin, two of the staunchest fighters against pornography, strongly supported these ordinances. Those opposed included the American Civil Liberties Union, with its insistence that free speech must mean, quite simply, free speech for *all,* and those feminists who felt on the one hand that they had a right to have access to pornography, and on the other that the connection between pornography portraying violence and actual violence had not been established. Furthermore, to blame pornography for men's crimes against women was to let men off the hook. Those opposed to the ordinances have also been alarmed by the eagerness of the Christian right wing to support such restrictions.[12]

Pornography is one of those rare subjects on which Steinem and many feminists disagree, though there is much of the disagreement that could be cured by information. For instance, the antipornography groups are not advocating "censorship," but activism and social pressure, and they are not "antisex," but in favor of differentiating pornography from erotica, like rape versus sex, and untangling violence from sex in other areas. Yet two admissions must be made by those who oppose any restrictions on pornography. One—the great majority of women who appear in violent pornographic films have already been sexually abused; two—the antipornography movement, and particularly the work of Andrea Dworkin and Catharine MacKinnon, has alerted everyone, on whichever side, to the true horrors of some pornography, and to its widespread influence.

Ms. ultimately dealt with the pornography question most fully in an article by Mary Kay Blakely, whom Steinem had called in 1981 after reading the "Hers" columns she had contributed to the *New York Times,* which were critical of a *Ms.* cover story about marriage. Blakely wrote a women's column for Fort Wayne, Indiana, newspapers, and Steinem wrote to her, saying that *Ms.*

---

[12] Canada recently passed a national law, for which Catharine MacKinnon was largely responsible, allowing erotic films, however obscene, but forbidding violence and assault. It is a fact of life in the United States, however, that the preservation of liberty has never been a popular cause; it is most unlikely that the Bill of Rights would be added to the Constitution were it put to a vote today. Perhaps restrictions on speech must be more assiduously guarded against here than elsewhere. (Jeffrey Toobin has discussed this in detail; see the *New Yorker,* October 3, 1994, pp. 70–79.)

needed her and inviting her to write for it. Eventually, when Blakely moved to New York, Steinem invited her to the *Ms.* editorial meetings; Blakely thinks Steinem wanted her there because she had a non–New York attitude.

Blakely summed up the debate for the April 1985 issue, in an article entitled "Is One Woman's Sexuality Another Woman's Pornography?" Read today, Blakely's article seems balanced, with quotes in sidebars giving each side a fair representation. Writing on a question as fraught and with two such clearly identifiable sides, Blakely produced the fairest possible article.

I ended up getting that assignment because I was the new kid on the block. I did not accurately understand what the issue was about to be in the feminist community. I also had formed a friendship with Andrea Dworkin, and had heard and followed Catharine MacKinnon, and I had just done a story on Minneapolis–St. Paul feminists [who were involved in pushing through an antipornography ordinance]. MacKinnon is an original thinker, and the law does not like original thinkers. Dworkin is an inspiring thinker; she's also a very difficult person; which is why *Ms.* assigned me the story, when everyone else had tangled with her. At the time they decided to do this story on pornography, it was like sexual harassment: We didn't yet refer to it by name. The main question about pornography was: Did it do harm? For the first time they were trying to articulate the question of whether safety is a right, and was there a connection between pornography and harm.

We had meetings at *Ms.* with Dworkin and MacKinnon, who came into the editorial offices and addressed all of the editors, so that we could all hear at one time what they were saying. And then we set up a similar meeting with FACT [Feminists Against Censorship Today], the ACLU people, and others vs. Dworkin. The animosity between these groups became terrible. They had to meet separately because they couldn't be in the same room at the same time. But we did get different points of view. We then got the transcripts of these two meetings, and a summary on the law, and a summary of what was happening as the ordinances were making their way in the various communities; we had to summarize all this.

This was where the collective process of editing broke down and didn't work; I had to write this article after talking to everybody. At first it was going to be a cover story, but then we decided it was too hot an issue. [Eventually, the article did appear as a cover story.] Since everyone had strong feelings about it, everyone had to read it.[13] It was a nightmare, for me and for Ellen Sweet, the editor who kept getting the changes. Sometimes the collective process strengthened *Ms.,* but sometimes it diluted it, and writers had to submerge egos. The article has since been anthologized all over the place; I think it unreadable with so many points of view in it; it ends up making no one happy. Dworkin and MacKinnon were angry, sometimes justifiably and sometimes not. But eventually both sides ended up using it.

It must be added that the whole process of editing changed over the years. By the time Blakely's piece was being passed around to most editors, the practice had become rare; because the topic was so very controversial, her article was given exceptional treatment. Too many editors was one of the problems Steinem and others at *Ms.* learned over time to control, just as they learned, by and large, to make the nonhierarchical structure work. But the problem Blakely describes of having to satisfy many points of view does reflect a genuine problem at *Ms.* for much of its history, and underlines the complaint of Willis and others that the magazine was run for the editors, not for the writers. *Ms.* was not alone

[13] Steinem, who had been on the road during the meetings, and mindful of the outside image of *Ms.* as "her" magazine, did not read this, or most other articles on which she was neither the writer or the editor.

25. Steinem and George McGovern during the 1972 campaign

26. A news conference at the founding of the National Women's Political Caucus in 1972. Bella Abzug, standing. Seated, left to right, Steinem, Shirley Chisholm, Betty Friedan

27. Brenda Feigen, who urged Steinem to give the Harvard Law School address, and with her founded the Women's Action Alliance

28. Steinem and Simone de Beauvoir in de Beauvoir's apartment in Paris, 1972

29. Bella Abzug and Billie Jean King in 1977 holding the International Women's Year torch, brought by women runners 2,610 miles to Houston from Seneca Falls, where the first Women's Rights convention was held in 1848

30. Steinem on her way to Louisiana to help organize the rural sugarcane workers, women who had worked on these plantations for generations

31. The women organizers understood that the workers needed their own homes; here Steinem meets in one of the homes the workers were now being helped to build.

32. A lunchtime conference with the sugarcane workers

33. Steinem and her mother in the 1970s

34. The Democratic Convention, 1984. Mondale and Ferraro have been nominated for president and vice president.

in this predicament; almost every feminist journal, including the learned quarterlies like *Signs* and *Feminist Studies,* fell into the same trap. In an effort not to unduly offend minority, gay, or other-than-upper-middle-class women, each article was read by many people.

This exhaustive vetting process was not without its benefits. Consultation is important for any writer involved in a movement, and certainly some feminists have made fundamental errors through a failure to consult any of their peers. But the practice soon went too far and involved too many consultants; the writer's voice was all but overwhelmed. Perhaps the wiser move, for *Ms.* and also for academic feminist journals, would have been to let individual voices be heard, and then, if necessary, answered. Those voices would have added color and variety to a collection of prose in real danger of becoming pallid.

Steinem certainly played an important part in the emphasis on many editors. She believed that each editor's input was valuable, and should be considered. Partly, she disliked, and therefore tended to shun, controversy; partly, she genuinely wanted to avoid offending people; certainly she wanted everybody to feel heard. That, however, was impossible. On the question of overediting at *Ms.,* Mary Thom has written:

> The lack of distance between the magazine and its readers encouraged an editorial process that was very, well, hands-on. After all, if our lives were the text, then we all were the experts and who couldn't have an opinion? It is absolutely not true that we ever subjected articles to a majority vote, or edited in a communal circle, or any of the other mythologies that grew up to explain what happened at *Ms.* But it is true that there wasn't the usual hierarchy of an editor at the top making all the decisions. There was a lot of input, particularly in the early, wilder days, before the staff [after 1980] settled into our various, fairly

well recognized areas of expertise—though we were still not differentiated on the masthead. Whether the process served us well is a matter of debate among the early editors of *Ms.*

Thom quotes Letty Cottin Pogrebin as an example of one who felt the process did serve them well. Says Pogrebin:

Looking back, it could have been seen as a kind of intimidation by group-think. But I loved being edited that way. It was rigorous. It forced me to think harder. I would get back one of my manuscripts with scribbles all over the margin, and I couldn't wait to get into it. You could always fight for your own thing. I don't remember anyone forcing me to say something I didn't want to say, or taking out anything I passionately believed in.

Many believe that Steinem and Carbine could have had their pick of women editors: The magazine was exciting, new, and wonderfully challenging. But they did not hire any editors with more than a few years' experience in magazine editing, because there were few if any feminist editors at that time. Indeed, Steinem, Carbine, Peacock, Levine, and Lyons all had previous magazine experience, and at *Ms.* there was not one "top" editor, as is usual, but five. Levine, however, was the editor who was more equal than others, and whose efforts were essential in shaping the magazine. When it came to the hiring of an art editor, Steinem and Carbine went for the most experienced. They hired Bea Feitler, who designed the early covers, and who gave them the best work available.

Several errors were made early in the magazine's history as the staff tried to balance purity of purpose with the realities of running a successful magazine. The nonhierarchical management tended inevitably to be inefficient. Not a few of the major crises in Steinem's affairs during the 1970s concerned women whom she had taken at their own self-assessment. Steinem's openness to people, their stories and their lives, has its shadow side: a willingness to accept volunteers as her personal assistants or assistants at the magazine on their own assurance of competence.

She made some notably bad judgments in hiring people. One extremely problematic woman left behind chaos, unanswered mail, and many bad vibes. Fortunately, her stay—a year—was relatively short. Steinem is notorious, even among those co-workers who most ardently love and admire her, for offering jobs to whomever she happens to meet, and then leaving others to cope with the resultant inefficiency and downright incompetence. This led, at best, to time-consuming muddles, at worst to something very close to disaster.

Steinem, aware of this failing of hers, categorizes it under the theme of Ms. Fixit, Ms. Rescue-Complex. The distinction between a sitting duck and someone willing to take the risk of helping others is a fine one; though, as a journalist, she would check stories carefully, as a private person Steinem is unusual, perhaps, in her willingness to suffer for her naïveté rather than ignore someone in need of help. Those who despise all group hatreds, all racial and sexual stereotypes, are more easily duped. Most people, certainly, lean the other way. She takes responsibility for her approach and harbors resentment against those who misuse her generosity only when they go on to misuse others in the same way. It nonetheless took her some years to overcome her reluctance to warn people about those who had double-crossed her, a reluctance she later came to regret and to remedy.

It is worth noting that Steinem was duped only by women, whom she trusted; never by men. In later years, her tendency to help people became somewhat tempered by experience and by the vigilance of her friends. And she eventually acquired good assistance, usually hired by someone else—for, as a freelance journalist, she had been accustomed to working on her own. Or, as

Steinem puts it: "If I got some excellent assistants at the magazine, it was because Joanne Edgar and others began to interview them for me."

The latitude Steinem allowed those who volunteered for unsuitable tasks can be contrasted with her outspoken criticism of groups and individuals she found hurtful, or slow to take up causes. An illustrative incident, still remembered with shudders by some who were there, occurred at the 1973 convention of the League of Women Voters, an organization that, in Steinem's opinion, had been damagingly slow in supporting the Equal Rights Amendment, claiming they knew too little about it.

After telling her audience that "we women have been much too docile, much too law abiding, and I think that period is about over," Steinem's speech went on pleasantly enough:

> I am especially happy and honored to be here at this organization which has played so important and courageous a role in the history of women. It is symbolic for me . . . because I have just discovered my own grandmother, who was a suffragist, and who died when I was five years old. She was somewhat covered up by the family in the forties and fifties, as that was not the thing to be.

But then there was warning of what was to come, as Steinem continued talking about her grandmother, who "was a member of the League in Ohio. I confess, though, that she left eventually because she was saddened by the fact that . . . women in the League had begun to deemphasize women's issues, and to the degree we voted, we voted like men and met male standards."

Then Steinem launched into the question of homemakers, warning that women must not adopt the male view of housework and child care. "Women at home work harder than anybody," Steinem asserted. "According to the Department of Labor, women work 99.6 hours a week, and are guaranteed no pay. They have to depend on the largesse of their husbands, and that's it." Then came the words that would continue to ring for many years in the ears of all those present:

> If we are to redefine work as dignified and human and important, whatever it is, what a woman does at home is important. If a man had to hire a housekeeper, male or female, he would have to pay a minimum of nine thousand dollars a year, and probably twelve or fourteen thousand dollars a year. That does not include, as the Department of Labor does not point out, part-time prostitution. That's what it is, if we are there because we are afraid to leave.

Almost everyone who heard that speech, and many who only heard about it, insisted that Steinem had accused married women of being prostitutes. Feminists who were there hoping to win over the League of Women Voters to feminism believed that Steinem had blown their chances. And Steinem herself makes an important distinction between that speech and later ones. "I never said married women were prostitutes, but I did compare traditional marriage to prostitution. I always took great care not to accuse women, but to address the institution." Steinem always did take great care never to accuse women, but to the listener at that convention, the distinction was a delicate one. There was a frightful controversy. However, over the next several years, the League did come to support the ERA, and its members wore bracelets that said women would be in chains until the adoption of the Equal Rights Amendment.

MARCH 1973 brought one of the most vicious attacks yet against Steinem in particular and feminism in general. Such outbursts increased as feminism attracted more converts and accomplished revisions in gender arrangements. In the March 19 issue of *Screw* magazine was a spread of a nude female who looked—the aviator glasses, the long hair—like Steinem. She was drawn, as Steinem would later put it, "in full labial detail," and headlined "Pin the Cock on the Feminist." The woman was bordered on one side by drawings of penises to choose from. The picture is obscene enough to depress a far less ebullient character than Steinem. But those who run pornographic magazines and clubs are well aware of the powers of their feminist enemies, who are feared and therefore demonized.

The magazine also printed *Ms.*'s phone number as that of a sex service, with results profoundly upsetting to the young woman at the switchboard, and was threatening to turn the centerspread drawing, already hung on display in newsstands, into a poster. When Steinem's lawyer, Nancy Wechsler, wrote to *Screw* to protest all this, the editor, Al Goldstein, responded by sending Steinem a box of candy and a note saying "Eat It." This was not the first or last time Steinem would learn that a public figure has little recourse in such a situation. As Steinem recounts in *Outrageous Acts,* "Only Bella Abzug's humor rescued me from my depression. When I explained to her about this nude centerfold with my face and head, she deadpanned, 'and my labia.' " [24]

At about the same time, a staff member at *Playboy* snuck out a memo Hugh Hefner had sent to the writer of a fairly reasonable *Playboy* article on feminism. Steinem quoted some of Hefner's comments in *Outrageous Acts:* "What I'm interested in," he wrote, "is the highly irrational, kookie trend. . . . These chicks are our natural enemies. It is time to do battle with them. . . . What I want is a devastating piece, a really expert, personal demolition job on the subject." [These comments were scattered throughout Hefner's letter to the writer of the article, but are a fair representation.] Steinem released Hefner's memo to the media, hoping that at least such bald-faced misogyny would raise some consciousness; her hopes were dashed. Chuckles were all Hefner's words evoked— What more did women deserve?

DURING THE mid-1970s Steinem was continually plagued by questions about her personal finances, particularly in light of her wide coverage by the media, and the public notion that "rich" and "famous" must go together. In July 1973, for example, she received a letter from a clinical psychologist, a woman unknown to Steinem. The psychologist, responding to a fund-raising letter from the Women's Action Alliance, asked why she should give money when Steinem "received millions to date for your writing," and why Betty Friedan's lecture fee was a thousand dollars "when I was making $200 a day." The woman reasonably pointed out that she had raised four children and put three husbands through graduate school; she wanted to support other women, but wished to know how much was being contributed by women like Steinem.

Characteristically, Steinem thanked the woman for writing the letter. "Too many of us just allow the mistrust to remain instead of getting it out in the air where it can be examined." She suggests that the letter writer ask Betty Friedan what she does with her book money by writing directly to her. As for herself, Steinem explains:

> I would like to assure you that my income—never startling, as a freelance writer, but enough to support me and my mother adequately—has gone steadily down since 1968 when I became fully (and joyfully—this is not meant as a complaint) involved in the Women's Movement. This has been true because 1) I simply have less time to do my own writing, 2) the publications I write for now are likely to pay less (*McCall's* used to pay as

much as $3,000 for an article, for instance; *Ms.* can afford only $500), and 3) the new money I receive from speaking seems to me to belong to the Movement, so I return most or all of it as contributions, travel expenses to help women candidates, prisoners, and others who raise funds, and . . . well, I'm sure you know how the money goes because you're probably doing the same thing.

Steinem mentions how the media delights in "turning powerless groups against each other as a way of expressing resentment of the little bit of power that women do have." She concludes by saying that she has contributed over $5,000 to the alliance, and more to other groups who "because of their localized obscurity and/or radicalism, are least likely to get contributions elsewhere."

Such a letter, the veracity of which is confirmed by every possible source from that time, is likely to arouse disbelief in those who dislike and distrust Steinem. It should, therefore, be emphasized that it was a private letter, not a public statement. When, in the later eighties, Steinem was finally convinced that she must make some financial arrangements for her future, it was clear enough that the greater part of her income in previous years had been given away. The shock, after the publication of *Revolution from Within* in 1992, of knowing she would have money "three months hence" took some getting used to.

By February 1974, Steinem was again threatening to stop speaking and get back to writing. She had taken up speaking because no one would publish what she wanted to write on feminism, but having once begun she found it impossible to stop. She also realized that she would never again be anonymous, which eliminated certain assignments that she may have dreamed of. John Brady interviewed Steinem that month for the *Writer's Digest,* and his opening paragraph indicated that nothing had changed much, from the press's point of view.

She calls herself "the great stone face." She is a friend of the rich, the famous, the powerful. She is a writer, organizer, speechmaker, editor and political gadfly. She has been called everything from "the thinking man's Jean Shrimpton" to "the reluctant superstar of the woman's movement" to "a royal pain in the ass." She goes her own way, doesn't depend on anyone, is beautiful and makes nothing of it. She is Gloria Steinem.

The interview indicated that nothing much had changed from Steinem's point of view either. She had lost both time to write and anonymity, though how much anonymity she had had since 1963 is certainly questionable. But she felt a loss: "When Joe McGinniss wrote *The Selling of the President,*" she told Brady, "I realized I would never be able to write that kind of book again or write that kind of article again—one which depends on being anonymous and kind of looking around you. And we had been on the same campaign plane."

What Steinem gave up by going around the country to speak to women over the heads and around the edges of the media (rather as candidate Clinton would do in 1992) is real enough. Whether, in fact, one ever gives up what one really wants to do, except if forced by extreme poverty or illness, is another question. By this time, however, two facts were evident: Steinem was a gifted speaker, and she believed in having opinions and expressing them. This last point was made sharply in answer to a question Brady asked about Barbara Walters. Steinem replied:

It's hard for me to relate to [her] kind of journalism because it's more television-based. Her pride, as I remember in [her] book, is that she has no opinions, that she betrays none and indeed that she has none. That makes for a blandness that I find it hard to relate to. It reminds me of the old newspaper journalism that is still alive but is changing slowly, where someone would go to the South, and report on a sit-in, say, in the sixties and they would report that X number of people were in prison and beaten up and so on. Then they would go to the sheriff and the sheriff would say, "No, they weren't." They would present these as two equal points of view.[14]

There is a proleptic irony here. "The old newspaper journalism," which was changing in regard to civil rights and racism at this time, would never, in fact, change in regard to women. Well into the nineties, if the mainstream media ever presented a feminist point of view, they found it necessary to present the antifeminist point of view simultaneously. The reverse of this, of course, was never seen as mandatory.

By the end of 1974, Steinem was quoted in *People* (under a typical headline: "Gloria Steinem Tries to Lower Her Famed Profile") as saying that she was tired of people writing about her, and had, accordingly, cut her public appearances from fifteen a month to five. Her current rule, she said, was "Don't do anything that another feminist could do instead." Her reason for this rule, apart from her own weariness, was realistic: "It's the practice of the media to set up leaders and knock them down, which is very damaging to movements. We need to have enough women in the public eye so that we can't all be knocked down." Again, she expresses her hope of going back to writing, by which it can be assumed she means books, since she was continuing to write, as well as edit, articles for *Ms.*

Shortly thereafter, Patricia Burstein, the author of the *People* story, wrote to Judy Klemesrud at the *New York Times,* coming to

[14] Steinem had written an admiring article about Barbara Walters in the mid-1960s, mentioning her as the first television reporter to do her own research. Walters, who worked both behind the scenes and on camera, was the first woman on the *Today* show other than beauty contest winners who served coffee. Walters always credited Steinem's article for having led to the *Life* cover story on Walters that started her famous career.

Steinem's defense in response to Klemesrud's letter to the editor, published by *People,* objecting to the Steinem story. Klemesrud had written:

> So Gloria Steinem is trying to "lower" her famed profile. Is that why her face is on the cover of *People,* one of the nation's largest circulation magazines? And is that why she agreed to be interviewed for a two-page spread that included three additional photographs? Good luck, Gloria, I hope you succeed.

Burstein's letter to Klemesrud, three pages long, is important because it so neatly summarizes the central tension of Steinem's life: her desire to come to the aid of individuals, and her position as an object of hatred in the press and, unfortunately, on the part of many women as well as men.

Burstein explains that Steinem had refused the interview, and had not posed for the cover photo, which had been taken at a public event and in which, Burstein observed, "Gloria looked like she had either a sandpaper face or delayed adolescent acne." [*People,* Steinem recalls, refused to print her own letter explaining that she had neither posed for the cover nor cooperated in the interview. When she called Richard Stolley, then editor of *People,* to ask why, she remembers him saying, "I don't know any editor who would undermine his own story."] Burstein suggests that if Steinem were as tough as she, Steinem "would have an easier time of getting off the treadmill of the media trap. . . . Before I had the chance to know her a little better, I had considered her to be just another 'commercial act,' but I do not think this anymore." Burstein concludes:

> Someone would have to be enormously dedicated to put in the mileage she has done these past few years. These are hardly pleasure trips. . . . In a sense this has been a sacrifice. Her

intense involvement in the movement has canceled out the possibility of some, say, t.v. commentator job. No news operation
would touch her with a ten-foot pole. . . . What is most dis-
turbing is that women who feel this way about Gloria are really
devaluing themselves. They are saying, in effect, "Who does
SHE think she is? She's just shit like the rest of us."

Accusations of martyr-playing inevitably await those who over-
schedule themselves and then complain of their weariness. Perhaps only those who have achieved the limelight learn to loathe it;
here Steinem, of course, was caught in a cleft stick. She needed
the limelight to spread her message, while resenting the personal
sacrifice fame exacted. Those less successful and still convinced of
the glory of the limelight will always believe that anyone so pre-
eminent must be some variety of louse, and that complaints about
the burdens of fame are patently insincere.

Toward the end of 1973, *Today's Health* had asked Liz Smith to
interview Steinem "to discuss the ten men she most admires, identifying, along the way, the characteristics that distinguish them as
exceptional beings." Few of the ten would have surprised anyone
who knew Steinem. She cited the late Bobby Kennedy, because of
his sympathy for the powerless; John Kenneth Galbraith, because
he was always willing to change his mind, and did, about women;
Ralph Nader, because he seemed interested in people regardless of
their sex; Cesar Chavez, who went against the masculine mystique
to use nonviolence to achieve his goals; Olof Palme, the prime
minister of Sweden, because he was the only chief of state in the
world who said it was the prime responsibility of government to
humanize sex roles as the root of violence; Frank Thomas, who
through his urban development work, Steinem believed, changed
the lives of so many black people; Ron Dellums, congressman
from California, who won his seat through the support of a coali-
tion of the "outs"; Martin Abzug, Bella's husband, a very support-

ive man who would have loved to see his wife become president of the United States; Rafer Johnson, who was gentle and could be depended upon to be human and to help people; and Bobby Seale, who in his book *Seize the Time* included a chapter on his thoughts about women and the position of women as a political issue.

By 1975 Steinem had met another who could sympathize with the less powerful: Stan Pottinger, the first lover younger than she. In late 1974, when Steinem met him, she still had hopes of a different kind of life. She was tiring of the relentless schedules in response to the many requests she felt she must continue to honor. To a certain extent, she felt in flight from her current life, yet during that flight she was still buffeted by others' needs. She was aging, not obviously, but questions that arise with age—Am I always going to be doing this, and if not this, then what?—must have occasionally occurred to her. Pottinger was a kind and sensuous man who would provide a refuge for Steinem in 1975, the year in which the hatreds of those who felt pushed aside by her would erupt.

TRASHING

IN 1975, *Ms.* noted that the United States was halfway through a decade that had begun with Cambodia and the shootings of students at Kent State and Jackson University in 1970; that decade would end with the election of Ronald Reagan. In retrospect, Nixon's resignation under fire in 1974 and Jimmy Carter's subsequent election would come to be seen as mere interludes in a conservative sweep. As with the riots at the 1968 Democratic Convention in Chicago, intellectual and liberal outrage became overwhelmed by the country's general anger, not at the shooting of students but at the protesters themselves. The staff at *Ms.,* and their many contributors and readers, began to question whether the seventies would indeed produce that more caring, democratic, less violent society that the sixties had promised. For Steinem personally, the middle year of the decade was for the most part harrowing.

Her anguish was, however, somewhat mitigated when she became involved with Stan Pottinger. Although Pottinger worked in both the Nixon and Carter administrations (he was head of the

Civil Rights division of the Justice Department when she met him), he was clearly a liberal anomaly within that hardly liberal group—he had fought for school busing cases and reopened the Kent State investigation, among other accomplishments. Whether Steinem, rooted in feminist and radical politics as she was, allowed herself to be seduced by the attractive, like-minded Pottinger, or whether she was searching for some calm in a year that provided little enough tranquility, is not a question easily decided.

Like all the men in Steinem's life, Pottinger was caring, supportive, and intelligent, and fundamentally compatible with her politics. No man would ever be absolutely central to the structure of Steinem's life, and if her involvement with an official of the "enemy camp" drew some sniping, certainly the emotional support Pottinger offered against the barrage to come more than compensated, and proved the measure of his appeal.

Pottinger had been the director of the Department of Housing, Education and Welfare's Office for Civil Rights in the first Nixon administration, starting in 1970; he worked for HEW Secretary Elliot Richardson. Pottinger felt that he had been unfairly criticized while at HEW by feminists who said he was fighting race discrimination but not discrimination against women. As historian Winifred Wandersee writes, "The lackadaisical performance of HEW, and the reluctance of civil rights chief J. Stanley Pottinger to enforce the rules of compliance, led to frustration on the part of feminists. The department's sluggish performance was caused by a lack of staff, an unwillingness to apply sanctions, and difficulty in obtaining vital employment data from universities." [115] Regardless of the overall ineffectiveness of HEW at that time, Pottinger, as the person overseeing civil rights in education, was himself educated by the radical women on campuses throughout the country during the three years he was there. He would bring some lessons learned to the Justice Department.

In 1973 Richardson and John Ehrlichman were responsible for

convincing an apparently reluctant Nixon to appoint Pottinger to the post of assistant attorney general for civil rights in the Justice Department. (Pottinger was told that Patrick Buchanan vehemently opposed his appointment.) It appears Nixon was so busy with other matters—Watergate was already looming, among various other presidential distractions—that he ignored the civil rights office; the change of attorneys general to head the Justice Department also allowed Pottinger to do pretty much as he liked, investigating many of the country's domestic crimes that Nixon condoned.

When Pottinger joined the Justice Department, he discovered to his astonishment that Justice, unlike HEW, didn't even know there was a "women's problem." So he decided to create a task force in an attempt to change the government's attitude toward women. The first person he thought of was Steinem, whom he had never met, and he called her.

It was Steinem who arranged for Ruth Bader Ginsberg and Brenda Feigen to join her in a meeting with Pottinger in New York in November of 1974. She came late, and he was surprised to find her pale and with little vitality: "The first time I saw her I was stunned; she looked really emaciated." Overwork, even then, had taken its toll.

Nevertheless Pottinger clearly found her attractive. During the meeting, a secretary interrupted to let Steinem know she had to leave for an appointment in Hartford. Pottinger got up, excused himself, went into an office, and called Hertz to get a car. As Steinem was leaving, Pottinger said, "I'm going to Hartford, too, can I drive you?" And so he drove her to Hartford where she was to give a speech to women on the insurance companies there. On the way they discovered they were both from Ohio, and both lovingly remembered Vernor's, a golden (not dry) ginger ale, described by Pottinger as "a special, unique elixir in the Midwest."

A prespeech press conference astonished him by its hostility. He recognized that, for him, press conferences were about his position; for her they were about her persona. For the first time he understood the difference. "If anyone had jumped on me as they jumped on her, I'd have been shocked." The first question was "Do you have lots of boyfriends?" Pottinger sat in the back of the room, appalled. Steinem was trying to have a serious discussion about sex discrimination, and was regaled with such questions as "We know you came in with a man; will you tell me who he is?" Steinem told Pottinger he didn't have to answer. He identified himself as an assistant attorney general, and that he and Steinem had just met on business. He remembers being outraged by the vitriol. "I would have objected, but she said she was used to it."

Pottinger drove Steinem back to New York, where they went to Elaine's for dinner. He dropped her off at her apartment and asked if they could have dinner some other night. "Life is complicated," was her answer, which he, newly divorced, interpreted as meaning she was involved with someone else. He sent her a case of Vernor's, and thought that was the end of that. But a few months later, while in California on business, he read that she too was there, so he called. She remarked that she had never heard from him; he mentioned her comment about life being complicated. Together, however, they attended a fund-raiser for the National Women's Political Caucus in Washington the following week, and thus the affair began. He was thirty-four and she was forty.

Pottinger was then living in a house in Washington; two of his young children lived with him. He was the custodial parent, though they also visited their remarried mother, with whom Pottinger was on good terms and who had the care of their youngest child. Steinem enjoyed the house, which was a real home, not like her New York apartment and even less like Toledo—there was a cookie jar in the kitchen, always filled—but for their first few years together she was with Pottinger only on weekends; or when he came to New York, where he stayed in her apartment; or on her rare vacations.

Shortly after Pottinger moved to Justice, the new J. Edgar Hoover Building was built for the FBI. Justice staffers who had been housed across the street from the Justice Department, Pottinger included, moved into the old FBI offices, where Pottinger was given the office that had formerly been J. Edgar Hoover's. This was an opportunity he and Steinem could hardly refuse. They renamed the adjoining conference room "The Martin Luther King, Jr., Room," and provided it, in addition to a picture of King, with African paintings they borrowed from a Washington museum.

At the time of their first meeting, when Pottinger had planned to hire Steinem as a consultant, his office requested her FBI file.[1] A goodly percentage of her file consisted of clippings, plus, she recalls, "an anonymous report of a conversation in which I defended the Black Panthers (which I recognized), and a note that I had traveled to Cuba as part of the Venceramos Brigade organized by Castro to help harvest the sugarcane crop (which I didn't do but wish I had)."

Though the FBI is only supposed to supply information on potential appointees, it can make recommendations, and it advised Pottinger not to hire Steinem. "I was controversial and antigovernment, so why take on that baggage when he, as head of the civil rights division, would have to go up to the Hill on appropriations and be questioned? By then, however, Stan and I had become personal friends."

It is worth adding here that during this time, an assistant FBI director admitted to the Senate that the Bureau had indeed watched Steinem. He claimed, however, that the surveillance had

[1] Unlike the censored version of files obtained through the Freedom of Information Act, those given internally are complete.

ceased.[2] Steinem was also told by Paul Altmeyer at NBC News in New York, who could not reveal his source but was confident of its accuracy, that the Internal Revenue Service listed her among those subject to special surveillance. Steinem was also, of course, on Nixon's Enemies List, and on many other similar lists compiled by right-wing publications.

The June 1977 issue of *Ms.* carried a cover story by Letty Cottin Pogrebin entitled, "Have You Ever Supported Equal Pay, Child Care, or Women's Groups? The FBI Was Watching You." From 1969 until Watergate, J. Edgar Hoover's FBI practiced surveillance against the women's liberation movement, known as WLM to the Bureau. Using the Freedom of Information Act, Pogrebin was able to get all the reports on "WLM"; and a sorry waste of time and incomprehension they are—all paid for, of course, with tax dollars. Pogrebin called this particular FBI story a "paranoid's fantasy come true. 'They' kept tabs on 'us' with the aid of special agents, informers, observers, infiltrators, other law enforcement agencies, and Red alert signals from conscientious citizens."

One of the few existing memos in Hoover's own words overrules field officers who suggested that active investigation of the women's movement was unwarranted and should be put into "a closed status." Wrote Hoover: "The Bureau does not concur with your recommendation. . . . It is absolutely essential that we conduct sufficient investigation to clearly establish subversive ramifications of the WLM and to determine the potential for violence presented by the various groups connected with this movement as well as any possible threat they may represent to the internal security of the United States." Pogrebin went on to place this memo historically:

[2] About this time, John Kenneth Galbraith told Steinem that when he saw his FBI file, he couldn't figure out why they kept saying he wasn't a follower of Dr. Nair. He finally discovered that a friend had said he wasn't a follower of "doctrinaire" beliefs. The bureau, Pottinger wryly observes, was not then known for its political sophistication.

Hoover wrote that memo . . . on May 7, 1970, three days after the National Guard killings at Kent State, one week before
police murdered two students at Jackson State, and four days
after Richard Nixon commenced United States efforts to bomb
Cambodia off the map. One can't help thinking that tax dollars
would have been better spent investigating the National Guard,
the police, and Richard Nixon.

Analyzing the file, Pogrebin identified three principal reasons
why the FBI was watching the women's movement, motives that,
as she said, have guided our "secret police" for years (and which,
it may be noted, would long remain in full force for the radical
right). First, fear of social change and unrest; second, fear of affili-
ation with "dangerous" or "subversive" groups (Hoover was
clearly unaware that the earliest members of the "WLM" had, in
fact, become disaffected precisely with groups he might describe
in that way); third, fear of some deep erosion of the American
way of life (a fear vitriolically expressed later by Pat Buchanan at
the 1992 Republican Convention). As Pogrebin summed up, "The
Women's Movement introduced sour ingredients into American
apple pie, not to mention the idea that Mom might stop making
it." It is, of course, doubly ironic that against such a backdrop a
few members of the Redstockings were shortly to mount their
persistent campaign against Steinem as a CIA agent assigned to
subvert the women's movement.

POTTINGER'S TENURE at Justice came to an end in April of
1977, after which he remained in Washington to practice law. In
1982 he moved to Riverdale, a suburb of New York City, with his
two children, and the following year bought an apartment in
Manhattan. Steinem often stayed with him but, as was her wont,
she left only sufficient belongings for a change of clothes.

In an interview for the London *Times* in 1983, Pottinger was asked if other men ever commented on Steinem to him. Pottinger offered a story that was one of his favorites:

> I was at a convention for presidents of business organizations. Gloria and I were both there and both giving some talks. I was talking about civil rights, and Gloria was talking about feminism, and I came into the room where Gloria was giving a lecture . . . and just sat down in an empty chair next to the door. At this point Gloria was saying that a really just and fair society ought to be constructed in certain ways including the elimination of inheritance. Everybody ought to have an equal place at the starting line. Well, this organization was made up of presidents of businesses, 80 percent of whom had inherited their positions—either they had inherited them from their own fathers or from their wives' fathers. The guy next to me, who was one of those people, turned to me when he heard Gloria make the comment and said, "You get the cross and I'll get the hood."

Pottinger went on to say that most of the remarks made to him about Steinem by men who did not know he was her friend concerned her politics, not her personal life. He denied that being "a lover of a symbol of women's freedom must be a little, occasionally, like being prince consort for a queen," as the interviewer phrased the question. He also denied that Steinem had any "bad habits," but admitted: "Sometimes she spreads herself too thin."

Pottinger contributed an article to the January 1978 *Ms.:* "The Bakke Case: How to Argue about 'Reverse Discrimination.' " Allan Bakke, a white man, sued the University of California, alleging he had been denied admission to medical school because of his race. Pottinger's argument was that colleges and universities had always kept places for people with special qualifications, from football players to the children of alumni and large donors, without being the subject of such suits. Why not, therefore, for minorities, whose inclusion benefited the nation, and had been mandated by Congress, as football players and children of the rich were not.

Perhaps Pottinger's most important service to Steinem, however, was to be there for her when she faced the most damaging and protracted attack that had yet been mounted against her, an attack that was all the more hurtful because it came from within the movement itself and called into question her allegiance to her own most cherished principles and causes. It was in May of that year, that the Redstockings—particularly Kathie Sarachild—brought their charges against Steinem and *Ms.*

The story is a complicated one, but two facts are clear: Steinem suffered serious emotional damage from the experience, and the accusations were without substance and often ridiculous. Like most attacks, the Redstockings' allegations built upon some real events and feelings; at the same time they indicate the immense confusions whirling around radical feminism at that time. Steinem became the easy target of feminist rage—rage that the radical aims and energies of the early feminist movement had been diluted and made more palatable to more conventional women. All the events of 1975 that were so painful to her arose, in large part, from misdirected fury. The hard question, unanswered in the nineties as it was in the seventies, is why, as their frustration and anger mounts, women attack one another rather than the establishment in any of its myriad forms. In the case of those whose main aim is publicity, one of the answers is that an attack by women against women, and particularly against feminists, will instantly attract the media.

Kathie Sarachild had become angered by a disagreement with the magazine over a book about consciousness-raising. At Ellen Willis's suggestion, Steinem had sought out Sarachild, who, Steinem thought, deserved recognition for her early role in establishing consciousness-raising. After *Ms.* had published its own guidelines for CR groups and found it the most-requested reprint, the editors wanted to publish an anthology on that topic and gave Sarachild an advance to undertake an outline for it, and then the book itself. When *Ms.* withdrew, finding the book too "East Coast" and otherwise unpublishable—that is, too limited to the experiences of the white middle-class woman in New York, as well as too disorganized—they allowed Sarachild to keep the advance, to be returned only if she got another publishing contract for the book. Apparently, she never did. Though it was not exclusively Steinem's decision, it had fallen to her to explain this arrangement to Sarachild.

Sarachild's subsequent anger at Steinem, intense and continuing, has perhaps best been explained by Barbara Ehrenreich.[3] Women like Sarachild and the Redstockings, Ehrenreich believes, took Steinem "as a symbol of bourgeois feminism." These early leaders, Ehrenreich points out, "never got a lot of credit, never became household names." Ehrenreich believes it is one of the failures of the feminist movement that it did not provide forms of recognition for such early leaders; unfortunately, much bitterness has resulted.

The Redstockings launched their initial assault in May 1975 at a convention sponsored by the journalism review *MORE.* They called a press conference announcing that as the true founder of the women's liberation movement—which in many vital ways they were—they were accusing Steinem of having a ten-year association with the CIA, and alleging that *Ms.,* "founded and edited by her," was "hurting the women's liberation movement." Their major points of attack were Steinem's work in "setting up a CIA

---

[3] *Ms.* had provided Ehrenreich with her first big opportunity, allowing her to write things she couldn't put in other magazines, and to do her first cover story, in October 1979: "Housework—How to: Do It Less, Get Paid for It, Get Men to Share It, Psyche It Out, Wipe Out Guilt Buildup."

front, the Independent Research Service," and Clay Felker's relationship to both *New York, Ms.,* and "a newspaper published by this CIA front." *Ms.* was further accused of "blocking knowledge of the authentic activists and ideas" of the women's liberation movement. "It is widely recognized," this particular accusation continued, "that one major CIA strategy is to create or support 'parallel' organizations which provide an alternative to radicalism."

Most frustrating to Steinem was the fact that the Redstockings pretended to have "discovered" facts about the Youth Festivals and the Independent Research Service that she had long ago made public and that had been published in newspapers and newsmagazines. To these facts they added certain absurd accusations: that Elizabeth Gould Davis, author of *The First Sex,* was part of "a pattern of alliances of matriarchists with the ruling elite"—this because her sister, Dita Beard, was an ITT lobbyist and because Davis herself had been a Navy intelligence officer for six years; that Wonder Woman, the comic-strip figure whom *Ms.* had featured on their cover as a feminist heroine, was described as reflecting "the anti-people attitude of the 'liberal feminists' and matriarchists"; that *Ms.* undercut Simone de Beauvoir's contribution as a "feminist pioneer"; that Kay Graham, *Newsweek,* and the *Washington Post* were all part of the conspiracy.

They amplified their charges by observing that the National Black Feminist Organization shared an office with the Women's Action Alliance and "presumably Gloria Steinem has access to their files too." She was, by their lights, supposed to be betraying to the CIA the movement and the fight against racism to which she had dedicated her life. When she eventually responded, Steinem said that this accusation was not only racist but had been made with no attempt to check with the black women involved. (The NBFO had moved out a year earlier.)

The Redstockings also questioned the motives of the Women's

Action Alliance, saying that the Alliance's claim to be merely "an information and referral network" was deceptive. "In view of Steinem's secret CIA work, her failure to disavow it, and her continuing cover-up, we question how all this information is being used."

After claiming that *Ms.* was putting forth "an anti-woman ideology," the authors arrived at what was, unquestionably for them, at the heart of the matter: "Women's liberation's popularity and groundbreaking successes preceded the installation of Gloria Steinem as the movement's 'leader' by the rich and powerful. Today all the trappings of the radical upsurge remain, but the content and style have been watered down. We have reached a point when the movement must have a revival of the radical ideas and leadership which marked its early growth and success."

Much of the effect of the Redstockings' accusations arose from the evolving view of the CIA from 1958 to 1960 and from 1972 to 1975. As Frank Thomas sees it, one must distinguish these phases in perceptions of the CIA: "When Gloria considered her whole role in the Independent Research Service, she looked back on a period when she was engaged in what seemed to her a noble cause: a cause that meant connecting with people from other societies, building bridges, deepening understanding, and identifying similar concerns. I don't think she thought much about the funding at the time. Her motives were pure, she was working with people who had similar motives; she was doing something governments were unable to do. That was the power of the mission, it was universal."

And then, Thomas continues, the CIA got a bad name for its later activities—in Chile and Vietnam for example[4]—and "suddenly, this conspiracy notion starts to float around, and it

[4] That the CIA engineered the coup in Guatemala in 1954 did not become public knowledge until much later.

emerges in the seventies at a time when we all concluded that government could not be trusted with people's rights, when deep pockets in government were doing evil things that were bad for human rights both in this country and in the world. The CIA became the embodiment of the deep, dark secret actions of government. If you could link someone you disliked in the seventies with this evil force, you could wipe them off the map of high esteem."

To say that Steinem was a tool of the CIA as the CIA was perceived in the seventies was a terrible accusation indeed. The Redstockings made a very clever move against a woman they perceived as having usurped their movement and the celebrity owed them.

Following the Redstockings' press conference, there was no immediate response in the general press; the *Village Voice* printed an article on the *MORE* convention, not unfavorable from Steinem's point of view. Some of the feminist press, however, grabbed at the subject and began demanding interviews. Through Joanne Edgar at *Ms.,* Steinem responded to the feminist press, simply saying the charges were false and ridiculous. She was out of town through most of this period, so Edgar as the spokesperson fielded questions.

At first, Edgar thought the Redstockings' 1975 accusations were funny. She put up a sign on the office door reading CIA. But the humor soon wore off. Before the effects of the Redstockings' attack were over, Steinem had agonized for the whole summer over her response, growing thinner and thinner, and worrying all those who cared for her. Pottinger remembers that she was "on the verge of going to pieces." The real damage, of course, as Pottinger puts it, was not the accusation, but "what it did to Gloria's head." (There was one saving factor: The terrible isolation usually felt by a victim of this kind of assault was not Steinem's; friends from all over stood by her and tried to persuade her that matters were not so dreadful.)

Edgar believes this low-key public response would have worked if the women's movement hadn't kept putting on more and more pressure, and if Betty Friedan hadn't discussed the accusations in the *Daily News* and at the International Women's Year Conference in Mexico City. Edgar reports that "while I was acting as spokesperson, the articles—although they were really negative and terrible—were limited to the feminist press and underground papers. But once Betty's name was involved, it appeared on the wire services and thus in major newspapers all over the U.S. and as far away as Australia and the Philippines."

Even so, Steinem was reluctant to answer, certain that any statement would be picked up by the mass media and readers would remember only the charges, not her answers, or assume this to be a major division within the women's movement instead of one confined largely to small groups in New York. Three months passed. Finally, however, as the pressure from many in the women's movement increased, Steinem gave in. The result was a long-worked-on, six-page letter released only to the feminist press.

The feminist press printed the letter on September 6, and thereafter seemed to quiet down. Edgar reports, however, that the Redstockings did not. According to Edgar, since May the group had been pressuring Seymour Hersh, then a reporter at the *New York Times,* to cover the story, but he refused to do so without an interview with Steinem. *Newsweek* planned a story as well, but they took a hard look at the accusations and answers and also abandoned the idea. On August 29, 1975, though, what Steinem feared happened. Lucinda Franks wrote a long article—Steinem had refused to be interviewed—for the *New York Times,* repeating the accusations all over again. This was syndicated throughout the country.

Steinem had never denied the CIA funding of the youth festivals.[5] As she wrote in her response to the Redstockings:

> Because the "release" uses these long ago festivals to cast suspicion on the current work of other feminists . . . I will repeat the facts one more time. I worked on two of the World Festivals of Youth and Students for Peace and Freedom (to give them their proper name), held sixteen and thirteen years ago in Vienna and Helsinki, at which some of the American participation was partially funded by foundations that were in turn funded by the CIA; I was told about this indirect source of funding by the National Student Association people who were working on the festivals, too; and I naively believed then that the ultimate money source didn't matter, since, in my own experience and observation, no control or orders came with it. (It's painfully clear with hindsight that even indirect, control-free funding was a mistake if it couldn't be published, but I didn't realize that then.)

Sadly, the Redstockings also greatly upset Steinem's mother by bringing up her habit of denying her divorce and her poverty during the Toledo years. Steinem had long and without success asked reporters to leave her mother out of their stories. Her response to the Redstockings noted their press release's "breathtaking personal viciousness":

[5] Steinem's connection to the CIA had been noted once before, in 1967, when the *Washington Post* ran an article revealing that young Americans' participation in the World Youth Festivals had been subsidized by the CIA. A few days later the *New York Times* picked up the story. Steinem was quoted in both articles, explaining that the CIA had partially funded the students, many of whom did not know of the CIA funding. These articles aroused no great interest, and were indeed forgotten until the Redstockings accused Steinem. (Those who did know concluded that it was therefore not "un-American" to attend the Youth Festivals in the hope of converting other young people from communism.)

Though neither [my mother] nor events described by her have anything at all to do with the political charges being made, her altogether understandable words are used to make it seem that I have lied about my childhood: that we were never poor; that our Toledo neighborhood did not have rats; that she and my father were divorced but got remarried.

If the writer(s) of this "release" don't understand the socially enforced feelings of my mother and others that poverty and hard times are a personal fault to be repressed or concealed, than she/they understand nothing at all about class—particularly people who have seen better days only to *become* poor. (She/they reprint the sadness of my mother's protest that yes, we were both bitten by rats—but they weren't *our* rats, since they came from next door. Even that doesn't seem to touch a human chord.)

And if the writer(s) don't understand that divorce is supposed by society to be a woman's great and personal failure (and therefore why my mother might choose to claim remarriage and ignore my father's marriage to another woman before he died), she/they don't deserve to be called feminists at all.

Every page of this meandering "release" contains other distortions. To answer each one would be like to definitively shake hands with an octopus.

It was only much later that Steinem could appreciate the prominent French feminist Claude Servan-Schreiber's disbelief back in 1975 that Steinem could take this whole matter so seriously. To a French woman, inured to and used to taking pleasure in such attacks, the whole affair seemed silly in the extreme. The French, to be sure, have never been able to understand U.S. scandals. But at the time, neither Servan-Schreiber nor anyone else could divert Steinem from the pain of being trashed.

Alice Walker wrote to Steinem with empathy:

Your trouble reminded me of how *wounded* I was in Mississippi by people who accused me of not being black. What could I possibly *say* to such a charge? It was entirely painful and indelible and, having lived through just the anxiety it caused, I think I may never be hurt so deeply again. Deeper hurt is hard to imagine. It was as if those accusers took my whole life and tried to turn it into shit.

Walker, by the way, wasn't altogether right about the effects of "having lived through" that accusation. When she was later attacked in demonstrations and forums against her book *The Color Purple,* she was deeply hurt again, though perhaps she bore it better than she might have without the Mississippi experience. But for Steinem, too many attacks came in the same year before she could store up courage from one to sustain her in the next.

The next blow came from a long, negative piece on *Ms.* magazine by reporter Jean Carper in the October 5, 1975 *Washington Post*. Carper used the Redstockings' accusations and the Harris suit to bolster her account of *Ms.*'s history, and to evoke current criticisms of the magazine within the woman's movement—i.e., "The *Ms.* myth is waning." This article, too, was syndicated all over the country. Both the *Times* and *Washington Post* articles were noticed and commented on by *Ms.* advertisers. Celanese executives even passed the articles around in their company. During these months, Friedan continued her assault, especially on television programs where she announced she would not talk about Steinem and the CIA and then proceeded to do the opposite.

All of this confirmed Steinem's original conviction that she ought not to have answered the Redstockings. The media people she has known say to this day that answering them was her mistake. When shortly thereafter, Random House determined to republish all the allegations in the Redstockings book, *Feminist Revolution,* Steinem sent a routine lawyer's letter, and Random

House did take out these libelous accusations. The correspondence with Random House over this certainly suggests a curious eagerness on their part to include the Steinem material. This may, of course, have merely reflected their sense that her name sold books. In any event, when the book was published the cover declared it to be an "abridged edition."

Of all the articles rehashing the Redstockings' accusations, only one other deserves mention. "Ms. Steinem, Are You Now, or Have You Ever . . . ?," written by Mary Perot Nichols, appeared in a new journal called *New Dawn,* illustrated with drawings of Steinem as variously dressed paper dolls. Its subtitle was "An Investigation into the Connection Between Gloria Steinem and the CIA," and the story was extensive, reviewing much of Steinem's life. The *Florida Sentinel Star* asked Steinem to respond to the article, on which they reported. Steinem replied that she hadn't read the story, and added that *New Dawn* was not a feminist magazine, but was "put out by a men's skin flick mag." She was right about that, according to the *Florida Sentinel Star:* "*New Dawn*—for 'liberated' women—is published in conjunction with *Gallery,* a *Playboy*-type magazine, founded by attorney F. Lee Bailey."

In the April 1976 *Ms.,* "Joreen" [Jo Freeman] republished an earlier movement essay, her now famous "Trashing." An editorial introduction explained that "in 1968 and 1969, Joreen herself was 'trashed,' and since then she has spoken to many others with similar experiences." Steinem was not one of those Joreen spoke to on this subject, nor did she have Steinem in mind. All the same, however unintentionally, she did identify the attack on Steinem as "trashing."

Joreen began by observing that she had "been watching for years with increasing dismay as the Movement consciously destroys anyone within it who stands out in any way." She continued:

Trashing is a particularly vicious form of character assassination which amounts to psychological rape. It is manipulative, dishonest, and excessive. It is occasionally disguised by the rhetoric of honest conflict, or covered up by denying that any disapproval exists at all. But it is not done to expose disagreements or to resolve differences. It is done to disparage and destroy.

Joreen quoted Italian-American feminist Anselma Dell'Olio, who had recently spoken on the same subject: "The most common and pervasive [form of attack] is character assassination: the attempt to undermine and destroy belief in the integrity of the individual under attack."

In September 1976, *Ms.* printed a representative sampling of the enormous reader response to Joreen's article (Pat Schroeder wrote that "women have not yet learned the game of 'rumps together, horns out.' ") Steinem also wrote (without specifically referring to her own case): "Joreen's article captured a basic truth about trashing: it is not meant to teach but to destroy. Just as men victimize the weak member of their group, women victimize the strong one." (This insight applies not only to Steinem's own case but to all trashing since the early days of the movement.) Steinem added two other ideas worth recalling: "Lack of self-esteem leads to a voracious need for approval from others. Among feminists, this frequently takes the form of claiming to have invented, or otherwise to 'possess,' some publicly successful part of the Movement or even the entire Movement itself." She also observed that those women who, because of a basic lack of self-esteem, cannot achieve the recognition they crave must make certain that no other woman can have it either; hence, such women trash and destroy.

Since Betty Friedan seemed to do more than any other individual to spread the accusations against Steinem, it seems possible that Steinem, writing her letter, had both the Redstockings and Friedan in mind. The irony here, of course, is that the Redstockings and Friedan had always been on opposite ends of the feminist spectrum; but in this case they joined against someone whom they perceived as a common threat.[6] And that threat, Steinem suggested fifteen years before her book on the subject, came from the lack of self-esteem: the inability of some women ever to gain enough assurance that they were, indeed, of value.

It is, of course, always possible that, as Vivian Gornick observed, the feminist movement was simply in danger of following the pattern of the old left. In a *Village Voice* article in November 1975, Gornick wrote:

> It is dismaying, almost tragic, that after a few years of near silence the invaluable group of radical feminists known as the Redstockings—the group that coined the terms "consciousness raising" and "the politics of housework"—should have re-emerged with its great revolutionary energy focused on denouncing Gloria Steinem and *Ms.* magazine as dangerous enemies of the women's movement. Dismaying because bringing charges against Steinem is so wrongheaded an action. (I looked at those tabloid-sized charges and I thought, So young, and already we have our first purge.) Tragic because it is so meaningless an exercise in terms of feminist activity.

One other observation casts light on the possible motives of those who brought the Redstockings' accusations. Early feminists of the second wave, their names now forgotten, bore the brunt of the opposition against them in academia, in religious institutions, in the corporate and legal worlds, and won ground for their successors at great personal pain to themselves. As Virginia Woolf once wrote of the great English composer Ethel Smyth: "She is of the race of pioneers, she is one of the ice breakers, the gun run-

---

[6] Echols observes that the Redstockings had by the time of their attack on Steinem developed "an antagonism toward lesbian feminism that verged on the homophobic."

ners, the window smashers. The armoured tanks, who climbed
the rough ground, drew the enemies fire, and left behind her a
pathway—not yet smooth and metalled road—but still a pathway
for those who come after her."[7] There are too many early heroes
of this, as of other revolutionary movements, whose heroism is, if
not unrecorded, at least uncelebrated, and little known.

Alix Kates Shulman, the author of *Memoirs of an Ex-Prom
Queen* and *Burning Questions,* a novel about the early feminist
movement, who has edited the writings of Emma Goldman, is
someone who has no rancor against Steinem; she speaks of the
whole Redstockings affair in measured tones. Apart from the fact
that Steinem did not immediately answer the charges, which
Shulman considers to have been a mistake, Shulman understands
that Steinem was chosen as a target because she was a public
figure, like Kate Millett and others whom the radical movement
shot down in its earliest days. The problem, as Shulman sees it, is
that Steinem "has done a lot of important work for feminism, but
she's been represented as the voice of feminism. She is not a
movement person, she just became part of the movement." Shulman admits that Steinem has never said anything she, Shulman,
couldn't subscribe to, but at the same time Shulman does not feel
that Steinem has ever represented her. Shulman feels that
Steinem's "relation to the radical movement was problematic
from the start. Then, when she refused to answer the [Redstock-
ings'] accusations, that blew it."

Alix Kates Shulman's criticisms of Steinem can be seen as fair,
certainly as understandable. She feels "a certain amount of distress
over the turn of the women's movement, [recalling how] the radical movement which had turned the world on its head through
audacity, imagination, was being ardently attacked. The best part

---

[7] Quoted in *The Pargiters,* Mitchell Leaska, ed. (New York: The New York Public
Library, 1977), p. xxvii.

of the movement, the part that dared to imagine a feminist transformation of the society was being attacked as crazy. Radical
women who had said this is where we have to change the world,
at Miss America for example, [were] being labeled ugly, crazy."
Since Steinem was not at the time associated with this radical part,
Shulman suggests, "it did look bad for the feminist revolution
when the uptown middle-class, nice-girl look was embraced and
represented by Gloria, who seemed to love it. The police were
destroying the radical movements, so people had reason to be
alarmed by the possibility that there was a conspiracy here."

Ultimately, while Shulman, who had been in the more radical
feminist movement from its beginning, clearly saw feminism differently than did Steinem, her major criticism arose from
Steinem's failure to respond.[8] When "charges came down from
people with impeccable radical feminist histories . . . it seemed
as if they might all be true: There was a big confrontation at that
time between the government and all radical groups." The only
challenge one might reasonably offer Shulman is why she insisted
that "they weren't charges, they were questions. . . . There
wasn't anything but a question raised initially." The Redstockings' press release scarcely looks like mere "questions" today, nor
did it look like questions in 1975.

At the time of the Redstockings' allegations, Shulman was at
Sagaris, an experimental feminist college in Vermont, which
played a vital part in the accusations against Steinem. As is so
often the case in any complex history of allegations and counteral-
legations, accounts of Sagaris differ significantly, depending on
who renders them.

Sagaris was one of the dreams of a place for feminist education,

---

[8] Shulman withdrew an article she had written for *Ms.* because of Steinem's initial
silence.

without hierarchy, patriarchy, or the rigidity of received ideas. In its brochure, Sagaris described itself as

> an independent institute for the study of feminist thought. Its purpose is to provide a framework for women with prior involvement in women's issues, to study with some of the important feminist thinkers. . . . There are now many feminist programs within degree-granting colleges. SAGARIS because of its independence and excellent faculty will reach beyond the scope of what can be accomplished within more traditional institutions.

The original faculty included Rita Mae Brown, Charlotte Bunch, Mary Daly, Bertha Harris, Ti-Grace Atkinson, Alix Kates Shulman, Barbara Seaman, and Susan Sherman, among others. Susan Sherman, in her book *The Color of the Heart,* has provided a moving account. After describing the "bucolic scene of Vermont in the summer," she continues:

> It seemed almost too perfect. And perhaps a more experienced, less enthusiastic observer might have predicted from the beginning that isolating over one hundred women of all ages, interests, and levels of emotional stability along with some of the strongest, most diverse and opinionated voices in the feminist community on an isolated hill top for a period of five weeks would itself be a dangerous thing to do. [105]

At its start in 1975, Sagaris had received $5,000 from the Ms. Foundation; over two months later, they requested another $10,000. This was granted at what happened to be Aileen Hernandez's first meeting of the Ms. Foundation board, to which she had just been elected. Since the foundation always evaluated those to whom they made grants, and since Hernandez had been chosen to undertake the evaluation at Sagaris, she took the check with her when she went to Vermont.

She walked into a maelstrom: The Redstockings had just issued their charges. Since Hernandez did not take the allegations seriously, she delivered the check. A discussion ensued because the money was "tainted," and a public debate erupted among all those at Sagaris. Hernandez did not stay for the entire discussion; she left, as she put it, "a little bit surprised to have this reaction, since it wasn't usual then for feminist groups to get ten thousand dollars from anybody." But, as Sherman writes, because Steinem had not answered the allegations, "some members of the Sagaris faculty, because of political stands they had taken and statements they had signed, could not possibly have accepted part of their salaries from the Ms. Foundation." [106]

One of those who commented on the controversy mentioned that Sagaris had no problem, apparently, accepting money from the historically hardly blameless Carnegie Foundation, but whether that is true or not is less to the point than the possibility that Sagaris was already so divided and troubled that any cause for dissension would have sufficed. "The fight over Ms. Foundation money," Sherman notes, "function[ed] as a catalyst that brought the internal contradictions which had plagued Sagaris since its inception to the surface: that Sagaris, rather than being an alternative, was in reality a caricature of the traditional educational system." [107]

Ultimately, the fight came down to resentments deep in some East Coast groups of the original women's movement, a movement begun by radical women and eventually, as they saw it, diluted by women who had come out of the male left. What is confusing about this with respect to Steinem is that her lifelong identification with the dispossessed and her inherent dislike of middle-class culture would seem to recommend her to the feminist left. However, Steinem's association with *Ms.* apparently undermined that appeal. When we add to this Steinem's attention from the media, it is clear that she was, for both sides, a ready target.

Unfortunately for Steinem, Betty Friedan continued to help keep the CIA matter alive. Friedan's *It Changed My Life* appeared in 1976, and with its publication any question of Freidan's goodwill toward other women leaders of the movement, particularly Steinem, was laid to rest. A certain amount of brouhaha preceded publication, because *Ms.* had accepted an ad for the book before anyone there had read it, and the editors now wished, on the advice of the magazine's lawyers, to be sure that would not affect any suit Steinem might consider bringing against Friedan. Steinem had seen prepublication galleys of the book—full of denunciations of her—and she received transcripts of Friedan discussing, or pointedly refusing to discuss, her on various television shows. In the event, Steinem brought no suit—not because Friedan let up on the attacks but because after that point, Steinem's resignation overcame any hope of change or redress; this was the last time that she would be profoundly troubled by Friedan's attacks.

Indeed, to judge by its pages, Friedan appeared to know herself as little as she knew Steinem, although she did correctly perceive that they "seemed to be operating from quite different places, in some fundamental way." In 1973 Friedan told Paul Wilkes of the *New York Times* that she saw herself—as the *Newsweek* researchers had, for different reasons, seen Steinem—as "Joan of Arc." "I don't think there is another woman in America who could muster more votes [than I, running for the Senate]. . . . I don't want to sound corny about it, but . . . well, you know about Joan of Arc and the voices that guided her? I think I hear voices sometimes, too. It is no more than your own sixth sense telling you what is best." Friedan did not run for the Senate. In April of that year

Friedan had told Rhoda Amon of *Newsday,* "The defeat [of the ERA] showed the degree to which we have allowed the women's movement to be taken over by extreme groups. Like *Ms.* magazine, for instance." It is, of course, interesting to contrast this with the complaints from some readers that *Ms.* was not radical or extreme enough.

In *It Changed My Life* Friedan wrote that she felt "I was no match for [Steinem], not only because of that matter of looks— which somehow paralyzed me—but because I don't know how to manipulate, or deal with manipulation, myself." [179] Manipulation is in the eye of the beholder. Friedan reported that just before she left for the 1975 International Women's Year Conference in Mexico, "Someone came to see me to ask me to hold a press conference in Mexico, to expose the links between Gloria Steinem and the CIA, which had recently been documented and released by the Redstockings group." Friedan mentioned that she also began to receive anonymous threats, but had "no idea whether Gloria Steinem had anything to do with these calls." [343]

It Changed My Life is a monument of innuendo. Stephanie Harrington, reviewing the book for the July 4, 1976 *New York Times Book Review,* quoted many of Friedan's accusations against Abzug and Steinem and countered some of them. "Well," Harrington wrote, "this is heady stuff. Is she saying Steinem and/or Abzug have CIA and FBI connections? If so, why doesn't she say so plainly?" Harrington ended on a humorous note: "You can't be too paranoid these days. However, some beguiling pedestrian answers to Friedan's exotic charges, stated or implied, are available." Harrington then offered some "pedestrian answers," concluding: "If most of this space has been spent questioning Friedan's version of events, she cannot complain, since she has raised politically sensational questions that she must know will not go unnoticed, and she has failed to spell out or document her answers. She has

driven me to defend Bella Abzug, although I have often considered moving to Michigan so I could vote for [Congresswoman and
ERA supporter] Martha Griffiths."

In the ensuing years, the *New York Times,* under the direction
of Friedan's friend Abe Rosenthal (who had known Steinem in
India and agreed with her throughout the Vietnam War), continued to regard Friedan as *the* feminist, a fact that makes even less
comprehensible her continued attacks on Steinem. By 1981, when
Friedan's *The Second Stage* appeared, she had isolated herself from
almost all other feminists. John Leonard reviewed the book unfa-
vorably, accusing Friedan of blaming the victim, of "identifying in
reverse" with the rhetoric of the antifeminists, and of "[l]icking
the hand that batters you." (As a result of this review, Leonard
reports, he was taken off the roster of daily book reviewers, and
eventually left the *Times.*)

In an interview in 1991, Friedan claimed to have no animosity
toward Steinem. But "Can a Feminist Be Beautiful?" her article
on Naomi Wolf's *The Beauty Myth,* appeared in the March 1991
issue of *Allure* at the same time as the interview. Friedan wrote:
"It used to amuse me when feminist voices like *Ms.* told women to
wear makeup or pretty clothes or shave their legs. All the while,
there were reports of Gloria Steinem having her hair streaked at
Kenneth and, according to an apocryphal story, hiding under a
hair dryer, holding *Vogue* in front of her face." What the point
can be, other than ill will, of telling an apocryphal story is difficult
to determine. Equally apocryphal are the positions attributed to
Ms.: The magazine had discussed questions of makeup and body
hair, but not been prescriptive.

By the time Friedan published *The Second Stage* in 1981, she
had lost the greater part of her feminist following. The reasons
are clear enough to historians of feminism. Zillah Eisenstein
writes:

Friedan interprets the theory of sex-class oppression to mean that all men, individually, hate women. She says this is nothing but man-hating propaganda. She denies the reality of sexual-class conflict between men and women by reducing this theory of patriarchal privilege to a theory about individual men, and then dismisses it. . . . Although Wollstonecraft and Stanton never said that man was the enemy, they never said he was not. Neither Wollstonecraft nor Stanton ever tried to deny that men are privileged as men and that they benefit from their privilege. Friedan inadvertently denies male privilege by denying that antagonism exists between men and women as sexual classes. . . . How one creates new institutions without dislodging the existing power arrangements is unclear. It must be unclear to Friedan, who acknowledges that people do not voluntarily give up their place in the sun and at the same time embraces the pluralist vision of power and social change. [182]

In fact, as Winifred Wandersee succinctly puts it: "Americans never felt a collective guilt for their sexism as they did for their racism; they never accepted collective responsibility for the centuries of discrimination and the consequential secondary status of women within society. Indeed, one of the major tasks of feminists was to convince women *themselves* that they had a right to their freedom, and that women's issues were justifiable political objectives." [xv] That was the primary task, together with the fight against racism, that Steinem undertook and still undertakes. It was the task that, once it began to arouse a male backlash, Friedan abandoned. Ironically, Friedan was so far from what the radical innovators of the women's movement conceived as important that she was not even available as an object for its anger.

An obsession like Friedan's with Steinem is most notable for the harm it does to the cause of feminism. There is no reason why an accomplished woman, like an accomplished man, should not acquire enemies in the course of a public career. What makes the continued enmity between women particularly regrettable is the eagerness of the media to publicize it. Even Nora Ephron found Friedan's anger at Steinem, like Steinem's anger at Gary Hart, amusing, and well worth a clever article.

An account of Steinem as an object of feminist hatred is important because it is a part of the history of feminism, and must be taken note of. Steinem never attacked or spoke out against Friedan publicly; when she was herself attacked, she responded only minimally to specific allegations. When she abandoned this principle to respond to the Redstockings, she suffered repercussions and great anguish. But even though Steinem did not attack Friedan, the perception of public battles between feminists defeats the cause both wish to serve.

IN JUNE 1975, whether coincidentally or not it is impossible to determine, Elizabeth Forsling Harris sued Steinem, Carbine, and the *Ms.* corporation for $1.7 million, alleging stock fraud. This was, of course, delicious to the print media. The story was widely reported, sometimes along with the accusations of Steinem's "CIA connections." When, some months later, the suit was dropped because Harris failed to pursue it, there was no publicity; resolutions or the abandonment of suits, unlike the suits themselves, seem merely to be tedious. But Harris's action remains of interest because she is Steinem's most lasting, most intractable enemy.

Pat Carbine reports that on May 9, the day of the Redstockings' press conference, "I had a call from a reporter on the *New York Times* who said, 'How do you feel about the lawsuit?' I said, 'What lawsuit?' She said, 'You and Gloria are being sued for fraud by Betty Harris.' I said, 'You've got to be kidding, I'm learning this from you.' It turned out that Betty Harris that day had lunch with somebody at the *Times* and said, I'm suing Gloria and Pat for fraud."

Since Harris did not follow through on the suit, her motive appears to have been a desire for publicity and injury to Steinem rather than any hope of proving fraud. Initially, Carbine and Steinem did not take the matter seriously, but when summonses were served on them at the *Ms.* office, they realized that Harris apparently meant to go through with it. But not, it subsequently appeared, for long. Following the erratic pattern that had characterized her behavior in the early days of *Ms.,* Harris asked for two postponements of her deposition; the court granted these, but when she failed to appear for the third time, the case was dismissed. Molly Ivins, reporting on the case for the *New York Times,* quoted Harris as saying, "I saw no point in pursuing it. I instructed my lawyers not to proceed." Ivins also reported that Pat Carbine intended to "countersue Harris on a charge of having maliciously sued the magazine." Unfortunately, few of the hundreds of other newspapers that had reported the suit followed Ivins in also reporting its dismissal.

The countersuit, also filed in the federal court, asked for $287,000 in actual damages, asserting that the Harris suit had been brought "with the intention and for the purpose of causing dissemination of false and libelous information about the defendants." Philip Mandel, the lawyer for Carbine and Steinem, has said, "In those days, I was imbued with a very strong sense of justice, and I felt that anytime someone brought a baseless action they should be made to pay for that." But Harris appeared on her own behalf—without a lawyer, probably at her most persuasive, pitiful, and broke—and the judge found she did not have to pay. Mandel, however, interprets this as only a nominal victory; the real case had been put to bed some months before. Harris, however, claimed that she had won a moral victory.

Harris made Steinem into a kind of bogey and determined, with an almost frightening intensity, to bring her down. In 1985, Harris signed a contract with New American Library to write a biography of Steinem, but the publisher eventually canceled the contract when Harris failed to deliver. Nonetheless, she went on talk shows to castigate Steinem as man-crazy, a judgment picked up by the *New York Post*'s notorious Page Six on August 10, 1990. "Why Was Book on Steinem Killed?" the headline read. Identified as "the founding publisher of Steinem's *Ms.* magazine," Harris was quoted as calling Steinem "a 'man-izer' with a yen for rich men. She has a remarkable ability to manipulate men, to get them to do what she wants them to do." Perhaps Harris was referring to the men like Mandel who supported Steinem against her. Steinem was quoted in the same article as saying she had nothing to do with complaints about the book, and the publisher confirmed that it was canceled because the author did not submit the completed manuscript by the agreed date.

Harris's accusation that Steinem is a "man-izer" is worth considering, since Harris said aloud what many women have whispered. Three factors rendered Steinem particularly vulnerable to this attack: her beauty; her attractiveness to men; and her liking for men and the sexual experiences and satisfactions they can extend. There has long existed, even beyond Hollywood, the belief that women who get ahead do so in exchange for sexual favors. As Steinem is wont to remark, If women could sleep their way to the top, why aren't more women heads of companies? The truth in Steinem's case, and no doubt in others, is that the combination of talent and beauty is a kind of affront to some women unblessed with this combination or even one of its components. The average man, too, finds it easier to deal with one or the other —often ignoring the talent if it exists together with the beauty. Steinem was lucky, or perceptive, in most of the men she chose as lovers.

Women, alas, seem to have found it hardest to deal with Steinem's particular combination of gifts. Such looks and such radical and feminist ideals are rarely enough conjoined, and when they are publicly exhibited they seem to instill a simmering indignation in even the most generous of women. Those less generous, or those who are the victims of envy, find it easier to credit the men who have loved Steinem rather than Steinem herself for her achievements and fame. Steinem, like every person, can be criticized and even disliked on various grounds; but the accusation that she has got where she is through men undermines both feminism and the right of feminists to be both beautiful and profoundly sexual. Steinem herself has found the charges of government agentry and getting ahead through sex to be connected. When women, who have internalized society's estimate of their group, see a woman doing what they cannot, they assume she must have the benefit of a sinister male force behind her. This also justifies cutting her down; what the Australians call "the tall poppy syndrome," or African Americans call "crabs in a basket."

Oddly enough, feminists in the nineties, including Steinem, were to find themselves trashed by women, some of them self-declared feminists, who apparently ached for the publicity Steinem seemed able so easily to evoke. The most ironic aspect of this was that some of these women—Christina Hoff Sommers, Katie Roiphe—seemed to base their assaults on their defense of men against the hatred feminists of Steinem's generation supposedly felt for men. Attacks on feminists veer preposterously—always absurd but, alas, constant.

Steinem found the Harris suit and Friedan attacks worse, in certain ways, than the Sarachild accusations, because Friedan and Harris had more credibility in the world at large. Some might find it strange that she did not seek therapy at that time when she was so under siege. But therapy would not occur to her as a possibility for a decade. Meanwhile, her friends served as a support group. All report that they had never seen her more agonized; despite staunch reinforcement from the *Ms.* editors and from Pottinger, she suffered to so great a degree that she was perhaps the readier for therapy when she came to it.

The question remains why Harris's dismissed suit should have caused Steinem so much pain. Analyzing her response twenty years later, Steinem attributes it to an unrealistic trust of outsiders. She had early developed a way of treating the outside world as if it were her family, because her family world was much more undependable, empty, and nonprotective than the world beyond it. She now realizes that even before the years alone with her mother, she had come to expect from friends, acquaintances, and even strangers the understanding and support that one would usually expect from family. Most people, including Steinem's sister, are more upset by attacks from family members than by collisions with others. Steinem, on the other hand, regards family problems as emergencies that she can handle, as she handled them for Ruth in Toledo.

She had this irrational faith in people and circumstances on the outside, because, she believed, they made her "real"; she felt less real than other people, she believes, because she was not the focus of anyone's attention when a child. And therefore, when the outside world profoundly misunderstood her and condemned her wrongfully, it hurt much more than it should have: It made her feel invisible, annihilated. To some extent, she admits, all women think they can become valuable only by being useful to other people. But Steinem believes that she had a double dose of this problem because of the way she grew up.

This question will be reconsidered at the point in Steinem's life when, already over fifty, she experienced a kind of hitting bottom, and for the first time entered upon a course of introspection, including therapy. Suffice it for now to suggest that her explanation of the problem, while not without a certain veracity, seems rather too simplistic; those who eschew introspection tend to look for simple explanations. In the area of psychological response and reaction to rejection and hostility, explanations are inevitably complex. Like many others, however, Steinem was at this particular historical moment imbued with a newfound feminism and had let her barriers down. A faith in sisterhood was in the air; Steinem recalls that even Kathie Sarachild, three years earlier, had praised the preview issue of *Ms.* magazine, the only issue Steinem was responsible for every part of, as a triumph. Nor, as Joreen's 1976 article testified, was Steinem the only one to be trashed. She was, however, the most famous and the most publicized, therefore the most ardently hated. Steinem's pain resulted in part from her failure fully to digest the fact that having only "good" motives and working hard for "good" causes was insufficient to protect one from such assaults. Her naïveté would never wholly vanish, but it would, from this point on, diminish. And on this side of maturity, the experience of being falsely accused made her far more careful in documenting her own writing, as well as more skeptical of rumors and accusations.

HOUSTON

IN APRIL of 1976, when Steinem was forty-two years old, the journalist Susan Epstein asked famous people what they would do if they suddenly found themselves broke. Those asked ranged from John Lennon to Ronald Reagan to Julia Child. (Reagan replied that he would breed and raise horses.) Steinem answered: "I would try to keep working somewhere as a writer. Failing that, I would open a diner with red gingham curtains, selling scrambled eggs by the side of the road, someplace with sunshine and a little friendliness for anyone who stopped. With maybe a few revolutionary feminist cell meetings in the back room for *real* support and good cheer." There is something sad yet earthbound about this fantasy: The revolution would continue in the back room; strangers would be encountered; and there would be sunshine by the side of the road.

Steinem's answer is indicative of a conflict that would only grow more intense as she moved through her fifties, but that would never altogether subside. She was a political creature; she believed in action and the validity of experience—particularly the experience of those who lived and worked beyond the eye of the media. Yet in fulfilling her political aims, she had committed herself to a wandering life, to a home that was more like a dressing room, and to having little chance to write except under the enormous pressure of journalistic deadlines. Nonetheless, Steinem felt that feminism and its relationship to the world had to be rooted in the populist experiences of those who stopped for eggs and conversation, not in theories. Throughout that year she in fact thought more constantly about the possibility of actually writing of such feminist experiences.

First, however, were the demands of Democratic party politics before and after the 1976 Democratic Convention, which was held in New York City. Steinem's views on the convention were summarized in a July 26, 1976, "City Politic" column for *New York* (she would still occasionally contribute to that magazine): "Kissing with Your Eyes Open: Women and the Democrats." The article began with an admission that, after the two previous Democratic conventions, she had every intention of avoiding this one, "finding some faraway spot, with no television, no newspapers, and no reporters" with banal questions about feminism. She had, as she reported, paid all her activist dues before the convention, "by testifying at the Platform Committee hearings, going to strategy meetings of the National Women's Political Caucus, working on the Democratic Women's Agenda '76, and generally helping with the various mechanisms feminists have invented in a long-term struggle to make the Democratic party behave democratically." Then, she planned "to get the hell out of New York in July."

Of course, she didn't do so. While, like all the women who had been at the 1972 convention, she felt like the walking wounded— "We hadn't even admitted to ourselves the emotional battering of years past"—she nonetheless understood that by 1976 women were no longer on the outside, but were now accepted by the party as a recognized pressure group "and occasionally, a majority that wins."

Steinem's column reported on the convention fights over delegates and the abortion issue, and mentioned the women on the caucus's Democratic Task Force, who operated so successfully at the convention: Millie Jeffrey, its chair; and Bella Abzug, Patt Derian, and Koryne Horbal, whose grassroots political genius in Minnesota "helped to turn that [women's democratic] caucus into such a powerful force that the governor of Minnesota staked his reputation on trying to oust her from office at a recent Minnesota convention." (The governor lost.)

Even the media seemed a bit more informed. Steinem was not asked in New York, as she had been in Miami, if women really suffered discrimination in the United States. In addition, all the women delegates were willing to meet with each other and identify as a constituency: "Whatever the disagreements internally, we bargained as a unit, and were treated seriously by the candidate as the same."

Practically, convention life was a lot easier in New York in 1976. "In Miami, we had trouble maintaining an office in a cockroach-infested hotel. Here, we had a hospitality suite, a sophisticated press operation, and a big benefit at Lincoln Center to pay for the whole thing." Steinem reckoned that in Miami the life of a woman activist was shortened by four years, but in New York by only six months.

She ended the article with a warning to Robert Strauss, chairman of the Democratic party, who had compared the Democratic party to his "favorite girl friend . . . deaf and dumb and oversexed and the owner of a liquor store." Well, Steinem retorted, our liquor store is beginning to pay, and we aren't your girlfriend anymore.

Indeed, by the end of 1976 Steinem was in Washington, speaking at the press conference of the National Women's Political

Caucus. While she celebrated the appointment of economist Juanita Kreps as secretary of commerce, Steinem had critical words for President-elect Carter, finding nothing further to celebrate after the Kreps appointment. Carter and his staff had, like many before and after them, expressed difficulty in finding qualified women to fill government jobs, although women's organizations throughout the country had inundated them with résumés. The NWPC press conference, Steinem explained, was held in the hope that Carter and his staff might "still be willing to listen." Abzug, Steinem, and others were concerned because the women's constituency was the only one Carter had not consulted personally, despite many requests by women for such meetings. She concluded: "In short, we did not work and vote for a Carter Administration in order to get appointments that might have been made by President Ford." She was concerned, not only with the sex of Carter's appointments, but with their ability and willingness to listen to women, their "majority." (Carter did, in fact, come to appoint many women to important posts.)

DURING THE remainder of 1976 and the early part of 1977 Steinem was still constantly on the move. She appeared as guest speaker at the tenth anniversary of the New York chapter of NOW; she delivered a talk to the American Marketing Association Conference in New York about the potential impact of women in the workforce; she was the keynote speaker at a conference on battered women and did benefits for many smaller, grassroots women's groups. In addition, she spent more and more time working for the passage of the Equal Rights Amendment. The right wing was mobilizing hard against the feminist movement, particularly in the Sun Belt. While speaking in Tampa, for example, Steinem was assailed with posters featuring pictures of herself and other campaigners "Wanted Dead or Alive." (Thus were right-wing tactics against abortion foreshadowed.) "The religious opposition [to feminism] goes very deep," Steinem wrote to Jo-anne Williams, a reporter who interviewed her for the *Pacific Sun*. "Religions have enshrined the white male political ethic. The movement has diminished male supremacy. There are a lot of junkies out there who can't get along without their male suprem-acy; it's like an addiction." Steinem was, of course, aware that there are a great many nonwhite junkies of male supremacy else-where in the world, but it was American fundamentalist religion against which she fought.

Beginning in March, Steinem became substitute radio colum-nist for Murray Kempton on a CBS show called *Spectrum*. *Spec-trum* provided views from both the right and the left on various social and political issues of the day. For two months, twice a week, Steinem used this forum to discuss unequal pay scales for women, battered women, the Carter administration position on choice (he supported it but not for poor women who requested Medicaid), and homophobia, among other topics. Her impression was that CBS was not sorry to see her go. Orthodox rabbis had objected to her pointing out that homosexuals had also been put in concentration camps by the Nazis, and her last "essay," the now-famous, comic "If Men Could Menstruate," elicited much feed-back from outraged station affiliates, some of whom refused to carry it. Such was Steinem's visibility, at this point, that the *Na-tional Observer,* a conservative paper, ran an article featuring her as one of "the new Socialists." (Others listed included Harvey Cox, Julian Bond, and Michael Harrington.)

On March 28, 1977, four days after Steinem's forty-third birth-day, President Carter announced the appointment of Bella Abzug as presiding officer of the National Commission on the Observa-tion of International Women's Year. Many prominent women, such as Maya Angelou, Betty Ford, Coretta Scott King, Millie

Jeffrey—and Steinem—were named to the commission. From this point on, the National Women's Conference in Houston, a result of International Women's Year, would take up most of Steinem's time that year. Never before had federal money been allotted for such an undertaking by American women.

In the months before the convention itself, Steinem's role was almost entirely that of a mediator, compromiser, and unifier, helping to organize sessions in different states throughout the country as they elected delegates to the conference. All state sessions were open; consequently, the right wing, particularly Phyllis Schlafly's Eagle Forum (and male-led busloads of women organized by the Mormon Church), was able to mount well-organized assaults to elect their own. It was necessary, therefore, while assuring the right wing honorable representation, to make certain that they did not dominate the state-by-state proceedings. Lindsay Van Gelder, covering the conference for *Ms.,* reported that the Wichita state session to elect the Kansas delegation had a particularly rough time of it. At that session, the right wing had warned its supporters to vote "against any recommendation using 'neutral gender' words like 'person' or 'spouse.' "

The New York session in Albany, another huge two-day meeting of more than 3,000 women, was also under such pressure. The organized Mormon vote was led by a man wearing a white glove, to make sure his hand was visible. Together with Bella Abzug, Mary Anne Krupsack, and others, Steinem stayed up for three consecutive days and nights, collating handouts and passing out leaflets defining the feminist platform. Finally, in a profoundly moving scene, many hundreds of women stood in line for more than six hours to vote the platform in.

The response of the far right to the Houston conference was the first national evidence of the strength and organization of the enormous backlash to be mounted against feminism. Since the conference was being funded by tax dollars, it was especially threatening to the right wing. No longer was this just women meeting in their living rooms. Indeed, when the sessions to nominate delegates were over, religious fundamentalists, right-to-life groups, the Eagle Forum, the John Birch Society, the Ku Klux Klan, and the American Party had won an estimated 15 to 20 percent of the delegates. Thus, Van Gelder reported, Mississippi, one third of whose population was black, was represented by an all-white delegation, seven of them men.

Steinem was to write that "Houston and all the events surrounding it [became] a landmark in personal history, the sort of milestone that divides our sense of time. . . . Was it before or after Houston?" It is doubtful if this "landmark" really persisted for many years in Steinem's life, although her estimation of all that Houston accomplished would never diminish. She delighted in the fact that despite the efforts of the right wing and the composition of the Mississippi delegation, the three-day event was "the most economically, racially, and geographically representative assembly this nation had ever seen." As Van Gelder reported, for the first time in any such conference:

> if anyone was under represented (among the 2,000 delegates; 15,000 were in attendance) it was the white upper-middle class. Whites were 64.5 percent of the elected delegates, as opposed to 84.4 percent of the general female population, and women with family incomes of more than $20,000 a year were 14.1 percent of the elected delegates, compared to 25.7 percent nationally. It may be the only conference in which delegates-at-large had to be used to . . . achieve racial balance as mandated by the public law creating the conference—by adding white women. It was like a supermarket checkout line from Anywhere, U.S.A., transposed to the political arena. . . . We were an all-woman Carl Sandburg poem come to life.

The conference opened on November 18, 1977, with the passing of a lighted torch that had been carried by women's relay teams across twenty-six hundred miles from Seneca Falls, New York, where the first Women's Rights Convention had been held in July of 1848, and where the Women's Hall of Fame now stands. Fifteen thousand women from all over the country, two thousand delegates among them, were in attendance.

Few who were at Houston and who witnessed the impressive, unique, and triumphant outcome fail to mention Steinem's role. Steinem's actual assignment was to help draft the resolution concerning the handicapped, but her most extensive work was in connection with the minority caucus. There were, according to the *Official Report on the Conference,* chiefly written by Caroline Bird and Mim Kelber, "black women from almost every State and Territory; Hispanic women, including Chicanas, Puerto Ricans, Cubans, and other Latinas; an Asian American caucus of Chinese Americans, Japanese Americans, Filipinas, and others; American Indians from different tribes as well as Alaskan natives; and Pacific Americans from Hawaii, Guam, Samoa, and other trust territories." To say that there were differing priorities among them is to state the obvious. African Americans varied from older well-dressed Deltas to young street women in military surplus; California's Congresswoman Maxine Waters played a role in bringing diversity together that Steinem wouldn't forget. By all reports it was Steinem who, in a spirit of compromise, then helped the many different groupings to hammer out a resolution to which they could all subscribe. (Or, as Steinem herself puts it, "I was their scribe, finding shared issues, language for the shared issues, and adding special ones at the end, e.g., Indian fishing rights—and saving great Indian language about the Great Goddess—but they did it.")

Steinem, perceiving how many issues were shared, helped the minority caucus to create an umbrella of unifying language. As the *Official Report on the Conference* summed up: "For the first time minority women . . . were present in such a critical mass that they were able to define their own needs as well as to declare their stake in each women's issue." Steinem's contribution was exactly the central objective of all her feminist efforts, and also, in her words, "the best revolutionary function of a writer; to forge language that doesn't divide."

The plan that the conference produced had lasting influence, although the evidence of that took some years to manifest itself. Among the twenty-six issues solidified there were, in Steinem's words: "The economic rights of workers, including homemakers; a 'minority women's plank' that included Native Americans and the full spectrum of women of color for the first time; a 'sexual preference plank' that made discrimination against lesbians a shared issue; and 'a national health security program'; those were just a few samples of a plan that crystallized a majority consensus among U.S. women, became the agenda of a grassroots women's movement, and led to a growing gender gap in favor of candidates of either party who represented its issues."

The inability of the media, however, accurately to present a feminist event was devastatingly confirmed by the Houston conference. Van Gelder's article included a summary of the conference's media coverage. She paints a sorry picture of the media's insistence on giving "both sides of the story." Mainstream articles about the conference often made it appear that 80-20 votes against right-wing positions were 50-50 votes. The media, for example, never investigated how many tax-exempt churches paid the transportation bills of those attending the Schlafly rally or really explained that the Schlafly forces were demonstrating against an elected conference.

In addition, the press considered feminism to be a white, upper-middle-class movement, and therefore failed to report that at Houston one third of the delegates were minority women, or that there were more Native American women from different tribes than had ever met together before. The *New York Times,* eschewing any pretense of seriousness, ran a feature on the few men at the conference. And so on.

It is disheartening to read Van Gelder's reports against those in other newspapers and journals; only right-wing papers like the *Washington Star* covered the conference extensively—damning it, but nonetheless paying attention. In truth, the many reporters who flocked to the conference had hoped that it would turn out to be a war between the radical right and feminism, a struggle they never worked hard enough to understand and whose outcome they never explored.[1] They were disappointed in this hope.

One surreal moment stood out for Steinem among the three hectic days she spent at the Houston conference. Operating on adrenaline and little sleep, she was hurrying through the halls under the convention center and happened to pass a ringing telephone on a table. She picked it up, only to hear the voice of Gloria Carter, the president's sister, asking to speak to her or to Bella Abzug. Momentarily stunned by the coincidence, Steinem heard Carter go on to say that she had just converted Larry Flynt, the publisher of *Hustler* magazine, to Christianity and that an important part of such a conversion was to apologize to everyone he had injured. Flynt therefore wanted to apologize to Steinem or Abzug for all the damage he had done to women over the years.[2]

Steinem had received a peculiar letter from Flynt the previous October: "I feel I may have been wrong in my attitude toward

---

[1] See *The Media and Women Without Apology,* the winter/spring 1993 issue of *Media Studies Journal,* for an account of how the print media continues to misrepresent feminism.

[2] When Flynt left Christianity, he published a list of women who, if they posed "nude in *Hustler's* inimitable 'open-pussy' style" would be paid one million dollars. The list included Patty Hearst, Raquel Welch, Barbara Walters, Caroline Kennedy, Julie Nixon Eisenhower, Susan Ford, Sally Struthers, Mary Tyler Moore, Gloria Steinem, and Cher Bono Allman.

you and certain aspects of the feminist movement," he wrote. "Perhaps we could meet so I might explain my feelings." After the Houston conference, Steinem declined to meet with him, but suggested that a contribution of one million dollars or so to the ERA struggle would be a way of apologizing. She never heard from either Carter or Flynt on the subject again.

FOR STEINEM HERSELF, the Houston conference would remain incontrovertible evidence of the possibility of women's getting together, working together, and agreeing, eventually if not readily, on their goals. Returned from the conference, Steinem wrote to Jacqueline Onassis (who, beside the ailing Pat Nixon, was the only living wife of a president who had not attended), telling her that the prospect of being in Houston had filled her with dread: "I think I not only believed the press about [the conference's] failure and the strength of the ultra right forces, but also thought somewhere inside that women couldn't pull off such a big, populist event. If I had known how very wrong I was, I would have urged you to go. Now I'm sorry that I didn't." Steinem went on to report how—this was December 2—she was "trying to wade through work in time to start a Woodrow Wilson fellowship in two weeks. I can't quite imagine what I will do in a quiet room, but only those frightening, blank sheets of paper will tell."

Steinem planned during her Woodrow Wilson fellowship to write a book on the impact of feminism on political theory. She had decided to devote herself to the search for "some theoretical ways for feminist transition [into the political structure] that was not intimidating." Steinem had always been seeking, and would continue to seek, a way that feminist theory could arise from female experience, rather than be inserted into a male theoretical system such as Freudian psychoanalysis. She considered that academic feminists had to write in the language of jargon that might win them advancement in their scholarly profession, but would not make their discoveries accessible to women in general.[3]

The dream of solitude in a quiet room, facing blank sheets of paper, would sustain Steinem throughout the whole of that frantic 1977. But, as ever before for Steinem, solitude—at that point in her life—would remain a dream while other commitments, small and large, followed one upon the other. *Ms.* had convinced PBS to let it produce a *Woman Alive* series featuring important issues for women and profiles of important women in history. Steinem was the first host, introducing a magazine-style show that included a report on a couple trying to make an equal marriage, the union-organizing activities of Crystal Lee Jordan (the real "Norma Rae"), and the first television appearances of Lily Tomlin and Melissa Manchester. Bella Abzug had begun her courageous (but ultimately unsuccessful) run for mayor of New York City, and Steinem became deeply involved in that campaign. Steinem held the Bible—a copy of the Woman's Bible, by Elizabeth Cady Stanton—when her friend Koryne Horbal was sworn in as the Carter-appointed U.S. representative to the U.N. Commission on Women. She appeared before the Judicial Conference of the Second Circuit to testify in favor of the ERA at the invitation of and together with Ruth Bader Ginsberg. In a letter to Abe Rosenthal regarding the *New York Times* coverage of this issue, she pointed out that a recent piece by Judy Klemensrud presenting both sides of the argument was still lamentably inaccurate. "The ERA," she wrote, "has nothing to do with whether gays adopt children, does not increase the power of the Federal government, does not lead to unisex toilets; it increases the rights of women who work at

---

[3] It is worth noting that the change in the 1990s, when prominent academic feminists somewhat shifted their focus to their own experiences and away from male-identified disciplines, suggests that others may have taken up Steinem's struggle.

home, etc." In addition, Steinem stated that neither she nor anyone else in the feminist movement was "pro-abortion." "No one
in their right mind is pro-abortion. It's like being pro-appendec-
tomy. The accurate phrase is pro-choice." For a while, "pro-
choice" did appear in the columns of the *New York Times,* but old
habits returned.

And, as always, there were the demands of *Ms.*

In August of 1977, *Christopher Street,* a gay magazine, published
an interview with Steinem by Dorianne Beyer. Of particular interest to Beyer was whether any advertisers had withdrawn their
business from *Ms.* as a result of its coverage of lesbian issues.
Steinem responded:

> I can't remember if there was any problem with advertisers
> over the lesbian issue or not—there've been so many problems
> with advertisers it's hard to remember them all. There was
> some problem with something Flo Kennedy said—I think she
> was quoted as saying, "Nobody ever died from a blow job,"
> [this was, of course, before AIDS] and that was just too much
> for a car manufacturer, and he canceled his ad. There was also
> a painting by a woman—a very realistic, kind, nonsensational,
> good painting, which included nude men, and an airline pulled
> out. Of course—the ruling class does not like to be seen without
> its pants on! . . . The woman who does *Savvy* was asked to
> describe the difference between *Savvy* and *Ms.,* and she said that
> *Savvy* was for executive women and so on, and *Ms.* was for
> black lesbian farmworkers. These things happen all the time.

A short note that Steinem wrote to Jacqueline Onassis indicates, however, that there were blessed moments when Steinem
did relax. "I forget," Steinem had written, "what a great luxury it
is—no, more like a necessity, but one in short supply—to realize
in the middle of a conversation that *everything* is understood, that

we can talk shorthand, and not worry about being mistaken, or somehow later betrayed in small or basic ways."

As 1977 came to a close, Steinem was attempting to juggle the myriad demands of the feminist movement, the populist causes to which she had devoted her life, and her own personal desire to write. "What I really want to know now," she wrote to Liz Smith, "is how in hell you discipline yourself enough to write a book." This challenge was on her mind, especially in the light of the unrelenting demands for her help, and her unwillingness to refuse the greater part of them. "Somehow I question my powers of concentration," she wrote to media specialist Dick Clark. "That's always been a problem for me in isolated sessions of writing, and is generally a state of mind I achieve in an emergency: a deadline imposed from outside, concern about some upcoming event, something happening to a friend, etc. The idea of being able to marshal that intensity at will seems unlikely, and greatly desirable."

Her insight here was prophetic, and there is some question as to whether what she called the ability to "marshal that intensity at will" would ever be fully developed. Over the next two decades she would write books and much else—but all achieved in an "emergency" state of mind. Most significantly, she was not yet ready for a life of contemplation.

So Steinem herself, as her dream of release at the Woodrow Wilson Center indicates, must have become aware of a certain inner conflict, or worked very hard not to become aware of it. Perhaps she thought that a year off would somehow allow all these elements—her television persona, her continuous politicking on behalf of feminism, her desire to write a book about the sources of real feminist theory—to coalesce. If the Woodrow Wilson Center was the carrot, the stick was Steinem's own struggle with her inability to turn away those she felt were fighting for a righteous cause. The carrot and stick represented a fundamental contrast that would, in her fifties, ameliorate, but that would never altogether vanish.

Steinem was not the first woman, and hardly the last, to anticipate a year away from her usual duties as both possible and productive. The Houston conference may have seemed a landmark to her, but the hope she sustained for what could be accomplished during her year of facing blank sheets of paper was a more vital mark of her changing perceptions of her frantic and ever less easily bearable existence.

ANY PORT IN
A STORM

THE WOODROW WILSON CENTER opened in 1970 as a meeting place for scholars and others involved in a broad range of contemporary affairs who could benefit by access to the Library of Congress. It is officially affiliated with the Smithsonian Institution, but, like the other affiliates, the center has its own board of trustees and its own policies.[1] When she formally took up her

---

[1] Even at this writing, the current board of trustees of the Woodrow Wilson Center, largely appointed during the Reagan-Bush administrations, is heavily weighted toward the radical right, as the appointment of Lynn Cheney, head of the National Endowment for the Humanities under Bush, indicates. Also on the board are Gertrude Himmelfarb, author of among other works a biography of John Buchan, a best-selling early twentieth-century author who wrote, among much else, the famous *Thirty-Nine Steps*. Together with her husband, Irving Kristol, and with Norman Podhoretz and his wife, Midge Decter, Himmelfarb is one of the main components of the New York branch of the neoconservative movement, and among the very few Jews at home in a movement also accurately described as the *Christian* right, and fairly represented by Pat Buchanan, Pat Robertson, and William Buckley, Jr.

For a detailed, scholarly discussion of the radical right, its national presence, its financial support, and the intention and execution of its academic influence, see Ellen Messer-Davidow, "Manufacturing the Attack on Liberalized Higher Education," *Social Text* 36 (Fall 1993), pp. 40–80.

fellowship in December 1977, however, Steinem soon learned that the center took seriously the 1846 congressional mandate forming the Smithsonian Institution as "an establishment for the increase and infusion of knowledge among men."

It did not take Steinem long to guess at the degree of male domination, although the true extent of right-wing control was not yet evident. Other problems were immediately apparent. By March, she was writing to Paula Kassell, the editor of *New Directions for Women:*

As you know, the Wilson International Scholars have been overwhelmingly male. Indeed, I could find only one woman in the listing before I applied, and she was studying the law of the sea. (Barring a revolt of female dolphins, an event greatly to be wished, I guess they thought that was safe.) As you can imagine, this exclusion was one of the reasons I chose to apply to this program above others that have already admitted women. Opening up new territory—and not competing with other women for the stipends already available—seems to be a function that some of us should serve. There was some small improvement this time (three out of twenty-one "fellows" in my group are women) but part of our function should be as catalysts.

Of course, I have nightmares of sitting there for a year and not producing anything, thus disgracing women (not to mention "practitioners," by which they mean all non-academics, since my other sin is having only a B.A.), but that's probably exactly the kind of pressure I need to get myself back to writing again.

Steinem was altogether astonished at the lack of any interest in or attention paid to gender by the other researchers. The man in the next office, a former head of the National Institute of Mental Health, who was reputed to be enlightened, was doing a project on standards of mental health in the Soviet Union. He seemed to have no idea that gender could enter into ideas of mental health. Steinem remembers him also as a collector of pornography, which he assumed to be proof of his liberal credentials. "The nicest man," in her memory, was a collector of labor songs; he tried to calm the fears of his scholarly male colleagues by saying of Steinem, "She's just an anarchist." In addition, the center had only one "women's" office, lately occupied by the previous year's only woman fellow, neoconservative Gertrude Himmelfarb, and now assigned to Steinem. Himmelfarb left behind a copy of a paper she had produced there; Steinem remembers it as "saying that the idea of poverty was an invention of recent well-to-do societies; that historically the idea of poverty only arose as affluence arose."[2] Two women with fewer ideas in common than Steinem and Himmelfarb would be difficult to find.

Steinem, characteristically, had not found time to apply to the Woodrow Wilson Center until after the deadline for applications. Her first letter to them, dated October 15, 1976, mentions that she is on a lecture tour and cannot get her application in on time. This was worked out, as was the date for starting her fellowship. She was awarded a stipend of $30,255; $2,400 of which was for expenses and travel. The application itself, wholly typical, nonetheless should have induced some unease in Steinem: After the usual questions about her age and education, it asked her to list "academic, scientific, and other honors received." Steinem duly listed them, but it is notable how slight a view of her qualities they give: first woman lecturer, National Press Club of Washington; Woman of the Year, *McCall's* magazine; Penney-Missouri Award for Journalism, among others. No one could possibly deduce from this application the woman Steinem was. Her recommendations, how-

[2] Himmelfarb's most recent book is *The Demoralization of Society: From Victorian Virtues to Modern Values* (Knopf, 1995).

ever, were unbeatable, including those of a college president, a
provost, a prominent woman lawyer, and one man, John Kenneth
Galbraith.

Steinem described her own project in a many-page "outline"
entitled "Feminism and Its Impact on the Premises and Goals of
Current Political Theory." The short description she provided
reads:

> What are the long-term implications of feminism? In societies
> no longer based on the fact and philosophy of a sexual caste
> system, how many institutions and values can be expected to
> change? These questions are the basis for inquiry in a book
> consisting of eight major areas: The View of the Individual;
> Nationalism and Property; Childhood and Community; Reli-
> gion and the Sense of Time; Definitions of Work; Human Or-
> ganizational Forms; The Question of Ends and Means; As-
> sumptions of Duality. Though this work would take into
> account major political philosophies of the past, it would be
> cross-cultural to the greatest degree possible.

The striking fact about this project is that it was, indeed, carried out: not in a book, but in Steinem's life. The eight questions
were all ones she repeatedly asked, and worked to answer: some
sooner; some later; none, of course, finally. But all were central to
her life's work. In outlining a project for a book she outlined the
project of her very existence. By the 1990s she would recognize
her writing ambition to be "Express, don't persuade"; she reminded herself of this by keeping the motto posted on her bulletin
board at home. But throughout her life she would feel compelled
to do both, often persuading simply by her presence. As a journalist, she had always written. In seeing this particular idea as a book,
however, Steinem was primarily seeking to reach the same ends
while withdrawing into solitude and research. "You do realize

that this book is a project that would take almost daily work, four to eight hours a day, for a full year," the novelist Rita Mae Brown wrote to Steinem. In reality, however, the project was far too ambitious. It would certainly have taken even a devoted academic with no other responsibilities far more than a one-year sabbatical to finish it properly. As Brown also wrote, "I think you can do it but you are going to have to drastically reorder your life."

Of course, Steinem was in no way ready to reorder her life, drastically or otherwise. And it must soon have become clear even to her that if she spent Thursdays and Fridays in New York, the spillover of her other work onto the Woodrow Wilson days would be inevitable. Another reason Steinem found it difficult to write at the center was that it was very social. There were lunches every day, which the fellows were expected to attend, and seminars at which attendance was almost mandatory in order to create a "collegial" atmosphere. As one of the few women, her presence was even more ardently expected. She had always found night the best time to work, so she asked for a cot in her room to nap on. The center found this request bizarre; news of the cot leaked out, and the press treated it as a sex joke. Since she spent time each week at the *Ms.* office in New York, undertaking more sociability at the center was not what she required. And she found the cast of characters frequently wanting her to explain "women's point of view." That same year, Steinem remembers, the Woodrow Wilson Center applied to the Ford Foundation for a grant, and the foundation, as was its custom, asked for a breakdown of employees by race and gender. The center administration was, Steinem recalls, very upset by this. All the executives were white males (except for one black executive whose duties were more involved with catering receptions than academics), all the secretaries were white women, all the cleaning personnel who used floor waxers and other machines were black men, and those without machines were black women.

The hierarchical structure of the center was no more hierarchical, of course, than any other academic institution at that time, but it was nonetheless antithetical to Steinem. She therefore requested that all women working there be invited to the talk she, like all fellows, was scheduled to give; this, of course, meant mainly cleaning women and secretaries. The idea both surprised and horrified the center, as well as the union to which the cleaning personnel belonged; the few secretaries did, in fact, attend, as did the few cleaning women after getting union permission—including one, an ex-army person who frequently stopped into Steinem's office to discuss her plans to become an auto mechanic. The center was further disturbed by Steinem's encouragement of a young woman complaining of sexual harassment.

If Steinem was scarcely prepared for quite so patriarchal an institution, the institution was even less prepared for her. James H. Billington, the director of the center, was certainly bemused and not a little disturbed by Steinem's actions and attitudes, and above all by her schedule. Certainly he had the right to expect that anyone accepting a fellowship at the center would abide by its rules. He wrote to Steinem in March 1978, and his letter clearly indicates how at odds she was with the center's arrangements. She had wanted a place to write undisturbed, and the Woodrow Wilson Center, like every other such association of fellows, saw the community as central to, and no less important than, the individual work of the fellows. Billington expostulated with her in a memorandum:

> You mentioned that you have been taking two days a week to New York for board meetings and things of that kind, and suggested that this was the equivalent of a weekend. I wanted to make clear that I do not think it is in keeping with the spirit of agreement for full-time research in Washington which all our fellows undertake to spend that much time away from the

city. The fact that those two days may be in place of a weekend might be relevant if we did not think of a certain amount of collegial presence as part of the normal expectation of a fellow here. It is clear that taking as many as two days a week with any degree of frequency away from the Center cuts into the minimal collegial presence that is expected of all fellows.

Billington pointed out that it had not been their practice to "regulate the life and work style of each fellow," but that the strain of traveling to New York each week was certainly taking its toll on her. He concluded: "Apart from my more general and informal advice about beginning to write as early as possible, I would be inclined to encourage a slight increase in participation and collegial activities here." Reading this correspondence years later, including Steinem's extensive answer to him, leads one to the conclusion that, while both were unswervingly courteous, their aims were sufficiently disparate to suggest a marriage that should never have been thought of, let alone performed.

Steinem responded to Billington's letter graciously but firmly. She explained that while she understood his point, the demands upon her were such that she could not possibly rearrange her schedule. She made clear that while she valued one-on-one contacts at the center, the collegial lunches were a chore. More often than not, she remarked, she found herself having to respond to rarely sincere requests for information about what women really want; she saw no profit in reacting to baiting and to scarcely veiled attacks on the women's movement. Steinem was, she said, pleased to serve as "a bridge or reference," but clearly she had not come to the center to conduct elementary classes in feminism. Though she, of course, does not mention it, others' recollections of her appearances at similar institutions suggest that the eagerness of the male fellows to talk with so attractive a woman on any subject was a burden not to be discounted. Finally, Steinem told

Billington, the fight for the ERA and against right-wing attacks on reproductive freedom continued to demand her attention.

The following September, in fact, Steinem threatened the right wing enough to cause reverberations that led all the way to the Vatican. Harvey Egan, then the revolutionary priest of St. Joan of Arc Church in Minneapolis, invited Steinem to present a homily to his congregation. (He had never met her, although he had heard her speak some years earlier at the University of Minnesota.) She was far from the first activist, liberal, pacifist speaker Egan had invited, nor was she the first woman: Maggie Kuhn, the organizer of the Gray Panthers, had been a speaker in his church.

Harvey Egan is an extraordinary man and priest.[3] Steinem particularly appreciated the fact that Egan always attributed his courage and imagination to his mother. She was a remarkable widow, admonishing him to beware of conformity, committees, and insurance policies, to be punctual and orderly but to bet on long shots—which certainly stands among the best maternal advice that has ever been recorded. "Risk-taking may keep you moving and give the system a little goose," she said. Clearly, he took her advice to heart. But asking Steinem to deliver the homily in his church provided more than a little goose. The chancery had been troubled before; there had been some rumbles that were tolerated because Father Egan was so popular with the liberal Catholics of Minnesota, but Steinem was something else again. Local outrage, even before Steinem spoke, was a worthy preview of the right-wing, antichoice shrieks that would culminate in the Republican National Convention of 1992. The news that she would present a homily was sufficient to bring out the mobs,

---

[3] Father Egan has written his own story as a priest whose mission was inspired by the Second Vatican Council convened by Pope John XXIII in 1962–65. In *Leaven: Canticle for a Changing Parish,* published in 1990 under the more rigid Pope John Paul II, Egan recounts the considerable pressure he has come under; probably none of which was as publicized as the brouhaha over Steinem's sermon in his church.

complete with huge graphics showing a fetus in a bottle and cars circling the church with loudspeakers bellowing: "She is a murderer; Gloria Steinem is a baby-killer."

Steinem's homily, which had to be given at two services that Sunday due to the large size of Egan's liberal Catholic flock, did not mention abortion; she declared that the right to have or not to have children, without government interference, was as important as the rights of freedom of speech and assembly. She spoke of the tragedy that most institutionalized religions have perpetuated a message of sexism and racism:

> I am not suggesting to you that God from now on should be a woman. I am suggesting that there are political motivations for the fact that God, in our memories, has been a man—usually a white man—and that the function of the great religions of the world has very often been to support, enshrine, and make sacred this concept and system. Women will no longer be controlled by patriarchal institutions.

The event was blazoned on front pages across the country, and responses were remarkable in their volume and number, and both Steinem and Egan defended themselves and his church on CBS national morning television.

Twin Cities archbishop John Roach called Steinem's speech an affront to the thousands of people who have prayed and fought for the unborn. But the Reverend George H. Martin of Saint Luke's Parish in Minneapolis wrote to the *Minneapolis Star* [Sept. 23, 1978] defending Steinem's homily and noting: "If we listen only to people who agree with us we shall become as mild as milk toast and as meek as lambs." On October 13, Martin wrote to Steinem directly to tell her how welcome she would be to speak at his Episcopalian church, "which has been actively seeking to affirm the role of women in the church. As a result of the controversy which followed your sermon," he said prophetically, "it is highly doubtful if the church diocesan chancery would permit your speaking in another Roman Catholic parish."

An October 4 item in the *Detroit Free Press* nicely summed up the whole matter:

> Gloria Steinem brought Minneapolis priest Rev. Harvey Eagan [sic] lots of secular glory and plenty of ecclesiastical grief. The renowned feminist preached at two masses at St. Joan of Arc Church last month. Letting the non-ordained into the pulpit goes against canon law, and Archbishop John Roach told Father Eagan this week that future lay speakers will require episcopal approval. That's not sitting well with the pastor, who said the parish committee was having trouble lining up speakers. "So far," said the priest, "they have found Mickey Mouse, Little Lord Fauntleroy, Peter Rabbit, and Lawrence Welk."

Throngs of Christians, hearing that Egan's parish believed in women and in the consideration of significant social issues at contemporary masses, came to the church. A handful of worshippers walked out; many more joined. The archdiocese seemed finally to have retreated into silence, probably because Egan's was the most popular church in the state.

Pope Paul VI, however, had not retreated. He actually addressed the issue—although not mentioning either Steinem or Egan by name—on the front page of the *New York Times,* decreeing that laypersons could no longer give homilies, something that had not been forbidden until then. Steinem found it amazing to wake up to the pope speaking to her from the front page of the *Times.*

* * *

BY OCTOBER, poor Dr. Billington was forced to complain once again to Steinem: "I was awakened a little before three last night by a call from the Smithsonian security people who had found an unauthorized person working in your office, with your key and your I.D. card." (Steinem's crime had been to lend her I.D., on the same chain with the key to her office, to Henri Norris, a black woman lawyer who had been helping Steinem with her research.) Then came another of Dr. Billington's worries: "I have been reading of your outside activities with some frequency lately and I would appreciate your reassurance that none of your absences is of longer duration than three days."

Steinem's response was apologetic but not altogether without a touch of irony. "I do apologize for the phone call. I shall be more respectful of Government-Style security in the future. Both Henri and I have late night work habits that might well seem unusual to a non-journalistic guard." She concluded that she had been planning a weekend trip to Japan to give one speech and a seminar, then she would return. The trip would provide an opportunity to address women of the Japanese movement, and to do one interview that would be helpful to her project. "I was about to succumb to the temptation of going, but I will be happy to cancel it if you think it unwise to go to such a faraway spot while still a fellow." She ended by saying that she was *so* sorry for the late phone call, and mentioned that the Japanese trip would entail four days of absence from the center.

Billington responded, courteous but dazed. He appreciated her asking him; he found that even the thought of going to the Far East and back for a weekend left him exhausted, but he offered his blessing. He still hoped for time to have a talk with her about her work.

How, indeed, was her work going? On Christmas Eve she wrote to tell Billington that she was talking to publishers about a book, and that if she was successful she would be accepting an advance and signing a contract in the hope that it "will keep me from sinking back into the temptations of traveling, speaking, and disappearing into conservative state legislatures." She offered to return some of the advance, if she got one, to the center in the form of a contribution. Were it not for the center, she writes, "I would most certainly have done twelve more rallies and no reading, thinking, or writing. I really do feel enormously grateful for this year, and for your help and confidence." And, yes, in response to his request, she would be happy to speak at Billington's son's school in Washington.

Some of the essays in *Outrageous Acts* would be the result of her work at the center, notably the article on genital mutilation. She wrote, two years after her fellowship, to tell Billington about it. "As you will see, we [the article was co-authored with Robin Morgan] also tried very hard to make clear that this practice is done in varying degrees and ways in most patriarchies—whether the methods are Freudian and psychological, or much more physical—and thus to escape the posture of moralistic outsiders commenting and pointing fingers of blame." She emphasizes the work that Third World women contributed to the article. And again, she tells Billington how much the year has meant to her. One wonders how astonishing the subject of clitoridectomies and infibulations may have seemed to the director of the center.

DURING STEINEM'S stay in Washington, the Air and Space Museum of the Smithsonian had shown a film called *To Fly;* its director arranged for Steinem, Stan Pottinger, and his two children to take a balloon trip. Finding herself aloft in a balloon is not a bad metaphor for Steinem's year at Woodrow Wilson. However, if there was an inevitable passenger aloft with her, it was again, as ever, *Ms.* magazine.

At this point *Ms.* was in desperate shape, deeply in debt to its printer, and losing a little bit more money every month. Steinem and Carbine could have gone out and tried to find investors, who would demand a majority interest in return, thus losing control of the magazine, or they could have tried to sell it, in which case it would certainly not continue to be feminist but would become just another women's magazine as even Kay Graham, whose Washington Post Company was a buyer they had approached, warned them. They had even hoped to split the stock among the employees, under a type of plan called an employee stock option transfer, or ESOT. For a time, the *Ms.* staff wore humorous buttons saying: "I Have a Piece of the Pebble." Steinem remembered this period as hair-raising.

Finally, Steinem, Carbine, and others concerned with *Ms.*'s survival came upon a solution: The magazine would have to become a nonprofit foundation, a subsidiary of the Ms. Foundation for Women. There were advantages: The magazine could accept tax-deductible donations, and its mailing costs would decrease considerably.[4] In addition, both Dorothy Schiff and the Ford Foundation were prepared to make substantial contributions, but only if *Ms.* became a nonprofit organization.[5] Together Steinem and Carbine consulted tax experts, and eventually used the firm of Mortimer Kaplan, who had been head of the IRS during the Kennedy administration, to help them undertake the transformation; *Ms.* was the first case of a company becoming, rather than starting out, nonprofit. The process took until August 1979 to be completed. Steinem would ultimately compare the entire transformation to

[4] Postal rates for nonprofit journals rose under Reagan, but in the 1970s the difference in rates for profit and nonprofit journals was significant.

[5] Steinem, at this time, found Dorothy Schiff, then the owner and publisher of the *New York Post,* different from her reported persona. Steinem had heard that Schiff would not help, that she was a "queen bee," uninterested in other women's projects. But Schiff was generous with Steinem, who concluded that this reputation was the result of protective coloring. She gave $300,000, which qualified the new Ms. Foundation for Education and Communication for a matching grant from the Ford Foundation.

leaping in slow motion over a large chasm, not knowing if they would reach the other side.

That Steinem had chosen the year leading up to *Ms.*'s reorganization and the beginning of the magazine's downward race to financial disaster to "dramatically reorder her life" is sad, funny, and characteristically Steinem. If she had clearly perceived not only her need to get away, but the punishing demands of the magazine she had helped to found, the vision of the Woodrow Wilson Center as a refuge might have seemed comical. But those in desperate need of refuge rarely undertake a close examination of the refuge offered.

GETTING TO FIFTY

ALL PUBLIC FIGURES, it has been said, live on parallel tracks, one for the public, the other for the private self. For most prominent figures, who are male, married, and with children, the leap between parallel tracks is seen as between public and family life. When, for whatever reason they retire, they can be counted on to announce that they want to spend more time with their families; the public or busy man looks, as it were, beyond his present intense working world to another, more serene life.

Yet a deeper division between the public and private self often exists for women. The private self is one that may, with increasing fervor, wish as the years pass to have time to be alone, to regain composure in silence, to—in the words of Virginia Woolf—let oneself down into one's mind, eventually to write, to paint, to create not on demand.

The private self is, for women, likelier to hold the promise of new experiences, new discoveries of the self and its potentialities, new chances for creativity and contemplation; above all, this private self is mysterious, an unexplored country, waiting for the adventurer to reach its shore. Steinem may have been unusual in enjoying a more public life than most women, and in not feeling, as many women do, split between public and familial demands. Yet like the woman imprisoned in domesticity, unable to picture herself in a more public world, unable even to guess how that public world might, without terrible disruptions, be encountered, Steinem could not quite imagine abandoning the many demands upon her, nor, looking from the frenzy of her public life, could she clearly envision the private, quiet existence for which she longed.

At this point in her life Steinem's two selves were further apart than at any other time. During the five years before her fiftieth birthday, she appeared to be more enviable, more beautiful, more successful than ever. But Steinem was suffering physical and emotional exhaustion, no less profound for being largely invisible to herself. She still tried to rescue anyone who came to her for help; she worked full-time, and more than full-time, for the causes that needed her now more than ever. And meanwhile the financial needs of *Ms.* magazine relentlessly dragged on.

Ronald Reagan's presidency increased Steinem's activity in the public arena. Funding for social programs was fast eroding, Supreme Court decisions threatened to reverse gains for minorities and women, progressive social legislation was overturned, federal agencies like the EEOC and HUD were instructed not only to discourage compliance but to ignore or oppose antidiscrimination suits. The EEOC fell into such disarray under officials such as Clarence Thomas that business and local government bodies often found themselves maintaining affirmative-action campaigns against the wishes of the body that was supposed to be enforcing them. Year by year, life in the inner cities deteriorated, the environment was assaulted, the plague of guns and drugs increased, abortion clinics were besieged and bombed, and laws assuring women's control over their bodies were limited to exclude poor women and young women, and even to impose waiting periods and other impediments on those who were neither. The groups Steinem valued most were desperate for funds; her efforts on their behalf were ever more urgently required; her life became harsher, more hurried, and more desperate, as she was forced also to devote more time to fund-raising for the magazine.

While Steinem made her abhorrence of the Reagan White House clear in many interviews,[1] she was slightly more tolerant of the First Lady. Although she considered Nancy Reagan the first "Total Woman" in the White House—a Total Woman being one who had succeeded in totally merging her own ego into that of her husband—Steinem sympathized with Nancy Reagan because "she had a very insecure childhood and felt she had to be socially respectable—and she's done it with a vengeance." [*Daily News,* April 18, 1981]

IN 1979 Steinem was forty-five, and interviewers and photographers continued to marvel at how much she didn't look it, at how she was as feisty as ever. But the feistiness was, perhaps, beginning to recede. "I'm old news," she told Gail Sheehy, suggesting the journalist write about other leaders. "Who?" Sheehy responded. The resulting *New York Times* "Hers" column continued:

> That was just the point. Everybody who lived through the last decade's earthquake in gender knows the name Gloria Steinem. On the outside, functioning as the stage manager, she recognizes that if the movement is to have a long run, women must be represented not by a few stars but by a full cast. Despite the fact that her style is not imitable—one can stand in the dressing

[1] In August 1984, Joan Rivers asked Steinem on the *Tonight Show* to name the most destructive person she knew of. Steinem replied, "Ronald Reagan," and turned her thumb down.

room for hours trying to be Gloria Steinem and come out looking like just another aviator needing a haircut—she is tireless in
her attempts to transfer her own star power to other women.

Into this maelstrom of a life came an almost universal experience: the death of the mother. It has been suggested, most ele-
gantly by Nancy K. Miller,[2] that the death of a parent carries
special meaning to a childless woman or man. (In *Patriarchy,*
Philip Roth recounts the death of his father and the experience of
becoming his parent's parent.) Does every childless woman feel
the mother's death with particular profundity? Certainly Simone
de Beauvoir, the least sentimental of women, who never wished
for children and did not particularly care for her mother, has
captured with exquisite delicacy in *A Very Easy Death* the experience of her mother's dying, and the sudden profound sense of loss.
Was it in any way the same for Steinem?

Steinem's mother died in July of 1981, after suffering a stroke
and just before her eighty-second birthday. Ruth had been in a
nursing home for two years; her death was neither unexpected
nor wholly unwelcome. Steinem and her sister alternated staying
with her in the hospital—Steinem, who had not been present
when her father died, was determined not to repeat that experience with her mother. She writes sadly that she lied to her mother
"one last time," when the dying woman said "Please take me
home," and Steinem answered that she would. Ruth Steinem's
memorial service was in the Washington, D.C., Episcopalian
church she had loved, as Steinem wrote in "Ruth's Song," "because it fed the poor, let the homeless sleep in its pews, had

---

[2] I have been greatly helped in this account of Ruth Steinem's death by discussions with
Nancy K. Miller, whose forthcoming book from Oxford University Press clarifies with
great intelligence and originality both the experience of the death of parents and literary
accounts of that experience.

members of almost every race, and had been sued by the Episcopalian hierarchy for having a woman priest." [143]

In a way, as we have seen, for Steinem, her mother had died years before. In some women's lives, in a process still largely unexplored, the mother's power over her daughter is dispersed, losing its cogence and leaving behind affection and disengaged kindnesses. (Needless to say, any residue of rage against the mother negates the possibility of this occurring.) Perhaps because of Steinem's childhood role as her mother's mother, perhaps because of her later ability to engage with her mother without anger, Steinem was able to detach herself from the maternal bond. What guilt there was was probably defused by her continuing attentions and gifts to her mother, and by hours spent, on vacations and travels, in her mother's company. Ruth's death was not a meaningless event for Steinem; a mother's death can never be that. It was, in fact, a kind of gift, enabling Steinem to be present and caring, and at the same time releasing her to recreate the past, to begin to write what she felt without fear of the injury to the ever-fragile Ruth Steinem.

"While she was alive, I couldn't talk about any but the most routine, sanitized, good-news parts of our life together," Steinem says. "She couldn't bear to see sad movies, much less to be reminded of hard times in her own past, which could send her off into days of severe depression, 'black days' as she said. At a more superficial level, there was also her reluctance to admit that we had ever been poor—at least, other than during the Depression when it was no shame—so a great deal of life was off limits."

There can be little doubt that writing "Ruth's Song" was an important emotional beginning for Steinem in coming to terms with Ruth. "I remember sitting at my old rolltop desk a few months after my mother died," she continues. "Those unsaid words must have been stored up in me. I'm a slow and laborious writer, but for this one and only time in my life, the words, even the structure . . . seemed already to exist. . . . I was observing in much the same way I did when I read my homework in the midst of my mother's crises, a book in one hand, keeping her from running out in the street with the other. After I had finished writing the essay and no longer needed to hold back the tide—in order to write, to keep from sinking into my mother's sadness; to *function*—I couldn't bear to read it. Not for years."

Steinem did eventually bring herself to reread what she had written and, through therapy, come to terms with her mother's death more profoundly. The essay also reveals how much Steinem owes her political and social beliefs to her mother, who, whatever her inabilities to cope with life during Steinem's childhood years, never wavered from her belief in the equality of all peoples and the importance of understanding those suffering because of their race, or class, or religion. It was later that Ruth Steinem would learn from her daughter to add to that list: or their sex.

THE OUTSTANDING event of the next year was the publication, in 1983, of her first collection, *Outrageous Acts and Everyday Rebellions.* The book instantly made the national best-seller lists. *Outrageous Acts* was a selection from her many articles, with the addition of an introduction, which summed up her experience of being on the road with feminism, and "Ruth's Song." All but one of the twenty-seven reprinted essays in the collection are like touchstones of Steinem's major concerns over the preceding twelve years. They range from accounts of her individual experiences as a fighting feminist, whether as Playboy Bunny or troublemaker at her twenty-fifth Smith reunion, to her discoveries of major feminist issues; the lives of certain women, as dissimilar as Marilyn Monroe and Alice Walker, whose destinies caught her lasting attention; and her recollections of collective feminist efforts to transform politics.

One of the essays reprinted from *Ms.* in *Outrageous Acts,* "The Real Linda Lovelace," represents Steinem's bitterness toward violent pornography (as distinguished from erotic productions). Lovelace had starred in the pornographic film, *Deep Throat,* released in 1972 which was based on the premise that she had a clitoris in her throat and therefore enjoyed having penises thrust down it. As Steinem described it: "By relaxing her throat muscles, she learned to receive the full-length plunge of a penis without choking, a desperate survival technique for her, but a constant source of amusement and novelty for clients."

Steinem recalls that at the height of the movie's popularity, Nora Ephron wrote an essay about it, assuming Linda to "be a happy and willing porn queen who was enjoying a piece of the profits" (which, of course, she was not). Ephron was not delighted with the film, but wrote off her own reaction as that of a "puritanical feminist who lost her sense of humor at a skin flick."

Steinem did not blame Ephron, who did not know ("How could any interviewer know?") that Lovelace was punished by Chuck Traynor, her manager, for any comments he considered inappropriate. In fact, Steinem reported, "She had been beaten and raped so severely and regularly that she suffered rectal damage plus permanent injury to the blood vessels in her legs." She had also been brutally gang-raped and made to pretend to have enjoyed it.

It is doubtful that many disagreed with Steinem's sympathetic reporting about Linda Lovelace, although some of those closest to Steinem thought she rather overdid her attention to that unfortunate woman. Steinem had reinvestigated the case to report its credibility, and gone to the rescue, as she had dreamed of doing in girlhood, and this time she did help a hideously exploited woman to be believed and to regain some control over her life, to arrange later for a liver transplant that she needed because of the beatings, and to speak out about her terrible experiences during the filming of *Deep Throat* and beyond. There are still women, to say nothing of men, who believe that rape victims "ask for it," that women enjoy being brutalized, and that battered women could easily escape if only they wanted to. Only recently has opinion begun to change on these issues, and Steinem's defense of Linda Lovelace was a small part of that revision.[3]

A revision, however, that was not universal. Linda Lovelace's successor, Marilyn Chambers, featured by Chuck Traynor in subsequent porn films, declared in an interview in the *Seattle Times* in 1990 that she was perfectly happy, that women like to be submissive, and that "women libbers are too ugly to get a man who'd want to be in charge of them." Larry Fields, a columnist for the *Philadelphia Daily News,* had reported, however, that "when Traynor was answering questions on Marilyn's behalf, she asked his permission to go to the bathroom. Permission was refused. 'Just sit there and shut up,' Traynor said to her."

Steinem's ability to sustain her identification with an assaulted woman long enough to defend her and eventually help to rescue her is, as we have seen, related to Steinem's own childhood experiences. These left her far more able to believe the stories of victims than is perhaps possible for those with less aberrant childhoods.

The publication of *Outrageous Acts and Everyday Rebellions,* with its subsequent book tour, escalated to new heights the media's attention to Steinem. The "gorgeous" woman was now not only a best-selling author, but close to fifty years old and, as when she had turned forty, not looking it. One of the evidences of this came with a photo of Steinem reading a manuscript in a bubble bath, published in *People* magazine. The photographer was a woman. With this classic nude-in-the-bubble-bath photograph

---

[3] It is, alas, necessary to report that Katie Roiphe in her book *The Morning After,* published in 1993, again finds fame and fortune by blaming the rape victim. Katha Pollitt has written a brilliant refutation of Roiphe's book and research: "Not Just Bad Sex," *The New Yorker,* October 4, 1993, pp. 218–224.

Steinem again fell afoul of feminists, this time not without reason. Her miniskirts were often criticized on the same grounds, that she was giving status to being a sex object. Steinem long ago regretted the bubble bath photo, but her view on miniskirts was that women ought to wear what they damn well please.

As to the bubble bath photograph, however, there seems to many people to be here a degree of naïveté or ambiguity, certainly more than Steinem herself perceives. Modesty before women has never been a Steinem attribute; more than one acquaintance has noticed the unself-conscious way she undresses in rooms she shares with other women during her travels. There must be considered, also, Steinem's self-confessed inability to learn from previous experiences—an inability that she was finally forced to face up to at the time of the publication of *Revolution from Within*.

Once *Outrageous Acts* was published, Steinem's schedule—as usual—got seriously out of hand. The book tours were certainly punishing, and Steinem used the travel as an opportunity to speak at local benefits for *Ms.*, battered women's shelters, and so forth. From the middle of September, for example, she spoke in New York, Boston, Chicago, Minneapolis, Atlanta, Memphis, and Miami, usually with two days and many engagements in each city. She appeared on many major television talk shows, in addition to making bookstore appearances and giving magazine and radio interviews. And the pace only increased thereafter. She also attended various conferences and fund-raisers during her trip, was frequently away more than she was home, and was unavoidably involved in *Ms.* business when she *was* home.

Reviews were many and sometimes critical; among them, an October 9 front-page *Washington Post Book World* review by the late Angela Carter was harshly acerbic, though it began with the statement that nothing that followed "should be taken as demonstrating on the part of the reviewer any lack of sympathy with Gloria Steinem's philosophy of social justice."

Steinem's refusal to sound more learned or knowledgeable than her audience would always simultaneously grate on intellectuals and inspire large parts of the reading public. It is worth noting, however, that Angela Carter alone among reviewers objected to "Ruth's Song," which she saw as "subtly warped by . . . self-satisfaction. For what right has Steinem to assume she knows what song her mother would have sung, had the woman's movement existed at that time to provide the score?" Carter finds "a certain blindness to history" in Steinem, an odd comment, surely, on a woman who lived through almost all the history she records, notably without blindness.

With the publication of *Outrageous Acts* in view, Steinem was urged by her lawyer, Robert Levine, to think about her financial future. The year before she had begun putting small sums into a retirement fund. Now, for legal and financial reasons, she formed a corporation, named East Toledo. This would enable her, among its other benefits, to create a pension fund for herself. The creation of East Toledo was, quite literally, her first act of financial responsibility. As she told an interviewer on a cable-TV money management show, "Up to now I've saved not one penny. I [either] look at my bank account or not. If my checks bounce, then I stop spending." As Steinem explained, she didn't have time to spend money; she didn't want a second home, a car, or a lot of clothes. She liked to give money away because "there are so many individually talented people who just need a little boost," and because she wanted to back community projects. But she was also beginning to realize that her humorous prediction of being a bag lady in her seventies was becoming too plausible for comfort.

Steinem explained the name of her corporation to Robert Benton, in a letter thanking him for his praise of "Ruth's Song." Benton had always liked Ruth, and had written Steinem a loving condolence letter, remembering particularly the card games

Steinem and her mother used to play in stiff and affectionately laughing competition. Steinem told Benton:

> When I went back to Toledo to speak three years ago, a man called the television station and called me "a whore from East Toledo." While that would have killed me in the past, I suddenly realized that I would like to have that line as a kind of celebration on my grave stone. When I had to start a small company [I] named it East Toledo Productions. If only it didn't take so long to come home and see it in a new way.

And she thanked Benton again for his effect on her life.

> You made—and so continue to make—a big difference in my feeling that maybe I *could* write, and maybe I didn't *have* to pretend to be someone else. I wish I had behaved better then, or at least told you all the brand new energies that began because of you. But I hope you'll forgive me that, and I hope you know now. We are probably more each other's family than "real" relatives, and I hope you will call on that.

Defining family as friends, or friends as family, would be a continuing theme in Steinem's life. This is in sharp contrast, for example, to the thoughts Calvin Trillin expresses in his 1993 book *Remembering Denny,* about a Yale classmate who had recently committed suicide. Trillin found major lacks in Denny's life; he had wanted what most people want, Trillin wrote, "a lasting relationship, a person he could share his life with." [191] "For those of us who define our lives in terms of our families, he was unimaginably alone." [209] But Steinem was neither unimaginably alone nor desperate for "a long relationship." Her new definition of *family* may indeed be more widespread than is usually realized;

what is perhaps characteristic of Steinem is that her "family" is so large.

Along with a reconsideration of her finances, Steinem also took up fitness for the first time. As her fiftieth birthday approached, she announced to a *Washington Post* interviewer that "muscle is more important than fat." Exercise and an attempt at a new, healthy diet marked her public recognition of her middle age, all at the same time that she was flying around the country at dizzying speeds to help bring her first book to the attention of a national audience.

THE FINANCIAL condition of *Ms.* magazine continued to be perilous. Even though, as a nonprofit corporation, *Ms.* could now solicit contributions to make up its deficit, advertising revenue was still necessary. During that year, Steinem and Carbine went to Norway for the Magazine Publishers Conference, and also to look for compatible European investors. (They found none; European women's magazines were just as commercial and were expected to produce fashion and beauty articles.) She also visited France, in a vain attempt to get L'Oreal to advertise in the magazine.[4] In between her search for advertisers, international feminist concerns persisted, and provided some relief. She traveled to Egypt, where she met with women leaders and movement groups from both waves of feminism (who sat on the stage with her as

---

[4] On an earlier trip to France in the late seventies, Steinem had been introduced to Simone de Beauvoir by *Ms.* European consulting editor Claude Servan-Shreiber. At that time Beauvoir, despite having written *The Second Sex* thirty years earlier, had not yet become a feminist, so their talk was about class and the possibility of women uniting across class divisions. When Steinem told Beauvoir Lee Grant's story of having been married to a fascist and a communist, neither one of whom took out the garbage, Beauvoir really laughed. A picture of the two of them together hangs in Steinem's home. *Ms.* had published an interview with Beauvoir in 1977, and urged her to come to Copenhagen for the Mid-Decade Conference in 1980 and to consider allowing them to organize a tribute to her. She declined the honor.

she spoke, a protection against Muslim fundamentalists that was necessary even then), and interviewed Jihan Sadat, whose feminist influence was being felt throughout her husband's presidency. The search for advertisers to help cover inflationary production costs had become frenzied, and Carbine and Steinem, together with saleswomen, went out ever more desperately to persuade possible buyers of ad space. The food industry, for example, with its tremendous advertising revenues, was an industry *Ms.* had made little headway with in the past, but persisted in trying to crack. Stan Pottinger tells of an episode that, while extreme, is consistent with the sort of resistance Steinem faced:

> So she went for her umpteenth meeting with the head of the Avocado Growers Association. I was there [California] on business; she said, could you do me the favor to come with me to this dinner? Why? Well, because of what they think they know of *Ms.* magazine, and because I'm not married they think it's risky and we're a bunch of lesbians. Gloria was always conflicted on this issue; trying to say but it's a great choice. Here she was saying I don't want to give in to this prejudice, but we need the ad. I got there late; I came over to the table and gave her a long kiss. She turned a little pink. This guy sitting across the table and his women friend started into stories about sex. I thought Gloria was right. She and the ad person [from *Ms.*] were good on telling facts. The head of the Avocado Growers Association was drinking; by the time of the entrée he was drunk. They turned on Gloria, saying things you wouldn't believe. Not only had they lost track of where they were, their language was foul, they were saying your magazine is garbage, it talks about people fucking. The woman said I wouldn't read your magazine, much less tell him to advertise in it; I think it's garbage. And they turned on her about the kiss. I couldn't believe this. Gloria sat there and took it; I would have been gone. She kept saying I think you're wrong and I'll tell you

why. The woman said you've got an ad for condoms, and the condom is an awful thing to advertise. The crap she took; when it was over I said I don't know how you do it. It's bad enough that most of your life is pursuing ads. She had to beg for it and people were shitting on her. I said you'll never get credit for what you go through to keep this magazine going. They went so far beyond the bounds of decency, and the poor magazine picked up the tab. I told Gloria that while negotiating school segregation plans in the South I'd been called a child-molester, a nigger-lover, a mongrelizer in print; but nothing had been said to me as bad as what those people said at that fancy restaurant.

If her fame and looks got her in to see the advertisers, their antagonism was not overcome once they had met her. There is, however, an epilogue to the story. Six months later, *Ms.* got the ad. Pottinger thinks maybe it was because she had kept at it. It was a breakthrough with the food industry. But, he wonders, was it guilt, admiration for her sticking it out, or what? The truth appears to be that a representative of the man's advertising agency, who was also at the dinner, was so embarrassed that he gave *Ms.* the ad.

Steinem wrote to the owner of a feminist bookstore and restaurant who had taken the time to explain her refusal any longer to advertise in the magazine because she had been put off by what she characterized as a "fashion cover." (Perhaps she had interpreted the picture of a woman's suit being dumped in a trash can with the line: "You Don't Have to Dress [Like a Man] for Success" as a "fashion cover.") As she explained:

There are still many advertisers who won't even make appointments with our saleswomen, much less take an ad. ("I'll advertise in *Ms.* after *Pravda*," as the Gallo wine owner put it.) And in general we are suffering a great deal from the economic and generally hostile pressures of both anti-woman liberals and the right wing.[5]

In addition, rising printing and mailing costs added to the financial problems of the magazine. And to make matters worse, school boards, like supermarket newsstands and other such outlets for sale, continued to introduce problems of censorship. Steinem continued:

> [The] major and by far the most serious objection to *Ms.* is that we are too serious, too "anti-male," too feminist, too radical, etc. We are now fighting several court battles against schools and libraries that have banned us under religious or right-wing pressure.

During this time, *Ms.* was also continuing to hear complaints from its readers that it was too white, middle class, and heterosexual, often based on the imagery in ads, and that it was "selling out" to its advertisers, as well as complaints that its editorial content included too many lesbians, women of color, and poor women. These advertisers, of course, were a contributing force who were enabling the magazine to reach so many women readers for whom it was often a first introduction to feminism, and their only continuing link to it. Nor had *Ms.* changed its editorial policies or taken to selling out. Chiefly, it suffered from underfinancing. The dilemma was, and remained, where did cooptation overcome the feminist need to give voice to what could be read nowhere else?

Another consequence of Steinem's unremitting search for

---

[5] As far back as 1974, the Bennington, Vermont, school board voted to ban *Ms.* Carbine told Amy Erdman Farrell; also newsstands in the South had refused to display the January 1973 cover because a black woman, Shirley Chisholm, was shown with a white woman, Sissy Farenthold, as her running mate. Farrell points out that Chisholm's being a black woman with power doubtless added to the perceived threat of the cover. [164]

funds, alternating with her political speeches, her fund-raising for women's causes, and her support of the ERA and Voters for Choice, was that she paid less attention to the editing of *Ms.* She maintains that she had never been a full-time editor because she was too often on the road, and often missed even the weekly editorial meetings. Whether or not this absence had any meaningful effect on the magazine is uncertain; Suzanne Levine and others kept the magazine going, and even reserved space for Steinem's (always late) articles. What is clear enough, however, is that Steinem herself was paying far too high a personal price out of a kind of unthinking devotion to the magazine, a conditioned reaction, it would later seem to her, to her years of responsibility for her mother.

Many of Steinem's letters during the first half of the eighties are sincere regrets. For example, she had to miss a benefit for Judy Chicago's grand art project *The Dinner Party* because she would be in Washington "tap dancing hard for contributions to women's community projects." Ann Hornaday, then a new college graduate, was Steinem's assistant for two years, from 1983 to 1985, and she reports that time as a kind of perpetual triage. Her memory is a blur, of unrelenting tension between what needed to be done and the insufficient time in which to do it. Steinem was working to get ads, attending business meetings, and continuing to work for the women's movement that demanded an arduous speaking schedule from her. "It was always a balancing act trying to live up to her commitments," Hornaday recalls, "and at the same time Steinem was always aware of not having enough private time off, enough time to collect herself." Hornaday's distinct memory is of Steinem run ragged.

Steinem now questions whether she ought to have given up on *Ms.* sooner, let others take over, or let the magazine be sold. At the time neither of those options seemed practical or possible, for they all seemed like letting down the movement. But if she never really considered giving up, she probably should have at least tried for a better balance in her life. That she hung in far too long for her own mental and physical health is certain.

As Steinem's private self seemed ever less accessible, she ignored its demands, determined also to ignore her own weariness. The widely quoted admonition of the Red Queen to Alice that she must run as fast as she could to stay in the same place no longer quite applied to Steinem. Running as fast as she could, she was losing ground, eventually committing the cardinal error against which she would, in *Revolution from Within,* warn other women: She found refuge in a man, believing, however temporarily, that if she could rescue him from similar problems, they could together find the space and time for recovery that she could not find by herself.

ON MARCH 25, 1984, Steinem turned fifty. At forty, she had famously said, "This is what forty looks like." She applied the same remark at age fifty, followed by the less frequently quoted words "We've been lying for so long, who would know."

Turning fifty, both in anticipation and actuality, is a watershed in a woman's life. Nor is this metaphor merely cliché. A watershed marks that place where waters run toward opposite seas. Rivers that once arose from the event of birth become different rivers, moving toward the sea of death. Wallace Stevens has written that "death is the mother of beauty," but certainly in Western culture youth is the prized gift, and aging, the deprivation of youth, is regarded as cruel loss. First comes despair at the aging body, and particularly at the aging face, a despair whose alleviation can be sought either by impersonating youth with the aid of drugs, surgery, or makeup, or by abandoning all hope of a youthful appearance and accepting with wry humor the inevitable expanding and sagging. (This acceptance, of course, means that one must move against a dominant youth-fetishizing culture into an as yet scarcely defined world.) Only recently and gradually has the possibility emerged in female consciousness that something might be gained for women at the cusp of fifty. To face aging as a different experience, differently lived and wholly unnoticed and unhonored in Western culture, does not yet present itself as widely acceptable; the urge to attempt to retain the appearance of youth has all the force of our culture behind it. What is inarguable, however the onset of fifty will be faced, is that its approach and its arrival surpass in impact most other junctures in a woman's life. Consciously or unconsciously, early or late, that juncture must be anticipated and confronted. For the woman turning fifty, then, the reconsideration that surrounds that moment may and often does provide sufficient impetus profoundly to reenvision her life.

For Steinem, contemplating the inevitable physical symptoms of aging—although in her case they were hardly obtrusive—was not a significant problem. Her slimness persisted; her hair color, achieved by streaking, remained the same; and her legs still allowed the wearing of short skirts. She was more aware of the inner turmoil, the sense of having no control over her life, that was beginning to manifest itself. Turning fifty was not for her, in itself, a powerful metaphor. What was powerful was the coincidence of that birthday with the slowly growing realization that she could not continue her life in the same depleting and self-abnegating pattern.

Steinem's fiftieth birthday was marked by a more grandiose event than that of most women. As has since become a tradition with her birthdays, it was celebrated two months after the actual date, on May 23—a primary fund-raising month—as a benefit for the Ms. Foundation, this time in the grand ballroom at the Waldorf-Astoria. Even her birthdays were used as occasions to raise money. Marlo Thomas, opening the proceedings with Phil Donahue, who played host during the toasts, noted that "it is unusual to be holding a feminist meeting in such a clean place." To say everyone was there is, for once, hardly an exaggeration, if by "everyone" one means all those likely, at any time, to turn up in a Liz Smith column, plus as many, including those who had worked with Steinem on the grape boycott, who had never heard of Liz Smith. The columnist herself was, of course, there, and called the party "a social 'love-in' on a grand scale." Steinem was escorted by Pottinger; most of the men from her past life were there—still her friends.

Herb Sargent did much of the arranging for the party, including Bette Midler's hilarious performance, a gift (Steinem had written an interview for *Ms.* with Midler years before and they had remained friends), although, as Herb Sargent observed, "the band always gets paid." Phil Donahue moved from table to table, handing the mike around for toasts. Bette Midler was at her most comical, or in Liz Smith's words, "funny and sexy," including a rendition of the sorts of songs Steinem had liked in her youth, in as unfeminist and simpering a manner as possible. She did her number with huge breast balloons designed to purge sexism forever, and guests danced accompanied by an all-female band in tuxes. Joanne Edgar, Dorothy Pitman Hughes, Flo Kennedy, Suzanne Levine, and Pat Carbine sang a song with tailor-made lyrics. It was a party simultaneously glamorous and down-home. About a third of the guests went often to the Waldorf, and two thirds of the people would never otherwise go there—which made the party memorable.

There was a glossy birthday book of Gloria Steinem from birth to bubble bath, containing almost every extant picture of her childhood and youth. The press lavishly covered the party, which, in hindsight, can be seen to have ended one phase of Steinem's life and suggested the need for new beginnings. But according to long articles on her in *Esquire* and *Cosmopolitan,* Steinem was at the apex of her life, professionally and personally: Wasn't she still beautiful?

Among the letters accepting invitations to the party, and offering to help arrange it, was one from the Boston real estate magnate Mortimer Zuckerman. While Pottinger's appearance as Steinem's escort at the party was in the nature of a last hurrah, Zuckerman attended the celebration alone.

STEINEM HAD FIRST met Zuckerman in Boston in the late seventies at a National Women's Political Caucus benefit held in his home, and later she and Pat Carbine approached him—as Steinem said, "along with everybody else in the Western world" —to cosign a loan for *Ms.*[6] Carbine remembers that the three of them met in the Polo Bar of the Westbury Hotel in Manhattan to discuss it. He did agree to cosign the loan but, according to Steinem, he and Pat Carbine later had a misunderstanding about its conditions. Also Zuckerman objected, perhaps with good reason, to having to reveal his financial holdings to NatWest, *Ms.*'s bank, as other cosigners had done. The question of the loan was resolved when Zuckerman arranged it through his own bank in Boston.

In recording Steinem's relationship with him, it is important to resist the temptation to write a brief life of Mort Zuckerman. He is so relentlessly reported upon in magazines, the daily press, and occasionally in memoirs, that pasting together a media-based account of his career would be a simple matter. From clippings gathered unsystematically, one learns that he is widely disliked but admired for his business smarts, that he is worth something in

---

[6] Banks had refused a direct loan to *Ms.* because it was variously deemed too small to be worth the trouble; its asset of a subscription list wasn't tangible enough, and foreclosing on it would be too unpopular.

35. Steinem picketing in an antiapartheid protest outside the South African Embassy in Washington, 1984

36. Steinem being arrested outside the embassy

37. Steinem with Linda Lovelace Marciano, whom Steinem helped after Lovelace had made the film *Deep Throat*

38. Steinem receives an honorary degree from Hannah Greenberg, the provost of Wheaton College in Norton, Massachusetts.

39. Steinem with Stan Pottinger, who offered important support during the attacks on her in 1975

40. Steinem with Bette Midler, who performed at Steinem's fiftieth birthday celebration, a fund-raiser —as were all her birthday celebrations—for the Ms. Foundation

41. Steinem and Mortimer Zuckerman, a "romance" rather than a love

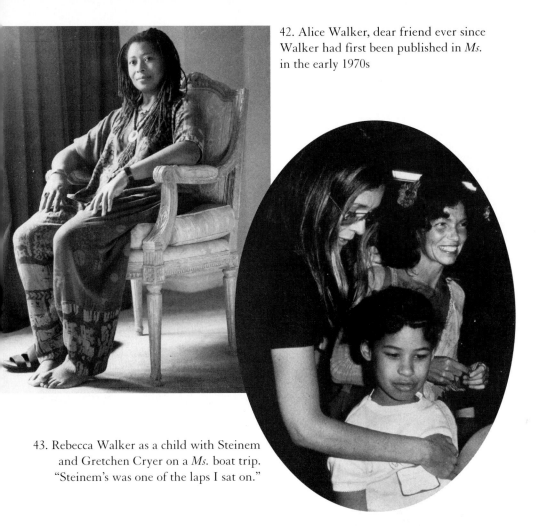

42. Alice Walker, dear friend ever since Walker had first been published in *Ms.* in the early 1970s

43. Rebecca Walker as a child with Steinem and Gretchen Cryer on a *Ms.* boat trip. "Steinem's was one of the laps I sat on."

44. Some of *Ms.*'s founding editors, photographed in 1987 at the time of the magazine's sale: seated, Mary Thom, Letty Cottin Pogrebin, Pat Carbine; standing, Steinem, Suzanne Braun Levine, Joanne Edgar

45. Steinem campaigning with
Bill Clinton in 1992

46. Steinem with
Rebecca and the cat
Magritte, in her
newly decorated
and expanded
home, 1992

47. Steinem at the
start of her sixties

the neighborhood of $400 million, which he made as a real estate developer, that he owns two first-rate journals, the *Atlantic Monthly* and *U.S. News & World Report,* as well as the *Daily News,* and that he has never married. His friends reportedly call him a Jewish Gatsby—that is, a man who has invented himself. He has long squired many intelligent and attractive women, few if any of whom remember him with noticeable affection or admiration. Clearly, he can be very entertaining: He is part of Long Island's elegant and arty East Hampton society, he owns many houses, he skis, he is a fierce competitor at softball, and he has probably exceeded his own fantasies. Though he had told other women he wished to marry and have children, whether he has or ever had a genuine desire to marry is certainly debatable.

In any case, his bachelorhood joined to Steinem's made for a pleasant companionship. Of course, soon after she and Zuckerman began seeing each other, a few friends urged her to marry him and use his money for her magazine or for other causes. This was obviously unrealistic advice for many reasons, not least because she intended never to marry, an intention not mitigated even by this uncharacteristic infatuation, but also because he had in other cases demanded a prenuptial agreement that would have left the woman almost no money in her own right. Steinem had learned the financial and emotional condition of so-called "rich" women —women who have inherited or married money, not those who have made it on their own—and felt no temptation to join their ranks.

Steinem's sympathy for rich women has always puzzled feminists, and does indeed require explanation in light of her own lifelong devotion to the dispossessed. What Steinem had come to realize, however, was how intensely many rich women have internalized their assigned role in paternalistic, patriarchal families; how deeply incapable they are, by and large, of questioning, let alone changing, their subordinate roles; how little money, apart from credit cards, they actually have in their own power to spend; and, above all, how likely they are to be abused and sexually assaulted in childhood in these families, in which the difference in power between women and men was often greater than in poor or middle-class families.[7]

Zuckerman agreed with Steinem about rich women. As he put it, "She wrote an article in *Ms.* magazine about women who come from wealthy families. That article is so intelligently thought through that I remember reading [it] and being dazzled by it; it was such a brilliant insight into a subculture, I don't know of anybody else who could have done that." (The article in question, "The Trouble with Rich Women," appeared in June 1986; for many years Steinem planned to turn it into a book.) Zuckerman considers Steinem brilliant in other ways. "She has a great human intelligence that is quite remarkable. She has a capacity which I admire beyond measure of seeing people in ways even those people didn't see. . . . I never met anyone like that." He also believes that they are both wrong not to have married, that they have missed a lot in what is for each, all appearances to the contrary, a lonely life. He has reportedly said as much—and reiterated his desire for children—to every woman he has dated. Yet, three years younger than Steinem, he has passed his mid-fifties without marrying.

The relationship with Zuckerman can in retrospect be seen as a symptom of Steinem's state of mind at the time that she met him. Her emotional health was precarious, and she had not yet awakened to the necessity of getting help to transform her life. Steinem, however, sees Zuckerman more as the protagonist in a romance,

---

[7] Sally Bingham's *Passion and Prejudice,* an account of her rebellion within a rich and powerful family, confirms Steinem's views, as does the immense campaign undertaken by Bingham's family to discredit her account. In fact, the brutal treatment of Bingham after the publication of her book discouraged many rich women from cooperating with Steinem in the book she had hoped to write about them.

not a love story, understanding her early attraction to him not as a symptom of her starvation for fun but as a return to how she had felt as a sixteen-year-old. This return to what she would later describe as "immature romance" came about, she believes, not only because she was so tired but because he presented himself as having had a deprived childhood, despite the fact that he was the only son, after three daughters, from a very comfortable Montreal family. His sense of deprivation comes from the fact that his parents spent every winter in Florida from the time he was four, due to his father's heart condition, and the boy felt deserted. In the memory of one of his sisters, Mortimer was treated like God in his childhood. Their mother referred to him as *"he,"* no name needed. Nonetheless, he believed himself to have suffered deprivation in childhood, and it is what one believes that matters. In 1984, to the weary Steinem, his childhood, or what he offered of it, sounded in essence much like hers, and made him one more object of her rescue fantasy. She hoped that if he found a more useful way of living he would become a happier, more generous person. This last she characterizes as her big mistake.

Zuckerman's account of *Ms.*'s problems is realistic and accurate from a commercial point of view; he considers Steinem's approach foolish. What it came down to was that Steinem put feminist principles above economic ones, or in Zuckerman's terms, she had editorial genius but not economic know-how. He found it depressing, as did everyone who knew her, that she was "tap-dancing" all over the country trying to get advertising and charitable contributions when, he believed, there were business decisions that could have helped. He tells a story he recognizes as unfeminist, but apposite. A woman came home with $18.25 after an evening working the streets, and was asked who had given her twenty-five cents. She said, "Everybody." Zuckerman understood that "Gloria was unbelievably dedicated to that magazine, that the magazine came first, what it stood for, the women with whom she worked who constituted her family." But, as he saw it, business advice could not operate in the face of feminist ideology. He was a man who believed that "you can't solve all the problems of the world if you don't have the financial resources to enable you to be totally unconcerned about whether or not [your magazine] is financially viable. . . . That thing was a huge hole." He has pointed out that he spent over $35 million to keep the *Atlantic Monthly,* with circulation similar to, or smaller than, *Ms.*'s, afloat, and that it only began breaking even in its eleventh year under his ownership.

In 1992, eight years after, in a section of *Revolution from Within* that was barely four pages long, Steinem gave her interpretation of her attraction to Zuckerman although she didn't name him; a commotion ensued when *Vanity Fair* named him, though it is doubtful that the rest of the world would have failed to identify Zuckerman. To her dismay all the reporters and television interviewers harped on those four pages where she described the causes of this ill-suited "romance," which she was attempting to show was different by definition from love, the first being two half-people looking for the rest of themselves, and the second being two whole people who accept each other as unique individuals.[8] She had warned, some pages earlier, against falling "in love when you're feeling vulnerable or not so good about yourself." She had previously chosen "kind men with good hearts who loved me back . . . and so we remained friends even after the intensity of romance was gone." It is significant that the relationship with

---

[8] It is symptomatic that the press never tried to determine the identity of another man discussed but not named in the section on romance—the man she had been deeply in love with, Frank Thomas. They were happy with the Zuckerman story because it could be used to demonstrate to their satisfaction that feminists can't have good relationships and are treated badly by men—and this despite the additional fact that Zuckerman had hardly treated her badly.

Zuckerman was her one extended relationship that did not evolve into friendship or "family."

Steinem went on to describe the treadmill life she was living, "with less and less time to replenish lost energy," when she met Zuckerman. She identified the two most important elements making this defective romance initially so attractive: He was "someone I *couldn't* take care of," and concomitantly, he was able to take care not only of himself but of her—superficially, it is true—making decisions, offering wonderfully staffed houses, and, she reported in *Revolution from Within,* sending a limousine to the airport to meet her after one of her endless trips to raise money for the magazine.[9] Her exhaustion and burnout had, she later determined, made her particularly susceptible to a man who amused, entertained, and coddled her, and above all with whom she loved to dance. That she had to ignore all the aspects of his life that were not and could never be attractive to her became evident, as happens in romance, only later. "Having for the first time in my life made a lover out of a man who wasn't a friend first—my mistake, not his, since I was the one being untrue to myself—I had a huge stake in justifying what I had done."

What she had to explain, of course, even years later, was not only how she could have loved a man who supported policies she had worked all her life to change, who advocated trade with governments she had publicly protested against, who gave dinner parties at which her closest friends would have felt ill at ease—these were part of her original misconception that she could change him, or that somehow all these differences could be made

---

[9] This limousine meeting her at the airport loomed rather large in media responses to her book. This is particularly ironic, since, in fact, Zuckerman never again sent a limousine to meet her, never knowing exactly when she would return. Steinem invented the limousine in place of another occurrence that would have made him too recognizable. What is also ironic is that Steinem had tried, repeatedly and unsuccessfully, to persuade Zuckerman to substitute vans for his limousines.

not to matter. While it is not hard to explain her original attraction to Zuckerman, it is much harder to explain the condition, however desperate, that allowed a woman such as she to align herself with a man like him.

They were not altogether different: that would have been impossible. He was capable of respecting, if not of sympathizing with, her views on the world. He was highly intelligent, as she was; fun; a good teller of jokes; fond of dancing and partying; and able to provide attentive material care no one in her life had ever provided before, though many may have offered it. She had not, until now, been tired enough to consider such care desirable. If one is very ill or painfully fatigued, even a hospital bed can be a relief. In all probability, the fact that Zuckerman's care was provided by paid employees, not by him directly, made it easier for her to give way to it. But what made him ultimately irresistible was that he also presented himself as miserable and wanting her help in changing his life. Thus she could both indulge her rescue fantasies and tell herself that once happy, he would give all his money to the poor—an alluring combination.

In the eyes of many of Steinem's friends and acquaintances from that time, she did in fact fall in love with him. Not with what she first thought him to be, nor, certainly, with what, having recovered some of her equilibrium, she discovered him to be. But at that time of her great tiredness, her weariness of caring and worrying, the charming Zuckerman appeared in a distinct glow of attractiveness, and she seems to have been far more infatuated with him than she is now quite willing to recall. Stan Pottinger, with whom she was, at this time, undergoing the transformation from lover to friend, definitely remembers her telling him she had found her double in Zuckerman. He, in short, remembers exactly how much of a "romantic" falling in love her original infatuation with Zuckerman was.

Another factor Steinem appears now to minimize is the appar-

ent ease with which, however reluctantly, she moved in Zuckerman's social circle. They have been described as like the heads of
two states, in great demand and, together, high on the hierarchy
of social importance. When in 1985 the TV movie of *A Bunny's
Tale* was broadcast, Mort Zuckerman was photographed with
Steinem for (of course) *People* at a screening of the film. The
caption of another picture of Steinem and Zuckerman in *People*
the following year reported that Steinem "makes do with an income near six figures from royalties, speeches, and her pay as a
Ms. editor." This was characteristically inaccurate on the part of
the media, but nonetheless brought Steinem outraged letters from
hardworking women who contributed to the women's movement
from far smaller incomes than hers was reported to be. Steinem
wrote to *People* as well as to her correspondents, pointing out that
"it's more rewarding to watch money change the world than to
watch it accumulate. That's why most of my royalty and speaking
income is given to the Women's Movement, why my editing at
Ms. is unsalaried, and why I am happy to make do with a fraction
of the income you imply." However, there was little hope, then as
now, of making any dent in the media's view of a famous figure,
however inaccurate, however unfair. "Rich and famous" has become all one phrase, so that it is hard, if not impossible, to be
perceived as "poor and famous."

The social circle was for the most part Zuckerman's, not hers.
It is a measure of Steinem's profound fatigue that she did not
immediately reject the East Hampton scene as undermining all
her previous convictions about class, but instead clung to her belief that she could change minds and raise money there; indeed,
that Zuckerman's earlier support for the NWPC and Democrats
like Gary Hart would stem his rightward swing as he moved up
in the echelons of real estate and publishing power. She would
soon become sadly aware that East Hampton was not a place in
which she could picture Alice Walker or many of her other closest

friends. At first, however, those of her friends with a foot in that world thought she seemed to enjoy it, to enjoy dinner parties needing no preparation or planning from her, well-kept houses in which she could simply relax, beaches on which she could loll. Close women friends noticed that, in the beginning days with Zuckerman, Steinem again looked wonderful—she was more carefully made-up and took a renewed interest in clothes. She acted, in short, like someone in love. Looking back over the affair, Steinem, like many a woman before and since, forgets or minimizes the early, violent attraction in the light of later knowledge of the lover's drawbacks and her own state of need when they met. The fact remains that she was "in love" with someone she had made up, and that the need to be "in love" had come for negative reasons.

Steinem fell into Zuckerman's world with a kind of desperate, unthinking relief. Once she began thinking again, the relationship was doomed. In certain ways, her time with Zuckerman resembled her time at the Woodrow Wilson Center. Both seemed to offer what, at the moment when she accepted their offers, she thought she desperately needed. Neither turned out to be what she had hoped for, or what she had at first envisioned. Lives are not changed by writers' colonies or by lovers. They are changed, as Steinem would eventually put it, by revolution from within.

That the press has never forgotten Zuckerman's connection with Steinem is hardly surprising; she is mentioned at every run-through of his female companions. Yet the absurdity of them as a pair can be summarized in a trifling fact: In 1992, Zuckerman was among the seven celebrities who chose Miss America at the same Atlantic City pageant where, by some accounts at least, today's feminism began in 1968.

By the time she wrote the "Romance versus Love" chapter in *Revolution from Within,* Steinem explained the relationship by saying that she was "empathy sick." She had to face the fact that she had spent so long relating to others that she knew other people's feelings better than her own. This was undoubtedly true, if one adds to her habit of empathy her lifelong avoidance of introspection, of examining what she herself was feeling. She had finally to face the need to look within herself, to try to discover, as her book would recommend, what *her* needs were. Zuckerman, therefore, was both a symptom and a catalyst. As she wrote: "The only problem was that, having got [Zuckerman] to fall in love with an inauthentic me, I had to keep on not being myself. . . . This relationship became a final clue that I was really lost."

But as the media's fascination with Steinem's four anonymous pages on her affair with Zuckerman testifies, reality undergoes a double definition: once in the media, once in the lived life. It is easy enough to portray Zuckerman unsympathetically even as one damns Steinem for having taken up with him. They are both news.

Zuckerman, however, represents one of the few occasions in Steinem's life when her account of "reality" may differ significantly from both reality itself and the media's version of it. The problem here is not only that Steinem, seeing Zuckerman as one of the most blatant symptoms of her fatigue and despair, may underestimate the force of her original attraction to him, but that her need to write about him, even camouflaged, in *Revolution from Within* indicates her compulsion to tell the story of that relationship in an attempt to gain control of it. She says she included this nameless anecdote because she thought it was important for women readers to know, "that even if you're as old as I am and never wanted to get married, you can still neglect yourself so much that you fall into romantic mistakes." She can publicly proclaim that her affair with him was a "mistake" and a symptom, but she must also repeatedly assert that her original infatuation—

or "romance," as she chooses to call it—was less powerful than it probably was.

None of this is to deny that Steinem's interpretation of the events, apart from the force of her original attraction, is inaccurate. Where she and Zuckerman differ on the facts, she is usually correct—as is he. For example, they disagree on the length of the affair; he has been reported as counting it as four years, she as two. The difference here, according to Steinem, can be explained by the fact that as long as they were still seeing each other, he counted it as a relationship, while she restricted it to the time in which she (and probably he) was not also seeing others. She, who had never decisively broken off a longtime affair, continued to see Zuckerman, slowly moving away from the relationship until its abrupt end in 1988 after an incident involving Alice Walker's daughter, Rebecca, who had, by this time, become a veritable daughter to Steinem. The incident shows up as sharply as possible the different worlds Steinem and Zuckerman occupied, and the situations that aroused their most ardent responses.

Rebecca and a group of fellow Yale students were making a film about people of color at that university and other Ivy League institutions. Steinem had asked Zuckerman if Rebecca and her two associates could work at his Manhattan triplex while he was out of town. Zuckerman agreed. But one morning, when one of the filmmakers had fallen asleep on the couch, he was found by Zuckerman's housekeeper, who then addressed all three in racist terms, suggesting that they go home to Harlem where they belonged, or words to that effect. Rebecca, outraged, reported to Steinem, who demanded that Zuckerman ask the housekeeper to apologize and allow the three to remain. Her point was that if the housekeeper had told Jewish guests to go home to Israel where they belonged, the housekeeper would have been discharged, but to tell people to go home to Harlem was acceptable. Zuckerman did not countermand the housekeeper. Instead his sympathetic secretary arranged for Rebecca and the other filmmakers to stay at a corporate apartment owned by his company. This last case of many in which Steinem had witnessed Zuckerman treating others less than well—even though he behaved differently with her— caused her never to go out with him again. As Steinem considers it now,

> I felt I was walking on eggs all the time; I was always worrying about how he had treated past women friends, who told me alarming stories, and how he often treated his executives and even his friends. After I had screwed up my courage and dis- cussed this with him many times, I kind of gave up. . . . By two years after we were seeing each other I had given up on the idea that if this man became a happier person he would also become a nicer one. I realized, as so many women have, that the idea that I could "change" a man was the female version of a fantasy of power.

The giving up on Zuckerman was also accompanied by a dawning event of greater significance. In 1986 a diagnosis of can- cer precipitated profound changes in Steinem's life.

IMPERATIVES
FOR CHANGE

IN THE MIDDLE of the American adult female life, women may undergo a failure of spirit. They must decide either to continue life more or less as one has always lived it—if circumstances cooperate in this ambition—or to renew one's life by asking fundamental questions of it.

But for Steinem, reaching the middle of her adult life was not a sufficient jolt. As though life had contrived to turn her around as in a game of blindman's bluff, the magazine to which she had given fifteen years of her life was perilously close to failing; and a terrible weariness from the incessant seeking of ads—or contributions to make up for lack of ads—and the equally incessant responding to demands from the many causes she served overcame her. In the past twenty years there had, after all, been only one week when she was not in an airplane. She also awoke from an entirely unsuitable infatuation to find herself coupled in the minds of the media and her friends with a man whose values were fundamentally opposed to her own. Given such a concentration of events, collapse is likely, often inevitable. Her world was changing from color to shades of gray, a common sign of the beginning of deep depression. Though Steinem, with her characteristic ability to keep on keeping on, avoided a breakdown, she was among the walking wounded.

In addition, in November of 1985 Steinem felt a tiny lump in her breast. She went immediately to the mammogram center Dr. Ruth Snyder had established in New York. Snyder examined the lump, which presented itself as a fibroid adenoma, a benign tumor. Steinem's mammogram registered nothing, and with so much else going on in her life at the time, she accepted the negative results without question.

Shortly thereafter Steinem went for a routine checkup to the Women's Medical Center in Hempstead, Long Island, run by Dr. Penny Budhoff. According to Steinem the center provided "one-stop shopping—all your body parts at once." There Steinem had a sonogram. Again, the sonogram revealed nothing untoward. Again, Steinem accepted the negative results without question.

Steinem had always taken her health, which she credits to good genes, wholly for granted. As she was to report in *Revolution from Within,* she often went without sleep, bore enormous stress, and occasionally consumed quarts of ice cream or whole Sara Lee banana cakes at a time. There had, moreover, been no history of cancer in her family, and, at the time, neither the mammogram nor the sonogram indicated that any invasive procedures were necessary. Steinem, like her doctors, was falsely reassured; she kept on as before. *Ms.* was in desperate shape and she felt her responsibility, as always, was to help insure its survival.

Seeing the exhausted state she was in, Suzanne Levine and her husband Robert urged Steinem to consult a therapist. Because Steinem recognized how weary she was, and because the Levines knew her so well, she was more inclined than she ever could have been before to take their advice. So in May of 1986, some months after her book *Marilyn* was published, Steinem began to see a woman therapist when she was in town and could make the time. Thus, she was beginning therapy while dealing with the book's publication and, of course, much else.

Steinem had written *Marilyn* the previous summer, opting out of the social scene in Zuckerman's house in East Hampton by saying she had to work. She had written *Marilyn* to satisfy *Ms.*'s debt to her publisher Holt, Rinehart and Winston for copies of *Outrageous Acts* the magazine had used as a subscription premium. Dick Seaver, then Holt's publisher, had called her to say that he had photographs of Monroe taken by George Barris in her last year of life. Would Steinem write the text? No woman had ever written extensively on Monroe.

To Steinem, it seemed better to satisfy the Holt debt by writing than by "begging for money in someone's living room." She had, in fact, met Monroe in 1956 during a visit to the Actor's Studio, when she had been taken there by David Shaber, her Smith instructor in theater, to see Cheryl Crawford, the famous producer who had also taught at Smith. She had also been persuaded by Harriet Lyons, in the first years of *Ms.,* to write an essay marking the tenth anniversary of the actress's death. "The Woman Who Died Too Soon" appeared in the August 1972 issue. The essay emphasized the causes of both Monroe's doom and her continued fascination for so many people after her death.

Steinem supposed it was captions that would be expected, perhaps a thousand words for each photograph at most, but when the contract arrived she discovered it called for sixty thousand words of text. Steinem wrote the book quickly, chapter by chapter, like a journalist fulfilling an assignment, never seeing the whole until the book was in print. It is unlikely that, without the motive of fund-raising, she would have chosen to write a book about Monroe at this time.

The book does serve, however, to emphasize many of the themes that had always entranced Steinem, and many themes that she was beginning seriously to consider in connection with her own life and her new ideas about self-esteem. Steinem found that all the classical female experiences were Monroe's, although Monroe suffered from them more intensely than most.

Steinem's earliest fantasies had been of rescuing people, and Monroe's need of rescue had long been palpable. She appealed to many women as susceptible to rescue by them, had they been given the chance, had Monroe known and trusted them. Indeed, the few real friends Monroe had were women, but they could not save her. No one could. Steinem quoted Diana Trilling—one of the few women to write an essay among the dozens of men who wrote books about Monroe—mourning Monroe's lack of friends, "especially women, to whose protectiveness her extreme vulnerability spoke so directly. But," Trilling added, "we were the friends of whom she knew nothing." [18]

However Steinem may have wished that Monroe had, in fact, been rescued, and however assiduously she worked in this book to rescue Monroe's reputation, she never believed that she, or anyone else, could have saved Monroe. Steinem now considers that, because of the necessary hurry, she failed to give Monroe enough credit for surviving as long as she did. Had she known Monroe as a friend, Steinem sees, she would have found her *too* needy: trying to fulfill that need would have been like throwing oneself into a vortex. This perception is notable in the context of Steinem's extensive efforts to help Linda Lovelace. Eventually Lovelace did escape from her own vortex, did cease being a victim, did make a life for herself. This, Steinem knew, Monroe never could have done without the changes in social consciousness wrought by a whole movement, not just a few women friends.

Monroe was never in control of her life professionally or any other way, even though she tried her best to rebel against Hollywood. Although the Barris photographs were supposed to have been lovingly done, they are all examples of the male gaze, as elucidated by John Berger in *Ways of Seeing:* "Men look at women. Women watch themselves being looked at. This determines not only most relations between men and women but also the relation of women to themselves. The surveyor of women in herself is male: the surveyed female. Thus she turns herself into an object—and most particularly an object of vision: a sight." [47] Monroe believed she existed, Steinem understood, only because men saw her with delight.

Steinem recognized Monroe's conviction that she was invisible, except when seen by others. "Children who are not the focus of loving attention may come to feel they are invisible. They fight to be noticed to prove they exist" was how Steinem explained it. [137] About the same time she was writing the Monroe book, she began to wonder if that insight might not describe her own situation as well.

Monroe was constantly drugged. Often the power of the drugs had been enhanced by alcohol. In these matters Monroe was unlike Steinem—but in addition, Monroe was treated by Freudian analysts who, Steinem feels, seem to have exacerbated rather than reduced her anxieties. Steinem had no respect for the Freudian treatment of women; the disinclination to believe that women had suffered sexual assaults in childhood from male family members is merely the most obvious instance of what she saw as Freud's inability to trust women's experiences or believe women's words. Finally, the famous men who laid claims upon Monroe and interpreted her by their own standards of female desirability and victimization could never have the same effect on Steinem.

Yet she identified with Monroe as many women do, hating her vulnerability and aching to release her from a seemingly hopeless bondage. Monroe combined a fatal combination of blessings and curses, almost as though the good and bad fairies of legend had had equal access to her at birth. She was not only beautiful, but could also be remade, with plastic surgery on her jaw and nose (though not, she was proud to say, on her breasts), into greater perfection. Her hair was bleached, her teeth were fixed, and mincing mannerisms and a kind of breathy speech (so that you could never have guessed, Steinem observed, that she was an athlete) were taught to her. Above all, she exuded a kind of sensuousness, a unique sexual attractiveness that persisted in its appeal long after her death. There was something about her that was tantalizing, ultimately innocent and unreachable.

Unlike Steinem, but like many women of that era, Monroe both wanted and feared pregnancy. She had many abortions, and then failed, when married to Arthur Miller, to carry a child to term. She wanted a child so that she could treat it as she should have been treated, and feared having a child who might repeat the pattern of her life and perhaps force her into womanhood. Above all, as Steinem recognized, Monroe searched continually for a self that did not exist, and that could not be created by the attentions of others. Did her remarkable physical endowments serve her well? The answer, surely, is that they did not, that even as she reassured herself by the continuing force of male desire, she longed for a self-assurance and seriousness that was not dependent on that male desire.

Inevitably, Monroe was terrified, above all else, of aging; in this, as in everything, she was the woman as victim. As Steinem put it, "The restriction of her spirit in the airtight prison of her beauty was so complete that she literally feared aging more than death itself." [157] Monroe appears in Steinem's book, in a text subtly and very unobtrusively at war with the photographs, as a woman with the conventionally best and actually worst of all possible female destinies. And while Steinem identified with Monroe, she remembered her initial reaction to her: She had, in her teens, walked out of a Monroe movie because she could not bear the sight of Monroe's vulnerability. And if, more than thirty years later, she had more sympathy for that vulnerability, she also un-

derstood it, understood above all that Monroe was like those battered women who, as children, have come from battering homes
and few of whom, as adults, can manage to escape from their
belief that their battering is their deserved fate. Monroe had been
so damaged by her childhood that escape was probably never a
possibility in the culture of the 1950s. Steinem determined, in her
next book, to suggest ways of making possible such an escape.

   She dedicated the book to "the real Marilyn" even as she,
Steinem, began to question her own reality.[1] But the differences
and similarities between Steinem and Monroe must have struck
her as she contemplated this idolized victim of female destiny.
Steinem did not share that destiny; but had she, in her own childhood, suffered similar neglect, if not damage like Marilyn's? This
was a question she would explore with a therapist, but it is poignant that a comparison of her life and Monroe's did not seem to
offer sufficient reinforcement of her ability to control her own
destiny.

IN MAY OF 1986 during another regular checkup at the
Women's Medical Center, Dr. Budhoff, head of the clinic, determined, despite all the negative indications, to excise and examine
the lump in Steinem's breast. Dr. Virginia Maurer, a surgeon who
worked at the clinic one day a week, gave Steinem a shot of
Novocain and excised what Steinem described as "this tiny little
pink piece of flesh." While Steinem waited, Dr. Maurer ran across
the street to the pathology lab of the Mid-Island hospital. When
she returned, it was with the news that the "tiny little pink piece
of flesh" was malignant. The benign tumor had masked malignant, hypoplastic cells within it. Steinem was shocked, but no less
shocked than her doctors. Mammograms are inaccurate 15 percent

---

[1] Barris dedicated his part of the book to "a gentle, fragile Marilyn."

of the time and Steinem's mammogram had shown nothing. Steinem remembers returning to New York, sitting in a car thinking, "Isn't it interesting. So this is how it's going to end." She said she felt like she was "looking at herself from the outside."

In the midst of this—adding a bizarre, even absurd, characteristically Steinem note—the day after her diagnosis she had to honor a commitment as substitute host for the vacationing Jane Pauley on the *Today* show. She had undertaken the *Today* assignment mainly to conquer her fear of television. "It was like a dare, like doing the thing you fear most." After the week was over, Steve Friedman, the producer, told her she had done badly. "I felt," Steinem recalled, "like saying, 'Well, not too badly considering I just got a diagnosis of breast cancer.' " [2]

But she didn't say this to Friedman, nor to anyone other than a few close friends, because she was fearful that public knowledge of her illness might cause skittish advertisers to withdraw from *Ms.*

IT IS WORTH noting that ten years earlier, before pressures by the women's health movement and before *Ms.* magazine's early crusade against unnecessary surgery, Steinem would have had a mastectomy. She had garnered much information about breast cancer from previous *Ms.* articles—particularly a September 1973 article by George Crile, "Breast Cancer: A Patient's Bill of Rights," which disclosed that lesser procedures were just as effective as radical mastectomies, in which, along with the breast, the chest muscle was removed. When the lump was small, only the

---

[2] In March she had had some fat removed from above her eyelids; this enabled her to wear contact lenses first thing in the morning, before television cameras, which swelling had previously made impossible. This was a minor in-office procedure, taking little time, and her only cosmetic (if it was cosmetic) alteration. She had never, in fact, been in a hospital for any reason before the cancer.

breast might be removed; lumpectomy was until 1973 performed only rarely. (So many women took this article to their doctors that the *Medical Newsletter* shortly thereafter published an article on the subject.) "At that point," says Steinem, "there was no Internet." So, faced with her own cancer, she used her journalist's skills: She telephoned informed people, got hold of books and articles, and learned what, at that time, could be learned. "If there is one thing I have taken away from this experience, it is never to trust tests," she says today.

She went for a second opinion to the Dana Farber Cancer Institute in Boston, which confirmed that further surgery was needed to make certain the whole lump was gone, to make sure the margins around the tumor were clear, and to take a sampling of the nearby lymph nodes under her arm—a surgical procedure to see if the cancer had spread beyond its primary site. The next question was where to have the procedure done.

Because of her research Steinem had come to believe that a lumpectomy, rather than a mastectomy or any form of radical surgery, was an option she would choose. New York's Sloan-Kettering, a hospital that, in Steinem's opinion, performed "draconian surgery" would not therefore have been her first choice. On the other hand, Dr. Sam Hellman, a radiologist from Boston who believed in a more moderate form of breast cancer surgery, had just become president of the hospital, so Steinem went. After her examination Steinem heard Hellman in the hall outside the office door, arguing with the famous surgeon who would be in charge of her procedure. The surgeon believed "a quadrant" of her breast would have to be removed. Recognizing that the man hadn't much experience in doing less, Steinem finally chose to have the procedure done at Boston's Beth Israel Hospital, where first the pioneering Dr. Oliver Cope, then Dr. William Silen (mentor to Dr. Susan Love, who had by then left Beth Israel), had become famous for treating women with breast cancer in an enlightened way. Silen would be her surgeon.

Suzanne Levine accompanied her. They had been working together for twenty years and loved each other as friends; Levine would know what Steinem wanted, should any decision have to be made during the operation if anything went wrong.

The postoperative protocol was also conservative, in another contrast with Sloan-Kettering, whose postoperative procedures were the same for a lumpectomy as for a mastectomy. Steinem was hospitalized for only two days altogether, had no problem with her arm, and had the surgical drain in only briefly.

After Steinem returned to New York, she went to Sloan-Kettering early every weekday morning for six weeks, for radiation treatments (for which Zuckerman offered his hated limousine even though it was only a few blocks, and Steinem accepted). She was still secretive about her cancer at this time—she even underwent treatment under the name of her grandmother, Marie Ochs —because she feared to endanger the magazine's chance to find investors.[3] It was only in 1988, when ABC made a film on breast cancer, that Steinem spoke publicly about her own experience. (The film was a rare media event: Because of the writers' strike in 1988, this unusually intelligent exploration of a serious subject actually got on the air. Most of those connected with it, including the technical and camera people, had had breast cancer.)

Throughout this period, from her brief surgery through radiation and thereafter, Steinem worked—on behalf of the causes she believed in, and particularly, as always, on behalf of *Ms.* She was also working with her therapist, and for the first time, looking within.

---

[3] Years earlier, when Steinem had answered the phone while working in the *Ms.* office late at night, the news got out in an ad industry newsletter that *Ms.* was in trouble because Steinem was answering the phone: *Ms.*'s nonhierarchical staffing methods were rarely understood.

For Steinem, the beginning of the breakthrough came fast. She quickly understood that she now had to look after herself as she had always looked after others, and this realization took a material form. The very early visits to her therapist enabled her to accept encouragement from a friend, Filippa Naess, a designer who, in Steinem's words, took Steinem on "as a charity case." This included going with Steinem to buy "old-fashioned" cotton sheets, in place of the synthetic colored sheets she had used all her life. Buying elegant cotton sheets like her grandmother's was almost, as Steinem describes it, an "orgasmic experience," because she was doing it for herself, to make the home she never had. This was the first indication of a turnaround in her life.

Remodeling her home quickly made her physical life more comfortable, but a remodeling of her mental and emotional state required a much longer process. To go to a therapist is, inevitably, to look back, to reconsider one's childhood and one's parents, to seek to remember what one had, perhaps, chosen to forget. Steinem did not easily undertake this necessary task. She was afraid of what she would find—afraid, as perhaps she had always been, albeit unconsciously, that she would discover an abyss, fall into it, and never come out.

Despite this fear, three important perceptions emerged from her therapy. First, Steinem realized that she had not been allowed to be a child but had been forced at too early an age to be the mother. In a sense she had always known this, and attributed her lack of a wish for children to it. Having taken care of one child, her mother, she had no wish to repeat the performance. Recent feminist critics have observed that some women who have had highly charged and difficult relations with their mothers decide either to avoid motherhood for fear of repeating the experience or embrace motherhood to prove that they can do better. In Steinem's case, one senses a certain stubborn need to hold on to the basic logic of her decision not to bear children; like many oldest children in large families who do not, in turn, become parents, she had, as Huck Finn said about being civilized, been there before.

Second, Steinem came to believe that escaping from the "Toledo" relationship with her mother, or determining not to repeat it, was not as simple as she had assumed. Surely the tenacity with which she accepted, long after sense dictated giving it up, the responsibility for *Ms.* and its financial survival suggested that the magazine had become like her invalid mother. She had, perhaps for that reason, averted her eyes from, and avoided any feelings about, its dire condition and had just gone on doing what she assumed had to be done; there was no choice, just as there had been none in Toledo.

As she has described it, she had learned from her childhood to solve things by taking action outside the home. And taking action made her feel real, gave her back her self; but she had, at the same time, built a brick wall between herself and her childhood. She had become an optimist as a result of that childhood: Nothing as bad could ever happen again. As a result of all the crises in recent years, her childhood began to seep through the carefully constructed brick wall. She was, in therapy, undertaking a process that most individuals attempt either earlier and constantly or not at all. Her analogy for this experience was that her childhood was like dehydrated milk, and suddenly someone was pouring water into it.

Third, if until her therapy she had believed that her childhood was all past, she was now forced to realize how continuously she had reproduced many of its characteristics: never owning anything, never saving anything, neglecting herself as she had been neglected as a child, eating terribly, not exercising, not sleeping enough. And there had always been her father's cures for troubles: going to the movies or having a malted milk as the only alternatives to her mother's course of giving up her work and self.

Facing the hardships she had endured on behalf of *Ms.,* Steinem was also able to recall hardships from her childhood that had been forgotten: looking for dirt tracks on her arms to know if it was time to heat water on the stove for a bath; washing a blouse for school each morning and then ironing it dry; seeing her mother lying helpless on a bed talking to demons in an unseen world; repeated nightmares of boys taunting her mother mercilessly; fearing that her mother, forgetting that Gloria had told her where she was going, would report her missing to the police, and she would again fear sirens meant police coming to find her. Much that was, as she mildly said, "fairly terrible."

These things, Steinem came to see, had helped to determine the course of her life. Are her memories accurate? To a therapist, such a question is meaningless. "What is truth?" they ask with Pilate, and agree to accept what presents itself as truth to the client. We must assume that reexperiencing her mother in more detail than she previously had was both necessary and healthy. Having written "Ruth's Song" perhaps freed Steinem to speak of the years with her mother more openly.

In a certain, carefully defined sense, Steinem remained an adolescent for over five decades. That is, she retained all the dreams and eagerness and risk-taking of adolescence, without what we think of as its excesses: self-indulgence, overindulgence, arrogance, and indifference to the needs of others. Because she never had a child—and children serve, if in no other way, to push us into the next generation—she never lost that youthful determination to change the world nor the youthful courage to try. Perhaps, to put it differently, she passed through the difficulties of adolescence in the years following her fiftieth birthday, having never before had the opportunity of its uncertain confusion in all its frightful glory.

We must, however, consider this: If she had had a child or husband and then left them, we would call her selfish. Since she has neither married nor had children, but continues to be remarkably generous in a world not notable for generosity, we call her selfless. Perhaps it is our definition of "self" that is too limited. Certainly in caring for her mother when she was a child—and should have been being cared for as a child herself—in not marrying or having children, she dares us to discover the cause of her "abnormality." When we see, in addition, that she enjoyed dancing with smart and successful people, enjoyed dressing up, and learned to deal with the powerful in connection with her political causes, her journalism, and *Ms.* magazine, we begin to accept that perhaps the events of her childhood in no way undermined her pleasures or inhibited her endless personal efforts on behalf of those aims she considered vital.

DURING THIS TIME, however, there were moments of comic relief. President Reagan, apparently as unaware of her feelings as he was of so much in the country, called Steinem—a call that seemed to her as peculiar as the one from Gloria Carter during the Houston conference in 1977. This is what happened: In 1986 Steinem went to Paris on behalf of the *Today* show to interview Patrick Kelly, a black designer whose fashion was populist— denim instead of expensive fabrics, and buttons and bows instead of beadwork—and who had become the first U.S. designer accepted by the French into their inner fashion circle. But since Steinem only got to interview less than world famous people if she also interviewed really famous personalities (she had used a rare interview with Robert Redford to trade for a report on a child care center for sick children in Minneapolis, for example), she went as well to the south of France to meet with film actor and singer Yves Montand. She was at a small inn there, trying to take a nap, when she got a message to call Ronald Reagan. (His office had first called *Ms.,* and when Steinem was told that, she thought the *Ms.* people were kidding.) The White House operators are, of course, renowned for being able to find anyone, anywhere.

And so she heard the familiar voice of this man for whom she had such disdain launch into a story at least five minutes long. The upshot of the story was that he was sitting in the Oval Office in the White House calling people to ask them if they would do television spots for a foundation unconnected with the government, which was trying to promote the peaceful use of space technology. The theme of these spots, produced by a Hollywood producer Reagan had once worked with on Westerns, was to have two people who had otherwise agreed on nothing, say they agreed on this. Reagan wanted her to do a spot with Charlton Heston. "I'll have him call you," he said.

To Steinem, the call was bizarre not only because of Reagan's meandering verbal style but also because he clearly had no idea she was his adversary and she couldn't even make him laugh at the unexpectedness of this exchange. He was simply following a provided list of names. (In the end, Steinem did do the spot with Heston, both of them agreeing on the importance of peace and the environment. Jesse Jackson talked her into it, because he was doing a similar spot and he thought it important that he and Steinem turn up in these sorts of places.)

During these years of intense work and great pressure from many needy organizations serving the poor, the oppressed, and those who had slipped through Reagan's "safety net," the media continued to take Steinem less than seriously, or any rate to undercut her and the real issues of the movement. Andy Rooney's 1984 attack was typical when he criticized her for appearing on an NBC comedy special, *The News Is the News,* with streaked hair and makeup, claiming this to be inconsistent with her role in the movement and stating that if Charles Kurault wore a toupee he would look as ridiculous as a fifty-year-old woman who dyed her hair blond and tried to look eighteen. Steinem answered, meeting this sort of attack, not for the first time or the last, and, of course, to no avail: "After years of being criticized for too little makeup and changes of fashion, Mr. Rooney's unique complaint is almost restful." She said Rooney was naive about the impact of a few blond streaks ("It's revolution that keeps me young"), about male wearers of toupees, from Jack Paar to Howard Cosell, and about the dangers of blaming the victim. "Women will keep on fighting until we can appear on television even if we have Mr. Rooney's age and paunch—and his poor eyesight." She added that everyone, both male and female, on the show, which was live, was wearing the same makeup, put on by the same person. But neither Rooney nor anyone else would be stopped from attacking feminists for how they looked, however they looked. Indeed, her name also appeared on the "Worst Dressed" list, on which she commented: "I was disturbed until I realized there's only one thing that's worse—appearing on the 'Best Dressed' list."

Even as Steinem was deeply engaged in introspection and life changes, she continued to function in her public tasks. In 1986–1987 she had been asked to serve on the Citizens Committee on AIDS for New York and northern New Jersey; this commission had been created by approximately fifteen foundations in New York City, with Carol Levine, a specialist in bioethics, as its executive director. Two of those on the commission whom Steinem remembered with particular affection were John Jacobs of the Urban League, and Tom Stoddard, a lawyer and gay activist she encountered again in 1993 when he was working on behalf of gays in the military and she was serving as a moderator at a meeting on the subject, which he had organized. They were both amused to find themselves entering to military music. As they met again, he let her know he had become HIV positive, and he was moved by her loving response. He spoke of their earlier acquaintance, when he had so admired what he called her genius for moderating. Here, though a pacifist, Steinem was supporting the rights of women and gays to be in the military. As Steinem put it, "Shit equally divided is always better than shit unequally divided."

The 1987 commission produced reports critical of government at all levels. The most important thing it did, however, was to develop for employers guidelines on employees who had HIV, which became the basis for all others nationally and in other countries. Steinem, Stoddard remembered, was mainly interested in the underestimated HIV problems of women (those, for example, with bisexual or drug-using partners), and was very active on the commission. "She has a way of raising points trenchantly, but never in a way that frightens and offends people." Stoddard believes that, like Dr. Martin Luther King, Jr., did, Steinem recognizes the need to fight injustice personally as well as abstractly. She was always deeply respectful of other people, and Stoddard feels that his illness taught him how rare her kind of consideration and firmness was. "She is a wonderfully skillful moderator; she knows exactly the tone to use.

"We live at a time without heroes," Stoddard says. "Perhaps we know more about people than we did. But to meet someone like this is reassuring and inspiring. The media has no model for women heroes. Straight white men have much to learn from gay men and women, especially about breaking open. It is hard for me to be a gay man because I find women more evolved. She is a peacemaker, an extraordinary combination of change-maker and peacemaker. I was stunned to find a celebrity who was genuinely humble and kind."

Not the least ironic aspect of this ardent praise is the difficulty one faces in repeating it. Nevertheless, Stoddard's opinion suggests that Steinem continued, throughout this period, to function as she had always functioned, still expressing empathy for others and working on their behalf, even as she would, in therapy, begin to understand at what price that empathy was given.

Steinem's therapist once joked to her that perhaps, given her then weary outlook on life, she should learn from a public figure named Gloria Steinem. To appear close to ideal to many, and to feel oneself lost in a colorless world, is hardly unique to Steinem, but her way of taking control and seeking help was unusually effective and practical.

BY THE SPRING of 1987 the situation at *Ms.* looked quite hopeless. Steinem and others had persevered for many years trying to keep the magazine afloat. Advertisers were still skittish, to say the least, and could only be recaptured, if at all, with a huge rise in the number of readers; but money was needed to send them subscription invitations, and there seemed no hope of getting it. Financial experts estimated that over $10 million would be required to save *Ms.* A renewed search had begun for investors, though it was not, finally, investors but buyers who materialized at the last possible moment.

At the urging of two prominent Australian women—the feminist journalist Anne Summers and her publishing partner Sandra Yates—Fairfax, an Australian media firm, bought the magazine. *Ms.* was happy to sell to Anne Summers, a far better alternative than purchasers here who would turn *Ms.* into a conventional woman's magazine. She would take the helm as editor in chief. Steinem was more than willing to offer Summers any help that might ease her passage into the editorship, but Summers made it clear that she wanted to begin with complete control. Some senior editors, such as Mary Thom, Joanne Edgar, Ellen Sweet, and Gloria Jacobs, stayed on. But the makers of editorial policy were the Australians. Although Steinem and Carbine were listed on the masthead as consulting editors, they were never consulted.

By the time of this sale Steinem was almost past regretting any action that would release her from the terrible burdens of recent years. It is always possible to suppose that with relief, however ardently desired, comes some sense of regret. In this case, however —probably because she was able to pass the magazine on to true feminist leadership, and because of her exhaustion—her regrets, if they existed at all, were confined to anger at the unfairness of the past.

In 1988, with the magazine no longer requiring her help, Steinem took up a post at Random House as a contributing editor. She now also had two contracts for books, with large advances. (These contracts were for the proposed book on rich women and the masculinization of wealth—eventually transmogrified into the book of essays that was published in 1994 as *Moving Beyond Words* —and for *Revolution from Within.*)

If the word "cancer" and the experience of the illness woke her up, she was still not ready to face the state she was in, living cramped in two crowded rooms, almost never seeing her neighborhood in the daytime, caring for herself not at all. Kristina Kiehl, a Washington feminist/activist who had moved to San Francisco, gave Steinem essential help, urging her to abandon her cardboard cartons and acquire furniture; together they put the contents of the cartons onto shelves or hung them on walls. It took the urging of friends and their actual, practical help to move Steinem out of her current state.

Her book advances had, at last, allowed her enough money to renovate her two rooms—the apartment she had moved into with Barbara Nessim all those years before—and to annex two rooms below them in order to have a real study and a guest room. This provided space for Rebecca Walker to occupy in the summers, and a backyard—a home, in fact, instead of a place to crash. By the end of 1989 she had actually had the apartment wholly decorated. It is filled with Indian fabrics, many drapes, shelves holding earrings, shoes, books, and so forth, a bed with a canopy from which flowing red cheesecloth draperies descend. Her former loft bed acquired floating white material resembling a baby's bassinet, and in Alice Walker's view it represents the much-cared-for-baby Steinem believes she never was. Steinem also acquired a blue Persian cat named Magritte whom she cherishes, hugs, cuddles, and leaves alone while traveling less than she did Crazy Alice, the cat of earlier times. (Crazy Alice had ultimately gone to live happily in a house in Queens with a backyard.)

IN 1989 Steinem saw *Ms.* taken over by Lang Communications. At this time *Ms.* became an ad-less, bimonthly magazine; the struggle for and with advertisers was over. The magazine would now depend on its subscribers for support. Robin Morgan became editor-in-chief. The Australian regime had failed. Despite the fact that Summers and Yates were strong feminists with backgrounds in publishing, the death of the head of the Fairfax empire and its subsequent reorganization undercut their efforts. Also, in changing the editorial content to please advertisers—that is, in adding articles on fashion, gardening, new products, and the like—Summers and Yates succeeded only in annoying readers without enticing advertisers. They failed to make the magazine pay.

That same year Steinem began to be squired about by Gil Shiva, a handsome Israeli widower whose wife, Susan Stein, had died of cancer. They were more friends than lovers, took tango lessons together, and Steinem watched over his daughter, Alexandra, who worked at *Ms.* before entering college.

In those two years leading up to the publication of *Revolution from Within,* Steinem continued much as before to devote a good deal of time and energy to causes and political commitments. In 1992 she campaigned vigorously for women candidates, and took part in a number of conferences supporting Anita Hill and publicizing the newly exposed question of sexual harassment. Steinem was a particularly devoted and generous supporter of Carol

Mosely Braun, but her effort on behalf of all women candidates, as well as Clinton, was notable. Then, when Ted Weiss, the long-time congressman from New York's Upper West Side, died, she helped Bella Abzug in a fight to be named to fill his seat. Despite the wide field of candidates, the committee, dubbed by Steinem "a Dracula committee: It only lives when someone dies," selected a party regular, Jerrold Nadler, to fill the seat. [*NYT,* Sept. 23, 1992]

The Nation asked Steinem to write one in a series of articles called "Why I'm Not Running for President." She explained that she thought the presidency was chiefly a bully pulpit, and that changes had to come from below. "Clinton can't and shouldn't make change *for* us. Unlike Bush (who, with Reagan, is the first president to turn back the clock on equality), Clinton won't stop us—and that's what's important. By listening, he will help citizens to know that we are worth listening to."

THE PUBLICATION of *Revolution from Within* at the beginning of 1992 was the culmination of Steinem's belated bout with therapy and her obsessive reading of all she could find on the subject of self-esteem. When the book was published, she was widely perceived to have abandoned the public life for self-examination or, as several reviewers put it, for "me." The irony here is that she had chosen to write this book in order to connect internal authority to the overthrow of external authority, but in an "either/or" culture, "and" is difficult to accept. In an afterword to the paperback edition she tried to make that point clear.

Revolution from Within is, in fact, a book about self-esteem: its importance as the source of both personal well-being and political revolution, how to get it, how to keep it, how to unlearn the past and reshape the future. It provides a meditation guide and recommendations for how to rediscover and therefore reshape the unchosen patterns of one's childhood. The section entitled "Romance versus Love" is only thirty-five pages long; its purpose is to warn women against substituting a man and his desires for one's own self and one's own desires, and—in keeping with Steinem's constant intention to speak of women as "we," never as "they" or "you"—to demonstrate that she, too, when her self-esteem was low, had made that mistake. Her original version of *Revolution,* as she recounted in her preface, had been devoid of any mention of herself. When she realized this she determined firmly to place herself and her own experiences into this book, whose creation represented the triumph of her therapy and her ability—that is, everyone's ability—to survive the terrors of aging, illness, the wrong love, and the loss of one's professional structure.

Many newspaper headlines called *Revolution from Within* the revelation of a "midlife crisis," and this cliché, of course, is near the truth of the case. But as we have seen, for Steinem the crisis was not just the fear of aging—which our society does everything possible to induce in all women—but an inevitable change of outlook and emphasis for women and men.

Certainly Steinem's unusual resistance to introspection made her sudden decision to change her life seem to suggest some profound fault with what had gone before. But what had gone before was not at fault; it was simply no longer relevant to her needs. Had her book been not on self-esteem, but on the need for a woman to change her life at fifty or thereabouts, there would probably have been few objections to it. Steinem, however, believes that her sin was to use herself as an example, and to link the internal and the external in a world that considers one "soft" and the other "serious," one "feminine" and the other "masculine." It can also be said with some assurance that the media, while they would still have salivated over the Zuckerman bits, would not have been able to produce lines like "Little Gloria, Happy at Last."

Revolution from Within reveals many truths that, with the help of a highly intelligent and sympathetic therapist, Steinem was able to contemplate and accept: ideas such as the recognition that women's cultural diseases are "empathy sickness" and depression while men's are anger and narcissism. When Steinem writes, "I finally began to admit that I, too, was more aware of other people's feelings than my own," she has discovered something profound about her earlier self—and about why women are persuaded not to fight on their own behalf.

A controversial piece in the January 1992 *Vanity Fair* by Leslie Bennetts contributed to the skewed reception of the book. Steinem had gone along with her publisher's belief that the interview would be helpful. It was, as Steinem later explained, typical of her refusal to learn from experience. As Steinem tells it, this time she should have refused firmly on the basis of her previous experience with *Vanity Fair* and Tina Brown, then its editor. *Vanity Fair* had run a negative review of *Marilyn,* suggesting that Steinem was just another person profiteering off the dead Marilyn Monroe. Steinem had mentioned in the book that money she personally made from the project, after the *Ms.* debt was paid, was going to services for abused children. She pointed this out to *Vanity Fair* and was told that there was no space for corrections. At another time, the magazine sold a picture they had agreed to use only once, of Steinem in a short skirt, to *Playboy.*

"You would think," Steinem commented, "that these two experiences might have alerted me to the fact that I should be somewhat cautious and perhaps even unwilling to do an interview with them." But when Brown called her, and assured her the interview would be about the book, she agreed. This was a perfect example, Steinem explained, of "believing against all previous experience that the outside world is going to be fair." The nub of the disagreement between Steinem and Bennetts was over Steinem's negative response to Bennetts's query about whether Zuckerman had ever given any money to *Ms.* (Steinem managed, in time, to joke about the fact that women are supposed to get in trouble by saying yes, but she managed it by saying no.) Zuckerman, understandably offended by reading that he had given nothing to the magazine, documented what loans he had cosigned, what charitable donations given, and threatened to sue *Vanity Fair.* Brown and Bennetts blamed Steinem, rather than a lack of routine fact-checking to catch such mistakes. The rumpus, picked up by the *New York Observer* and Liz Smith, who found herself unhappily entangled in the matter because she, too, had talked to Leslie Bennetts, continued through the early part of 1992. Steinem and Bennetts each wrote letters to the *Observer,* which gleefully printed them, as well as a front-page article that condemned Steinem as "The Ivan Boesky of Nookie," on the grounds that she must only have gone to bed with Zuckerman for those contributions, thus insulting them both. Whoever was technically correct, Steinem or Bennetts, the *Vanity Fair* article's clear aim, like that of so much of the ensuing publicity, was to attract readers by rehashing the conflict between two public figures, not to discuss a new book.

Then came two new waves of response to the book. Steinem went on a strenuous book tour, speaking to exultant crowds—some of whom camped out overnight in the rain to be able to catch her at a book signing at the same time letters from all over the country poured in praising *Revolution* for having helped women to change their lives. Simultaneously, the reviews in major New York and London publications began to appear. They were either gleeful with amazement—*she* has self-esteem problems?—or downright critical. Subsequently, favorable reviews began to appear in other U.S. and Canadian papers—many of these defending her against the earlier unfavorable reviews. In March, *Time* magazine featured Steinem and thirty-something Susan Faludi, author of *Backlash,* on its cover—testifying to feminism's strength in spanning the generations.

The reviews in notoriously conservative publications like the *Wall Street Journal* are neither surprising nor interesting; only the tones differed. The *Wall Street Journal* sneered that "having a serious leader like Gloria Steinem run around town talking about her low self-esteem is rather like having Lenin show up on 'Nightline' touting primal scream therapy." Antifeminists like Sally Quinn in the *Washington Post* seized the opportunity to attack Steinem, feminism, and lesbians in her article "Feminists Have Killed Feminism," happily aligning herself with William Safire and Betty Friedan in the latter's weaker moments. Even when the reviews were, on the whole, favorable, they sometimes had snappy headlines like "Book Offers Pop Psych's Greatest Hits."

Steinem felt they had all misunderstood her and failed to read the book properly, but, as uncertain as most authors, the reactions made her wonder if she had written what she thought she had written, or if she really had enough self-esteem to write a book about self-esteem. When the paperback edition came out a year later, she included an afterword, answering many of the reviews. A blurb from Alice Walker on the back of the paperback edition pointed to one of the factors that had disturbed reviewers: "Gloria Steinem has dared to look behind the bravely smiling face she presented to the world for many years to encounter a not-so-bravely smiling inner self." This was the message many disappointed reviewers had taken from the book, together with regret for the effect such an admission would have on feminism. The other major criticism was that Steinem had used what some call "psychobabble."

It was, however, the response from intellectual feminist women that most disturbed Steinem. With wide-ranging evidence—and even feminist intellectuals could offer such evidence from women they personally encountered—of how many women had been helped by her book, Steinem found these reviews carping, and she observed in the new afterword that the "intellectual establishment seemed to find the subject too soft and intangible to be taken seriously." She had also noticed that "the more obscure the review the more favorable." Well, had she not always wanted to reach obscure people rather than the "intellectual establishment," which she had with good reason found slow to understand? The only problem in this case was that her critics were not the Smith graduates whom she had described in her book as far slower to comprehend feminism than her Toledo high school peers; these were genuine feminists, genuinely sympathetic with all she had previously done, and heretofore her admirers. What was the problem?

That Steinem had chosen never to be an "intellectual," let alone a member of the "establishment," was obvious. Yet there was an intellectual problem here that Steinem was unwilling or unable to face up to. She summed up, in her afterword, what she characterized as the main misreadings of her book: "that my interest in internal concerns must mean I had . . . regretted my earlier years of activism; that the pages most deserving of critical attention were the three personal ones in Chapter Five's romance section; [that] journalists on both sides of the Atlantic theorized that I must have deserted serious political pursuits to write a self-help book for personal gain." And she went on to again emphasize the distance she had encountered between reviewers and readers. This is a distance well worth noticing in all cases; no literary critic, for example, who has studied the contemporary reviews of great writers can imagine for a moment that reviewers have better sense than readers. What they do have is more clout, for a short time. And certainly the media, as Steinem said, was describing a different book than the one she had written; this is, alas, a frequent complaint. In addition, and most important, Steinem noted that "by far the most consistent response came from women who had been active feminists for years before retreating, and from women who'd been turned off by the women's movement." These women, she understood, were glad to discover that "feminism is about strengthening women from the inside too."

What, then, are the possible cogent intellectual criticisms of the book? The strongest centers on the self-help language in which the book is couched. Steinem came to appreciate the self-help industry late; she came to self-awareness even later. Because she had valued the unexamined life—and, unlike many other fifty-year-old women, had lived in the public eye—she fell upon intro-spection like a thirsty desert traveler upon water. Surely, she seemed to think, everyone else had also been waiting for this. But Steinem's was hardly the first word anyone had heard on the subject. Although they came from a renowned feminist—and that fact did much to bring many women back to, or simply to, femi-nism—none of these methods or ideas was new. However sound her research, *Revolution from Within* fitted neatly and successfully into the self-help mold. As one reviewer pointed out, the self-help section in bookstores now occupies more space than the feminist or women's studies section. Steinem's failure to see how many of her ideas would therefore appear familiar—or even tired—was surely naive.

At the same time, she defended *Revolution from Within* as new in one important way: It was not an either/or book. New Age self-help books maintain that you can solve personal problems without changing the outside world, which is, in Steinem's judgment, "feminine bullshit"; political writers, on the other hand, say that by changing the outside circumstances you will fix it all, with no introspection, attention to child-raising, and so forth, which is "masculine bullshit." Steinem set out to demonstrate that neither the inner nor outer approach works without the other.

A survey of the favorable reviews can leave no doubt that Steinem's book did in fact appeal strongly to three groups of women: first, to women who needed to hear that they ought to stand up for themselves; second, to feminists who had worked hard for feminism and other causes but were burned out and glad to receive from Steinem permission to pay long-delayed attention to themselves and their depleted strength; and third, to women who had been frightened away from feminism because it seemed so external and public, and who were now won over to it upon learning that it also had a softer, inner, more personal side.

Nonetheless, intellectuals remain suspicious of self-help for two reasons. The first, excellently set forth in Wendy Kaminer's book of that same year, *I'm Dysfunctional, You're Dysfunctional,* is that the self-help movement has brought in its wake a public far too willing to be told what to think and how to react. This is politically dangerous, and unsatisfactory in other obvious ways. Some self-help programs are admirable: Alcoholics Anonymous, for example. Most are not, or not in the long run. They may even be detrimental, leading to impermanent successes.

The second reason for suspicion is that most intellectuals, certainly most academic intellectuals, have learned the necessity of processing information, of interpreting reactions, of questioning motives and thoughts. To them, Steinem's sudden discovery of the value of the examined life must have seemed, if not naive, both uninformed and unhelpful.

And to them as to many others, the announcement that Steinem lacked a healthy self-esteem and self-authority was simply not credible. Not that Steinem gave that impression dishonestly. Her modesty, by all accounts, is genuine; no one who has known her well, with the exception of Betty Harris and some disaffected Redstockings, can doubt it.

While *Revolution from Within* contains many good ideas, there is another major intellectual problem with the book: its dependence on childhood experience. No one can discount childhood experience; neither can it be denied that we now know much more about molested and abused children than we formerly knew, or admitted we knew. Originally it was Marilyn Monroe, with her miserable childhood, who had set Steinem off in search of the "inner child," a subject she hoped to discuss in *Revolution from Within*. When she mentioned this interest to her therapist, the therapist referred her to Nancy Napier, a writer and expert on the concept; Steinem saw Napier three times.

It is highly questionable, however, whether searching for the inner child is the best way to go about remaking one's life, and to some readers it will look like too simple a way of explaining, as Steinem does, the evil done by Saddam Hussein or by the wavering of George Bush. When, in addition, Steinem quotes Hugh Missildine, child psychologist and author of *Your Inner Child of the Past,* as saying, "The childhood of persons who suffered from neglect usually reveals a father who somehow wasn't a father and a mother who somehow wasn't a mother," [36] she relates this to herself, but hardly seems to realize what conventional standards of parenthood lie behind such a statement, or that Missildine and so many other psychologists have long used this sort of analysis to explain male homosexuality and other unconventional behavior.

Childhood cannot be ignored; repeated patterns call for its examination. Steinem herself remembers her very early childhood as happy on the whole rather than otherwise. Indeed, she did not need therapy to know that the time in Toledo with her mother was harrowing. What remains noteworthy about those childhood years is that they did not prevent her from becoming the politically effective woman she is, or from serving so admirably the cause of feminism.

The revelation about herself that Steinem learned from feminism is in itself worthy of special remark:

> But though I was rescued by feminism, it had one result for which I was ill prepared: finding myself referred to as "the pretty one"—jeans and all. Rationally, I knew it was a response of surprise, based on what the media thought feminists looked like (if a woman could get a man, why would she need equal

pay?), and this was particularly clear to me because I was judged much prettier *after* I was identified as feminist than I had ever been before." [235]

This is both true and disingenuous.

Steinem had to have known she was good-looking. What she seems to be trying to say here is that she does not want to believe her looks are counted as more important than her years of work, and she hated also the scorn this cast on less attractive women. One reason why she never responded to Friedan's attacks may have been because she recognized that Friedan was too often sneered at because she was not the media's idea of beautiful. Also, aware as Steinem was of how men honor women only for their looks, she felt a genuine impulse to deny including herself in the category of "looker." And doubtless she no more than any woman over forty escaped fears about how good-looking she still was. Yet even in 1990, when Steinem was fifty-six, Susan Hauser, a writer for the ever-cynical-about-feminism *Wall Street Journal,* went first to a Miss Oregon USA contest, and then, as she puts it, to salve her conscience, to hear Steinem speak. When she got close to Steinem, the reporter concluded, she observed that "Ms. Steinem wore a miniskirt that wouldn't quit. Her abdomen was flat, her hips nicely rounded, her bust firm and her figure well-proportioned. Her long, shapely legs look like they were on a moon launch. I gave her a 10." [Nov. 1990] When a woman has enough of this, she may well come to question what her looks have done for her, and eventually question the looks themselves.

Steinem's greatest strength is her instant identification with "common" people, as the word was used by Samuel Johnson and Virginia Woolf in the phrase "the common reader." She even leaves spaces in *Revolution,* as she does in her speeches, for the audience to express its own thoughts. She has scorned intellectuals for many good reasons, but when she is allowed to explain her book, even to them, she is in many ways more convincing than the book itself.

In the end, *Revolution from Within* made many profound and excellent points. The romance section, so perversely dwelt upon, was never sufficiently appreciated for its understanding of what women want from romance, and why they defeat themselves so in pursuing it. Her knowledge that there is only one true inner voice, and that women especially should learn to trust it is, though often repeated, no less valuable now than ever. Finding that true voice is not a simple matter, and there are many ways to it. It is particularly important that it be found after a woman has passed fifty.

Ultimately, what must be said about *Revolution from Within* is that it is wholly a feminist book. That is an important judgment these days and one brought into greater clarity by, of all people, Camille Paglia. As the *Times Literary Supplement* quoted Paglia: "Like I said when I was talking at Harvard, who is the better role model for women—Gloria Steinem . . . with [her] self-esteem problems or me? I have no self-esteem problems . . . [I am] a better role model for women today than all these sex-phobic women." Sex-phobic as an epithet for Steinem is chosen with Paglia's usual delicate inaccuracy.

What *Revolution from Within* does demonstrate is what a good role model Steinem is. In trying to persuade us that in a male-dominated system even a woman with her success and looks has self-esteem problems, she may have somewhat misstepped, but her message is clear and, separated from the self-help lingo, impor-tant: that anyone, however successful or unsuccessful, whatever her past triumphs or defeats, must at midlife be ready and able (if outer limitations are not too great) to seek out a new and different life.

Recognizing after fifty the symptoms of exhaustion with one way of life and the necessity for remedies and for a different pacing, Steinem had herself changed markedly. If many read her book principally for its autobiographical revelations, it nonetheless affected and encouraged many of those readers. Steinem set out to give her readers the courage to change, and she often succeeded in doing so.

EPILOGUE

STEINEM TURNED sixty on March 25, 1994. She had, to a certain extent, altered her life from its previous pattern of every week in flight or on the road—not entirely abandoning her old ways, but achieving more balance. What she had, in fact, discovered was a new freedom—a new ability to be herself. Like many who have crossed the boundary beyond middle age into that period in a woman's life for which we have no single satisfactory phrase, she was able to welcome, and cherish, a sense of life as play—serious play—and not as compulsion. (Her humor remained: At a 1995 celebration for Bella Abzug, Steinem said that she had reached the age when to remember something is better than an orgasm.) The language for what may be discovered by the aging person's delight in life is new, awkward, and largely undeveloped. Just as Anne Elliot in Jane Austen's *Persuasion* would say that in speaking of love, men had always held the pen in their hands, so we may say that the young, in speaking of life's joys, have determined the vocabulary. Those in the springtime of old age know what Germaine Greer has called "bliss," and Steinem has called "freedom," without any expectation of convincing those not yet there, or miserable to be there. What they never tell you about age, some pundit once observed, is that it's such a delightful change from being young. The secret is to view the passing of youth as gain, not loss.

Here, again, Steinem is both exemplary and exceptional. She may notice her changing features, but to many resenting their own aging, she seems enviably to have retained a youthful face and figure. Yet the men who worked with her at *Esquire* and who testify to having first been dazzled by her beauty would not, now, be so beguiled. Today she is an aging woman, and in our society aging women are not there to be noticed: Steinem has found ways to rejoice in this and see it as freedom.

Intense, continuous devotion to any one person, whether lover or friend, together with the clear exclusion of others from this special category, is not Steinem's mode; there is not, and in all likelihood will not be, a constant male companion and lover in her life. She has, furthermore, shocked many people in frankly stating that her sexual drive has diminished, though she can still find sex enticing when she encounters it.

Steinem is particularly notable for having run the gamut of possible responses to conventionally attractive men. At twenty-two she had the strength to withstand the enormous appeal of Blair Chotzinoff; at fifty she sparred romantically with a man who, as marriage to Chotzinoff would have done, locked her into a period of inauthenticity. It is possible that all women must, at one stage or another, fall into the trap of what Steinem calls "romance versus love," just as all women must sometime undergo a period of arduous introspection. Steinem, encountering these two necessary experiences in combination, did so at a time when she could gather her forces and begin to relish what Margaret Mead called "postmenopausal zest."

Steinem's life suggests that postponing certain valuable experiences until the last third of life may be a pattern worthy of emula-tion. Not, to be sure, that one consciously postpones one experi-ence for another; even those "successful" men who work sixteen hours a day and tell themselves that they'll get to know their children soon are not consciously postponing the nurturing of children until their grandchildren arrive to serve the purpose; that is merely how it often turns out. (Perhaps this is why so many "successful" men marry young women and produce their own "grandchildren.") Steinem hardly set out to live a youth and mid-dle age pulsating to what seemed to be demanded in order to change the world, and not responding to what "ought" to be experienced at that stage; unconsciously, she "postponed" the more contemplative, introspective life, even as she never surren-dered to the appropriate. Life, as though admiring renegades, will frequently offer alternative experiences at another time. E. M. Forster, one of Steinem's favorite authors, wrote (intriguingly, in the Steinem context, in *A Passage to India*) "that life never gives us what we want at the moment that we consider appropriate. Ad-ventures do occur, but not punctually"—and certainly not always at the moment society considers inevitable or desirable. Steinem has noted that women grow more radical with age; they may in fact, she seems to suggest, grow in any way they find alluring if they are willing to abandon the suitable.

If Steinem slowed down, it was to a pace that most people would consider arduous: as she frequently remarked about any situation, "Compared to what?" Compared to her old way of life, she now lives somewhere in the lower range of what is possible for workaholics. Book tours, for both the hardback and paperback editions of *Revolution from Within* and then for the publication of *Moving Beyond Words* in 1994, took her again from bookshop to bookshop and city to city. In addition, she had become the con-sulting editor of the new, ad-free, reader-supported *Ms.,* which continued to feature her books as premiums for subscriptions; she was still the best-selling point the magazine had.

She continues to work with enormous diligence for the causes and candidates representing her ideas and needing her support, before the 1994 elections and since. Her inability to meet deadlines, long recognized at the old *Ms.* and still evident in her endless revisions of her books even when they are already in proof, continues, as does her refusal to turn down the request of an old friend or companion in arms, even when the request is less than wise. All this remains unchanged. Those who know her well, and have known her long, are occasionally overcome with the desire to shake some sense into her. Sure, she's nice to me—I deserve it— but need she be so nice to everybody? There is a price to be paid for such responsiveness, and Steinem has paid it in dissipated energies and excessive expenditures of time and vitality. She now pays it less, however, and in the long months of working on *Moving Beyond Words,* she was, for Steinem, in virtual seclusion. This adoption of an alternative pattern is probably characteristic of all women who welcome their sixth and seventh decades as opportunity rather than penalty: the movement to more or less activity on behalf of others varies, of course, with each woman.

Moving Beyond Words is a collection of six essays; three are original—one on Freud, one on revaluing economics, and one called "Doing Sixty." The other three—"The Strongest Woman in the World," "The Masculinization of Wealth," and "Sex, Lies, and Advertising"—are expanded versions of works earlier published in *Ms.* This book does not represent a new enterprise for Steinem; rather, it is a summation of ideas already formed, or in the case of "Doing Sixty," with its memories of India, newly rediscovered; it did not achieve the commercial success of her two earlier books, *Outrageous Acts* and *Revolution from Within,* having followed the latter of these perhaps too rapidly. One of the difficulties was that *Moving Beyond Words* did not have, as did the earlier two, a coherent theme, but was rather a collection of what Lionel Trilling once called "fugitive essays": what they were fugitive from was unity. In addition, the book did not command a distinct or identifiable audience; however excellent each of the essays, they did not, together, arouse any single chord of response.

The essay on Freud displays Steinem's humor and witty reversals at their best: in turning Sigmund Freud, with all his excessive sense of male superiority, into "Phyllis" Freud, Steinem was able, in hilariously deadpan, "scholarly" fashion, to celebrate, among much else, the now-obvious—to Phyllis—superiority of female genitals. It was, in attacking Freud's theories on women, however, that she marched to a phantom band from years well past: Few other than the most religious Freudians today follow these precepts slavishly. And at the same time, the essay ignores the original Freudian structures that contemporary psychoanalysts—Jessica Benjamin's *The Bonds of Love* is an excellent example—use as the basis for transforming Freud not by mockery but by building on his formulations. "Feminism," Benjamin writes, "has provided a fulcrum for raising the Freudian edifice" and illuminating the way in which Freud's analysis "gives domination its appearance of inevitability." This, Benjamin understands, "starts us on a new approach to grasping the tension between the desire to be free and the desire not to be" [8,10], a formulation Steinem has embodied rather than explored. It is particularly ironic that Steinem, in 1994, was still attacking Freud as though his grip on the American imagination had not altered since the 1950s. Freudian psychoanalysis, which Hannah Arendt had labeled in the 1950s "an American madness," began to loose its tight grip on women's minds over the years in which *Ms.* flourished. Clinical psychologists and other therapists actually examined women's experience and, astonishingly, actually listened to women instead of trying to fit their experiences into Freudian narratives such as the Oedipal conflict and penis envy. Women and their therapists now sought new narratives to describe their condition. Steinem had always been a great believer in this reform.

In college, Steinem had learned a lesson from a large mud turtle, a lesson that would become a touchstone for her. On a field trip for a geology class, she saw a large mud turtle resting at the edge of a paved road, and Steinem feared that it was about to cross the road and be hit by a car. She picked up the turtle and carried it to the bottom of a hill beside the stream from which it had, presumably, wandered. Her instructor, for the moment abandoning geology, pointed out that it had probably taken the turtle weeks to reach the mud at the top of the hill where she would lay her eggs. Now, thanks to Steinem's help, the turtle would have to begin the long journey all over again. It was a lesson Steinem never forgot, and the motto "Ask the turtle" was ever after with her.

Steinem's essays, each in its different way, give the impression of having hovered in her consciousness for a long time, waiting to reach print. *Moving Beyond Words,* therefore, may well be seen as the closing account of one phase of Steinem's intellectual life, and the promise of another.

Steinem has spoken all her life of her desire to write. Yet she has until the last few years almost never written except under pressure, either from assignments with deadlines or from book editors facing publication dates. She explains her need for pressure by saying that we are all scared of doing what matters to us most; thus truly explained or not, the need has so far persisted. Had Steinem wanted to be married, she would be married; no one, interviewing the men she has loved, can doubt it. The compulsion to marry was shed early in her life. But the compulsion to write without doing so in response to an assignment has not been shed; what has perhaps changed is her ability to write at her own pace, or at least to attempt to do so.

Solitude is not a state necessary to Steinem, though she is capable of enjoying it, like sex, when it occurs. Her house is almost always available to those who need a place to stay and cannot pay for hotel space. She finds it difficult to understand why longtime associates of hers, who apparently have space to spare, do not wish to share it with passing strangers or even acquaintances. If she does not assume responsibility for the daily needs of her guests, she also does not fail happily to accept their presence. Young women (sometimes with friends) stay with her, as do some of her assistants and associates. The world is her family, which, of course, means that other than the world there is no constant family at home.

Steinem is a remarkably open person, yet beyond this openness there is something that is accessible to no one, probably not even to herself. Although she commands intense loyalty, her personality remains elusive, even to her closest friends. All those who have known her intimately, including her therapist, recognize this apparent wall beyond which no one can look. It may be that her life has been so focused outside of herself that to peer intently inside is not easy, perhaps not possible; more simply, it may be that one does not come by intimacy easily if one did not learn it in childhood. She is a person simultaneously brave and vulnerable, who long ago learned to get on with it, to do the best she could, and to look neither backward with regret nor forward with trepidation. She seems to have been able to decide to be only herself and to respond to whatever comes, but always protecting, keeping inviolate, that precarious self.

On the part of many women as well as men, Steinem has inspired lust or passionate desire. Aware of this, she neither repels nor responds to it. Women have urged her to love affairs, but have not pressed beyond her clear, if kindly, rejection. Like many obviously desirable women, she has developed physical rejection to a fine art, where kindness and firmness are merged. With women, as with men, Steinem has often transmuted passion into friendship. What is notable is how seldom men have made passes at her. Late in 1992, when Senator Robert Packwood, having just been reelected, was accused of sexual harassment by a number of women, Steinem, who had helped Packwood in his earlier campaigns when he ran against an anti-choice candidate, was asked by many if he had ever harassed her. Steinem had to say that he had not. The reason she offered, and probably the reason she was generally less bothered than many by sexual harassment, was that Packwood and other men were not in positions of power in relation to her. The greater part of sexual harassment in the workplace occurs between powerful men and less powerful women.

Steinem sometimes muses that she has lived the unlived life of her mother; perhaps all the accomplished women of her generation have tried to live their mothers' unlived lives. In doing so, they have sought, like Steinem, to preserve the threatened self. It is notable that Steinem herself was not what any therapist or psychoanalyst would call properly or ideally mothered. Ruth Steinem was never, certainly after the early years and probably at no time, a "good enough" mother. We cannot know what sort of mother Steinem would have been to her own biological daughters had she had any, but there is evidence that as a surrogate mother she transformed or benefited from her own maternal lacks. It is just possible that she learned mothering, if she learned it at all in childhood, not from being mothered but from mothering her mother—an opportunity open primarily to the children of single mothers, and contrary to popular belief, often for the good.

Certainly, Steinem has long since been content with the absence of her desire for children. As she so often said, and truthfully, her friends were her family, and her childlessness did not haunt her. Indeed there is a distinction between the desire to bear one's own children and the desire women may feel in their middle years to nurture and mentor young women who become "surrogate daughters." Steinem has, however, deviated from her generation less in choosing not to have children than in welcoming into her "family" life young women whom she has served in a maternal role. She can be seen not only to have eluded cultural pressures toward maternity, but also to have enacted her own ideas of maternal love. Steinem's life offers an example of a new definition of family; a new, more open version of serial monogamy; a new definition of devotion to the young. Certainly, she has lived a life of benefit to others well beyond what most of us ever achieve.

Women who make different choices are caught in a no-win game: if they are good, they are unbelievable or mysteriously flawed; if they are bad, they are unwomanly, or ignoble, and disappoint us with their lack of consistency and perfection: Simone de Beauvoir is a prime example. When it transpired that she had served Sartre and remained in some way dependent on him, her claim to our regard was declared compromised. The question about Steinem becomes: what is the fatal flaw? If there is a lack of self, is this reflected in her decision not to marry, not to have children? Steinem's own response is that she didn't "serve Sartre" on the principle that, as a member of an oppressed group, nothing she did would be right so she might as well do what she wanted.

Her daily rounds are now enriched by several surrogate daughters, young women who clearly know her as intimately as anyone can. Since Steinem began writing, and revising the essays that would appear in *Moving Beyond Words,* Amy Richards, now twenty-five, has worked with her, traveled with her, and served in every capacity from research assistant, to arranger of dinner parties to raise funds for beleaguered women candidates, to cat-sit for Magritte when Steinem travels alone.

Rebecca Walker is a daughter—in fact, better than a daughter, for few daughters find their own mothers as unproblematic as a surrogate mother can be. Probably all children should have several unrelated adults available to them beyond the usual nuclear family or single parent, and Steinem serves happily in that capacity.

Rebecca's mother, writer Alice Walker, is a far more private person than Steinem and considerably less open to strangers and admirers. The friendship between Alice Walker and Steinem is a vibrant one.

Rebecca's account of Steinem's place in her life can serve as a model for how one can perform mothering acts toward the daughters of other women and—in a way not always possible to actual mothers—mentor a young woman entering adulthood. Mothers who have raised a daughter since babyhood have established a relationship of great intensity and importance, but its very emotional history of identification and separation preclude the daughter's accepting certain lessons from that mother. Only a surrogate mother or mentor can, without evoking tempestuousness or resentment, offer them. As Rebecca recalls it:

> She was my champion, my support, she opened many windows for me, always showing me, introducing me to new worlds, showing me a certain tactic, a certain kind of strategy about how to get one's point across. My first year at Yale [I used] a lot of my own energy, and it wasn't all used as wisely as it could have been, and from Gloria I learned a certain efficacy; she would sit and talk with people I thought were detestable, she would be very calm, she stayed calm, decisive, clear, and spoke lovingly and gave them her information even when they said, "You're crazy." And I think her approach really allowed them to hear it—if not at that moment, still I always thought it reverberated for them in a way that my kind of screaming didn't. And I also felt that it created a lot more room for humanity, that kind of civility, and so I started to take that into my own life. I came into her life at that point when she was shifting from not wanting to examine her life to opening up. I started living there in the summer of 1988. I remember just sort of being aware of that transformation as it was happening . . .

I could almost sense her trying to get more in touch with herself.

I think that this transformation was a lot about giving herself
permission to be like herself when she got up in the morning.
She started to allow herself to have more options.

The point here is not so much Steinem's particular qualities as
a parental mentor—but rather the contribution an unmarried,
childless woman can make to the next generation if she is readily
available to it.

Her hopes for her life past sixty include seeing the Ms. Foundation for Women have an endowment large enough to assure its
survival as a permanent feminist institution. Steinem has long
considered the Ms. Foundation to be as important to her as the
magazine, a feeling perhaps more pronounced today. Since 1993,
the Ms. Foundation has successfully launched Take Your Daughters to Work Day, the most visible part of the National Girls
Initiative; in the past it has helped to organize women who were
trying to get jobs in mines, aided the first battered-women's shelters, and encouraged economic empowerment—that is, programs
allowing women self-determination and jobs through the creation
of cooperatively owned businesses. Steinem wants the foundation
to expand sufficiently to embody many of her earliest, long-held
ideals, including an unusual board primarily of activists, a few of
whom are women of wealth; the chance to introduce new ideas to
the foundation world; and a risk-taking support of emerging issues and self-help grassroots efforts. In addition to her work for
the foundation, Steinem plans, as she puts it, "if I have one more
start-up in me, to start a school for organizers."

In *Moving Beyond Words,* Steinem described herself as "beginning to realize the upcoming pleasures of being a nothing-to-lose,
take-no-shit older woman." Asked what, if she had only one wish
for social change, that wish would be, she answers that, while on

different days there might be different answers, "what I wish for on this day is that women would treat ourselves as well and take ourselves as seriously as we do others." Meanwhile, the struggle between the public and private world continues. Steinem still sees her wise woman therapist, whom she calls "the only thing in my life that causes me or encourages me to balance the internal and the external; everything else in my life pushes me toward the external, so I really value her for this." Differently worded, this can mean that having determined, as she approached sixty, upon a shift, in her case from public to private endeavors, Steinem provided herself with an individual who would support and encourage her in that shift. "Wise women" are seldom engaged to encourage us in what we do not really want to do. Steinem ended *Revolution from Within* with the words: "There is always one true inner voice. Trust it." Like everyone, she has had moments when the true inner voice was lost. But she has trusted it more steadily than most.

To anyone reviewing her life up to this point, it may seem that —quite contrary to her own view that her destiny has been largely to respond to outer assignments and requests, always functioning only on demand—there is a completeness, a steadfastness of purpose, a willingness to undertake risks and to work for chosen goals, and a firmness in maintaining her principles that can be discerned throughout her life. From her earliest years with her father (demanding to be given the nickel without having to say what it was for) through the hard years with her mother, the Washington summers at the "Negro" swimming pool, Smith, the journey to India, New York, journalism, feminism, the loving of men, a unique magazine, and the profound change after fifty, a pattern is evident.

But what of the future? How will she fit into the coming years of feminism, and what will that feminist time be like? One indication is her plan to go with Alice Walker and Wilma Mankiller (when she finishes her term as head of the Cherokee nation in the summer of 1995) to India, and most especially, to her, to return to Kerala, India, where there are still remnants of a female-run culture; they also hope to visit aboriginal areas in India where gender balance is greater than elsewhere. From this they may, all three in their different spheres, confirm in themselves new ways to encounter the world, much as Steinem was transformed by her first Indian trip.

The future of feminism has few outlines, but some are clear enough. The time of what white, educated American and European women have called history is past; we all live, women and men, in a world that cannot be confined within any cultural or national borders. The environment must become a paramount consideration on a planet hideously misused by male ambitions of domination, exploitation, and arrogance. Included in this attempt to save the environment must be the empowerment of women to control their bodies and their own destinies. Clearly, feminism must engage young women; Steinem's support of the "third wave" and of the feminist education of young girls, both in the inner cities and the wider country, is high on her agenda.

All of these aims will be hard fought by a worldwide backlash against feminism and against any weakening of patriarchy, whether defined by established religions or neoconservative ideals. How to counter this backlash, particularly in the light of its extensive financing and influence on the media, is the major question women the world over face now.

Steinem's answer is for women to speak more and more to each other, across all boundaries. She has commented that many women who call themselves feminists do not in fact *like* women. It is always in defense of men that such women speak, and it is by this defense that they can be identified. Their accusations that women like Steinem hate men are a neat reversal of their own hatred of women, unconscious though it may sometimes be.

Never mind them, Steinem now says. We feminists, she considers, have too long been accustomed to ignoring the hundred people in the room who agree with us and arguing with the five people in the room who do not. Our numbers are great, but we do not have church funds behind us, nor the wealth of right-wing foundations. What we have is one another—and it is to one another that we must speak and offer encouragement and support. In working for feminist candidates during the 1994 elections, Steinem found that countering the lies of the right-wingers when speaking to pro-equality women and men was the essential task, and the hardest. Would so many have voted as they did if they really knew what those candidates stood for? She thinks not.

Steinem has rarely lacked courage in grappling with the world, or with herself. Yet it is the sweep of her actions, the endless lending of herself to causes large and small, that remains so mysterious to many: What can the reasons be for so great an expenditure of energy? And, oddly enough, it is this unceasing fight for what she believes in that is resented by those, themselves well-known, who question her motives and accomplishments. She is most honored and most cherished by people throughout the country who remember her speaking, her helping to start their rape-crisis center, her timely support for their various burgeoning organizations.

To the media and those who live in its light, Steinem is, to various degrees, an enigma and, perhaps inevitably, a paradox. But to the many thousands she has helped or encouraged or rescued, she is, like the mythical Kilroy of World War II, essential and ubiquitous:

Steinem was here.

APPENDIX

Articles by Gloria Steinem up to the
Founding of Ms. *in 1972*

1957

"In the Camp of the Radical Humanists." *The Radical Humanist* (Calcutta, India), June 30, 1957.

1962

"How Far Behind the Scenes Can You Get?" *Show,* March 1962.

"The Return of the Figure." *Show,* June 1962.

"The Moral Disarmament of Betty Coed." *Esquire,* September 1962.

"Dateline: Helsinki, the Last Red Festival." *Show,* October 1962.

1963

"Comfort." *Glamour,* February 1963.

"A Bunny's Tale, Part 1." *Show,* May 1963.

"A Bunny's Tale, Part 2." *Show,* June 1963.

"Funny Ways to Find a Man on the Beach." *Glamour,* June 1963.

"How the Single Girl *Really* Spends Her Money: Your Guide to Personal Deficit Financing." *Glamour,* October 1963.

"How to (Put up with/Put Down) a Difficult Man." *Glamour,* November 1963.

"The Passionate Giver." *Glamour,* December 1963.

1964

"Music, Music, Music, Music." *Show,* January 1964.

"How to Find Your Type (and, If Necessary, Change It)." *Glamour,* February 1964.

"1964 Won't You Please Come In?" *Ladies' Home Journal,* February 1964.

"A Haircut by Sassoon." *Glamour,* March 1964.

"London: What's New." *Glamour,* March 1964.

" 'Visiting Englishmen Are No Roses.' " *The New York Times Magazine,* March 29, 1964.

"Meet the Real New York . . . and Real New Yorkers." *Glamour,* April 1964.

". . . the Girls in Their Summer Dresses." *Glamour,* May 1964.

"Marisol: The Face Behind the Mask." *Glamour,* June 1964.

"Culture and the Candidates." *Glamour,* July 1964.

"Shake Your Head Three Times: A Message from Mr. Kenneth." *Glamour,* July 1964.

"James Baldwin: An Original." *Vogue,* July 1964.

"College and What I Learned There." *Glamour,* August 1964.

"Mrs. Kennedy at the Moment." *Esquire,* October 1964.

"The Death of Cool and the Birth of Beyond-Cool." *Glamour,* October 1964.

"Very Basic Training." Book review of *Sex and the Office* by Helen Gurley Brown, and *Nine to Five and After* by Irene Silverman. *Book Week,* October 18, 1964.

" 'Crazy Legs': Or, the Biography of a Fashion." *The New York Times Magazine,* November 8, 1964.

1965

"Put Yourself First." *Glamour,* January 1965.

"Gernreich's Progress; Or, Eve Unbound." *The New York Times Magazine,* January 31, 1965.

"How to Leave Home Gracefully." *Glamour,* March 1965.

"Julie Andrews." *Vogue,* March 1965.

"Second Game . . . Secrets of Deception." *Glamour,* May 1965.

"Take the Good Taste/Bad Taste Quiz." *Glamour,* May 1965.

"Gloria Steinem Spends a Day in Chicago with Saul Bellow." *Glamour,* July 1965.

"It's a Young Man's Game." *Glamour,* August 1965.

"The Ins and Outs of Pop Culture." *Life,* August 20, 1965.

"How I Became a Writer." *Glamour,* October 1965.

"Who Has the Higher Morals I.Q., You or Your Mother?" *Glamour,* November 1965.

"Why I Write" series: "What's in It for Me." *Harper's Magazine,* November 1965.

"Nylons in the Newsroom." *The New York Times,* November 7, 1965.

1966

"She Will Not Vegetate in Gracie Mansion." *The New York Times Magazine,* January 9, 1966.

"The Adventures of Max and Jennie." *Glamour,* February 1966.

"The Adventures of Max and Jennie." *Glamour,* March 1966.

"The Adventures of Max and Jennie." *Glamour,* April 1966.

"A Visit with Truman Capote." *Glamour,* April 1966.

"The Adventures of Max and Jennie." *Glamour,* May 1966.

"Boy/Girl Morals Quiz." *Glamour,* May 1966.

"The Adventures of Max and Jennie." *Glamour,* June 1966.

"The Lefrak Way of Life." *The New York Times Magazine,* July 31, 1966.

"The Student Princess." *Glamour,* August 1966.

"Barbra Streisand Talks About Her Million-Dollar Baby." *Ladies' Home Journal,* August 1966.

"Maurice Joseph Mickelwhite—What's 'E Got?" *The New York Times Magazine,* December 4, 1966.

1967

"The Party: Truman Capote Receives 500 'People I Like.' " *Vogue,* January 1967.

"The New Place in the Sun." *Glamour,* April 1967.

"A Woman for All Seasons." *McCall's,* May 1967.

"The Establishment Game." *Glamour,* July 1967.

"Advice for Misfits." *Glamour,* July 1967.

" 'Go Right Ahead and Ask Me Anything.' And So She Did." *McCall's,* November 1967.

1968

"And Starring Lee Bouvier." *McCall's,* February 1968.

"The Inner Man." *Glamour,* March 1968.

"Ho Chi Minh in New York." *New York,* April 8, 1968.

"Paul Newman: The Trouble with Being Too Good-Looking." *Woman's Own,* May 25, 1968.

"Between the Lines." *New York,* July 8, 1968.

"Notes on the New Marriage." *New York,* July 8, 1968.

"Trying to Love Eugene." *New York,* August 5, 1968.

" 'Anonymous' Was a Woman." Book review of *Born Female* by Caroline Bird with Sarah Welles Briller. *The New York Times Book Review,* August 11, 1968.

"What the Kennedy Family Taught Me." *Glamour,* September 1968.

"Looking Around with Gloria Steinem: A Few Words from the Silent Generation." *Look,* September 3, 1968.

"The Smartest Girl in New York: 'Renata Who?' " *Glamour,* October 1968.

"In Your Heart You Know He's Nixon." *New York,* October 28, 1968.

"Helsinki: The Last Red Festival." *Show,* October 1968.

"The Black John Wayne." *New York,* November 11, 1968.

"The City Politic: 'Post-Election Diary.' " *New York,* December 2, 1968.

"The City Politic: 'Unions, Black People, and Mrs. Onassis.' " *New York,* December 16, 1968.

"Women and Power." *New York,* December 23, 1968.

1969

"Notes on the New Marriage." *Queen,* January 1969.

"The City Politic: 'Proust, Subway Sleeping, and the Poor People's Cabinet.' " *New York,* January 13, 1969.

"The City Politic: 'McCarthy, Ghetto-busting, and the Astronauts.' " *New York,* January 27, 1969.

"The City Politic: 'A McCarthy Poem and Kennedy Money.' " *New York,* February 10, 1969.

"The City Politic: 'A Racial Walking Tour.' " *New York,* February 24, 1969.

"The City Politic: 'A Nice Place to Live—for Revolutionaries.' " *New York,* March 10, 1969.

"The City Politic: 'Outside Advice.' " *New York,* March 24, 1969.

"Nonviolence Still Works." *Look,* April 1, 1969.

"The City Politic: 'After Black Power, Women's Liberation.' " *New York,* April 7, 1969.

"The City Politic: 'The Making (and Unmaking) of a Controller.' " *New York,* May 5, 1969.

"The City Politic: 'The Kafka Effect.' " *New York,* May 19, 1969.

"The City Politic: 'Room at the Bottom, Boredom on Top.' " *New York,* June 30, 1969.

"The City Politic: 'Doing Jackie In.' " *New York,* July 21, 1969.

"Link Between the New Politics and the Old." *Saturday Review,* August 2, 1969.

"Nelson Rockefeller: The Sound of One Hand Clapping." *New York,* August 11, 1969.

"The City Politic: 'After Teddy . . . Maybe George?' " *New York,* September 1, 1969.

"The City Politic: 'The Souls of (Lower-Middle-Class) White Folk.' " *New York,* September 15, 1969.

"The City Politic: 'Biafra in the Bronx.' " *New York,* October 13, 1969.

"The City Politic: 'The Lindsay Haters.' " *New York,* October 27, 1969.

"The City Politic: 'Vietnam in Queens.' " *New York,* November 10, 1969.

"A Close-up Look at Bernadette Devlin." *Glamour,* December 1969.

"The City Politic: 'Is Spiro Agnew Really W. C. Fields?' " *New York,* December 15, 1969.

1970

"That Woman in City Hall." *New York,* January 5, 1970.

"The City Politic: 'A Nixon Sunday.' " *New York,* January 12, 1970.

"Why We Need a Woman President in 1976." *Look,* January 13, 1970.

"The City Politic: ' "Hi There, I'm Ed Koch." ' " *New York,* January 26, 1970.

"Laboratory for Love Styles." *New York,* February 16, 1970.

"The City Politic: 'Rx for Miserable New Yorkers.' " *New York,* February 23, 1970.

"The City Politic: 'The Politics of Sex and Fashion.' " *New York,* March 16, 1970.

"The City Politic: 'New York Love Styles, Part 2.' " *New York,* April 6, 1970.

"Lindsay's Urban Strategy: The Opening Scenes." *New York,* May 11, 1970.

"The City Politic: 'The War Against Nixon.' " *New York,* May 18, 1970.

"Women's Liberation Aims to Free Men, Too." *The Washington Post,* June 7, 1970.

"The City Politic: 'The White Shirley Chisholm.' " *New York,* June 22, 1970.

"Didion Novel of How a Housewife Came to Cope." *Los Angeles Times,* July 5, 1970.

"The City Politic: 'Goldberg's Complaint.' " *New York,* July 13, 1970.

"What It Would Be Like If Women Win." *Time,* August 31, 1970.

"The City Politic: 'Misgivings About Ottinger.' " *New York,* September 21, 1970.

"What *Playboy* Doesn't Know About Women Could Fill a Book." *McCall's,* October 1970.

1971

"The City Politic: 'Is Lindsay Deserting Us? Do We Care?' " *New York,* April 5, 1971.

"The City Politic: 'What Nixon Doesn't Know About Women.' " *New York,* July 26, 1971.

"A New Egalitarian Lifestyle." *The New York Times,* August 26, 1971.

"The Machismo Factor." *The New York Times,* October 6, 1971.

1972

"Sex, Politics, and Marriage." *Redbook,* January 1972.

"Sexual Politics." *Newsweek,* July 10, 1972.

"The City Politic: 'Convention Tip-Sheet.' " *New York,* August 28, 1972.

BIBLIOGRAPHY

Bair, Deirdre. *Simone de Beauvoir.* New York: Simon & Schuster, 1990.

Baker, Liva. *I'm Radcliffe! Fly Me!: The Seven Sisters and the Failure of Women's Education.* New York: Macmillan, 1976.

Barry, Kathleen. *Susan B. Anthony: A Biography of a Singular Feminist.* New York: Ballantine, 1988.

Beauman, Sally. "Encounters with George Eliot." *The New Yorker,* April 18, 1994, pp. 85–97.

Berger, John. *Ways of Seeing,* pp. 36–54. London: Penguin, 1972.

Brownmiller, Susan. "Sisterhood Is Powerful." *The New York Times,* 1970. Reprinted in *Women's Liberation: Blueprint for the Future,* Sookie Stambler comp., pp. 141–55. New York: Ace Books, 1970.

Bly, Robert. *Iron John: A Book About Men.* Reading, Mass.: Addison-Wesley, 1990.

Capote, Truman. *Breakfast at Tiffany's.* New York: Random House, 1958.

Charlotte, Susan. "Gloria Steinem." In *Creativity: Conversations with Twenty-eight Who Excel,* pp. 365–80. Troy, Mich.: Momentum Books, 1993.

Clarke, Gerald. *Capote.* New York: Ballantine, 1988.

Cohen, Marcia. *The Sisterhood.* New York: Fawcett Columbine, 1988.

Coles, Robert. *Erik H. Erikson: The Growth of His Work.* Boston: Little, Brown, 1970.

Davis, Flora. *Moving the Mountain: The Women's Movement in America Since 1960.* New York: Simon & Schuster, 1991.

Doty, Joy Billington. Unpublished typescript of interview with Stan Pottinger. (The published version appears in *The Sunday Times* [London], February 19, 1984.)

Echols, Alice. *Daring to Be Bad: Feminism in America 1967–1975.* Foreword by Ellen Willis. Minneapolis: University of Minnesota Press, 1989.

Egan, Harvey. *Leaven: Canticle for a Changing Parish.* St. Cloud, Minn.: North Star Press of St. Cloud, 1990.

Ehrenreich, Barbara. *Fear of Falling: The Inner Life of the Middle Class.* New York: Pantheon, 1989.

Eisenstein, Hester. "Response to Alice Echols' *Daring to Be Bad.*" Paper presented at the Berkshire Conference of Women Historians, Douglass College, Rutgers University, June 10, 1990.

Eisenstein, Zillah R. *The Radical Future of Liberal Feminism.* Boston: Northeastern University Press, 1981.

Eisler, Bernita. *Private Lives: Men and Women of the Fifties.* New York: Franklin Watts, 1986.

Ephron, Nora. "Miami." In *Nora Ephron Collected,* pp. 41–49. New York: Avon Books, 1991.

Evans, Sara. *Personal Politics: The Roots of Women's Liberation in the Civil Rights Movement and the New Left.* New York: Vintage Books, 1980.

Farrell, Amy Erdman. "Feminism in the Mass Media: *Ms.* Magazine." Ph.D. dissertation, University of Minnesota, 1991.

Fishel, Elizabeth. *Sisters: Love and Rivalry Inside the Family and Beyond.* New York: William Morrow, 1979.

Flaherty, Joe. *Managing Mailer.* New York: Coward-McCann, 1969–1970.

Freeman, Jo. *The Politics of Women's Liberation.* New York: David McKay, 1975.

Friedan, Betty. *The Feminine Mystique.* New York: Norton, 1973.

————. *It Changed My Life: Writings on the Women's Movement.* New York: Random House, 1976.

————. *The Second Stage.* New York: Summit, 1981.

Friedland, William H. and Dorothy Helkin. *Agricultural Workers in America's Northeast.* New York: Holt, Rinehart and Winston, 1971.

Gatlin, Rochelle. *American Women Since 1945.* Jackson, Miss.: University of Mississippi Press, 1987.

Giddings, Paula. *When and Where I Enter: The Impact of Black Women on Race and Sex in America.* New York: Bantam, 1985.

Gilbert, Sandra M., and Susan Gubar. *No Man's Land: The Place of the Woman Writer in the Twentieth Century.* Vol. 2: *Sex-changes.* New Haven, Conn.: Yale University Press, 1989.

Gitlin, Todd. *The Sixties: Years of Hope, Days of Rage.* New York: Bantam, 1987.

Gornick, Vivian. "The Women's Movement in Crisis (1975)." In *Essays in Feminism,* pp. 147–154. New York: Harper & Row, 1978.

Halberstam, David. *The Unfinished Odyssey of Robert Kennedy.* New York: Random House, 1968.

————. *The Fifties.* New York: Random House, 1993.

Harrison, Cynthia. *On Account of Sex: The Politics of Women's Issues, 1945–1968.* Berkeley, Calif.: University of California Press, 1988.

Haskell, Molly. *Love and Other Infectious Diseases.* New York: Morrow, 1990.

Hayden, Tom. *Reunion: A Memoir.* New York: Random House, 1988.

Hoff, Mark. *Gloria Steinem: The Women's Movement (A Book for*

Young People). Brookfield, Conn.: The Millbrook Press, 1991. (This book was done from clippings; it is inaccurate in many ways, but is good-spirited.)

Hole, Judith, and Ellen Levine. *Rebirth of Feminism.* New York: Quadrangle, 1971.

Kaminer, Wendy. *I'm Dysfunctional, You're Dysfunctional: The Recovery Movement and Other Self-Help Fashions.* Reading, Mass.: Addison-Wesley, 1992.

Kluger, Richard. *The Paper: The Life and Death of the* New York Herald Tribune. New York: Random House, 1986.

Koedt, Anne, Ellen Levine, and Anita Rapone, eds. *Radical Feminism.* New York: Quadrangle, 1973.

Kollontai, Alexandra. *The Autobiography of a Sexually Emancipated Communist Woman.* Edited and with an afterword by Irving Fetscher. Translated by Salvator Attanasio. Foreword by Germaine Greer. New York: Herder and Herder, 1971.

LeGuin, Ursula K. "The Writer on, and at, Her Work." In *The Writer on Her Work,* Vol. II, Janet Sternburg, ed., pp. 210–22. New York: Norton, 1991.

Linden-Ward, Blanche, and Carol Hurd Green, *Changing the Future: American Women in the 1960s.* New York: Twayne, 1993.

Mailer, Norman. *Miami and the Siege of Chicago.* New York: World, 1968.

Manso, Peter, ed. *Running Against the Machine: The Mailer-Breslin Campaign.* Garden City, N.Y.: Doubleday, 1969.

Matthiesen, Peter. *Sal Si Puedes: Cesar Chavez and the New American Revolution.* New York: Random House, 1969.

McPherson, Pat. *Reflecting on* The Bell Jar. New York: Routledge, 1991.

Middlebrook, Diane Wood. *Anne Sexton: A Biography.* Boston: Houghton Mifflin, 1991.

Miller, Russell. *Bunny: The Real Story of* Playboy. New York: Holt, Rinehart and Winston, 1984.

Millett, Kate. *Flying.* New York: Knopf, 1974.

Mills, Kay. *This Little Light of Mine: The Life of Fannie Lou Hamer.* New York: Dutton, 1993.

Morgan, Robin. *Going Too Far: The Personal Chronicle of a Feminist.* New York: Random House, 1968

————, ed. *Sisterhood is Powerful.* New York: Vintage, 1970.

————, ed. *Sisterhood Is Global.* New York: Doubleday, 1984.

National Commission on the Observance of International Women's Year. *The Spirit of Houston: The First National Women's Conference.* Official Report to the President, the Congress, and the People of the United States. Washington, D.C.: Government Printing Office, March 1978.

Redstockings. *Feminist Revolution: An Abridged Edition with Additional Writings.* New York: Random House, 1978.

————. "Redstockings' Statement." *off our backs,* July 1975.

Rennie, Susan, and Kirsten Grimstad, eds. *The New Woman's Survival Sourcebook.* New York: Knopf, 1975.

Rollin, Betty. *First, You Cry.* New York: Harper & Row, 1976; Signet, 1977.

Rose, Jacqueline. *The Haunting of Sylvia Plath.* London: Virago, 1991.

Rountree, Cathleen. *On Women Turning 50.* New York: HarperCollins, 1993.

Sherman, Susan. *The Color of the Heart: Writing from Struggle and Change, 1959–1990.* Willimantic, Conn.: Curbstone Press, 1990.

Shulman, Alix Kates. "Sex and Power: Sexual Bases of Radical Feminism." *Signs,* Vol. 5, No. 1 (summer 1980), pp. 590–604.

Sirlin, Rhoda. *William Styron's* Sophie's Choice: *Crime & Self-Punishment.* Ann Arbor, Mich.: UMI Research Press, 1990.

Snitow, Ann. "A Gender Diary." In *Rocking the Ship of State: Toward a Feminist Peace Politics,* pp. 35–73. Adrienne Harris and Ynestra King, eds. Boulder, Colo.: Westview Press, 1989.

Stacey, Judith. "The New Conservative Feminism," *Feminist Studies,* Vol. 9, No. 3 (fall 1983), pp. 559–83.

Steinem, Gloria. *The Beach Book.* New York: Viking Press, 1963.

———. "Statement from Steinem." *off our backs,* Sept.–Oct., 1975. (This statement was sent to other feminist journals.)

———. *Outrageous Acts and Everyday Rebellions.* New York: Holt, Rinehart and Winston, 1983.

———. *Marilyn.* New York: Holt, 1986.

———. "Sex, Lies & Advertising." *Ms.,* July–Aug. 1990, pp. 18–28.

———. *Revolution from Within.* Boston: Little, Brown, 1992.

———. *Moving Beyond Words.* New York: Simon & Schuster, 1994.

Steiner, Nancy Hunter. *A Closer Look at* Ariel: *A Memory of Sylvia Plath.* New York: Harper's Magazine Press, 1973.

Taylor, Robert B. *Chavez and the Farm Workers.* Boston: Beacon Press, 1975.

Thom, Mary, ed. *Letters to* Ms. With an introduction by Gloria Steinem. New York: Holt, 1987.

———. "The Personal Is Political—Publishable Too." In *The Media and Women Without Apology.* New York: The Freedom Forum Media Studies Center, Vol. 7, Nos. 1 and 2 (winter–spring 1993), pp. 223–30.

Toback, James. *Jim: The Author's Self-Centered Memoir on the Great Jim Brown.* Garden City, N.Y.: Doubleday, 1971.

Tolchin, Susan and Martin. *Clout: Womenpower and Politics.* New York: Coward, McCann & Geoghegan, 1974.

Trillin, Calvin. *Remembering Denny.* New York: Farrar, Straus & Cudahy, 1993.

Turow, Scott. *One L.* New York: Warner Books, 1988. (Originally published 1977.)

Wagner-Martin, Linda W. *Sylvia Plath: A Biography.* New York: Simon and Schuster, 1987.

Wandersee, Winifred D. *On the Move: American Women in the 1970s.* Boston: Twaine, 1988.

White, Theodore H. *The Making of the President 1968.* New York: Atheneum, 1969.

————. *The Making of the President 1972.* New York: Atheneum, 1973.

Willis, Ellen. "Radical Feminism and Feminist Radicalism." In *The Sixties Without Apology,* pp. 91–118. Sohnya Sayres, Anders Stephanson, Stanley Aronowitz, and Frederic Jameson, eds. Minneapolis: University of Minnesota Press, 1984.

PICTURE CREDITS

About the Author

Carolyn Heilbrun was Avalon Foundation Professor in the Humanities at Columbia University, where she taught modern British literature, the novel, and feminism until July 1993. She has had fellowships from the Guggenheim and Rockefeller foundations and from the National Endowment for the Humanities, and has served as president of the Modern Language Association, and as vice-president of the Authors Guild. Heilbrun is the author of *Toward a Recognition of Androgyny, Reinventing Womanhood,* and the now-classic *Writing a Woman's Life*, among other works of criticism. She is also the author of the acclaimed Amanda Cross mysteries and lives in New York City.

INDEX